BASED ON THE AMAZING TRUE STORY

THE INHERITANCE

POISONED FRUIT OF JFK'S ASSASSINATION

How One Man's Custody of Bobby Kennedy's Hidden Evidence
Changed Our Past and Continues to Shape Our Future...

CHRISTOPHER FULTON
& MICHELLE FULTON

INTRODUCTION BY DICK RUSSELL
Author of *The Man Who Knew Too Much*

This is a memoir; it is sourced from my memories, letters, and recollections. Dialogue is reconstructed, and some names and identifying features have been changed to provide anonymity. There is some informed, educated supposition about how actions affected historical events and meetings. The underlying story is based on actual happenings and historical personages.

Published by:
Trine Day LLC
PO Box 577
Walterville, OR 97489
1-800-556-2012
www.TrineDay.com
trineday@icloud.com

Library of Congress Control Number: 2018947033

Fulton, Christopher & Fulton, Michelle.
The Inheritance—1st ed.
p. cm.
Epub (ISBN-13) 978-1-63424-218-9
Kindle (ISBN-13) 978-1-63424-219-6
Print (ISBN-13) 978-1-63424-217-2
1. Kennedy, John F. -- (John Fitzgerald) -- 1917-1963 -- Assassination. 2. United States -- Politics and government -- History. 3. Kennedy, Robert F. -- 1925-1968. 4. Lincoln, Evelyn N. -- 1909-1995. 5. White, Robert L. -- 1949-2003. 6. Fulton, Christopher -- 1965- . 7. Conspiracies -- United States -- History. I. Title

FIRST EDITION
10 9 8 7 6 5 4 3 2 1

Printed in the USA
Distribution to the Trade by:
Independent Publishers Group (IPG)
814 North Franklin Street
Chicago, Illinois 60610
312.337.0747
www.ipgbook.com

Publisher's Foreword

No matter what the progress
Or what may yet be proved
The simple facts of life are such
They cannot be removed.

– Herman Hupfield,
As Time Goes By

Most welcome, bondage! for thou art away,
think, to liberty: yet am I better
Than one that's sick o' the gout; since he had rather
Groan so in perpetuity than be cured…

– William Shakespeare
Cymbeline, King of Britain

A Republic, if you can keep it.

– Ben Franklin

Personal testimony is something that TrineDay values highly. I first heard about Chistopher Fulton from Robert Groden. Later I spoke with Christopher myself. We talked about the book business and the JFK assassination. I wisecracked that unless he was writing a book that said "Lee did it," there wouldn't be much press coverage. We didn't talk much about his particular story. I asked if he had a manuscript. He said he was working on one. I told him that the Internet had roiled the publishing industry as much as anything, and there were now new ways to get a book to market that make self-publishing a viable option, mentioned other publishers that might be interested, and said to contact me once he had a manuscript.

Years later that happened, we talked some more, I asked him to send me his story. I received, sat down and read. Opened up Google, read, check, read, check. Wow! I was amazed that such an unknown narrative existed and appalled at the tortuous methods used by my government.

Fulton's story expanded and confirmed my understanding of the dynamics of the assassination, so I said, "Yes, let's do it, it needs to be done, for our country and . . . for our children and theirs."

The Inheritance: Poisoned Fruit JFK's Assassination is a must-read for anyone concerned about the future . . . and the past, for that is where our fortunes lie. Only with a true understanding of our history can we move forward in a proper way.

Yes, some names have been changed, some dialogue recreated, and there is some conflation of characters and minor events, but the story is very real. The question being: What will become of it? What will *we* do?

There will be those who disparage, those who will throw cold water on Fulton's tale, but then we have to deal, everday with those who say, "Lee did it," and those who wonder why anyone even cares about a murder that happened over 50 years ago.

Few of us who were alive when "it" happened, can honestly *not* forget what happened that day . . . and what has changed. For some, it gnaws at our souls, lurks in our minds and can keep us up at night.

There is so much controversy and divisiveness within our polity today. I welcome opportunities for a new grasp of reality, giving us a much-needed foundation upon which to act.

I heartily applaud the outstanding courage, fortitude, and downright grit that the Fultons have shown and their hard-won contribution to our ongoing quest for truth, liberty, and justice.

Being almost threescore and ten, which I grant is no great feat, has taught me, generally through hindsight, a few things: Listen to what folks have to say. Do *not* sell yourself short. And remember, there are many among us who wish a better world, a brighter future . . . a more perfect union.

TrineDay is humbled to have the pleasure to present Christopher Fulton's saga, *The Inheritance: Poisoned Fruit JFK's Assassination*. Our hope is that it will help us understand our history, behold our destiny, heal our nation, and revive our republic!

Onwards to the Utmost of Futures!

Peace,
RA Kris Millegan
Publisher
TrineDay
August 31, 2018

INTRODUCTION

By Dick Russell

The main character of this book is not a human. It's a timepiece: the gold Cartier watch worn by our 35th President, John F. Kennedy – on the day of his assassination. His wife, Jacqueline, handed the watch to JFK that fateful morning of November 22, 1963. He was wearing it when the shots rang out in Dallas. It bore ballistics evidence. And it was no longer on his wrist when his body was flown to Washington, D.C., for the "official" autopsy.

For many Americans, including myself, *time* stood still that day. The moment of hearing the news engrained itself in the memory, subject to instant lifelong recall. "Did you hear? Kennedy's been shot!" said the fellow student who informed me outside the high school cafeteria as everyone changed classes. The student wasn't a friend, barely an acquaintance. But I still recall his name and will never forget his face.

If we could turn back the clock . . . *and* that is what *The Inheritance* does, in an anguished plea for truth to will out, written by a man whose own sacrifice to the time-honored cover-up is stranger than fiction. The bizarre story of how a successful building contractor—not yet born when JFK was gunned down—came to briefly "inherit" the watch is mind-boggling enough. What happened to Christopher Fulton subsequently is downright chilling.

The reason comes down to this: JFK's watch was the single most compelling piece of evidence that Lee Harvey Oswald did not act alone, that someone else fired the fatal shot from the front, that a conspiracy existed—indeed that a coup d'etat may have taken place in Dallas. Forensics don't lie—but they can be buried.

It was a fatal shot that echoed far beyond Dealey Plaza, from the little boy issuing the unforgettable farewell salute to his father at Arlington Cemetery to the grown man whose own demise may well have been linked to his desire to expose the wrenching truth. His name was John F. Kennedy, Jr. Time cannot heal all wounds when the bloodshed is ongoing.

The book you are about to read is written in novelist style and, if the chronicle weren't so devastatingly real, one could hope it never happened.

Did the time bomb detonate for Christopher Fulton because he was in the wrong place at the wrong time? In retrospect, maybe so. But in his naivete, how could he have known? Did he have to endure years of false imprisonment in order to emerge one day to relate this saga?

Many who might have shed light are dead: the first keepers of the watch, a nurse at Parkland Hospital and two Secret Service agents; JFK's wife Jacqueline and brother Bobby; JFK's private secretary, Evelyn Lincoln; the would-be museum-keeper, Robert White, to whom the fate-filled timepiece was bequeathed; the son, John Jr., who sought to wrest the watch from the jaws of eternity, to rewind and let it *tell time*.

Fulton alone has survived to reveal its story. In the process, his curious destiny unfolded; secrets were unveiled. A Russian official, a Secret Service man, later two different fellow prisoners who offered their inside knowledge of what had transpired as JFK sought to move the nation away from nuclear annihilation and toward peace.

As the President once said: "We are not here to curse the darkness, but to light the candle that can guide us through that darkness to a safe and sane future."

I have long felt that this nation cannot truly move forward until the truth is faced about what really happened in Dallas. We saw our great leaders of the 1960s mowed down, men who would've helped us become an America vastly different than the bitterly divided and materially driven country we now inhabit. We have witnessed corruption replace compassion, Orwellian tweets supplant honesty.

The clock is running. Once upon a time . . . there was promise. Yet the legacy bequeathed here by Christopher Fulton recalls something else, the verse quoted by Robert Kennedy upon delivering the tragic news of Martin Luther King's assassination in April 1968. The verse was from Aeschylus. It resonated deeply with Robert Kennedy, who himself would be slain two months later. And perhaps it may serve as a fitting introduction to what Fulton describes of his life and those times.

> *Even in our sleep, pain which cannot forget*
> *falls drop by drop upon the heart,*
> *until, in our own despair,*
> *against our will,*
> *comes wisdom*
> *through the awful grace of God.*

Dick Russell is the author of thirteen books, including three on the Kennedy assassination.

To my mother,
who lost her life over the strain of these events,
and to Don Clark,
who finally convinced me on the 4th of July that this book
needed to be written.
***

I would also like to state my eternal gratitude for
President John F. Kennedy
and
Senator Robert F. Kennedy,
who sacrificed their lives for the betterment of the world.
Thank you.
***

I also dedicate this book to everyone who has served,
or is currently serving, in the Armed Forces of the United States.
Thank you for going above and beyond.

ACKNOWLEDGMENTS

Special thanks to Nanny Mason, who put her life on hold and traveled from another country—multiple times—to care for us, our children, our dogs, and our home, so that we could finish this book.

Thank you to our agent, Joe Kolkowitz, who told us this book was important; he has supported us with his professional guidance from the very beginning.

Thank you, Kris Milligan of Trineday, a true patriot publisher who works to make a more-informed and better world for all of us.

Thank you, Pat Boylan and John Lett, who—published authors, themselves—devoted a substantial chunk of their time to edit our book.

Thank you, Dick Russell, for your advice regarding this book and for writing the Introduction.

Thank you to the good men and women of the intelligence community who encouraged us to write this book.

And thank you to all of our family members and dear friends, the truest measure of a great life.

TABLE OF CONTENTS

Publisher's Foreword..iii

Introduction by Dick Russell v

Dedication..vii

Acknowledgments viii

Table of Contents ix

Prologue 1

1) What I Can Do For My Country 3

2) Inheriting Camelot 8

3) Material Evidence 13

4) The Approach 19

5) The Secrets Of Events 24

6) Under American Skies 36

7) Newton's Law 40

8) Legacy 44

9) Divided By History...47

10) Like A Game Of Chess..55

11) To Kill A Country..59

12) For All Of U.s. 70

13) Bonded By Blood 80

14) Liberty Knell...85

15) The Camelot Archives..90

16) The Secrets Man 95

17) Broken Promise..131

18) The Devil Cut In 134

19) Wings Of Wax 139

20) A Matter Of National Security 144

21) Unamerican 151
22) It's Not The Fall, It's The Stop 161
23) Letters To No One 170
24) Destiny Or Destruction 174
25) Slipping The Snare 182
26) Best Interests 185
27) Crossing The Threshold 187
28) Red White And Bars 195
29) Knocking At The Door 200
30) Most Wanted 204
31) False Flag 211
32) Extradition 216
33) Diesel Therapy 222
34) The Gauntlet 227
35) Temporary Bodies 231
36) The Color Red 237
37) Life 248
38) Fighting The Green Lion 251
39) Wisdom 255
40) Holy Sin 264
41) The Deal I Had To Make 269
42) When All The Stars Have Fallen, There's Nothing Left But Bars 275
43) Courage Rises With Danger 281
44) The Prophet's Clock 289
45) The Wounds That Never Heal 293
46) God Took A Holiday 302
47) Ameri-Can't 307
48) The Most Dangerous Man 318
49) A Glint Of Truth 327
50) The Keepers Of Secrets 332
51) Liberty And Justice For All 335
52) It's Nothing Personal 346
53) Just Being Alive Is A Gift 354
54) One Hell Of A Story 360
55) Time Waits For No One 367
56) You Can't Go Home 372
57) A New Future 379
Documents & Photographs 385
Index 511

Prologue

ASK NOT

November 22, 1963

Everyone's efforts were useless; President John F. Kennedy was dead.

Mr. O.P. Wright, the head of Parkland Hospital's security, was given a bullet; he placed it in his pocket. Soon after, he was given a gold wristwatch; he carefully wrapped it in his handkerchief.

The bullet was the foundation of the biggest lie in modern history, and the watch was secretly used to save us all from nuclear war . . .

WHAT I CAN DO FOR MY COUNTRY

MARCH 3, 1999

Today started out differently. I wasn't forced onto government aircraft controlled by the United States marshals, I wasn't stuck in cold holding cells for days, and my wrists and ankles weren't chained to a lock box at my waist. No one had died today, and no one was trying to kill me. I was put in an unmarked car and I could see out the windows; I hadn't seen outside in eight months. I was in the custody of IRS Agent Clara Mancini and FBI Special Agent Joe Callahan; they were driving me to the Federal Greenbelt Courthouse in Maryland. I had to go to the bathroom.

When we arrived I asked permission to relieve myself.

"Absolutely not," spat Mancini contemptuously.

"I'll take him," Callahan said. He led me down the hall, and aggressively pushed me through the door of the men's room. "Stand still." In the privacy of the facility his demeanor changed; he spoke to me like I was a human being and unlocked my steel bracelets. "Your files are stacked two feet tall on my desk. Why didn't you just come in?"

I rubbed my wrists; I was confused about his breach in protocol. Since my arrest, this was the first conversation with a government official that felt genuine, but I needed to know if he was trying to help me, or hurt me.

Callahan lowered his voice and spoke with more intensity. "The attorney general is going to bury you. I know about your letter to the president; can you save yourself?"

"I don't think . . ."

A loud knock broke my response and Mancini's aggravated voice came through the door. "Hurry up."

Agent Callahan quickly snapped the cuffs back on my wrists and walked me out of the bathroom. I never got to go.

Both agents led me through a security door and down a hallway. Callahan turned to Mancini. "You know we have to wrap this up before the Bush election."

Mancini gave him a distasteful look. "Yup." She spoke abruptly to cut him off

As we arrived at the end of a long corridor, my lawyer, Stephen N. Salvin, stood waiting outside another secure door. Agent Mancini punched a code in the keypad and walked through. Agent Callahan left, and I remained in the custody of a federal marshal standing beside me.

Salvin had a strained look on his face. "I can't go in with you," he said, "it's a closed interrogation. You've waived your constitutional rights, but it's the deal we had to make."

Deal was an interesting word to describe it.

"Don't hold anything back," Salvin instructed, "the government wants answers. At this stage they don't care whether you're a terrorist, if you've killed a thousand people, or if you've dealt with atomic weapons; it's all covered under your blanket immunity, in exchange for your cooperation."

My eyes locked on his. "You know I've never done anything like that."

He nodded. "Just remember, your family won't be touched now."

My family . . . I started to collapse within myself. I couldn't stay focused on what Salvin was saying; this was all too surreal. I knew I didn't fully trust him, but I was forced to take his direction under threat of even more terrible consequence: I had no choice.

"You're facing fifty years," Salvin said. "The Department of Justice's recommendation will mean everything. Just try to forget how you feel." He scrutinized me.

I knew how I looked: sallow, sleep deprived, nauseated, a shell of my former self . . . and this was a good day.

He advised me to put the misery aside and answer their questions directly and calmly. "Everything will be taken down for the record. It'll be classified, so we won't have access to it. Just try to remember as much as you can and write it down as soon as you get a chance. I know it's nearly impossible get anything to write with in the hellhole they're keeping you in—that place is *designed* to break people—but it's important you try." He looked at his watch. "It's time."

Too much was riding on this; my *life* was riding on this. I had to swallow my anxiety, my fear, but the question kept screaming in my brain: *What the hell am I doing here?* I took a deep breath and tried to appear composed, as the marshal escorted me through the door.

I was delivered into a small courtroom with a marble floor. The great seal of the United States hung above the proceeding. I walked through the center of the room to a podium. A federal judge and stenographer sat on my right, and a group of officials sat on the opposite side of the room. Their eyes followed me, emotionless. My cuffs were removed and Assistant District Attorney Stewart Barman ordered me to sit.

Barman addressed the room: "This is a proffer session debrief for Mr. Christopher Fulton. He has agreed to this session of his own free will. He will answer all questions put to him under penalty of perjury. He has agreed to plead guilty to the charges against him and is facing up to fifty years of imprisonment. The Department of Justice will recommend a reduced sentence based on his cooperation. The government has granted Mr. Fulton and his immediate family blanket immunity for anything that is said here today, or any other information or actions that are known, or become known, that occurred prior to this proffer. The United States Government will not bring any further charges against Mr. Fulton or his family, or assist any foreign government in charging him or his family." He turned to me. "Mr. Fulton, do you understand?"

"Yes." My mouth was dry, but I spoke clearly.

"Please state your name and occupation for the record."

He was really asking, *Who are you?* . . . but I didn't recognize myself anymore.

***

I grew up in Maryland, just outside the District. My mother was personable and smart, a stewardess, recommended by Howard Hughes to fly aboard the Lockheed Constellation shuttle between Washington and New York. Of the many important and interesting individuals she met, her favorite was Bobby Kennedy; they shared several long conversations together.

I learned from an early age about reputation and privilege, not from our family name or wealth, but from my mother's remarkable way with people. When I was two years old, she arranged a private tour of the White House for me which included the upstairs rooms. I even met President Johnson. I can't remember what he said to me, but I have a photograph to commemorate the occasion. From a very young age, I developed a great appreciation for history; my taste, desire, and love for it came from my mother's influence.

My family roots grow deep in the soil of a proud American military heritage. I'm the descendant of William Vaughn Jr., who fought with distinction in the Revolutionary War, and General John C. Vaughn, who fought in the Civil War. Most of the men in my family tree served in the United States Navy. My parents assumed I would follow in those footsteps. When I turned eighteen, an Admiral wrote a letter of recommendation for my acceptance into the United States Naval Academy, in Annapolis; it was a great honor. I was on my way, and my family was sure my future was set, but I wanted something different; I wanted to do the kinds of things my father had done.

My father was the Vice President of Weldcrete, a company that supplied NASA with the exceedingly hard concrete used to withstand the intense heat and powerful exhaust from the Apollo rockets. As a boy, I collected patches from the missions that my father helped make possible.

Although I was one of the first men in my family not to serve in the Navy, I eventually became successful in the commercial construction industry. It took years of struggle, hard work, and personal sacrifice, but I reached my goal and fulfilled my dream: I became an independent general contractor. I would always be proud of that, but the real thread of passion throughout my life, my love of history—particularly American history—never left me.

***

In this cold courtroom, I was about to be questioned by U.S. Assistant District Attorney Stewart Barman, witnessed by representatives of the secret agencies intended to keep our nation safe, and the military I would have been a part of . . . My childhood was an unattainable memory, and my future was about to be stolen.

"Mr. Fulton, please state your name," the prosecutor said again.

"Yes," I said, as I pulled myself back into the present, "my name is Christopher Fulton; I'm an independent general contractor."

"Mr. Fulton, when did you first meet Mr. Robert L. White?"

"1994."

"You were living in Maryland at that time, and Robert White was the friend of a friend?"

"Yes."

"When did you become aware of Robert's relationship with Evelyn Lincoln, President Kennedy's personal secretary?"

"1996."

"You're saying he kept that information from you for two years?"

"Yes," I responded. The panel looked doubtful, so I continued, "He had a deal with Mrs. Lincoln, to keep the information she shared with him secret until after her passing."

"Mr. White only shared information with you after Mrs. Lincoln died?"

"Yes, that's correct."

"Why?"

2

INHERITING CAMELOT

MID-1995

The judge sat behind the bench in her traditional black robes. "Mr. Robert L. White, do you understand why you are here today?"

Robert nodded respectfully. "Yes, ma'am."

The handful of people present looked on in silent anticipation. Robert didn't recognize any of them. He was concerned someone else would try to lay claim to his inheritance. His palms were clammy, he was nervous; this ruling could change his life.

The judge continued, "The matter before me is the evaluation of the wills of Evelyn Lincoln and Harold Lincoln. Harold Lincoln passed shortly after his wife. Maryland state law requires me to review his will; however, due to special circumstances I will review both wills to ensure the legality of their contents, to determine whether or not Mr. White shall inherit under their stipulated terms. At Evelyn Lincoln's instruction, copies of both wills were sent to the John F. Kennedy Library. Nothing has been filed in contention by the library in this matter. Let's proceed."

A calm voice came from the back of the courtroom. "May I approach the bench?"

Robert craned his neck as everyone in the courtroom turned to see who spoke. A silver-haired woman stood in the aisle; she was in her eighties and impeccably dressed.

"Do you have something to add to this proceeding?" the judge asked.

"I do, Your Honor. My name is Angela Novello; I was Robert F. Kennedy's personal secretary." She spoke with an air of competence that was well suited to her previous work. The room hushed.

"Please approach the bench, Mrs. Novello."

Novello, with all eyes on her, walked towards the front of the courtroom. Standing before the judge, she removed an envelope from her purse, and placed it on the desk. "This is for you," she said quietly.

The judge examined the envelope. There was a handwritten note on the front: "This letter is only to be opened upon my death." It was signed: "Evelyn N. Lincoln, secretary to the late President John F. Kennedy." The back of the envelope was secured with wax and stamped with the seal of the office of the President of the United States. The judge placed her hand over the microphone. "What is this about?"

Just above a whisper, Novello responded. "This letter was given to me in case Mrs. Lincoln's will was contested, or required to go through any court process. I was instructed to give it to the presiding judge for their eyes only."

The judge put on her reading glasses and weighed the gravity of breaking the seal. She understood the presidential seal was used for the private correspondence between the President and the U.S. Senate, but this was a unique situation. She broke it, and carefully opened the envelope. The letter inside was typed on White House stationary. She read in silence:

> To whom it may concern,
>
> As the private personal secretary of President John F. Kennedy, I, Evelyn N. Lincoln, was trusted with matters of the highest national concern. The intent of my will is to accomplish the best interests and directives given to me by the president's brother, the late Robert F. Kennedy.
>
> Following President Kennedy's assassination, the citizens of our great country were left deserving information which they could not receive. In 1965, I took careful instruction from Robert Kennedy in regards to gathered and non-relinquished evidence in his custody, in relation to the assassination of President Kennedy. As instructed, I kept Robert Kennedy's intentions secret to ensure the safety of the remaining Kennedy family.
>
> In 1992, I bestowed upon Mr. Robert L. White, of Catonsville, Maryland, by way of gift, an important artifact worn by President Kennedy the day he was assassinated. I received this item with instructions from Robert Kennedy. I gifted it to Mr. White to ensure its transfer and safekeeping. A sealed letter, such as the one presented to you today, is included in my estate and must now accompany that artifact as a matter of law. That letter details the special circumstances of that item.

Upon his inheritance, Mr. White's plan is to open a museum dedicated to President Kennedy. It would lie outside the jurisdiction of the National Archives and Records Administration and the John F. Kennedy Library. It is my hope he will be successful in that endeavor; however, the opening of his museum is not preclusion to his inheritance.

It is my intent that the materials saved by me, as President Kennedy's secretary, and passed to Mr. White, shall not fall under the control of the CIA, the FBI, the NSA, the Pentagon, the National Archives and Records Administration, the John F. Kennedy Library, the White House, or any other branch of government or agency.

If my will is contested, or ruled upon in any way that results in Mr. White's failure to receive as per my wishes, I have made arrangements, as directed by Robert F. Kennedy, for copies of all sensitive information in my keeping, related to the national security interests of the United States, to be published by a foreign press.

My final wishes are for this letter to become a permanent part of the record of my last will and testament, and be placed under seal.

Evelyn N. Lincoln
Personal secretary to the late President John F. Kennedy

The judge put down the letter, removed her glasses, and looked at Mr. White. A heavy burden had been placed upon her: based on her ruling, security interests of the United States could be exposed. "We will take a recess while I review the wills in chambers; court will adjourn for two hours." She hammered down her gavel.

Everyone in the room was intrigued by the mysterious letter that prompted the recess. Robert rose from his seat to speak with Mrs. Novello but his wife, Jacquelyn, put a restraining hand on his arm. "Now's not the time," she said. Robert felt uneasy; he would have to wait even longer to find out if the items bequeathed to him, which once belonged to President John F. Kennedy, would legally be his at the end of the day.

Precisely two hours later, Mr. White and his wife sat nervously in the courtroom when the bailiff said, "All rise." The judge entered from chambers, and took her seat on the bench. Wasting no time she stated, "In the matter before me today, as aforementioned, I find the last will and testaments of Evelyn Lincoln and Harold Lincoln to be legal and sound. I find that Mr. Robert White will inherit according to the Lincoln's wishes." Again her gavel struck the sound block; to Robert the sound was like music.

***

FBI Special Agent Joe Callahan left the will hearing immediately, and drove to FBI's headquarters in downtown Washington D.C. After writing his report, he walked to the office of Director Louis J. Freeh.

"My report, sir," Callahan said, as he placed it on the director's desk.

"Anything out of the ordinary?" Freeh asked, while looking at the report.

"Yes, sir. I believe our Russian counterpart was there, and Robert Kennedy's secretary approached the bench. She gave a letter to the judge."

Freeh looked up sharply. "And?"

"The content of the letter was not read aloud. White inherited."

Freeh made a guttural acknowledgment before saying, "Now this is a concern for national security. I'll have a judge approve a wiretap for White's residence; I want you to monitor it."

"Yes, sir."

***

President Bill Clinton sat at his desk in the Oval Office reading over the CIA's morning brief. Something unusual in the report caught his attention:

> A large amount of non-reviewed and non-classified materials, belonging to former President John F. Kennedy, formally secured by his secretary, Evelyn Lincoln, has been willed to a private citizen following Lincoln's death on May 11 of this year. These materials were transferred to Robert L. White of Catonsville, Maryland, by judicial order. At this time, the extent of materials in Mr. White's possession is unknown, as are his intentions, although he has been an avid self-promoter in the press. There are strong indications that the materials contain information regarding the policy of the United States with Cuba, and evidence in the assassination of President Kennedy. These materials require above top secret classifications; they were originally withheld from that process by Robert F. Kennedy. This transfer is a national security concern. The code name assigned to this matter is: "The Evelyn Lincoln Project."

President Clinton telephoned former Presidents Bush, Reagan, Carter, and Ford to notify them. Former President G.H.W. Bush told President Clinton that the best course of action was to order the Assassination Records Review Board to meet immediately with the FBI, the Department of Justice, and the National Archives, to discuss the security concern and arrive at a course of action. They would report directly back to President Clinton who, in turn, would keep his predecessors informed.

3

MATERIAL EVIDENCE

MARCH 3, 1999

The courtroom was cold and unforgiving. "Robert kept everything secret until Evelyn Lincoln's passing, because that's what she instructed him to do."

Barman asked his next question with sudden intensity. "Do you work for, or have you ever worked for, the Canadian Security Intelligence Service?"

"No."

"Why did you meet with one of their former agents?"

"I met him by chance."

"What did he tell you?"

"That I had something the CIA and Mob had been looking for."

"Did he tell you why they wanted it?"

"No."

Attorney General Janet Reno had personally requested that Stewart Barman conduct Fulton's interrogation; she wanted this handled. He was good at his job, trained to keep the pressure on and keep the enemy very motivated to answer his questions.

"Your wife's name is Shauna Fulton and she resides in Vancouver, Canada?"

My pulse quickened. "Yes." Any questions about my family made me very uneasy.

"Your wife first met Robert White in New York in 1998?" Barman pressed.

I knew I had to respond to any questions posed to me. My family's protection shackled me to the government's resolve, and Barman knew it. "That's correct," I answered.

"We know you have only spoken with your wife twice since your arrest. What role did she play . . . re-phrase . . . what was your wife's part in the development of the assassination evidence?"

I looked straight at Barman, whose job it was to tear me into small pieces of my former self.

"Nothing . . . she has nothing to do with this."

MAY 1995

I was living in British Columbia, Canada, indefinitely, working to modernize the downtown core of Vancouver by building new skyscrapers. The work was exhausting, sometimes a twenty-four-hour-a-day headache, but it was a beautiful city, and my hard work was about to become worth it. I had met a girl; I had met *the* girl.

Shauna had appeared in my life while I was walking my rescue dogs: Leo, a white and brown husky; Kelley, a black and brown English shepherd; Tao, a chocolate Dalmatian; and Bear, a 130-pound black lab. I was throwing a ball down the beach for them at Ambleside Dog Park, when a wide throw sent the ball flying into the water. I thought my dogs would splash in after it; instead, they just stood at the water's edge and stared at the ball, then stared back at me. "Don't look at me," I said, "that's your job."

"I'll get it," an unfamiliar voice rang out. I turned to see an attractive young woman, with a warm smile, jump up from the bench behind me, and hurry onto the sand.

I protested, "You don't have to do that."

"But I want to," she said.

"No, really, wait a minute," I said, trying to untie my laces and get my shoes off quickly.

"But I want to!" she exclaimed again, already in the shallows.

It wasn't how I was raised; I should have been the one in the water. But I stood there, anchored in that moment. The water lapped the bottom of her skirt as she stretched out her arm to retrieve the ball.

"Here you go," she called back, and threw it towards the shore, to the great excitement of my dogs. They clambered over each other to get to their beloved toy. I looked at her and smiled, and in return she gave me a smile I would never forget.

Suddenly she lost her footing on the slippery rocks and splashed into the chilly waters. She completely submerged before bouncing up with a look of surprise on her face. Her clothes clung coldly to her skin. My mouth dropped open in horror. I quickly waded towards her, but she burst out laughing. It gave me the warmest feeling, like I had known her since we were kids, and had always secretly been in love with her.

My dogs watched as we both made our way back to shore. Bear seemed to have a grin on his face, a clear communication that the pairing was alright by him. Once on the rocky beach, Leo, Tao, Kelly, and Bear all ran to her. Without a thought of being soaking wet, she crouched down to pet each of them and return their kisses. "Traitors," I said, enjoying the moment. I couldn't blame them; she had my undivided attention, too. "You must be cold." I moved to put my jacket around her shoulders.

"Not at all," she smiled, "The sun is shining; I'll dry. My name's Shauna." She looked directly into my eyes as she held out her hand.

Right then and there I knew: she was the one.

DECEMBER 31, 1995

Shauna and I were invited to attend a private New Year's Eve party aboard a charter yacht in Coal Harbor. It was hosted by Mehran Mikhailov, a Russian businessman for whom I was building a tower in the city. When we arrived at eight P.M., the alcohol was freely flowing, prompting much merriment in the partygoers. Shauna and I didn't partake; neither of us was particularly fond of the effects. But the lights and festoons glittered; they reflected elegantly in the gently rippling water, and the band was talented and energetic, heightening our enjoyment of the evening.

There must have been two hundred people there; some we knew, most we didn't. Early in the evening, the rise and fall of chatter drew us to a particular group of people that seemed more intensely concentrated than the rest. At its center stood a charismatic man I didn't recognize. As we moved closer, parts of his story reached us over the throng.

"I fought . . . Falklands . . . with the British . . . some time ago now . . . Souvenir." At that, he pulled up his shirt to reveal an array of small round scars that marked his torso. We joined the crowd to hear the rest of his narrative: "I was shot six times; I woke up in a body bag." A few women gasped, and a man shook his head in disbelief. As he finished his account, he lowered his shirt, and turned away from the crowd that was eating out of his hand. Before he walked away I stopped him. "We just caught the end of your story; it was fascinating! My name is Christopher and this is my girlfriend, Shauna."

"Cable Wade," he said.

"Somebody must have had great aim to hit you six times and allow you to live," I remarked, in awe of his survival.

Cable laughed. "Yes, I agree."

We talked for a while; he was interesting . . . different. He asked what I did for work. When I asked him the same, he said he was out of it for the time being. Then I inquired if he had any New Year's resolutions.

"Yes, a very important one." He half smiled, before taking a swig of his drink. "Next year, I'll be switching from Whisky to Gin."

Shauna laughed out loud.

"What about you?" he asked, his glass still hovering at his lips.

"Nothing so serious as yours . . ." I wasn't going to share my plans of marriage with Shauna standing right beside me. Changing tack, I asked him about the unusually large watch he was wearing.

"This is an Omega Marine Chronometer. When I bought it in 1976, it was the most accurate timepiece in the world. Jacques Cousteau has one . . . What do you wear?"

"I don't wear one, but I recently acquired President Kennedy's wristwatch . . ."

"Really? What make is it?"

I thought Cable would have been more surprised by my statement, but he remained un-readably cool.

"It's a gold Cartier."

"With his initials on the back?"

Did he guess that? "That's right."

Cable emptied his glass, before saying, "It was very nice to meet you, Christopher, Shauna. Have a happy new year." With that he walked away.

His departure seemed abrupt, but we had other people to meet so I didn't think much of it.

The rest of the evening had an enjoyable progression until the countdown to midnight: "3, 2, 1 . . ." Shauna and I kissed as noisemakers sounded and people cheered.

Shortly after the stroke of midnight we were making our way off the yacht when Cable approached, from seemingly nowhere, and stopped us in our tracks. "I'd like to speak with you tomorrow," he said, in a tone rather unsuited to the surrounding high spirits. I assumed he wanted to discuss a potential job opportunity. It seemed odd he would be so eager on a holiday, but perhaps he had reevaluated his New Year's resolution. "I'm sure we can work that out," I said, and handed him my card.

JANUARY 1, 1996, 8:00 A.M.

My doorbell rang. Sleepy and bleary eyed, I made my way to the front door. *Who on earth would call so early on New Year's Day?* I opened the door and was taken aback to see Cable Wade and a tall, slender woman with subtly greying hair. Cable was notably more somber and sober than the night before.

I was obviously missing something; the card I had given him only provided my name and phone number and now, just a few hours later, he was standing on my doorstep with a strange woman. I didn't know how I should feel . . . I was just confused. "How did you know where I live?" It burst out of my tongue-tied mouth before I even said hello.

"I haven't been totally honest with you . . ." Cable stood his ground on my doorstep and kept direct eye contact with me. "I have something important to discuss with you; can we come in?"

I found the change in his character intriguing. His stance and speech were authoritative but not threatening; I felt compelled to trust him. "Yes," I said, and fully opened the door.

Cable thanked me as he and the enigmatic woman made their way inside. We settled in the living room. "This is Sasha Luken," he said.

I reached out my hand. Sasha's long, delicate fingers just barely touched mine in something I would be hard-pressed to call a handshake.

"What did you mean when you said you weren't honest with me?" I asked.

"I used to work for CSIS, the Canadian Security Intelligence Service." He handed me his military ID and his security credentials. "When you told me you had acquired President Kennedy's Cartier watch, I immediately called my former CIA counterpart in San Francisco. After some discussion, we came to the conclusion that you are in possession of something very important, something the CIA, and the Mafia, have been trying to locate for the past thirty-three years. . . What do you know about the watch?"

I was caught off guard. "Not much, just that it was given to JFK by his wife as an anniversary gift and he wore it as a senator."

"Who did you get it from?"

"A friend . . . What is this about?

"Do you have the watch here?"

My instinctual reaction was to become defensive, but I wanted to know where this was going. "If I did?"

"Would you consider letting us see it?" I thought I sensed urgency in his request.

I contemplated for a moment; I wouldn't find out what this was all about if I didn't follow through. "Yes, it's here," I said. "Give me a moment."

I kept the watch in a box in the safe in my bedroom. After retrieving it, I placed the open box on the coffee table.

Cable looked at me. "May I pick it up?"

"Yes."

He put on a pair of reading glasses, fished a magnifier from his breast pocket, and carefully picked up the watch. He inspected it slowly and carefully, front and back. When he was finished, he placed the magnifier and his glasses on the table and handed the watch to Sasha. He observed her intently as she held it in her hand and closed her eyes. Cable politely gestured for me to remain silent. We both sat still and hushed, as if in prayer, waiting for Sasha. After a brief moment, she jolted in her seat. She opened her eyes and hurriedly replaced the watch in its original position on the table. She nodded to Cable.

"Christopher, I'm sorry," he said. "I've already tipped the first domino, but I had to be sure."

"What are you talking about?"

"There is no doubt about it . . . JFK was wearing this watch when he was assassinated."

4

THE APPROACH

EARLY 1996

Jacquelyn White hurried down the steps of the basement. "Come quick!" she said breathlessly to her husband. "There's someone on the phone for you." Robert registered both shock and excitement in her voice.

"Who is it?" he asked, wondering why she had bothered to come down the stairs, rather than just yell like she usually did.

"It's Ronald Reagan," she said, with urgency.

"President Reagan?"

"Yesssss," she hissed, "President Ronald Reagan . . . just get the phone. Hurry up!"

Jacquelyn was on Robert's heels as he ran up the stairs to pick up the receiver. Still thinking it had to be a prank, he said, "Hello?"

"Hello, Mr. White." There was no mistaking the voice. "This is Ron Reagan calling you from California."

"Hello, Mr. President, how . . . how are you, sir?"

"Fine, fine, thank you, Mr. White. I'm calling you because a little bird told me President Kennedy's secretary left you the majority of her estate."

"Yes, that's correct."

"Well," Reagan said, "I'd like you to come meet me in Beverly Hills, so we can talk in person about it. The whole trip will be taken care of; you don't have to worry about a thing."

"That would be an honor, Mr. President." Robert paused for a moment; he wondered if he should ask. "Would you mind if I brought my son, Zac? It would mean the world to him to meet you."

"Yes, yes, that would be fine, Mr. White. Bring him with you."

***

One week later, Robert and his son walked through the front doors of an office building in Los Angeles, to meet the former President of the United States. Robert's heart pounded in his chest. They were greeted by a smiling Ronald and Nancy Reagan, who bid them sit down in the comfortable lounge area. Robert had brought something with him he hoped the former president would appreciate. He handed Reagan a white box; it contained three wallets. Two were JFK's, and one was Abraham Lincoln's. Reagan took out a black leather wallet. "That one's President Kennedy's," Robert said.

"Really, Robert," Reagan exclaimed, "I think these are the nicest gifts anyone has ever given me."

Robert froze. He swallowed audibly. How could he tell the former president that the nicest gifts he had ever received were not intended as gifts at all? They were among Robert's most prized possessions. This was not a good start. Robert broke into a sweat. He searched the room for inspiration. What could he say to get the wallets back? He made eye contact with a Secret Service agent standing nearby. The agent merely raised his eyebrows and shrugged.

Reagan broke into a huge smile. "Gotcha!" He chuckled. "But really, Robert, thank you for bringing these to show Nancy and me."

Robert laughed in nervous relief, but he also felt like he might throw up. He took a few deep breaths to calm himself as Reagan reverently inspected President Kennedy's wallet. "I have both wallets from his presidency," Robert said, "but this is the one he had with him in Dallas."

Reagan solemnly felt the supple leather before opening it to reveal the gold embossed initials "J.F.K." and a deep imprint where something had sat in the wallet for a very long time. Reagan handed it to his wife, as Robert passed him the second black billfold. It was heavier than the first; it had a large, solid gold St. Christopher money clip fastened inside. It was clear: the medallion was the source of the imprint in the previous wallet. "What's the significance of the money clip?" Reagan asked.

Robert was eager to share. "It replaced an identical one that Jackie bought for President Kennedy for their first wedding anniversary. They placed the original in the grave of their infant son, Patrick, in August '63."

Reagan closed the second wallet and passed it to his wife.

"Was John wearing it when he was shot?" Nancy asked, her voice thick with emotion.

"Evelyn Lincoln wrote a note for my museum that said President Kennedy only wore it for a short while, then discarded it. But she told me he always wore it in his breast pocket, over his heart. The unofficial story says it was in his pants pocket when he was assassinated.

Nancy visibly trembled. "This gets me so mad, Ronny. That was almost you; I almost lost you."

Reagan nodded his head. "It's OK, dear." He tried to comfort his wife from the unexpected distress the wallet and its story, had drawn from her.

Robert knew she was referring to the near-fatal attempt on President Reagan's life, outside the Washington Hilton Hotel, just two months after he became president.

"You need to tell him, Ronny." Nancy implored her husband.

Reagan nodded again, acknowledging her request, as he picked up the other wallet from the box. "Tell me about this one, Robert."

"That was President Lincoln's; he used it throughout the Civil War."

Reagan held it in his hand, and ran his thumb over the aged yet soft leather. He looked at Robert and said in a somber tone, "I want to talk to you alone for a moment; would you follow me, please."

It wasn't a question, so Robert rose and followed Reagan into the next room, leaving his son, Zac, with the former First Lady and the Secret Service agent.

Once alone, Reagan said, "I want to talk to you about your inheritance."

"Ok." Robert was excited to talk to a former president about his Kennedy items.

"What we discuss today must remain confidential."

"Yes, sir."

"My understanding is that you were left a great deal of material, and information, that never went through the assassination review process, or reached the National Archives."

"I guess that's possible, sir; I'm still going through it all."

"When Bobby Kennedy was assassinated in my home state, it hit me hard. I had debated him on *CBS Television* the year before. Bobby thought the problems of our country stemmed from corruption, and needed to be fixed from within. In my view, communism was the evil behind the weaknesses in the U.S., and our focus should remain on treating them as our enemy. Once I became president, and was shot, well, that experience changed me. I have embraced more of what Bobby was talking about in '68.

"The government pushed him hard to gather up sensitive materials regarding his brother's assassination. He did not cooperate . . . after his assassination, it all went quiet. Since then each new president is made aware they must publically agree with the findings of the Warren Commission.

"When the *Challenger* exploded, the national disaster that struck during my presidency, I made sure the American people knew all the facts . . . but to be fair, I wasn't facing issues of imminent war, as the Warren Commission was.

"Anything concerning President Kennedy's assassination, or of the policies of the Kennedy brothers towards Cuba, is treated as a national security concern; those materials must be placed in the custody of the National Archives. The President of the United States is directed as to when, and if, these materials will become public, or remain secured. I have been informed that much of the information on the participants in the assassination has long been destroyed; a CIA man named James Angleton took care of that.

"In 1992, George H.W. Bush created the Assassination Records Review Board, the ARRB, after Oliver Stone's movie *JFK* came out and caused a stir in the public. The board was meant to be just another pacifier for this generation, like the Warren Commission was in the 60's. It was established to make Americans believe they would get answers, but in reality, whatever had to stay classified would do so, by mandate of the intelligence community.

"But the ARRB really became operational under Clinton's presidency; he personally appointed the members of the board. It's become a useful tool to gather all information under one blanket . . . it's starting to shake the tree of the national security establishment."

"Sir, what does all of this mean for me?" Robert asked.

"There hasn't been much of a concern until Evelyn Lincoln passed away and the bulk of her items were willed to you, rather than the Kennedy Library, or the National Archives. You likely have evidence that was secured by Bobby Kennedy . . . that's a game changer. It puts you in quite the sticky wicket, Robert; you will be brought before the board to testify. If they find you have those materials, you'll be ordered to surrender them. They will be classified, and removed from the public indefinitely."

Robert started to panic at the former president's foresight.

Reagan continued, "It's important that no embarrassing information ever reach the American people through a foreign government, especially Russia; it would undermine our democratic process, and subvert our national security."

Robert didn't like what he was being told.

Reagan could see him struggling. "As Americans, we have to fix our own problems and acknowledge our own mistakes. We cannot afford to have a foreign government preach to the American people that our government lied to them, and worst case, offer up evidence in support. With all respect, Robert, you are not an institution, or a trusted member of government sworn to secrecy. There will be concerns and interested parties in this.

"In 1976, President Carter attempted to involve himself in JFK's assassination evidence. Bush, then Director of the CIA, told him it was need-to-know and Carter didn't need to know. President Nixon also involved himself with the assassination, thinking it could be used as leverage to help his position, but it ended up bringing down his presidency.

"Robert, I need you to understand what is riding on this. After you review your inheritance, you will know more about this matter than the current President of the United States. I would like to know your intentions regarding the materials in your possession."

Robert sat transfixed. He couldn't believe it; he'd just been told by a former president he idolized that his inheritance was of urgent concern to the government. He hesitated; it hadn't crossed his mind . . . *National security?* He had only ever looked at his inheritance as historically significant . . . but Evelyn Lincoln had willed these items to him; he had every right to keep them.

Reagan could see Robert was still trying to process, so he continued from a different perspective. "The government will question your patriotism if you refuse to cooperate with them. Releasing documented, hurtful truths could unravel the trust between the government and the people it's supposed to serve. Although now . . ." Reagan paused, deep in thought, "maybe we have become our own biggest threat. Government has not been the solution to the problem . . . government is the problem." He paused again and spoke quietly, almost to himself. "Maybe it *is* time . . ." his voice trailed off.

After a moment of silence he put his hand on Robert's shoulder and spoke, strong and sure. "I ask you pray about this matter Robert, and do whatever that prayer leads you to do."

Robert was uncomfortable with political agendas. Everything Reagan had told him felt threatening. He just wanted to keep his inheritance, and open his museum.

"Oh, one more thing," Reagan said, before leaving to rejoin his wife and Robert's son in the adjacent room. "Have you sold, or transferred, any of your inheritance to anyone else?"

5

THE SECRETS OF EVENTS

JANUARY 1996

I had the overwhelming feeling that Cable must have made some sort of mistake. I couldn't imagine a scenario where evidence in JFK's assassination would wind up in my hands. How could it be possible? If accurate, it had serious implications. I had to find out . . . I couldn't afford to be uninformed about something of this magnitude. I had to get in touch with Robert White.

When I called, he seemed eager to chat, but I was too anxious for pleasantries. "Robert, a former Canadian intelligence officer came to my house to inspect the Cartier watch I got from you. He told me President Kennedy was wearing it when he was assassinated, and that the CIA and Mafia have been looking for it for thirty-three years . . . could that be true?"

I was met with silence. Robert knew something, but didn't want to address it with me. He eventually answered in a very quiet and subdued tone, "I got it from Evelyn Lincoln . . . It's possible."

***

I needed to document the watch. I had to be sure of its provenance and I had to discover the sequence of events that led it into my custody . . . I decided to start by contacting the obvious authority: the John F. Kennedy Library.

I found the number for the library's head archivist, dialed, and got an answer right away. "Hello, This is June, Director of Archives for the John F. Kennedy Presidential Library. How may I help you?"

"Hello," I said. "I'm doing some research and have a question."

"I'll do my best to answer it," June responded.

"Do you have an official record of every item that President Kennedy was wearing the day he was assassinated?"

"His clothing?" she inquired.

"Not just his clothing, but very specifically *everything* he had on his person when he was shot."

"Hmm." I could hear her chewing on the end of a pen. "That would require some digging, but whatever I find I could fax to you."

"I would prefer something more official, is that possible?"

"I could photostat the originals we have on file, bind them, and put them under the National Archive seal as true and correct copies of our records. Is that official enough for you?"

"June, that would be perfect," I said. "I happen to be doing work in British Columbia, Canada, at the moment; could you send them to me here?"

"That's no problem; just give me your address and I'll make sure they get to you."

FEBRUARY 1996

I was very happy to find that June had stayed true to her word. When the manila envelope arrived, I opened it right away. A rivet went through each document and they were all bound together with a red ribbon; the National Archives seal was placed over top of the rivet and ribbon. It was very official.

The cover page said: "National Archives and Records Administration, by virtue of the authority vested in me by the archivist of the United States, I certify on his behalf, under the seal of the National Archives of the United States, that the attached reproductions are a true and correct copy of documents in his custody. Secret Service official case of the assassination of President Kennedy, 1963–4." It was signed by Steven D. Tilley, JFK Liaison Textual Ref. Div., The National Archives, Washington, D.C. 20408.

On the main exhibit page, under the heading: "Inventory of Clothing worn by President Kennedy, receipt by FBI to FBI Lab," was the definitive list of what President Kennedy was wearing and had on his person when he was killed in Dallas:

Grey suit, Brooks Brothers
Black Leather Belt, Farnsworth-Reed, size 34
Blue and White shirt, Dillon, custom made

White Shorts, Brooks Brothers
Black Moccasin Shoes, size 10.5
White Linen Handkerchief
Tortoiseshell comb, Kent of London
Blue Silk Tie, Monsieur Christian Dior
Cloth Back Brace

There was no mention of a watch. I turned to the next page and there it was. Box 16 folder: "Secret Service Official Case of the Assassination of President Kennedy, 1963–64" and a copy of the receipt with the National Archives seal on it:

> Received this date, December 2, 1963, from Robert I. Bouck, SAIC, PRS, gold wrist watch (Cartier), with black leather watchband, property of the late John F. Kennedy.

It was signed by Clinton Hill.

Something was wrong. I couldn't quite put my finger on it. I re-read the documents until it hit me: everything he wore on November 22 went to the FBI forensic lab, but his watch did not. *Why?*

I grabbed my coat, called the dogs, and flew out the door. I drove down to the used book store on Marine Drive, just past Fourteenth Street. It was a shop jam-packed with books, old and new, that would undoubtedly have what I needed. The shelves reached to the ceiling and made a labyrinth of worn paperback and hardcover spines, but I quickly found what I was looking for: *The Death of a President* by William Manchester.

The weather outside was half decent for February. I walked the dogs down to the beach, planted myself on the bench where Shauna and I had first met, and devoured the book while the dogs played on the rocky shore. Eventually the wind picked up, and the chilly waters of Burrard Inlet whipped until the waves were white capped, but I couldn't put the book down.

I withstood the cold, until the words jumped off the paper on page 627: "[...] a week after the funeral the Secret Service delivered the wristwatch [Mrs. Kennedy] had last seen in Trauma Room No. 1 [...]"

That was the exact date on the receipt that Secret Service Agent Clint Hill had given to Secret Service Agent Robert Bouck. *Why didn't the watch—that was material evidence—go to the FBI for testing? Why was it returned to Jackie ... and why did it take ten days to return it to her?*

I was now in possession of a piece of the puzzle ... but something didn't fit; I had to figure out what it was.

LATE FEBRUARY 1996

I needed to talk to the two Secret Service Agents named on the receipt: Clint Hill and Robert Bouck. I had no way to get in touch with them so I called Gary Mack, the curator of the Sixth Floor Museum in Dealy Plaza. Mr. Mack was audibly shaken when I told him what I had in my possession. He said he didn't have any connection with Hill or Bouck, but he did have a phone number for Forrest V. Sorrels, the head of the Dallas Secret Service in 1963. I copied it down and thanked him for his help.

I wasn't sure if Sorrels would talk to me, or if he was even still alive, but I felt a nervous twinge of excitement as I dialed his number.

A woman picked up. "Hello?" It was the voice of a sweet older lady with a Texas drawl.

"Hello, ma'am, I'd like to speak to Mr. Forrest Sorrels, please."

"I'm sorry, Dear, my husband isn't well. May I ask who's calling? I can take a message."

"My name is Christopher Fulton, ma'am. I'm in possession of the wristwatch that President Kennedy was wearing when he was assassinated. I'm documenting it."

"Oh! I assume you're working for the family?"

Her kindly question caught me totally off guard . . . I couldn't think how to respond, so I said, "I need to record its chain of custody." I think she believed my real answer to be, *Yes*.

"Please hold on a moment while I talk to my husband," she said.

I waited, hoping I wouldn't be shut down upon her return. When she did come back she said, "I told my husband what you need. He wanted me to tell you that you should speak with Mr. Roger Warner and Mr. Robert Bouck." My heart did a double beat at Bouck's name; things were starting to connect.

"Could your husband provide me with their contact information?" I asked, hoping one open door would lead to another.

The obliging Mrs. Sorrels replied, "I'm sure I can help you with that. I'll get the information and call you back. What's your number, Dear?" Once she jotted down my number, she said, "Ok, nice to speak with you, Mr. Fulton. I'll talk to you again soon."

"Thank you, ma'am." As we hung up, I feared I might never hear from her again.

It was striking that Sorrels knew exactly what I was talking about, even after all these years. He remembered the president's wristwatch . . . and whom I would need to contact about it. The enormity of what I was dealing with began to sink in and a vibrating nervousness pulsed through my veins.

Thirty minutes later, Mrs. Sorrels called back. "Hello, Mr. Fulton, I have the numbers you need."

"Thank you, ma'am."

As she read them to me, I noticed that Secret Service Agent Roger Warner's phone number had a 703 area code, not 214. Mrs. Sorrels explained that he was transferred to Washington D.C. after the assassination, and he moved to Virginia. Secret Service Agent Robert Bouck's number also had a 703 area code. I wrote down the numbers quickly. "I really appreciate your help, Mrs. Sorrels; please give my best to your husband and thank him for me."

"Oh, that's fine, Dear," she said. "You tell everyone you're working with that we said hello . . . and good luck." I heard a smile of approval in her voice and the click of the receiver as she hung up.

I smiled, too. I was eager to continue, so I dialed Roger Warner's number. Lo and behold, a gruff voice on the other end said, "Hello?"

"Mr. Warner? Roger C. Warner, former special agent with the Secret Service?"

"Who's speaking?"

I tried to keep a composed, flat tone. "My name is Christopher Fulton; I'm in possession of President Kennedy's Cartier wristwatch, the one he was wearing when he was killed. I'm documenting it as material evidence, and was told to contact you."

Warner realized that I must have had access to classified information. "Sir, may I ask who you're working for?"

The answer I gave could make or break the conversation; I had to think on my feet.

Encouraged by my exchange with Mrs. Sorrels, I took some liberty and replied, "Mr. Warner, don't worry about who I'm working for. I need you to fill out a notarized, sworn statement of your actions that involved the evidence, following President Kennedy's assassination." The authoritative voice I used for the job site served me well.

Warner's cautious attitude changed immediately. "Yes, sir."

I asked him to give me a detailed synopsis of what his role was that day.

"If I tell you verbally, does everything have to be put in the sworn statement?"

I thought quickly and said, "No, if I feel you've been forthcoming, we can limit your statement to the basic facts of your involvement."

He opened up. "I was interrogating Oswald when Agent Sorrels asked me to investigate a claim by the head of security at Parkland Hospital, a Mr. O.P. Wright, who said he had been in possession of the wristwatch since the president's death. We were sure all the president's possessions had been collected and accounted for aboard *Air Force One*, so I thought it was a mistake or a hoax.

"After Oswald was killed, I had time to investigate the watch and discovered it was not a mistake. I picked it up from Mr. Wright. He had initially received it from a nurse, Diana Bowron, in Trauma Room One. The watch had been documented in Parkland's logs, and Special Agent in Charge Sorrels contacted Washington to let them know they had missed it."

Although I remained calm on the phone, I was hurriedly writing down everything he said.

"When I picked up the watch, it was wrapped in a handkerchief. I unfolded it to verify the contents before leaving the hospital. It was unpleasant to see; the watch was encrusted with gore. I was careful not to touch it or change its condition in any way; those were my orders from Agent Bouck in Washington."

"Where is the report you filed?"

"It's classified."

"What happened once the watch transferred out of your custody?"

"Sir, I think you need to speak to Robert Bouck about that. Bouck was head of the Protective Research Section; he was the agent in charge of the most sensitive assassination materials."

"Mr. Warner, please make sure your statement is signed and notarized, and send it to me as soon as possible."

The call ended after Mr. Warner said, "Yes, sir."

The tumblers of the lock clicked into place. It was clear that agents responded to inside information. These men would do exactly what they were trained to do: loyally follow orders. Part of me felt bad for leading Warner, but I hadn't lied; I did have the evidence in my possession.

A close friend once told me, the most important thing to know in seeking information is what questions to ask. The information is almost always there; you just need to know what the combination is to unlock the answers. I wondered what door I had just unlocked.

I would wait to call Agent Bouck. I wanted to give Warner's affidavit a chance to arrive; I wanted to see what he put in writing.

MID-MARCH 1996

It was pouring with rain outside; it spattered loudly on the window as Shauna and I sat down to breakfast. It had been raining for a week. I was reading the Warren Report from 1964 on President Kennedy's assassination. Shauna sighed as I pushed my eggs and toast away to turn to a book-marked page in the volume in front of me. As I scanned it, I found the testimony of Diana Bowron, the nurse who had assisted in trying to save the president's life in Parkland Hospital on November 22, whom Roger Warner had mentioned. It was a transcript of her interview.

The commission posed question after question, asking her for detailed information about her personal awareness of the president's specific wounds, what happened to anything that the president's blood had touched, the people present at the hospital, and articles written after the fact that included her name. When they had finished questioning her, they asked, "Do you have anything to add that you think might be helpful in any way to the commission?"

"Yes," Bowron stated. "When we were doing a cutdown on the president's left arm, his gold watch was in the way and they broke it—you know, undid it. It was slipping down and I just dropped it off of his hand and put it in my pocket. I forgot completely about it until his body was being taken out of the emergency room, and then I realized. I ran out to give it to one of the Secret Service men, or anybody I could find, and I found this Mr. Wright."

"Was that the same day?"

"Yes—he had only just gone through O.B.—I was just a few feet behind him."

"Do you think of anything else that might be of assistance to the commission?"

"No, sir."

"Thank you very much for coming, Miss Bowron, thank you."

It seemed blatant to me: here was a young nurse notifying the commission—whose sole purpose was to investigate every possible lead in the assassination of President John F. Kennedy— that she had removed material evidence, that was subsequently left behind by the Secret Service, and they only asked her one inconsequential question about it. In fact, they stopped any further discussion of it all together. According to the commission, a linen hamper was of more interest to them than the president's wristwatch, which was direct evidence in the assassination and would have been required to go to the FBI for forensic testing

I decided I should try to contact Ms. Bowron. I spent the next few days trying to locate her. I knew she had been on loan to Parkland Hospital from England, so I was eventually able to find her hometown, but no phone number. I did the only thing I could think of: I called up the town's head constable.

"Hello, Police Department, Constable Taylor speaking."

"Hi, my name is Christopher Fulton; I'm calling from British Columbia, Canada." There was a strange echo on the phone where each word came back to me immediately after I said it.

"Oh, how is everything out your way?" he asked cheerfully. My granddaughter goes to university out there."

"Well, it's very beautiful here . . . except when it isn't, about nine months out of the year."

Constable Taylor laughed. "It seems the British Colony also has British weather."

I was glad he was in a good mood. "Constable, I was hoping you could help me; I would like to speak with Diana Bowron. I believe she lives in your town. Is there any way you could get me in touch with her?"

The phone went quiet; then he spoke abruptly. "One hundred thousand dollars."

"Excuse me?" I said.

Again the officer spoke boldly and without compromise. "I know the person you're interested in; I'll let you speak with her for one hundred thousand dollars. She's been in hiding a long time."

It was clear, I was on the trail of *something*. "Wow, that's a lot of money," I said. "Let me get back to you."

I hung up the phone and tried to figure out what had just happened. A joke? No, a real offer; he certainly sounded serious. Contacting Ms. Bowron was obviously beyond my resources. I would just have to move on.

***

My research also led me to contact the Office of Protocol in Washington, D.C.; Steve Landregan and C.J. Price, administrators at Parkland Hospital who knew O.P. Wright; O.P. Wright's widow, Elizabeth L. Wright, who told me her husband's report at Parkland Hospital on November 22, 1963, had been classified *Top Secret*; Nurse Hinchcliffe's daughter; Dr. Ronald Jones, who did the cutdown on President Kennedy's left arm; William Greer's widow, who told me that even though her husband was the limousine driver for Kennedy, he really disliked the president; and Joe

Hagan, the funeral preparer who had worked with three other men to prepare President Kennedy's body for burial. Hagan had personally picked up the president's remains from Bethesda. He told me he was given strict orders from the White House Secret Service detail and the FBI not to discuss any factors relating to points of entry of the bullets, or their effects.

**

I was excited when I finally received the letter from former agent Roger Warner. I tore open the envelope and a formal affidavit fell out.

> ROGER C. WARNER
> Special Agent, Secret Service
> Dallas, TX 1963.
>
> Statement given February 29, 1996.
>
> I was sent to pick up the president's wristwatch from O.P. Wright at Parkland Hospital. I did not look at the watch, I was not interested in seeing it. We were very busy at the time. I don't recall exactly how we sent it back to Washington. Because the watch was the personal possession of President Kennedy, we were not required to testify about it, so a specific receipt was not issued to me. But everything in the assassination went back and through PRS section of the Secret Service in Washington, D.C. where careful documentation took place. That was our clearance house for the items from Dallas.
>
> Roger C. Warner
> Date: 11 March, 1996
> Notary: Catherine M. Frank
> State of Virginia
> County of Fairfax.

I had just received a sworn statement from the Secret Service. *Incredible!* They were legendary for never providing any information in writing, especially regarding President Kennedy's assassination. I could see that Warner had worded the affidavit very carefully to protect the integrity of the service and himself—understandable, considering his report on the matter had been classified.

Now it was confirmed: a piece of material evidence from President John F. Kennedy's assassination had somehow slipped through the cracks of official investigation, and wound up in my possession. I could only imagine it would have overwhelming sentimental value for the Kennedy family, considering the president was wearing it during the last moments of his life. Why didn't the Kennedy family have it in *their* possession? Maybe they didn't want it for a reason. Did they not know about it? How could the Canadian and U.S. intelligence services know about it, but not the family? Something was missing; this was an enigma.

JUNE 1996

It was movie night. Shauna went to Frontier Video and picked out Oliver Stone's *JFK*. Back at home, we settled on the couch with the dogs and a bowl of popcorn. Something caught my eye when the opening credits were running. There was a piece of footage from Dallas: a flash of President Kennedy and his wife in the limousine, as it rolled along in the motorcade. I saw a glint of gold on the president's wrist. I hit rewind and froze the frame on that exact image. It was the Cartier wristwatch, revealing itself from under JFK's shirt cuff. The image was overlaid by the credit "SCREENPLAY BY OLIVER STONE & ZACHARY SKLAR." I wanted that image.

The next day I tried to contact Oliver Stone through his production company, but wasn't able to reach him. I thought if anyone else could help me, it would be the movie's technical assistant, Robert Groden. Luckily, Gary Mack of the Sixth Floor Museum also had his phone number.

When I got hold of Mr. Groden, he said he was extremely busy. I managed to get out that I was interested in obtaining a specific frame from the beginning of the Stone film. He said he was being pulled in too many directions and couldn't help me; a recent divorce had left him in financial crisis. Just before hanging up, he asked, "Why you are interested in that particular image?"

I was hesitant to tell him, but realized I couldn't expect something for nothing. "Mr. Groden, you can see President Kennedy's wristwatch in that frame; I own that watch."

He was surprised by my answer, and I was surprised by his. "Let me see what I can do," he said, and hung up.

It wasn't long before Mr. Groden called me back. "I did some research for you," he said. "That image is number 030..06,30 from the DCA film. I cut the original 35mm slide from my copy of the film, and I've had the image printed for you. Give me your address and I'll mail it to you; you can do whatever you want with it." Needless to say I was very grateful, and thanked him profusely for his efforts and generosity.

Mr. Groden went on to tell me about multiple films taken during the assassination. They gave different perspectives from diverse angles, and all of them had been withheld from the American public. We continued to talk in depth until I thought to ask him if his phone could be tapped. Without hesitation, he said, "Of course; my phones have been tapped ever since I published my first book."

With that I said, "It's been very nice speaking with you, Mr. Groden." and promptly ended the conversation.

I later received a kind letter in the mail, along with the original slide and printed image. I could see the round, gold watch protruding from President Kennedy's sleeve as he flipped his hair back with his left hand. Only a quarter of it was exposed from under his shirt cuff, but I could see it. In thanks for his time and assistance, I felt compelled to send Mr. Groden what I could afford, to help with his divorce.

That first image fueled me to find more photographs of JFK wearing the watch. I quickly found two snapshots by his photographer, Jacques Lowe. One showed Kennedy, as a senator, wearing the watch while smoking a cigar. It was on the cover of a 1992 publication of GQ magazine that featured an article on Oliver Stone defending his movie.

I called Jacques at his home in New York. He was standoffish, until I told him why I wanted his photos. I purchased two prints; he signed them both before sending them to me.

**

I had spoken with my mother about the events that had occurred since New Year's Day. As she had known Robert Kennedy, I found her to be a helpful sounding board.

I told her I wanted to get the watch back to the Kennedy family, but she said, "You can't just walk up to the Kennedys and say, 'I own something that should have been examined as material evidence in the president's murder. . .' They won't know where you're coming from. Any approach, without a trusted intermediary, could be construed as a possible angle for blackmail. You'll need to use a world-class broker to make this work, and they'll need to see your provenance before they contact the family."

A few months after that conversation, she called me back with an idea that illuminated a possible way forward. "The Jacqueline Kennedy Onassis Auction was just recently held by Sotheby's Auction House. They would be perfect to arrange a transfer of the Cartier. Once approached by Sotheby's, I'm sure the Kennedy family would be more than happy to compensate you for your time and expenses in exchange for the watch."

At my mother's suggestion, I felt like a huge weight had been lifted from my shoulders. Documenting the watch had been exciting and important, but I had gone as far as I thought I should. Events surrounding the watch had been classified; I had been fortunate to receive the affidavit from Agent Warner. I felt it was time to get the watch into the hands of the Kennedy family; they should be the people to decide to either continue documenting the evidence, or not. And now I had a clear way to get that evidence to them.

6

UNDER AMERICAN SKIES

JULY 1996

I was going to ask Shauna to marry me. I knew her family would want the wedding in Canada, but I was born with an American heartbeat. I had grown up in Washington D.C., so that's where I would ask her to be my wife.

***

It was Shauna's first time to the East Coast; I rented a convertible so she wouldn't miss a thing as we drove around the city. The Smithsonian museum was our first stop. She gasped at the enormity of the blue whale that hung above our heads as we entered the Natural History section. At the Air and Space Museum, I pointed out the *Spirit of St. Louis*. "That's the single-engine airplane that took Charles Lindbergh on the first transatlantic flight."

"There's no windshield," she said aghast.

I smiled. "I'm sure it's never easy to accomplish something great."

Then Shauna turned to me with a girlish grin plastered on her face and eagerly pleaded, "Can we see the Hope Diamond?"

"Of course." *Perfect*, I thought, as I patted the small box in my pocket for the hundredth time that day, *I'm going to give her a diamond, but first she wants to see one of the most valuable ones in the world!*

It was crowded, but we were able to get up close. Her mouth hung open for a moment as she peered through the glass. The gargantuan blue diamond was impressive, set vividly, surrounded by uniquely shaped white diamonds. "How much do you think it's worth?" she asked.

"I don't know. It was part of the crown jewels worn by King Louis the ... whatever." I rolled my eyes; I thought it was the sixteenth, but I couldn't remember for sure. Something about Shauna made me forget most of the historical facts and dates I prided myself on knowing.

"During the French Revolution!" she said.

"Yes ... that one. Did you know it glows red under ultraviolet light?"

"Really?" she whispered as she leaned in for a closer look. "I heard it's cursed."

"Lucky it's behind glass then," I said with a grin.

We could have spent a week in the museum and not seen everything, but there were so many other landmarks I wanted to show her. We walked down Pennsylvania Avenue until we reached its most important address: 1600, the White House. We stood together outside the black wrought iron fence, and took in the grandeur of the official home of the president. I wanted to sound clever, but I could only think of one story to tell: "Winston Churchill once stayed here," I blurted out. "Late one evening he walked out of the bathroom, naked, with only a cigar in his mouth."

"Uh-huh?" she said with a mischievous smirk.

"Well ... he saw the ghost of Abraham Lincoln, but the apparition was more startled by the naked Churchill than vice versa."

Shauna laughed.

"There's also a black ghost cat in the basement that's rarely seen, but when it is, it foretells a national disaster. Apparently it was seen right before Kennedy was assassinated."

Shauna looked at me and wrapped her arms around my neck, gave me a kiss, and said, "Thank you for bringing me here. It means the world to me."

It was a nice moment, but not *the* moment. "Hungry?" I asked.

"Yes!"

"Then let's go ... before we see that cat!"

We went to one of my favorite restaurants and had Maryland's trademark blue crabs for lunch. We talked for a while about the history of the nation's capital and my youth. Then I caught Shauna in a moment of introspection. "What are you thinking about?" I asked.

"Nothing really ... the ghost cat you mentioned at the White House ... your mom told me a story about a black cat that showed up at her door when she first found out she was pregnant with you. The cat came and stayed with her, sitting on her lap every day until you born, but when she brought you home from the hospital, the cat was gone and she never saw it again."

"She told you that story?" I asked, wondering why she would share such an obscure anecdote.

"Do you think it's real? The black ghost cat in the White House?"

"I don't know, President Reagan thought so."

"Christopher, what are you going to do with President Kennedy's watch?"

"I wanted to pass it down; I wanted to be able to show my future children that history really happened, it's not just in a book or a movie . . . but now I'll do everything I can to make sure it gets back to the Kennedy family."

Shauna warmed to my mention of future children. Suddenly she blurted out, "You should go."

"Go where?" I asked puzzled.

"Russia."

I had told Shauna about an unusual offer I had received from Mehran Mikhailov, the man whose New Year's Eve party we had attended back in '95. As Mehran and I were both lovers of history, we had shared our knowledge from both the American and Russian sides. He was pleased with the tower I had built for him in Vancouver and had asked me to go to Moscow to do some work for him there. I would be hired short-term, with great pay, to consult on the renovation of dilapidated apartments, but I had kept turning down his offer.

Shauna tried to persuade me. "Christopher, it's a once-in-a-lifetime opportunity. It will be a chance to experience a side of history you've never seen before, just like the experience you're giving me now."

"Yes, but it's Russia, not exactly the history I'm interested in!"

"Go on, you're fascinated by the history of humankind."

"I don't like the idea of leaving you behind; also, I'd have to get permission to go, I'd have to sub out contracts while I'm gone . . ."

"It's only a month, and you're being offered five times what you make here, paid in full before you even leave! That's enough money to put a deposit down on a house." She smiled coyly.

She made a good argument; maybe I would reconsider.

After lunch we walked to the Vietnam Veterans Memorial and looked on in silence at the 58,266 names etched into the gabbro wall. There was name after name, like typed pages of a roll call. Our hearts went out to their families.

As the sun started to set, everything glowed with hues of gold. I took Shauna's hand and we walked beside the reflecting pool; the still water mirrored the dramatic sky. We continued up the steps of the Lincoln Memorial, then stood in silence and admired the Great Emancipator, immortalized in marble, towering above us. I stared at Lincoln's words engraved into the wall: "That this nation under God shall have a new birth of freedom—and that government of the people, by the people, for the people shall not perish from the earth." I missed America, I missed home.

I knew this was my moment. Still holding her hand, I got down on one knee. "Shauna, everything I am, everything I have worked for, has been for you. I want the rest of my life to be for you, too." I opened the box and revealed the ring I had been inspired to design for her.

"Shauna, will you marry me?"

"Yes," she said breathlessly.

I slipped the ring on her finger and we stood holding each other. I felt the rhythm of our heartbeats change from two to one.

7

NEWTON'S LAW

MARCH 3, 1999

"**W**ho told you to sell the watch privately through Sotheby's Auction House?" Barman was trying to march me to the cannon's mouth.

"I wanted to get it back to the Kennedy family; my mother suggested I use an institutional broker."

"Your mother gave you direction . . . are you aware that your mother gave Linda Tripp direction on how to handle the media regarding the Monica Lewinsky scandal?"

Jesus! They must have tapped Linda's phone. "I had no knowledge of that."

"What is your mother's relationship to Linda Tripp?"

"They're friends."

"Does your mother hold a grudge against President Clinton, or his administration?"

"No."

"What other advice did she give you in regards to the assassination evidence in your possession?"

"None."

EARLY SEPTEMBER 1996

I called Sotheby's auction house in New York and asked to speak to the head of the department for U.S. historical items. I explained what I had and was informed that I should speak directly to Sotheby's Executive Vice President: Warren P. Weitman Junior. I was transferred immediately.

Weitman came on the line. "Hello, Mr. Fulton; my colleague explained to me that you are in possession of a very special item and would like us to handle a private sale for you."

"Yes, that's correct."

"Wonderful. Now, I will have a difficult time giving you an accurate estimate at this juncture; however, if you could send us any information you have, I will personally review it and get back to you as soon as possible."

In response to Weitman's request, I compiled several copies of my records on the assassination evidence and placed each in a light blue, leather-bound book. I had one copy mailed to Weitman overnight.

Several days later I received a phone call and heard the distinguished voice of Mr. Warren P. Weitman Jr. "Mr. Fulton, thank you for the book you sent documenting President Kennedy's Cartier wristwatch. After careful review by several heads of departments, we've come to the conclusion that Sotheby's would love to sell it privately for you, but we will require your legal release before we can contact the Kennedy family. Once we have a confidentiality agreement in place we can proceed. We've already prepared the release; all we require is your signature."

"Of course," I said, "but there must be several stipulations: one, nobody but the immediate family of JFK is to see the information; two, my name is not to be shared with anyone without my prior written permission; and three, the evaluation material I sent you is to be retained by you and returned to me at the close of the transaction, with no copies made." I thought if the family requested any further information or documents, we could draw up a contract specifying the care that would require.

"Consider it done," Weitman said. "I'll have the release faxed to you within the hour. Thank you, Mr. Fulton."

I was concerned about how the Kennedys would react. I was in a difficult position, but if the sale proceeded, the watch would find its proper place and I could get on with my life. Once the agreement arrived, I signed it and sent it back for Weitman's counter signature, along with a personal letter I had written for JFK Jr. It read:

> First, let me congratulate you on your marriage; I wish you nothing but happiness.
>
> I want to inform you that my corporation has acquired a personal item that belonged to your father, through his late secretary, Evelyn Lincoln. The auction Sotheby's held on behalf of your mother was so well done that I want to sell the item in my posses-

sion to your family through them. I want no publicity, so we have signed non-disclosure agreements.

The item in discussion is the documented Cartier wristwatch your father wore on Dallas November 22. Because of the highly personal nature of this piece, I wanted to contact you personally.

I suggest that 15% of the proceeds be given to the JFK library, and another 10% to a cause of your choice. Your concerns and/or suggestions are encouraged and appreciated. If you are not interested in purchasing this item, I would like Sotheby's to sell it publicly. If you are adamantly opposed to a public sale, please write a letter to Sotheby's stating your feelings as such, and I will honor your wishes.

Thank you, and best to you and your wife.

I didn't sign the letter.

Weitman called me two days later to inform me that Caroline Kennedy would be coming to Sotheby's New York office to review my book documenting the watch's provenance. He promised to contact me immediately following that meeting. The day and time of the meeting came and went, but I received no call from Mr. Warren P. Weitman Jr.

I decided to give it another day before I rang him back. "Mr. Weitman, this is Christopher Fulton, I was expecting to hear from you yesterday."

"Yes, my apologies, things got rather intense here. Caroline Kennedy came into our office and I personally handed her your book. She asked if she could read it alone. I acquiesced and left the room; she was in there for hours." He paused.

"So where are we?"

"I'm not exactly sure," Weitman said quietly.

I was perplexed. "What do you mean?"

"Why don't we give it a few days?" he dodged.

I reluctantly agreed and waited another few days before calling Sotheby's again; I needed closure. When Weitman picked up the phone, there was a great deal of apprehension in his voice; our conversations seemed to be getting progressively more difficult. "Mr. Weitman, where are we? It's been long enough; you should have an answer for me by now."

"Yes, you're right. I apologize for not getting back to you sooner, but you see, I have a slight problem; the situation has become somewhat delicate."

"Tell me exactly what you mean," I said.

"Legal has advised me to stall you for as long as possible, but I've personally decided it would be better if we spoke openly."

I didn't respond.

Weitman continued, "You see, when we contacted the Kennedy family about your material, we had very little time to prepare. Caroline Kennedy notified us that she would visit the office almost immediately. We didn't want to postpone the appointment, so we agreed. When she arrived and asked to be alone with the material, our hopes were to proceed with the sale, or, in a worst-case scenario, to be told there was no interest. Unfortunately we weren't given either response."

"Alright then," I said, frustrated, "send me my book back."

"Well . . . that's part of the problem," came Weitman's halting response. "You see, Caroline Kennedy took your book."

"I beg your pardon?" I said, taken aback, "We have a contract that clearly stipulates the book would remain in your sole possession and be returned to me as soon as our business was concluded."

"I know, but please see our position," he said defensively. "We couldn't just stop Caroline Kennedy from leaving the building."

"Let me get this straight: you're telling me that Caroline Kennedy has my research, has caused a breach in our contract, and has given no permission one way or the other for the sale to her family to go ahead?"

"She was adamant; she said she needed more time with your documentation and that she wanted her uncle, Ted Kennedy, to review it. By allowing her to leave with your material, it was my hope we could reach a favorable conclusion, but it does not seem to have worked out that way. Please, Mr. Fulton, what can we do to remedy this?"

"Did JFK Jr. make contact with you?" I wondered if Caroline had been representing all of the immediate family.

"No." It was an unhelpfully simple reply.

I was distraught. I had been sure that a private sale through Sotheby's was going to be the answer, but I had been completely stonewalled. I was also disturbed that Caroline had appropriated the information I had gathered; I clearly felt her lack of respect towards Sotheby's and myself.

It seemed I had nothing left to say to Mr. Warren P. Whiteman Jr., so our conversation ended with me being left devoid of my book of provenance and knowing I would have to continue to keep the evidence secured in my custody. Perhaps one of my earlier musings had been correct—maybe the Kennedys didn't want the watch for a reason . . .

8

LEGACY

JANUARY 29, 1997

Robert White's attorney, Jarrod Glazier, received an official phone call. It was from the Assassination Records Review Board requesting Robert meet with the board in April. Just as President Reagan had said, the request was in relation to his inherited Kennedy materials. Glazier knew the "informal" meeting would consist of federal lawyers questioning White to trap him, so they would have ammunition to pursue him with more vigor.

The board wrote an internal memo regarding that phone call:

> [. . .] [Glazier] was not cooperative in reference to the assassination materials we were seeking from White. We offered to send him some explanatory material and a copy of our legislation, purpose, and authority. Glazier said sending such material to him is irrelevant. He said, "I'm representing to you that my client does not have any assassination records as you describe them," and that he does not feel comfortable in any way about our approaching his client. We discussed possible avenues for gaining White's cooperation and Glazier mentioned the word "subpoena." Glazier reiterated that if we started asking questions, it may "open the door" to other parties seeking access to Robert White's collection.

On February 3 the ARRB sent a letter to Glazier:

> Enclosed is a copy of our letter sent to Mr. White [. . .]. The review board is attempting to contact Lincoln estate beneficiaries because we have reason to believe that the estate may have contained some

records that would be useful for understanding issues related to the assassination of President Kennedy that were dispersed by the terms of the Lincolns' wills. [. . .] Mr. White is in the best position to provide an overview of the contents of the estate and direct us to potential assassination records in the possession of other parties.

It was signed by the General Counsel of the Assassination Records Review Board.

On February 5, David G. Marwell, the executive director of the board, reached out to Robert personally:

Dear Mr. White: [. . .] The Review Board is not seeking to reach conclusions about the assassination [. . .].

As part of our effort to locate assassination records, we are contacting all of the beneficiaries of the estate of Harold and Evelyn Lincoln. Our review of the Lincolns' wills and the inventory of the Lincolns' estate indicate that some of the items left by the Lincolns may be assassination records. [. . .] diaries, notes, papers, correspondence, appointment books or other materials bequeathed by the Lincolns that may directly relate to or provide historical context to the assassination of President Kennedy. [. . .]

In further communication with the board, Glazier made it clear he would put up every possible obstacle to keep Robert and his inheritance protected. He put his reputation on the line to stop the board from even speaking to Robert. On February 24, he wrote: "[. . .] I can confirm that White did not receive nor is he in possession of any assassination related artifacts [. . .] from the Lincolns will [. . .].

[. . .] I regret that we cannot be of any further assistance to the committee in this regard."

The board responded on February 28:

[. . .] Although we have no reason to doubt his or your sincerity in this matter, it is of course entirely possible that information that may look unremarkable to him might be of significant importance to us in our work.

[. . .] It is our understanding that the U.S. Federal Government provided Mrs. Lincoln with an office in the National Archives after the assassination. During that time she had custody of materials that had been prepared at the autopsy of President Kennedy. These materials were subsequently donated to the U.S. Government by the Kennedy family. At the time the autopsy materials were inventoried, however, it was determined that some of the materials were missing. I am sure that you can understand that the U.S. Government has an interest in pursuing all leads relative to materials that had been in the custody of Mrs. Lincoln and that subsequently were found to be missing. For this reason, cryptic notes that might appear innocuous to one reader might be highly relevant to us. As a lawyer, I am sure that you understand that there may be a substantial difference between what a lawyer might (honestly) say about what he believes his client knows, and what his client might be able to describe to others.

[. . .] we continue to be interested in receiving a conscientious understanding of the records that Mrs. Lincoln left. [. . .] Most people whom we have contacted in the course of our work have been agreeable to such discussion. Others, because of the nature of their testimony, have requested that we issue subpoenas (we have also employed our statutory authority to provide witness immunity.) Although we prefer not to issue subpoenas unless necessary, we would be perfectly willing to do so if you believe that to be the most effective and advisable manner for us to proceed.

Again, we would simply prefer to have an informal discussion with Mr. White, but we are willing to proceed differently if you so advise. [. . .]

Again, it was signed by the general counsel of the ARRB.

Robert White agreed to meet the board on April 10. Glazier advised him that his testimony before the board would be reported to President Bill Clinton.

9

DIVIDED BY HISTORY

MARCH 3, 1999

"**M**r. Fulton, in 1983 you were on your way to being accepted into Annapolis Naval Academy, the most prestigious military academy in the world; why didn't you attend?"

I knew Barman was trying to establish a character flaw before the intelligence panel. "I wanted to follow in the footsteps of my father."

"But your father *was* in the Navy; he went to Cuba in the 1950's."

"Yes, he was in the Navy for ten years, but not as a career officer; he finished his service before I was born. His passion was architecture and construction."

"What did he tell you about his time in Cuba?"

"Nothing."

"Your father attended almost all of President Kennedy's press conferences. Why?"

"He worked for President Kennedy on a small task force and was invited to the White House."

"What did he tell you regarding his attendance?"

"He said he was very impressed with Kennedy, and the president was well respected by the press."

Barman paused before looking at me poignantly. "So you wanted to follow in the footsteps of a failed builder who filed bankruptcy, rather than serve your country?"

"I feel I've served my country in other ways."

"Your corporation for commercial construction is named The Twelve Global Ltd., correct?"

"Yes."

"Who are the other eleven individuals you're working with?"

"There is nobody else."

"Your father isn't one of the twelve?"

"No, he just worked for me as a consultant."

"Then why *Global*? Why *Twelve*?"

"*Global* because I work internationally, and *Twelve* for the twelve disciples; I based the name on the Bible."

"But you aren't affiliated with, or work on behalf of, any organized religion?"

"No, it's just a name. But I have donated my services to build synagogues and . . ."

Barman cut me off. "Tell me about your time in Russia."

MARCH 1997

My eyes opened and I was staring at a blank wall. The jet lag from the fourteen-hour flight to Moscow had taken it out of me, but Shauna was right, this was a once-in-a-lifetime opportunity.

Mehran Mikhailov, the man who had employed me, was running for the Duma, the Russian equivalent of the United States Senate, so I would be granted access to some of Moscow's greatest historic sites while I was working here.

I was ill-prepared for the cultural differences when I first flew in. There were girls in uniform on guard in the airport; they looked so young. They held machine guns and never smiled; I didn't know whether I felt more sad or concerned. Once I collected my luggage I found a driver waiting for me at the terminal. We sped off into traffic, where the rules of the road varied from driver to driver; even the roads themselves had no lines.

As we stopped at an intersection, I saw another young girl, likely no more than twelve years old. She was scantily dressed, exposed to the cold, and leaning provocatively against a brick wall. "Prostitute," the driver said. "Make sure you pay, or she will cut you." I was deeply saddened; she should have been playing with her friends, not trying to sell the last of her innocence on a street corner.

***

On my first full day in Moscow, I must have visited fifteen flats. My job, as I understood it, was to give a detailed analysis of what materials would be required to bring the flats up to grade-A American standards so they could be resold to international businessmen. I was amazed at the condition of the buildings; they were in a terrible state of disrepair. Many were what I imagined war-torn Europe looked like: cold, bare, dilapidated. Mehran told me that the building itself didn't matter, only how luxurious and esthetic the flats inside could be made. This was not Manhattan.

Mehran's cousin, Stanislav, "Stas," worked as my translator and bodyguard. Stas was in his mid-twenties; he was honest and spoke plainly. I believed he was a good man and I enjoyed his company, but having to rely on someone else to convey even the simplest of statements was arduous. Stas told me that under the communist regime, each individual had been assigned a flat. Since Russian politics had changed, the flats could be transferred in legal transactions. Mehran stood to make enormous profits by purchasing flats cheaply, upgrading them, then selling them to foreign businessmen, most of whom were involved in improving the infrastructure for Russian oil production. The market was hot, and buyers would bid and pay well above asking price.

Stas informed me in confidence that Mehran had managed to acquire at least one of the flats in exchange for a bottle of Vodka. That sort of unethical business practice was a direct result of the state of the country. The rich and powerful ran everything, and the poor were helplessly pushed and pulled by the enormous ebb and tide of the wealthy.

I was standing with Stas on the ground floor of one of the buildings, when a couple walked through the front door. The man saw us and immediately pushed his wife behind him. He walked backwards up the stairs, aware of my position, but keeping his eyes downcast, until his wife, nervously fumbling with her keys, opened the door to their flat. They disappeared inside, and the thick steel door shut with finality. I was confused by their strong response to our presence and asked Stas what it meant.

"Take no offense, he recognize you as foreigner," Stas said.

"How could he know that?" I asked.

"The way you dress, how you make eye contact; he know."

"What difference does eye contact make?"

"Christopher, please understand, this is not America; for many decades speaking with foreigner could mean being locked up by security services. Even relatives turned each other in for small reward; this man is trying to protect what he has because he is scared."

My heart sank; I had never experienced behavior ingrained in people from decades of misery. How does a country become like that?

***

A week into my work, Mehran handed me an invitation from the Russian Politburo, to sit in its reserved section for the showing of *Swan Lake* at the Kremlin Theatre. I was afforded the day to do some sightseeing before the performance that evening.

In the morning Stas accompanied me to the Kremlin. We passed by rows of Napoleon's cannons; each was adorned with a large N. If you asked the French, they would tell you the cannons had been abandoned when Napoleon returned home in the winter of 1812, because the Russians had burned their city and there was nothing left to conquer. If you asked the Russians, they would tell you they had captured the cannons while forcing Napoleon to retreat back to France. History depends on who's telling it.

I was enjoying the sights, when a sound cut through the air; the penetrating alarm pierced my ears. I didn't know whether to duck or run, so I froze and tried to figure out what imminent terror I was about to face. The air raid siren was painfully loud.

It was the blitz, or a cataclysmic earthquake . . . Were the missiles flying? *I was on the wrong side of the ocean!*

I noticed a distinct lack of interest in Stas, so I uncovered my ears and tried to ask what was happening.

"*Ni nado, ni nado,* don't worry," he said. "Siren was installed at order of Premier Brezhnev; is not indicating emergency."

I tried to reply above the atrocious sound. "What is it indicating?" If that noise had been heard at the White House it would have made international news.

Stas grinned. "Brezhnev was out on morning walk, and pigeon crapped on his shoulder. He ordered siren be installed to go off every day to scare pigeons away." Just then the siren stopped, and the pigeons returned.

We walked out into Red Square. St. Basil's Cathedral dominated the skyline; Mehran had arranged a private tour for me, but that would come later.

Stas and I were both hungry, so he took me to a little kiosk that sold snacks. I bought something for each of us. I noticed a stray dog in the square; he was thin, and I knew he would benefit from the food more than I would. Without observing the look of horror on Stas's face, I coaxed the dog over and fed him the remaining three quarters of my bar. I was alarmed when I saw Stas's contorted features. "What's wrong?" I asked.

"You don't understand," he said. "These are expensive, expensive candy; most Russians cannot afford such things, and you feed almost whole bar to stray dog?" Understanding dawned on me as I looked around at several drawn, pallid human faces looking on as the dog trotted back to his haunt with the last morsel already on its way to his skinny belly. "We should go," Stas said abruptly, and we walked out of the square.

Stas continued to show me around the city until we had to return to the flat to prepare for the performance at the Kremlin. We made our way back through the plaza where I had fed the starving dog. I had a sinking sensation when I didn't see hide nor hair of him. I got the distinct feeling that some of the more hungry-looking Russians had taken drastic action after seeing the dog receive such a handsome treat. I had severely under estimated the cultural differences here. With my guts hardened from unpleasant thoughts, we made our way back to the flat.

My host informed me we would be having a very special meal for dinner: chicken. As the pièce de résistance was revealed, something seemed off; the chicken looked skinny, not like the plump rotisserie chickens I was used to getting at the supermarket back home. Everybody reached to take a piece. As I grabbed a leg, I noticed it barely weighed anything. I tried to take a bite but it was just skin and bone. It reminded me of a tire with the air let out, and it tasted like one too. "Stas," I whispered, "what's wrong with this chicken?"

"What do you mean?" he replied.

"Well," I said, "it's dry, and meatless."

"That is way chicken is when it dies of old age, but you don't eat young chicken ever; they still make eggs."

If the thought of eating a chicken that had died of old age wasn't bad enough, I was totally turned off when Viktor, one of the men in the flat, went to the bathroom. The facility was a small room where the walls ended before joining the ceiling; it was open to the kitchen and eating area. We could hear every groan and bodily function as we tried to enjoy our old, dead chicken. Then the smell rose over the top of the short walls. That was it; I'd had enough. I got up and told Stas we would be leaving for the Kremlin early.

***

The performance was about to begin and a man came forward to usher Stas and me into the theater. We walked down an elaborately decorated corridor to a private elevator that was operated by a security key. "This is just for you," Stas said and stayed in the hallway as I stepped inside. The elevator rose quietly for a moment before coming to a jerky halt. When the doors slid open, I was on a balcony overlooking the stage below. Russian officials filled the lofty rows.

My guide gestured to an empty chair at the front and explained in English that President Boris Yeltsin could not attend, and would I like to have his seat. I paused for a moment. *What could I say?* "Yes," I replied, and sat down, inwardly shocked. I was in the private Politburo box reserved for top Russian government officials and VIPs, and I was sitting in Yeltsin's seat. I could tell the other members of the Politburo were curious to know who I was, but nobody was going to ask, and I wasn't going to tell.

The ornate theatre glowed with light reflected from the gilded walls. I looked down at the rows upon rows of people below; it was a full house. The lights dimmed, and the ballet began.

The power of the performers was nothing short of an example of their ability to defy gravity.

When the curtain closed, I expected a roar of applause, but instead, the audience below turned their heads to the balcony where I was seated; they were waiting for our expressed approval. I, along with the rest of the Politburo, rose and clapped, and like a reverse echo, the theatre responded. It was without a doubt one of the most memorable experiences of my life; I wished Shauna could have been there with me.

Later that evening I arrived back at the flat; it was dismal and sparse in comparison to the elaborate theatre. I was hungry, but there was no food. I sat alone and quiet at the kitchen table and looked out the distorted glass window. A cake had been set out to keep cool . . . *Ask and you shall receive.* I opened the latch and grabbed the cake. It was crawling with hundreds of small black ants; they were happily enjoying what could have been mine.

I found myself in an odd mood. Knowing there was no way to separate ant from cake, the ants didn't live to see another day, and I satisfied my craving. I found the juxtaposition comical: one moment I was sitting in the Russian president's seat at the Kremlin, next I was so hungry I gladly ate colonized ant cake.

***

A few days later, Mehran came by the flat in the evening to check my progress. It was the first time I'd seen him since I arrived in Moscow. We went over some figures; then he told me to get ready—we were going to the Easter celebration. Although I hadn't gone to church with any regularity since I was a boy, I still had a strong belief in God.

We could only drive so close to the church; five thousand people had congregated in the square outside, so we parked and joined the crowd. The event was televised for the entire country and anticipation was high. Although I was comfortable spending the ceremony on the fringe of the expansive crowd, Mehran began to push his way past people, making his way to the front of the church. It seemed disrespectful, bulldozing his way past everyone who had arrived there long before us, but I didn't want to get lost, so I followed in his wake. After several minutes of pushing and shoving, we arrived at the red velvet carpet that graced the front steps of the church. The whole area was roped off with more red velvet; it was a spectacle.

As we stood there, a priest emerged from the massive front doors of the cathedral and walked directly towards Mehran. They spoke to each other as if they were old friends. I looked out at the thousands of worshippers; they were trying to figure out who Merhan and I were.

"Follow me, keep up," Mehran said firmly. The red rope was removed and I humbly made my way to the immense cathedral, just behind Mehran and the priest. Ten thousand eyes were on us; we had bypassed everyone. We entered through the heavy wooden doors and slowly walked the center aisle. I looked for a place to sit, but every pew was crowded with parishioners. Another four thousand people watched as we walked the entire length of the nave. We didn't stop, turn left or right, but walked straight up the steps to the altar. We stood on the dais at the front of the cathedral, just to the left of the holy table. As thurifers swung their censors, smoke swirled around the bishop, priest, and deacon who stood on my left.

I surveyed the congregation in front of me; some individuals were deep in prayer, others looked directly at me; Mehran and I were the only non-members of the cloth standing in such a privileged spot on such a holy day. I didn't know why this honor had been bestowed upon me, but the position made me feel uncomfortable.

I was handed a burning candle and told not to let it drop under any circumstance. One woman in the front pew viewed me through beady eyes, set deep in her heavily wrinkled features. If I faltered, she looked as though she would use the last bit of her strength to strangle me. I stayed rooted to the floor as hot wax dripped down my hand. That intensity continued through the entire evening.

The experience was far more uncomfortable than I had bargained for. Instead of a unique outside worship among thousands, with the freedom to leave at any time, I was placed, with no explanation or forewarning, in front of four thousand devout Russians, alongside the holiest men in the church, to stand for five hours, during a service I didn't understand a word of. The evening was too extreme for me to enjoy; I was relieved when it was over.

LIKE A GAME OF CHESS

APRIL 10, 1997

Robert White and his lawyer entered a small room. At its center was a conference table and four chairs. One of two men stepped forward. "My name is Ryan Roth, I'm an attorney for the Assassination Records Review Board, and this is ARRB Senior Investigator Monty Davidson. Please, Mr. White, take a seat." Two other individuals sat in silence in the room, Senior Attorney and Analyst Kim Herd and Deputy Director Tom Samoluk.

Glazier introduced Robert and himself, before Robert took the proffered chair. "You don't mind if we tape the meeting?" Roth asked, as he placed a small recorder on the table between them. "Yes, we do," Glazier responded flatly.

"Not a problem," Roth said, swiftly removing the recorder and replacing it with a legal pad. "Mr. White, have you received all the materials you inherited under the wills of Evelyn and Harold Lincoln?"

"Yes."

"Have you reviewed all of the materials you received?"

Robert knew it was an important question, but he could only think about keeping everything he had been given; he just wanted to open his museum. "I received a lot," he began nervously, "especially documents, tens of thousands of them. I haven't been able to look at everything yet."

"Mr. White, please describe how your relationship with Evelyn Lincoln came to be, in your own words."

"I first wrote to Mrs. Lincoln in the early '60's; she sent me a letter back. I wrote to her again in the early 70's, and she sent me another letter; she included a PT109 tie clip."

"The kind President Kennedy gave out during the 1960 presidential campaign?" Roth interjected.

"Yes, exactly. Our friendship grew from there; we kept writing back and forth, and had some lunches together. She started to give me Kennedy memorabilia."

"Which graduated to more important items?"

"That's right."

"Why would she do that?" Roth asked, as he stared at Robert skeptically.

"Well," Robert said, "I helped her; I kind of acted like a buffer between her and other researchers. Everyone kept approaching her about President Kennedy, and wanted her to authenticate materials. Eventually, she only verified things for me."

"In other words, you became her way to transfer information to one source, rather than to hundreds or thousands of other people."

"Yeah, and she sort of, you know, expected me to be the one to carry on the name of President Kennedy."

"Interesting ... please continue."

"Well, by the '80's, the two of us had shared so much we were like family."

"What did she discuss with you about the assassination?"

Robert looked to his lawyer for guidance. Glazier said nothing, but gestured for Robert to state what they had previously discussed.

"Mrs. Lincoln rarely spoke about the assassination ... she was damaged by it. It continued to be a very traumatic and upsetting topic for her."

"So I gather, Mr. White, but I need more than that ..."

"Well," Robert hesitated, "she had some strange ideas about Lyndon Johnson ..."

Roth and Davidson looked up from their notes; the silence in the room was dense. Glazier put his hand on Robert's shoulder to cease further conversation on that matter and stated directly to the lawyer and investigator, "Evelyn never showed Mr. White any documents or evidence to support her ideas."

"Mr. White, are you in possession of any assassination-related materials that came to you through Evelyn and/or Harold Lincoln's wills?"

Robert's lawyer had prepared him for this question. As calmly as he could, he answered, "No." He looked nervous.

At this point, Deputy Director Tom Somaluk interjected and asked: "Mr. White, are you in possession of any dictabelt recordings or logs related to recordings?"

Again, Robert followed Glazier's instructions, and he responded, "No."

Samoluk had caught him in a lie. The atmosphere became tense, but it dissipated when Roth continued his questioning. "Mr. White, what can you tell us about the trunks and file cabinets dispensed by the Lincolns' wills?"

Robert looked to Glazier, who nodded in response. "After Mrs. Lincoln passed, Mr. Lincoln showed me where the file cabinets were. We couldn't open them because we didn't have the combinations for the locks. Mr. Lincoln died about a month later. Two weeks after his funeral I got the file cabinets open. I made an inventory, and the estate was appraised."

"What about Evelyn Lincoln's diaries and appointment books?"

"I sent them to the JFK Library."

"Please describe them for us."

"They were day-to-day journals with red covers, packed together in a box."

"What were the dates and contents of the diaries?"

"I don't know, I didn't read them." Robert sounded less than convincing.

Both lawyers looked at each other, incredulous, and made notes on their legal pads.

"Mrs. Lincoln said she burned them years ago," Robert added, trying to cover the awkward silence, "but I knew they still existed; she always referred back to a source to answer questions for me, and she did it in such great detail."

The agents continued to pause, waiting for Robert to break the silence again.

"I'm sure Mrs. Lincoln would have donated anything of historical importance to the JFK Library . . ." Robert's attempt at filling the silent space came off weak.

Roth and Davidson would have to report their findings to the president, and they still had nothing. White was either too thick or too naïve to succumb to the board's authority.

"Mr. White," Roth pushed, "fully understanding the board's obligation under law, do you have anything more to add to this meeting?"

Robert took a deep breath and said, "No."

That was his last chance.

Roth was disgusted. "Mr. White, I previously asked you about having dictabelts in your possession. We have it on good authority that you do indeed have those dictabelts. Have you been advised by your attorney of the penalties for obstructing a federal investigation, or lying to a federal agent?"

White immediately looked to Glazier who said, "My client would like to amend his answer to the aforementioned question."

"Well then," Roth asked again, "for the record, Mr. White, are you in possession of the dictabelts we asked you about earlier?"

White, defeated, said, "Yes."

"Thank you for your time, Mr. White; we will be in touch."

11

To Kill A Country

April 1997

Towards the end of my trip I got my private tour of St. Basil's Cathedral. As I walked through Red Square, I looked up at the spires; the colors stood out in sharp relief against the grey sky. Meant to emulate the kingdom of heaven, the nine chapels, corresponding to the points on a compass, reached upwards in chorus.

I thought I would be accompanied through the building, but the cathedral was closed for renovations; I was granted access to enter and explore by myself. Gold-leaf icons filled the cathedral, but the frescoes took me to a different place entirely. I imagined the artist smoothing on fresh plaster, then, precisely yet hurriedly, brushing the paint into the wet wall before it dried, creating a masterpiece that was one with the building itself. I was alone and unwatched. I held out my hand and touched the paint-infused plaster. I could feel the past centuries reverberate through the walls, through my hands and into my bloodstream. This building, like so many others, held history living inside it, stoic and absorbent as year after year passed inside and out of its bulwark.

In the 1930s, the Soviet architect Pyotr Baranovsky tried to appeal to Stalin to preserve the cathedral when it was in danger of being demolished to make more room in Red Square for the expansion of military and political demonstrations. He subsequently spent five years in the Gulag for the letter he sent to the leader of the Soviet Union, but ultimately succeeded in conserving one of the greatest landmarks in Russia.

Mehran met me when I returned from my tour. He said he had a friend who would like to speak with me about America, and told me to be at the Kremlin the next day at precisely one P.M.

***

It was quarter to one when Stas and I arrived in Red Square beneath uncharacteristically clear skies. We walked to the Kremlin and found the entrance to the building that Mehran had described. We opened the door and were met by two soldiers in uniform, their star and sickle caps at a sharp angle.

"Names," one said. When we responded, the other typed on a keyboard and nodded. We were guided through a metal detector, but any further security was bypassed; they had been expecting us.

We followed the first soldier down a series of corridors until he stopped abruptly at a door and knocked loudly. A directive was given from inside and the soldier opened the door, held it, and gestured for me to walk through. Stas went to follow, but the soldier held out a hand and kept him in the hallway.

As I walked into the expansive room, I noticed a tall, thin man in a suit standing to the right of the doorway. He was slightly balding and had a smirk on his face. He looked familiar, but said nothing.

Ahead, a stocky man in a charcoal grey suit and tie greeted me in Russian; he had a deep, bass voice. "*Zdravstvuyte.*" He walked out from behind a massive desk to shake my hand.

"Hello," I replied, and wondered who this friend of Mehran's might be. We were the only three people in the palatial room. The tall man stepped forward and said in English, "Please sit down." He gestured to the chair in front of me, and I sat. Suddenly, I realized why he looked so familiar: I had seen him in a building I had inspected . . . inside the Kremlin walls by Napoleon's cannons . . . in the square with the hungry dog . . . Now I knew this was not an impromptu meeting; this man had been keeping eyes on me since I had arrived in Moscow. I tried to not let the revelation show on my face.

The tall man became my interpreter. "Very nice to meet you, Christopher," the stocky man said in Russian, relaxing back into the chair behind his desk. "My name is Alexander Lebed; Mehran and I have been friends for many years. He speaks highly of you, and Mehran is not easily impressed."

"It's nice to meet you, too," I replied.

"How are you enjoying Moscow?"

"I've enjoyed it very much."

"Cigarette?"

"No, thank you."

Lebed lit a cigarette for himself, inhaled deeply, then pensively blew out a puff of smoke. "Forgive me if I seem forward, but I believe is American way, yes?"

"Sure," I said, wondering what he was planning on being forward about.

"How do you feel about America? Maryland, you lived in Maryland, yes? But now you live in Canada."

He knows an awful lot about me. "As you may expect, to me, America is the greatest country in the world, but I'm living in Canada at the moment because I'm overseeing construction in Vancouver."

"Hmm, I see." He placed a crystal apple on the desk in front of him. "New York."

I didn't know what he wanted me to say. "The Big Apple, yes, it's beautiful. Have you been?"

"This was gesture of friendship from your American construction king, Donald Trump. I met him in his Tower in January. I understand in '96 he wanted to partner with Brook Group, is owned by company you work for, Liggett-Ducat. I invited Trump to Russia, to be part of building projects in Moscow. He accepted. But you are one who is here . . ."

I thought this meeting was just going to be a simple, *Hello,* but Lebed's statements seemed to have a definite purpose.

He continued on a different note: "Mehran says you very much like your tour of St. Basil's, and watching Swan Lake; you enjoy, yes?"

"Yes, I've had unique experiences here I didn't expect."

Again, Lebed inhaled deeply, pulling the cigarette smoke fully into his lungs; his exhale painted the air. The corner of his mouth turned up. "You think anyone gets to do what you have done?" The tone in his voice had changed. "Sitting in president's seat, exploring Cathedral alone, standing at altar for Easter ceremony . . . ?"

It struck me: because Mehran was not yet in the Duma, this must be the man who had pulled the strings for my trip. Mehran was a tough businessman with a commanding presence, but his characteristics paled in comparison to the man sitting in front of me.

Since being in Russia, I had learned that a favor for a favor was status quo. *What did Lebed want from me in return for my experiences here?* I waited for the other shoe to drop.

Lebed must have read my discomfort; he broke into a huge friendly grin and said, "Don't worry, is fine." He flicked his cigarette ash. "Is fine." He laughed, but I still felt uneasy. "I saw how Yeltsin benefited greatly from your President Clinton's visit here," he said. "That is why I went to your country. I will be president of Russia in new millennium. I want to build free democratic Russia and end corruption in post-Soviet Union. When this happens, I need business support of West."

His forwardness and confidence unbalanced me. I wondered if he was all talk, or if the man I was having a private meeting with would, in fact, be the next President of Russia. If his personality was any indication, I believed he would achieve exactly what he said. He must have had an interest in me as a bridge to the western world; I was one of only a few Americans doing business in this country. *Why else would I be sitting here?*

"You are historian, I like history, too." He changed the subject on a dime and began restlessly drumming his fingers on the broad desk. Waiting for the tall man's translations must have been aggravating for him. He clearly had a goal in his sights and felt restrained by the necessity to take the required steps to reach it. "Mehran tells me you have interest in Cold War."

"Yes," I said, trying to be polite.

"Let us talk about that . . . During missile crisis, Robert Kennedy told our ambassador, Dobrynin, that if your President Kennedy could not resolve situation with our President Khrushchev quickly, American coup was anticipated in your government that would throw our countries to war.

"Your Pentagon was furious over incident with one of your submarines; is still classified today. We agreed to resolve crisis: President Kennedy promised never to invade Cuba, and we promised to pull back our warheads."

I just sat there, not saying a word.

Lebed smiled, and exhaled more smoke before continuing. "We informed Kennedy we left one hundred tactical nukes with Castro and our troops, which gave Castro ability to protect his island, but not capability to launch against continental United States . . . But Castro would not go along with your U.N. inspections."

I tried not to change my expression.

"Kennedy brothers became more desperate. If there could be no peace with Castro their last resort was Almeida, commander of Cuban army. Almeida agreed to kill Castro and his brother on December 1, 1963, and assume power after palace coup; he was paid on morning of President Kennedy's assassination. If President Kennedy had lived, he would have sent in American military to support Cuba's new regime. He had tried very hard to remove our position there.

"Your Pentagon and CIA continued wanting to invade Cuba to take our countries to war, but if President Kennedy's plans were successful, he made it very clear your CIA and Mafia would be, as you say, out-in-the-cold."

Lebed's dialogue was making me very uncomfortable.

"But coup did not happen in Cuba, it happened in America. Your President's assassination was problem for our government and placed our country in state of national alert. Robert Kennedy needed to communicate with Khrushchev; he sent Bill Walton to deliver message to Georgi Bolshakov—on I believe twenty-ninth of November '63—saying Robert and Jackie Kennedy knew it was domestic coup, and showed evidence. This information was passed to GRU, our military intelligence." Lebed studied me for any recognition, but there was none. "Robert Kennedy said Russia would not be held accountable and he would not pursue false allegations that would lead to war.

"Robert Kennedy told us once he gained White House, policies would return to more diplomatic tone; he would pick up where his brother left off with quest for detente. My government held Robert Kennedy's actions in high regard, and kept them secret. But in 1967, during Six Day War, my government sent teletype communications to your President Johnson that threatened to expose his position in your government's coup if he did not stop his false flag operations."

Alarmed, I asked, "Why are you discussing this with me?" I tried to be respectful in my interruption.

"Did you know," Lebed said, not ready to address my question, "that because of what Robert Kennedy showed us, we sent orders to our embassy in New York demanding to know relationship between Robert Kennedy and your new president, Johnson? Were they going to cooperate, or kill each other?" Lebed looked at me for any reaction.

I tried to remain silent, but Lebed required a reply. *Why was he engaging me with this matter? Why was he testing my knowledge on this subject?* "No," I said, "I wasn't aware of that." I couldn't tell if this conversation was about his ego, or something else.

Lebed continued, "Our intelligence confirmed that President Johnson and your FBI were concerned that Robert Kennedy might overthrow their new government with violence, leading to another coup. I think he should have done this." Again, he watched my reaction closely. "We felt your country was left without real leadership and your Pentagon might have fired missiles at us. Later we watched Robert Kennedy's run for president very close, but President Johnson did not keep his promise to Robert Kennedy, and so another Kennedy was murdered . . . but that's all ancient history now, isn't it?" he said with a smile.

I just nodded slightly in response. *What promise was he talking about?* This was the first time I'd heard this version of history. I was sure I shouldn't have been made privy to such information by this man. Again, I felt I was on the wrong side of the ocean.

"Our countries are not so different," Lebed continued. "I was also involved in coup in my country in '91; it was backed by KGB. I was ordered to send tanks to surround parliament, our White House, so that conspirators could overthrow Gorbachev. But I took no action; I did not follow orders," he proudly stated, and laughed again. "Now communist Russia is finished; conspirators are gone, and I am here."

Clearly, Lebed was not just some friend of Mehran's; he was a very powerful man in Russia.

Just then, someone knocked at the door. A soldier came in and stood at attention with a message in hand. Lebed impatiently waived him away and continued to speak once the door had closed. "There have been so many books written about American coup; it seems your country has never healed from its wounds. You are still so fascinated with this subject because you still don't understand. But these books are all opinions and speculations, aren't they?" Before I could form an answer, he said, "You and Mr. White are unique in this now."

My heart skipped a beat, and my mind raced to catch up. *Had I misheard him? Did he mean Robert White?!*

I was sure Lebed could easily read my recognition now.

"You possess key evidence, Mr. Fulton, evidence Robert Kennedy showed us to prevent World War III following your President's assassination . . . The important question now is: What are you going to do with it? Do you think your government will *welcome* your insight?"

If my heart had skipped a beat before, now it stopped all together. Every muscle in my body tightened in anticipation, but I didn't even know what I was anticipating; I just knew it wasn't good.

"Don't be alarmed," he said, seeing my anxiety, "this is friendly conversation." The wheels kept spinning in my head, but Lebed kept talking. "Is of great interest to both our countries. So from one friend to another, I ask you . . . What will you do?" Both Lebed and the tall man waited in silence.

My mind raced back to my meeting with Cable Wade. *I've got to get out of here.* "Mr. Lebed, please understand, I am simply a lover of history, nothing more. I feel you would be better served to have this conversation with someone of more importance."

Lebed stood, with a very serious look on his face. I began to stand too, hoping I could simply shake his hand and walk out of the room, but I felt the hand of the tall man crest my shoulder in a firmly placed gesture to keep me seated.

Lebed placed both his hands on his desk and leaned towards me. "I am offering you chance to make America, and world, aware of facts in murder of your president. Russia will not censor what you have; we will give you free reign to expose truth . . . Believe me when I tell you, you will not get such offer from your country."

I didn't want any offers. The only thing I wanted was the nearest exit.

"Understand," Lebed said, "such things, they have been hidden from your Congress and people, suppressed for many decades, still kept above top secret by your government. We know most important evidence, that Robert Kennedy collected, did not go to your National Archives; it went to Mrs. Evelyn Lincoln. Now you and your friend, Mr. White, have possession. So, we simply want to know what will happen."

I was not prepared to discuss anything about what I had to a Russian official in the Kremlin. I needed to retreat. If I possessed hidden evidence that Robert Kennedy had shared with Russia to prevent World War III . . . Well, I wasn't going to explore that question here. If I could find out the truth for myself, Alexander Lebed would not be along on my voyage of discovery.

I looked at the tall man, then stood up to depart. "It was very nice to meet you, Mr. Lebed." I reached out my hand. "Thank you for anything concerning my experiences here that involved your influence."

Lebed shook my hand. He gave me a look like we had played a hand of poker, and he thought I had just bluffed. I turned to exit, but Lebed's words continued in a question behind me: "It feels different when you are part of history, doesn't it?"

I hesitated. I was only steps from the door; I thought about the soldier on the other side. *Would Lebed allow me to leave?* I couldn't hide the anguish on my face, but I had already turned away from the two men so they couldn't see my state.

The tall man looked inquiringly at Lebed, but Lebed raised his hand in silent acceptance of my departure. "My door is open to you," he said in final farewell. "If you need anything, please, let me know. Is good to have friends."

With that I left as quickly as I could without looking like I was escaping. The soldier was still outside the door, and to my relief, Stas was too.

***

The door to the office closed and Lebed asked the tall man, "Was he there when the secretary's will was ruled on in court?"

"No."

"Well, now we will see. I believe their government will leave them no choice and they will run to us."

"They will both hang," the tall man said matter-of-factly.

***

Once we were outside, Stas said, "You look white like sheet. What happened?"

"Your cousin has very powerful friends; that man was someone of great importance."

"Who was in there?" Stas asked.

"He said his name was Alexander Lebed."

Stas veritably choked, "My God, you know who that is?"

"No," I said, baited for an answer.

"Shit, I hope he was happy when you left."

"Why? Who is he?"

"He is General Lebed, commander of all Russian army; he controls everything. Gorbachev would not have been in office without him, and Russia would not have opened its doors to rest of world."

Shit. I looked back at the Kremlin and felt very lucky I had been allowed to walk out. "I need to get home, right now!"

"Yes, but General Lebed controls airport."

I felt hollow. "Well, he let me out of the Kremlin; maybe he'll let me out of Russia, too."

***

I placed an international call to Shauna. I needed to tell her what had happened, but when I got her on the phone, I realized I couldn't say any of it over an open line. "I'm leaving early. I have a lot to share with you when I get back . . . I miss you." I don't know if she could hear the apprehension in my voice; I didn't want to worry her, I just wanted to make it back to see her again.

I had completed my work for Mehran; there were a few more estimates to finish, but I could send those in the mail. That was beside the point now; the whole trip seemed to have been nothing more than an arrangement for me to meet Lebed. I realized I had to go to Baltimore to see Robert before I could get home to Shauna. I went back to the flat and packed. I looked at my camera and left it on the dresser; I didn't want to give them any reason to detain me. I asked Stas if he would take me to the airport.

As we drove through the streets of Moscow, I looked out the window, taking in the sights of the city for what I hoped would be the last time. When we arrived at the airport, I moved to get out of the car but Stas put his hand on my shoulder and said, "Wait." He fished in his pocket and pulled out a small round medal. "This belonged to my father," he said, and handed it to me. "It was on his military cap. I want you to have it."

"No, I couldn't," I said. "It's far too personal."

"Please, I want you to remember Russia well. If all Americans are like you . . . well, you are good man, Christopher; I have enjoyed knowing you."

"Thank you, Stas." Just then a thought took me: I quickly shared my concerns over the conversation with Lebed, and hastily wrote down Shauna's name on a piece of paper. I handed it to him and said, "Stas, please, if anything happens to me before I arrive home, my fiancée will contact you. Tell her about Lebed. I didn't tell her, she would need to know."

"Yes," he said, "I will."

I held the small Russian medal in my hand and got out of the car.

***

I stood in the airport, the airport that Alexander Lebed controlled. When I had first arrived in Russia, I felt sad for the young girls with machine guns and no smiles; now they just made me incredibly uneasy, even though I had done nothing wrong.

My palms were clammy as I handed my ticket and passport to the Russian official at the window. "You're leaving us today, Mr. Fulton," he said.

"Yes, it's time to go home."

He did not move to give me his stamp of approval; instead he picked up the phone. I could feel the sweat bead at my forehead. He spoke in Russian; everything he said sounded menacing. *Please*, I prayed, *just let me get home.* The border guard replaced the receiver, looked at me, and said, "Mr. Fulton, you should be more careful."

A surge of adrenaline shot though my body. "What do you mean?"

"Your shoe," he said, looking down at my feet. "It's untied." With that he stamped my passport.

As he returned my documents, I realized I had been holding my breath. I turned and let the air out in a slow, measured stream as I walked briskly towards my flight gate; I was too tense to stop and tie my shoe.

It was a very long trip home. I dislike drinking alcohol, but I disliked flying more. By the time I left Heathrow, I needed relief; I asked the Aeroflot flight attendant to keep bringing me little bottles of booze. I passed out early on in the flight. When I woke we were making our descent to Washington, D.C. My head was spinning and my leg hurt. I rolled up my pant leg to find a black bruise that covered most of my right thigh, hip to kneecap. The attendant must have clipped me with her serving cart, more than once.

As soon as I disembarked at Dulles International Airport, I fell to my knees and kissed the ground.

MARCH 3, 1999

The prosecutor was expressionless, but I heard the disgust in his voice. "Why did you go to Russia?"

"I was hired to evaluate flats to bring them up to American specs."

"Who hired you?"

"Mehran Mikhailov."

"What is your association with Mikhailov?"

"My company was contracted to build a tower for him in Vancouver. He was happy with the result and asked if I would go to Russia to do some work for him there."

"Why did you agree?"

"The money was good, and I'd never been to Russia before."

"What is your relation to Alexander Lebed?"

My blood ran cold; I hoped they couldn't see all the color drain from my face. I hadn't even known who Lebed was when I met him. Did they think I was some sort of spy? That I was working for the Russians? *That's exactly what they thought.* I wished I had never gone. "I met him when I was in Russia."

"How did you meet?"

"He was a friend of Mehran's."

"So the man who you did work for in Vancouver just happened to be friends with one of the most powerful men in Russia, the head of their intelligence, and when you went to Russia you just happened to get a private audience with the man?"

"I didn't know who he was at the time."

"What did you talk about?"

I was being backed into a corner. I could feel the anger rising in me. I'd endured so much to this point, but I had to remain calm or they would lock me away for fifty years. I thought of Shauna. I couldn't let that happen; I wouldn't just give up. I swallowed it all back down and spoke slowly: "History."

"Did Lebed want you to do anything for him?"

"He offered to help Robert White and me publicize what we had."

"In Russia?"

"Yes," I responded.

"What did you say?"

"I told him I had no interest in his offer; I would never do that. I left the Kremlin and Russia immediately."

I thought back to that meeting when Lebed had asked if I thought my government would be happy with my insights. His meaning had become devastatingly clear.

"Did he ask you about Robert White?"

"Yes."

"Did he ask you about the items you received from Robert White?"

"Yes."

"Did he refer to anything as evidence from President John F. Kennedy's assassination?"

"Yes."

"Did he instruct you to present your evidence to convene a grand jury, to begin a murder trial for President Kennedy in the state of Texas?"

"No." *My God! That's what they're trying to shut down! They believe there's a plan to begin a murder trial.* If that was my intention, at the request of the Russian Government, it would explain their espionage concern and the fifty-year threat. A trial would also explain why Agent Mancini got upset when Agent Callahan talked about wrapping this up before the presidential election. A Kennedy trial in Texas would make international headlines and could affect the election results . . . I wanted to tell the panel everything, but I couldn't do that; I had made a promise. This was my pit, and the prosecutor was the pendulum; every question was a swing closer to my mortality.

12

FOR ALL OF U.S.

APRIL 1997

Once safe on U.S. soil, I called Shauna and told her not to meet me at the airport in Vancouver; I would be delayed at least a day, but I missed her and loved her, and everything was ok. Then I called Robert White. His demeanor was markedly warmer than the last time I had spoken with him. "I'm in D.C.," I said. "We need to talk."

"That's great!" he responded, obviously not reading the urgency in my voice. "You'll finally get to see everything."

"See what? What are you talking about?"

"My inheritance, it's here at the house!"

I rented a car and just over two hours later, I pulled up to a modest two-story brick house with black shutters and a white portico. Robert greeted me at the front door and welcomed me inside. He wouldn't stop talking. He rattled off details about his inheritance so quickly I couldn't follow everything he said, and I couldn't get a word in edgewise. He finally ended with, "Come, I'll show you."

We walked through the door that led to the basement. Robert flicked on a light switch at the top of the wooden stairs, and we descended. What I saw next was impossible for me to take in all at once. The basement was brimming with tables and shelves and cases, all laden with his vast inheritance. There were labeled boxes filled with official and personal correspondence from the White House; there were photos, and books, and important artifacts, all on open display. American history hung heavy in the air; I breathed deeply.

I could have spent months discovering the treasures housed there, but my concerns prompted me to address my recent revelations immediately. "I've got something important to tell you, Robert. I just got back from . . ."

"More important than this?" He cut me off, barely able to contain the excitement that had been building in him since I had arrived. He picked up a large flat box and handed it to me. "Open it," he insisted.

From Robert's demeanor, I could tell it contained something very special. I couldn't resist the force that called me to lift the lid. I removed the top of the box and gently pulled back the tissue paper. I just stared in awe.

"These are the flags that flew on President Kennedy's limousine on November 22, 1963," Robert said.

I ran my fingers across them to immerse myself. The fringe on the bottom felt stiffer than the top. I assumed it was caused by residue from wax, from where the flags had continually swept across the endlessly-polished fenders. I wanted to spend more time looking at them, but Robert quickly replaced the box lid, and held out another artifact for me to hold. "This is the handle of the camera Abraham Zapruder used to shoot the famous footage of the assassination." I respectfully took the proffered handle.

I held what Zapruder held and a chill ran down my spine. I was transported back. As the president rolled into view, I felt it: the exuberance before the absolute horror that changed the nation. Grace, power, and elegance were transformed to sheer tragedy in a few short seconds of vibrant color.

I had seen the footage so many times over the years; it was hypnotic. *We have never recovered from what was taken from us . . . if we still don't understand that event, how can we ever hope to move forward, and understand everything that has come since?*

I snapped out of my trance with a jolt when Robert said, "Look at this." He took back the camera handle and put Abraham Lincoln's wallet into my open hand. "President Lincoln carried this during the entire Civil War."

It was incredible to hold: in my right hand was the possession of a man whom many considered to be the greatest American who ever lived . . . then Robert placed a second wallet in my left hand. "This one is Kennedy's," he said, with hushed reverence. I stood there, hands outstretched like the scales of justice, weighing the immense importance of the two artifacts. Both my hands felt heavy.

The leather of Lincoln's wallet was well worn to a smooth finish, while Kennedy's had something in it I wanted to inspect more closely. It was a

71

large, solid gold St. Christopher money clip. "That St. Christopher was a gift from Jackie," Robert said. "President Kennedy used to wear it in his breast pocket over his heart. In 1962, he moved the clip to a new wallet, but I like to keep it in the original one."

Robert held his hands out to take both wallets back, and said, "I want to show you the thing that's most important to me." He reached over and handed me a well-worn Hermes briefcase. "This was President Kennedy's favorite; he took it with him everywhere. The newer wallet and that briefcase were with him in Dallas!"

"What? How do you know they were both in Dallas?" I asked. "How do you know the history of any of these items?"

"The letters; Evelyn Lincoln documented everything!" he said, with a smile that glowed like the Cheshire Cat's.

Documented everything? "But you weren't family; why did she entrust all of this to you?"

The reservation and silence he had originally employed when I told him about the Cartier being assassination evidence seemed to have all but vanished. He willingly shared. "I promised her I would keep her information and items safe during my lifetime . . . Mrs. Lincoln and I had written back and forth for years," he explained. "In 1975 she called me up to have lunch with her. We kept very close, but in 1986 something changed and she called me out to lunch again. She said she hadn't been invited to Caroline Kennedy's wedding; she had been snubbed and forgotten by the Kennedy family entirely, and it made her very sad. Then she told me she had 'strong personal reasons' for leaving me everything in her will. It was unreal, I couldn't believe it."

I listened intently and knew there must be more to the story. The items Robert had shown me so far re-confirmed that he had received part of the nation's hidden history; it was the very reason I needed to speak to him. I stopped Robert before he could show me anything else; I had delayed my intention long enough. "I think we both may have a serious problem, Robert."

"What do you mean?" he asked.

"Several months ago, I got an unusual job offer through my construction business to go to Russia."

"You went to *Russia*?" Robert exclaimed, completely taken aback.

"Robert, listen, I was introduced to a man in the Kremlin: Alexander Lebed. I didn't know it at the time, but he's a very important general and political figure; I think he heads up their intelligence, like our CIA."

"What did he want with you?" Robert asked, now realizing that what I had to tell him had serious implications.

"That's why I needed to see you immediately; Lebed brought up your name and knew that I had important evidence in JFK's assassination!"

Robert looked very troubled and took a seat. He paused before saying, "I got the watch from Mrs. Lincoln in '92. When she gave it to me, she told me a letter documenting it would come after her death . . . but I sold it to you when I really needed the money. I shouldn't have done that." A cloud of concern cast a shadow over his face.

The president's wristwatch had been entrusted to him by Mrs. Lincoln and he had simply sold it. It made him feel sick to his stomach. He tried to gauge the severity of his mistake. Robert remembered what President Reagan had told him. *Was the watch part of the evidence Robert Kennedy had saved? Would the government think he still owned it and come for it?* Well, now he could say he sold it and be off the hook.

"What did the letter say?" he asked.

"What letter?"

"Mrs. Lincoln's letter . . . Didn't you get it?"

"No, I don't know what you're talking about!" I said, starting to get exasperated.

"It was part of the inheritance. It was supposed to stay with the watch as a matter of law. It was sent to your attorney because you own the watch. You need to call him right now; I need to know what's in that letter."

I walked up the basement stairs and used the wall phone in the kitchen. "McRobie and Shaw," came the robust voice on the other end of the line.

"Hello, Henry," I said.

"Christopher, my boy!" he exclaimed loudly. "Where have you been?"

Apart from being my attorney, Henry was a close family friend. "I've been in British Columbia, Canada, working on contracts. Henry, I've just found out that you should have something for me; did you receive a letter . . ."

"Yes, yes, yes," he cut in. "That's right, it looked very official. It had the presidential seal on it. I tried to get in touch with you a few times; I sent word to your address but never heard anything back. Your phone number didn't work either, and I couldn't find an updated number."

"Ok, that's right. That's my error. I should have given you my current info; I didn't realize how long I'd be away. You still have the letter?"

"Oh yes, it's sitting in the safe, here in my office; if you give me your new address, I can mail it out today."

"No, no, I'm in town; I'll come see you."

I went back to the basement to tell Robert the letter was safe. He looked relieved and agitated at the same time. "Chris," he said, "serious things have been happening since I inherited from Mrs. Lincoln. Angela Novello, Robert Kennedy's secretary, was at the hearing for the wills. The next thing I know, Ronald Reagan calls me on the phone."

"President Reagan contacted you?"

"Yeah, then he flew me to California to talk about the government and their concern over Mrs. Lincoln leaving JFK's things to me."

"So, we've both been approached," I said.

Robert opened the drawer of the table that had sat next to the Oval Office desk when Kennedy was president. He pulled out a photograph and handed it to me. "I'm going to have it framed," he said proudly. The photo showed Robert and President Reagan shaking hands, while Reagan held the same wallets I had just held.

"What did he say to you?"

"He was worried information might be released by a foreign government. What did you say to the Russian, Lebed?"

"I didn't say anything."

"But he said my name?"

"Yes."

Robert was silent a moment before he continued, "Reagan also warned me that the ARRB was going to call me to testify."

"What's the ARRB?"

"The Assassination Records Review Board; they report to President Clinton."

"Will you have to testify?"

"I already did, a few days ago. They asked me if I'd inherited anything that was involved with the assassination. President Reagan told me they'd make me turn in everything for classification. The American people would never see it again!"

"Everyone wants to know what we have . . ." I said, trying to think it through.

"I, I told them I didn't have anything," Robert blurted out. "I needed to keep . . ."

"You lied?"

"Yes, I guess," Robert said defensively. "But I'm not going to let them take away my inheritance." We were both silent for a moment, then Robert added, "Reagan said maybe it was time for all of this to become public."

"He said that to you?" I asked, surprised.

Our unique experiences established a quick bond of trust between us. "Yeah," Robert said. "If he said it, who are we to hold back? Look, I just want to open my museum." He got up and pulled a book from the closest shelf: *Profiles of Courage*. "This is President Kennedy's personal copy of the book he wrote." He flipped it open and revealed photographs that had been tucked inside. "Look at this," he said, drawing me closer.

I tilted my head, trying to figure out what was going on in the pictures. "According to Mrs. Lincoln's letter, these are important," Robert said. "They are original photos documenting President Kennedy's reinterment on March 14, 1967."

"They moved him after the burial in '63?"

"Yeah." Robert handed me the photos. I flipped through the black-and-white and color images and saw Bobby Kennedy, Ted Kennedy, and Lyndon Johnson standing over the open grave of the former president. It looked like it was late at night, and raining lightly. It was eerie to see the eternal flame extinguished, and President Kennedy's coffin disturbed and exposed.

As I looked through the photos, Robert said, "Mrs. Lincoln told me the bridge to Arlington was closed off and three hundred troops stood around the outside, with another hundred troops on standby. Any trespassers—press or private citizens—would be arrested."

"I've never heard anything about that," I said.

"I don't think many people have. Mrs. Lincoln told me it was done in total secret. A military operation: a matter of national security. Look at this letter she wrote." Robert handed me a piece of White House note paper that read: "... Johnson and Robert Kennedy both agreed that New Orleans District Attorney Jim Garrison, who had been given leads by French intelligence, had to be kept in the dark about the reinterment. Garrison's grand jury was in session, and he would have forced an autopsy of the president's body if he had known it was exhumed ..."

"Jesus," I exclaimed. My country's history was being re-written before my eyes.

"Look," Robert said, flipping through the stack and pulling out several photos in particular. He pointed out a metal container sitting at Ted Kennedy's feet. The next photo showed Bobby Kennedy standing in the grave, placing the same container alongside the casket.

"What is he *doing*?" I asked.

"Mrs. Lincoln said Bobby Kennedy kept the president's brain in a metal container; it was evidence of what actually happened in Dallas. She said he put the brain back in the president's grave in '67 and when Bobby reached the White House, he would have re-opened the investigation..."

"Robert!" His wife called sharply from the top of the stairs. "You're not supposed to be showing those, you know what you promised Evelyn." Robert looked like a whipped dog. He hurriedly collected the photos from me, and put them back in the book. "Anyway," he said, "Mrs. Lincoln kept vigil over President Kennedy's grave every year until her own death ..." He glanced up to the top of the stairs; once his wife had moved away from the door, he continued quietly, "Mrs. Lincoln told me the eternal flame at JFK's grave was Bobby Kennedy's idea, not Jackie's. The family paid for it to keep control of the gravesite. Mrs. Lincoln kept constant watch over it."

I was shaken. I needed a moment to collect my thoughts.

I looked around at everything before us: wills, passports, thousands of White House memorandums and documents; this was the official and personal history of the 35th President of the United States, and it had never been seen by the public. "So what are you going to do?" I queried, trying to figure the next move.

"Like I said, I just want to open my museum, but I don't have the money. Look," he said, gesturing to the entire contents of the basement, "it's a treasury. If I could just get some money, I could quit my damn job, open my museum, and live out my days as a curator, like I've always dreamed."

"Robert, most of this belongs in the Smithsonian; it's important American history, it belongs in an American institution."

"Yeah, but it *belongs* to me; there is a collector's code ..."

"This goes beyond that."

"Mrs. Lincoln wanted *me* to have this." his features were stony.

I wasn't about to argue over Evelyn Lincoln's personal reasons. Robert's face suddenly lit up. "What about a book?!"

"No, I don't think ..."

"Just a picture book, showing some of what will be on display in my museum!"

Perhaps his inspiration was born out of what Reagan had told him.

Robert was excited by the idea. "The proceeds could help me open and promote my museum!" I thought he might burst, but he suddenly deflated. "But, there's still no money to make the book."

It struck me: *my savings, everything I had just made in Russia* ... without thinking, I said, "I might be able to help." I knew I needed that money to buy a house with Shauna. What would she think of the idea? As far as I could tell, a photo book would be instantly significant. I would have to talk to Shauna before I set anything in stone. "I need to make another call," I said.

I talked with Shauna at length about the idea, and she agreed it was worth the risk. "If you don't take this opportunity," she told me, "you will always regret it."

I got off the phone and told Robert the good news: he had my financial commitment. "I will have to keep control over negotiations and content," I stated, realizing much of the private correspondence and many of the government positions couldn't be published, and I couldn't trust Robert's discretion on those matters. "If that's acceptable to you, we have a deal: fifty–fifty."

Robert shook my hand and we drew up and signed a contract right then and there, witnessed by his wife.

Robert wanted to show me everything he thought would be good for the book, and we began to plan our venture together. I looked at, touched, and read the most personal pieces from JFK's life, like Jackie Kennedy's wills: she made a new one every time she travelled, or anytime she and her husband were apart. Jackie was extremely concerned, scared, about the distinct possibility of an assassination. Her worries began in 1962, just after the Bay of Pigs.

Robert handed me a piece of paper with the header *Air Force One*. In Kennedy's untidy hand it read: "Government reform, we are going forward." Evelyn's letter said it was the last thing the president had written: an addition to the speech he was going to give at the trade mart." Then Robert told me about another note Kennedy had written. It said: "A storm is coming. If God has a place for me, I am ready to meet him." Kennedy had written the immortal words of President Abraham Lincoln down over and over again. Evelyn had transcribed it, as Kennedy's writing was all but illegible.

I read countless documentary letters written by Evelyn; all were detailed and precise. However, there was a handful of letters, addressed specifically to Robert, that were contradictory. They held added information that was clearly never intended for public display. They shared incredibly personal and secret information, some of which pertained to the assassination. She had even written a letter to accompany the hand-signed copy of Dr. George Burkley's original autopsy report that had been given to Bobby Kennedy before the original had been burned by Burkley.

There was a thin, square, gold Omega wristwatch; it was a gift from Grant Stockdale, and had an inscription to the president on the reverse.

I read a secret telegram dated October 28, 1962, to President Kennedy from Khrushchev:

PEACE AND WAR

ALTHOUGH WE DISMANTLE OUR EQUIPMENT, WE AS-SURE CUBANS WE ARE STILL WITH THEM. WE WANT ONLY PEACE. WE WANT TO CONTINUE OUR DEVELOPMENT.

YOUR SPY PLANES FLEW OVER OUR TERRITORY. IN 1960 THIS LED TO THE WRECKING OF THE PARIS CON-FERENCE. THEN YOU CONDEMNED THE FLIGHTS BUT UNDER YOUR ADMINISTRATION A SIMILAR FLIGHT OCCURRED. YOU THEN BLAMED BAD WEATHER FOR IT. HOWEVER, THIS COULD BE AVOIDED IF NO FLIGHTS NEAR SOVIET BORDERS WERE MADE. HERE THE PEN-TAGON TO BLAME. A SIMILAR FLIGHT OCCURRED YES-TERDAY. I WOULD LIKE YOU TO TAKE MEASURES TO AVOID SIMILAR PROVOCATIONS.

FLIGHTS OF YOUR PLANES CONTINUE OVER CUBA. I KNOW THIS FROM MY OFFICERS WHO TRAIN THE CUBANS. I WOULD LIKE YOU TO TAKE INTO ACCOUNT THAT VIOLATION OF CUBAN AIRSPACE BY YOUR PLANES MAY ALSO LEAD TO A DANGEROUS SITUATION. ALL PROVOCATIONS MUST BE AVOIDED.

THE SOVIET GOVERNMENT WILL NOT LET ITSELF BE PROVOKED, BUT IF WAR IS UNLEASHED, THE SOVIET GOVERNMENT WILL NOT (SHRINK) FROM THE CONSE-QUENCES.

WE ALSO PROMISE OUR COOPERATION WITH U.

"Look at this," Robert said, and handed me a private love letter be-tween the President and his wife. It was very touching, written just before Dallas. The letter was unique in that it reflected personal sentiment be-tween them, rather than just recounting daily activities. It spoke of their reunion and their intention of having another baby.

Robert told me he had offered to give the letter to Caroline Kennedy, if she agreed to buy two other items from him for $650,000. She was deeply offended by his offer . . . I could see her point. Robert told me Caroline had demanded the love letter's immediate return without any compen-sation. She also demanded that her letter to Robert be returned, so there would be no record of it. That in turn infuriated Robert, and he refused to comply. It was clear there was no love lost between them.

"Christopher, I've always been in total awe of her father," Robert said, "but Caroline is *nothing* like her father."

I was surprised by the bitterness and hostility in his voice.

He continued, "If she had just asked me with decency and respect, I would have given her almost anything she asked for, but she was so forceful and demeaning, I'll never give her anything!"

Robert should have told me about the bad blood before I committed to funding the photo book. A feud between Robert and Caroline could make publication difficult. I was not amused he had chosen to share the information with me after we had signed our contract, but Robert didn't seem concerned.

He took a moment to find one box in particular, from which he unpacked a series of old dictabelts. "President Kennedy made these recordings in the Oval Office," he said. "There are meetings, phone conversations, and dictations of his memoirs made in '62 and '63. Mrs. Lincoln set them aside, so I inherited them. I haven't listened to them yet, but I've made one copy of them on cassettes. Some of the belts stretched and broke when I copied them. I don't think I can get all of the information off them a second time." With that he handed me six cassettes, "I want you to have these; use whatever information you can for the book. Take care of them," he said, "they are the only copies in existence." I felt honored.

***

I stayed the night at Robert's, and the next day I made some calls to hire a photographer.

We spent the next week taking large-format photographs and hammering out the details of the book. When we finished, it was time for me to get back to Shauna. Before I left, Robert also gave me a number of original photographs, and a pair of JFK's tortoiseshell sunglasses that had been sat on by a general. "I'd like you to have these as well as the recordings, in honor of our partnership," he said. The glasses had been poorly repaired, but I thought they were one hell of a gift.

13

BONDED BY BLOOD

EARLY MAY 1997

Before I headed to the airport, I had one more important stop to make. I parked my rental car and walked into the small, familiar building just off Route 40: the law offices of McRobie & Shaw. Robert had wanted me to pick up Evelyn's letter from my lawyer while I was staying with him, but after I heard about his feud with Caroline Kennedy, I decided it was best to review it by myself, on my way out of the country.

Henry saw me come in. "There he is," he exclaimed, as he stood up and walked out from behind his desk. "Well, let me see you!" He gave me a hug, then abruptly turned around. "Ok, where did I put that thing? I took it out of the safe for you this morning." He looked around the office, trying to remember what drawer or cabinet he had put it in. It wasn't until he looked directly down at his desk that his eyebrows shot up, and a smile creased his face, "Oh here it is. I didn't want to lose the damn thing; not with the seal of the president on it." Henry handed me the letter and watched as I turned it over in my hands, inspecting it.

"Well?" he said. "Don't leave me in suspense, open it up."

I stared at the envelope and the wax seal on the back. I hesitated; I wasn't sure I wanted to open it.

"You don't have to open it now," Henry said, "but it's a legal letter; you're going to have to open it sometime, so you might as well do it when you're here with me." His ruddy Scottish features lit with a coaxing smile; he really wanted to see what was in the letter.

"Alright," I said. Henry handed me a razor blade and I opened the end of the envelope to preserve the integrity of the seal. I drew out a typed letter that was several pages long. A handwritten note was clipped to the top:

Dear Robert,

On June 5, 1992, I gave you a round, 18k gold Cartier wristwatch which formerly belonged to President John F. Kennedy. It was the only piece of physical assassination evidence left in my possession and I needed to ensure you received it. I am sorry I couldn't have been more clear about this matter at the time.

Enclosed with this letter is an affidavit from the head of the Protective Research Section, Secret Service Agent Robert I. Bouck. If Agent Bouck is still alive, contact him; he worked closely with Robert Kennedy and he can give you much more information.

This letter and affidavit must be kept with the watch as a matter of law. The citizens of our great country were denied information they have a right to know. It will be up to you and Mr. Bouck how and when this will occur.

Evelyn N. Lincoln

The letter was typed on White House stationery:

June 5, 1992

I, Evelyn N. Lincoln, former secretary for President John F. Kennedy, hereby state: on November 20, 1963, my husband, Harold Lincoln, overheard a conversation at a bar in Washington D.C. Secret Service agents in Vice President Johnson's detail were discussing President Kennedy being shot at in Dallas, Texas. I was shaken, and pleaded with the president not to go, but he was fearless.

Following President Kennedy's assassination, my services were terminated by the new president, Lyndon B. Johnson. Robert Kennedy informed me that President Kennedy was murdered due to his efforts to prevent WWIII. That someday, everything would be made public, but for now, secrecy was vital.

I was scared, I didn't feel safe. My husband and I left the country. We sold our house in Bethesda, Maryland, and moved to Sierra Leone, West Africa, where we remained until 1965. I then received word from Senator Robert F. Kennedy imploring me to return home to give him assistance in securing evidence in President Kennedy's assassination. After I returned to Maryland in early April 1965, Robert Kennedy asked me to return to my office in the National Archives, although I was not employed there.

In late April of that same year, I received President John F. Kennedy's autopsy materials from Dr. Burkley. Included were x-rays and autopsy photos, President Kennedy's brain, blood samples, and paraffin blocks. I also received President Kennedy's Oval Office recordings. During 1962 and '63, Secret Service Agent Robert I. Bouck had delivered the president's earlier recordings to me.

The only people aware of the recordings at that time were Robert Kennedy, the Director of the Secret Service James Rowley, Agent Bouck, who installed the dictabelt system in '62, his assistant Chester Miller, and myself.

Robert Kennedy then visited me in person, along with Secret Service Agent Bouck, to give me President Kennedy's Cartier wristwatch, its original strap (which had been removed) a blood analysis report, photographic documentation, and an affidavit regarding the watch from Agent Bouck. He informed me that the wristwatch needed to be secured, that future agreements between himself and President Johnson would depend on these secured materials.

Robert Kennedy told me that none of these items were to be released to anyone without his written permission or approval. He advised me that the Federal Government, under Lyndon Johnson, was desperate to collect these items from him; he legally had one year to turn over any assassination materials in his possession. Lyndon Johnson and the FBI altered, suppressed, confiscated, and classified evidence—some of which would remain secured until the year 2039 under national security.

Robert Kennedy said the ownership of the materials, entrusted to me, would revert to me in the event of his death. He requested that I hold any evidence in confidence, for as long as possible, for the protection of the Kennedy family. This was witnessed by Secret Service Agent Bouck. Robert Kennedy told me it was important that the chain of custody of the evidence in President Kennedy's assassination stay protected.

Approximately thirty days after taking custody of the assassination materials, I received a letter from Robert Kennedy instructing me to forward all of the evidence—except the watch and affidavit from Agent Bouck—to his secretary, Angela Novello. She came to pick up the items from me in person. Robert Kennedy later informed me that he had surrendered the original x-rays and autopsy photos to the government, but had kept copies. He arranged for the remaining items, including the president's brain, copies of the x-rays and autopsy photos, photographs of the watch, blood report, and the original watch strap, which I had given to Novello, to be placed with the president at Arlington National Cemetery during his reinterment in 1967, in an effort to keep them out of the government's custody, and safe from suppression. I retained the watch, the affidavit from Bouck, and the Oval Office recordings during this entire period.

When Robert Kennedy was assassinated in 1968, Mrs. Novello and myself were left vulnerable. As he instructed, we both kept his intentions secret to ensure the safety of the remaining members of the Kennedy family. The round, 18k gold Cartier wristwatch, serial number 345090 that belonged to President Kennedy, which is now in your possession, was one of the items involved in the president's assassination. Robert Kennedy withheld it from the government for his own investigation.

Sincerely,
Evelyn N. Lincoln
Secretary to the late President John F. Kennedy

Stunned, I looked up at Henry and silently passed him the letter without uttering a word. As he began to read, I opened the affidavit from Agent Bouck.

At the request of Attorney General Robert F. Kennedy, I, Robert I. Bouck, SAIC PRS United States Secret Service, hereby state the following: On November 26, 1963, I received a call in Washington, D.C. from Secret Service Agent Chief Forrest Sorrels, in Dallas, Texas, stating that Secret Service Agent Roger C. Warner was in possession of President Kennedy's gold Cartier wristwatch, that the president was wearing November 22 when he was killed.

I notified Robert F. Kennedy, who instructed me to fly to Dallas immediately and retrieve the watch and bring it to him directly. He ordered me to inform Agent Warner that he would not have to testify about it, and thus I did not issue him a receipt. Agent Warner told me the watch was recovered from the president's wrist in Trauma Room One by a Parkland Hospital nurse, Diana Bowron.

Upon my arrival back in Washington, I delivered the watch to Robert Kennedy as I had received it: covered with the president's blood and biological material and wrapped in a handkerchief. Robert Kennedy personally took custody of the watch and issued me a receipt, but told me to keep it confidential. The watch was not to be turned over to the FBI for forensics; he would be overseeing tests on it.

On December 2, 1963, Robert Kennedy returned the watch to me, and requested I have it returned to Jacqueline Kennedy. The watch now appeared normal: the original strap had been removed and replaced with a new brown strap.

I instructed Jacqueline Kennedy's secret service agent, Clint J. Hill, to return it to her, which he did. He issued a receipt to me, describing the watch as it was prior to Robert Kennedy's tests.

Sworn December 2nd, 1963
SAIC PRS Robert I. Bouck

I passed the affidavit to Henry and stared at the floor while he leaned back in his chair and read the last document. When he finished, he cleared his throat and asked, "This is about that watch you bought a few years ago from the guy in Baltimore?"

I nodded my head.

Henry sat up straight. "I have seen a lot of things in my career, but this is the most amazing thing I've ever read."

"Do you have any advice for me?" I asked somberly.

"You may be a little young for this, but in the Marine Corps they used to tell us 'when the atomic blast comes, duck and cover.' That's my advice, kid: duck and cover."

I didn't know if he was talking about me lying low, or keeping the watch under wraps. I told him I had already been contacted by Canadian and Russian Intelligence and Robert had been contacted by President Reagan.

"Well, then my advice changes," he responded matter-of-factly. "Get rid of it as quickly as you can; this evidence and the people who surround it are explosive. It changes the government's official position, and history!"

Henry was ruled by common sense and I knew his advice was heartfelt. Apparently he could see nothing but trouble coming from this. "Henry, can you make me a copy of those documents, and hold the originals in your office safe?"

"Yes, for how long?"

"I don't know, but if I'm going to take your advice, I'll need you to forward them to whomever I transfer the evidence to."

"Christopher, just handle this as quickly as you can; you're holding on to the tail of a very large tiger."

14

LIBERTY KNELL

MARCH 3, 1999

Prosecutor Barman stared down his nose at me. "How did General Alexander Lebed first become aware of your involvement?"

"I don't know."

"Well, you have to know something!"

"I assume he found out through Mehran Mikhailov; I told him I had acquired an item from Robert White."

"Were you ever asked to sell, give, or transfer any object or information regarding the assassination of President John F. Kennedy to Mehran Mikhailov or General Alexander Lebed?"

"No," I said with conviction. Lebed had said if I ever needed a friend, his door would be open, but even while suffering at the hands of my own government, the thought of betraying my country had never crossed my mind.

"Any other foreign national?"

"No." I was angry; Barman's only agenda was to destroy me.

"Tell me about your book deal with Mr. White."

"Robert and I signed a contract to publish a photo book on certain items from his inheritance."

"You thought you could just publish a book containing non-reviewed materials?"

"We were only going to publish photographs of what would be displayed in Robert's museum. Robert White legally owned the items . . ."

"Were you aware of the government's position that Evelyn Lincoln did not have the legal right to transfer certain materials to Robert White?"

"No, as far as I knew, a judge had ruled . . ."

He interrupted me again. "Under the contract with Mr. White, you were in charge of what was to be disclosed?"

"Yes, but . . ."

"What about the Oval Office recordings? You were going to release non-reviewed recordings to the public?"

"No, the only segment that might have made it into the book was President Kennedy's memoirs, something he had *intended* for the public to hear."

Barman stared at me through brooding eyes. "Where are the recordings now??

EARLY MAY 1997

When I returned to Canada, the weight of my commercial construction obligations was oppressive. Everyone expected me to get right back to work after my time in Russia, but I wasn't going to. Following the unprecedented events that had occurred, I put off any further construction work to concentrate all my time on the photo book. It was a risky financial move, but I felt compelled to do it.

I had to work diligently; without any money coming in, our funds would drain quickly. It was literally a race to finish the book, get it published, and get a return on our investment so we could buy our house and Robert could open his museum.

I was eager to sit down and listen to the dictabelt recordings Robert had given me. He told me they hadn't been listened to in thirty years, and even then, only Evelyn Lincoln and Robert Kennedy had been privy to their content. This verbal history of the slain president had remained silent since RFK's assassination.

I prepared myself; this was a once-in-a-lifetime opportunity to be a fly on the wall in the Oval Office in the early sixties. It would surely be the closest I would ever get to travelling back in time. I felt a deep sense of honor as I pressed the button and began playback.

Kennedy's voice was much lower and slower than I anticipated, but it carried his unmistakable lilt. I used the fine adjustment on the tape player to speed up the rotations. All of a sudden, there it was—as if he was sitting in the room with me—President John F. Kennedy's voice rang out full and clear.

I listened as JFK talked to John McCone, the Director of the CIA, in early November '63. McCone said, "[. . .] There was a history during the administration of President Eisenhower when the Agency did play footsie with the opposition groups."

"Was that a true story . . . the CIA did do it?" President Kennedy asked.

"Sure," McCone said. "They supplied money, and they were involved in a plot against . . ."

JFK cut him off. "Christ, they did it in Indonesia, they did it in Laos, they did it in Cambodia."

I could tell he was agitated.

McCone continued, "[. . .] We are paying for it with our own people, in our own press and in our own Congress. The Agency in those days wasn't responsible to the State Department; the State Department didn't know about it. Every time I go to Capitol Hill I get this thrown in my face: 'Are you in control?' I told them I am, well I am, but it's hard to live with the past [. . .]. We have to buckle our belts and really take the ambassador's advice: get out gracefully on our aid program [. . .]. Our public position at the moment [. . .] is the categorical denials we have anything to do with the opposition there, their plots, or the assassination of Diệm, and Nhu. [. . .]"

JFK spoke again. "Yeah, are we going to say we are going to get out?"

"[. . .] Mr. President, I think we are past the stage of being able to turn it around."

"Well, it seems to me we're going to have to have a public, and probably a Hill, position on what we're going to do about withdrawing our aid. Ok?"

"Yes, sir."

I pressed *Stop* and sat in silence. On another tape, I heard the president speak with General Maxwell Taylor. Kennedy was going to pull back all U.S. personnel from Vietnam. He said, "After the '64 election I will be the most unpopular president in U.S. history." He must have been referring to his popularity with the intelligence community, not the American public.

Hearing the prophetic words from the president himself made my hand shake as I removed the cassette and placed another in the machine; it was dated September '62. There was a crackling sound, like what you would hear from an old phonograph record, and I heard a woman's voice. "How are you?" It was Evelyn Lincoln answering the phone at the White House.

Then I heard the caller; it was a man. "[. . .] Miss Lincoln, I've got a problem here. I have some information that has come into my hands that I sincerely hope the president is aware of—but I don't know whether he is or not—related to uh, uh, missile activity. I work with the contractors here."

"Mm-hmm," murmured Evelyn.

"[…] I'd like to impart this knowledge to somebody over there […]"

"Would you like to speak to the president?" Evelyn asked.

"I would. […] I'd love it if I could, because I've been worried about this […] and I think I'd like to tell someone about it."

"Ok, we'll give you a call."

"Ok. You have my number?"

"Uh, I imagine … Yup," Evelyn said, scrambling to make sure she had the right information.

"I think it's 128; my extension is 6674."

I was amazed; I could only assume that what I had just heard was what actually happened before the U2 spy plane was sent to take photos over Cuba. President Kennedy knew what was going on with the missiles in Cuba before October 1962 and was keeping recorded tapes. This small segment must have been saved to document the tip. I looked up the number; it was a dial code for the Advisory Commission on Intergovernmental Relations.

The history I was learning from JFK's recordings kept pushing me forward. The president's voice came through strong and sure on national matters, ongoing political agendas, dictated letters, and passages for his memoirs. My ears perked as I heard the young president dictate a speech; I was instantly pulled into the oration he had recorded just ten days before his assassination:

> It is important and desirable that people feel this way about politics and politicians in a free society. A politician's power may be great, and with this power goes the necessity of checking it.
>
> But the fact remains that politics has become one of our most abused and neglected professions. Yet it is this profession, it is these politicians, who make the great decisions of war and peace, prosperity and recession, the decision whether we look to the future or the past.
>
> Everything now depends upon what the government decides. The magic of politics is participating on all levels of national life in an affirmative way, in determining whether, in Mr. Faulkner's words, freedom will not only endure but also prevail.
>
> In 1964, my office will reach out to new generations of men and women, to lead and to encourage the citizens of this country to try harder, do better, and go farther. In our great nation, there are those who want to achieve ultimate control over individuals, eliminate freedoms, and change the basic values that we, as Americans. hold

truest in our hearts. This is inherently dangerous, and cannot be sustained.

Our world is changing, and we must change with it. I therefore am dedicating myself, while in the highest office of the land and with the power to effect change, to go forward with an immediate, systematic government reform to benefit the future generations of the United States. Following my efforts over the next four years, I see no better successor to this office than my own brother, Robert F. Kennedy, to continue this change and amplify the United States of America, and its people.

The tape crackled and clicked, and the narration was over. President Kennedy was changing everything, but with his death, most of his reforms were lost or reversed.

From what I understood, Kennedy would have pushed for term limits to allow the replacement of older statesmen who had become entrenched in wealth and privilege and commerce, and had lost touch with the people they were meant to represent. He felt improved diplomacy and cooperation were necessary and needed to be employed quickly, before being overshadowed by out-of-control men, and weapons of war, and the dark commerce that accompanied them. He wanted us free from national debt and was in the midst of reversing the bondage that the Federal Reserve had placed on the American people. He believed we should be free and independent and support the democratic processes of foreign governments fighting for their own stability. That we should not police the world through fear and show of force, as it couldn't be sustained, and we would gain more respect by our diplomatic actions, rather than our brute strength. President Kennedy also realized the seriousness of our divisions at home. He had only just begun to throw himself into the separation of race and poverty and gender, to establish stronger social and educational systems for everyone, not supporting an intentionally weak structure that allowed the moneyed elites to continue to pit American against American for their own gain. He knew what needed attention and restructuring. The loss of this great president and his ideals, left an encroaching shadow where there should have been light, and let darkness eclipse the luminosity that should radiate from all of us. The people behind the murder of President Kennedy not only robbed him of his life, but robbed the American people of a stronger future.

15

THE CAMELOT ARCHIVES

LATE JULY 1997

I was tirelessly writing excerpts that detailed each item from the Evelyn Lincoln Collection that would have an eternal place in the pages of the photo book. Names, dates, layouts, my office looked like a storm had blown through and rained down paper on every surface.

While I was putting the book together, Robert took pleasure in doing a series of interviews and press shorts about his inheritance. He did not come across as professional, and was presented in such a way that even I found myself thinking, *Who is he to own our history?* I needed to get the book done as quickly as possible.

I secured a highly respected literary agent in New York: Richard Curtis and Associates. Richard was very excited about the book, and its accompanying CD of memoir excerpts. As pages neared completion, I sent them to him for his opinion and approval. After one such submission, he called me. "Christopher, I don't think we should wait until everything is complete. No one has ever seen anything like this before; I believe it's going to be the first multi-million-dollar picture book. I've sent proposals out to several major publishers in New York; our expectations are very high." My hopes soared. It seemed my investment would return much more than I had anticipated.

Shortly after our conversation ended, the phone rang again. "Hello?" I thought Mr. Curtis must have forgotten to tell me something; however, I was surprised to find it was a business call from someone else entirely.

"Hello, Mr. Fulton? My name is Deirdre Henderson."

"What can I do for you, Ms. Henderson?"

"I got your number from Robert White; I hope you don't mind me calling you at home."

"No, that's fine; how can I help you?"

"The reason for my call is, well, I'm an author. I met John F. Kennedy at Harvard, and I worked for him personally in 1959 and 1960 as his research assistant. I was also his campaign aide in 1960."

"Really?" I said, intrigued.

"He gave me his European diary. I wrote a book titled *Prelude to Leadership*; have you read it?"

"I'm sorry to say I haven't."

"Well, I'm working on some new material, and Robert told me you're the man to talk to now. He said you're working on a book together, and that you have Kennedy's unedited recordings from the White House."

I tried to stop her there. "Ms. Henderson, I'm not sure that Robert should have told you that."

But she continued, "Is there any way you would consider working on a book with me?"

"Under normal circumstances I would say yes, but under my contract with Robert, I can't work on any other project regarding JFK until this book is done."

"Well then, in the meantime, I could send you some photocopies of my work; would that be alright?"

"I don't see any harm in that," I said, my mind turning: *This woman had known President Kennedy personally.* "Ms. Henderson, how about I play you part of a recording and you give me your opinion of it?"

"I'd like that very much."

"Alright, give me a minute." I picked up a tape and played a section which I thought was of no particular interest. "Can you hear this alright?" I asked, and I held the receiver up to the speakers.

"Yes," she said enthusiastically.

I let the small segment play, hit *stop*, then asked Ms. Henderson what she thought.

"Oh!" she gasped. "Do you realize what he just said?" She continued without waiting for me to respond. "President Kennedy just said that he, by himself, wrote a speech that Ted Sorensen took sole credit for writing! Sorensen is a liar, and you can prove it."

I thought it was interesting, but I didn't know who Ted Sorensen was. She perceived my lack of familiarity and said, "Sorensen was Kennedy's speechwriter. He was responsible for many of the famous words JFK said during his presidency. That recording would be pretty damning if it became public, at least for *his* career. He's a lawyer in New York now; if he lied about something as important as that speech, who's to say what else he's lied about!"

Now I understood the contents of these recordings had the power to change individual lives as well as affect history. "Well, thank you for your insight Ms. Henderson, and thank you for calling."

"Please, call me Deirdre."

"Alright, Deirdre, thank you. I'll look forward to reviewing the pages you send me."

"Yes, I am very interested in working with you in the future. I'll also include a very rare photo of Kennedy in Hitler's Bunker."

"President Kennedy visited the bunker? I thought it was destroyed."

"Kennedy was there in 1945 when the military brass inspected it; he was just an ensign in the Navy at the time."

I thought it was unusual that a young lieutenant—in the Navy in the Pacific theatre—would be in Hitler's bunker in 1945 while the Pacific War was still raging. I thought about the letters from Kennedy's girlfriend, Inga Arvad, a suspected German spy during World War II, in which she mentioned Kennedy running for President. It made sense: Kennedy was at the bunker because his father, Joseph P. Kennedy, the ambassador to England, had already begun grooming him for the presidency. "How did you get the photograph?" I asked.

I could hear Deirdre smile on the other end of the line. "Just take a look at everything I send you."

***

Because I had access to Robert White's collection of the president's personal photos, I was able to analyze thousands and thousands of images not in the public domain. The photos documented JFK's day-to-day life from around 1952 onwards. There were no photos of JFK wearing the Cartier watch as President of the United States, none . . . other than on the afternoon he was assassinated.

The pattern was the same in every photograph: John F. Kennedy wore his Cartier watch as a U.S. Senator and while campaigning for the presidency during 1960, all the way up to the night of the election results. But when JFK became president, he exclusively wore the square Omega watch that Robert White had showed me in his basement.

Late on the night of November 21, 1963, JFK was wearing the Omega watch as usual. He still wore it the next morning, November 22nd, at the breakfast in Fort Worth. Then something changed . . . During the motorcade in Dallas, JFK was wearing his round, gold *Cartier* watch. It was the only time he had ever done so as president. The last time he had worn that watch was the evening of the election results, November 8, 1960. *Why? Why did he switch watches only on the afternoon of his assassination?*

I was now almost solely privy to a secret that could impact the entire world. It only led to more tangled mystery, but I was at the forefront of unraveling it. The danger of it was overpowered by my intrepid sense of adventure, and I couldn't help myself; the thrill of discovery kept pushing me farther and farther into America's concealed past.

Despite Henry's warning, the written words of Evelyn Lincoln and Robert Bouck continued to haunt me. Robert Kennedy had started something he never got the opportunity to see to completion, and his unfinished business had found its way into my possession. I didn't ask for it, I didn't seek it out, but I felt as though *I* had been sought out: I had been sent on a grail quest.

There were still so many questions. With all that had been revealed to me thus far, and with my collective documentation in hand, I felt I needed to fulfill the obligation that Evelyn Lincoln had requested of Robert White. I was going to call Robert Bouck.

Agent Bouck had been the head of the Protective Research Section for the Secret Service in the White House since World War II, with Roosevelt. I learned that of all the presidents he had served, JFK was his favorite. According to Evelyn Lincoln, Bouck was a man of distinct loyalty and total confidentiality, who was intimately trusted by both Kennedy brothers.

My fingers touched the keypad. As the tones rang out, I held my breath waiting for an answer on the other end.

"Hello?"

"Mr. Bouck?" I asked.

"Who's calling?"

"Mr. Bouck, my name is Christopher Fulton. I'm calling you in reference to President Kennedy's gold Cartier wristwatch, the material evidence that was left at Parkland Hospital on November 22, 1963. I'm in possession of that watch and have been tasked with fully documenting it. I've already spoken with Mr. Roger Warner, and I have received a sworn statement from him on this matter. If you could, I need you to recall any and all information about the watch and relay it to me at this time." There was an uncomfortable pause. "Sir, do you remember the evidence in question?" I probed.

Without any further hesitation Bouck responded, "Please describe the watch to me, in detail."

I presumed he intended to ensure the watch was actually in my possession. "Round, 18k gold Cartier wristwatch with 'J.F.K. 9-12-57' inscribed on the reverse, serial number 345090, 156 is the three-digit Cartier code on the underside of the lug, 18-jewel movement, number 486411, originally had a black wristband with Cartier deployant buckle."

"Is the black strap still on it?" Bouck asked.

A test? "No," I responded.

"What band is on it now?"

"A brown strap that seems unworn; it's a Lord Elgin. I also have a detailed letter from Evelyn Lincoln . . ."

"Just one moment," Bouck interrupted, and the line went quiet.

I waited for what seemed like an age, but it must have only been about four minutes. At one point I thought we had been disconnected, but there was no way I was going to hang up the phone, not yet. Finally Bouck came back on the line and said, "Where can we meet?"

16

THE SECRETS MAN

AUGUST 1997

After a long train ride from Vancouver to Maryland, I arrived early at the spot designated by Robert Bouck: a little coffee shop in Bethesda, just outside Chevy Chase. The weather wasn't right for sitting outside, but I took a chair at the pre-arranged table on the terrace. Dark clouds gathered and it felt like rain; I was thankful for the patio umbrella. I hadn't been there long when a car with a Hertz license plate bracket pulled up. The passenger window slid down and an elderly gentleman called out, "Christopher?"

I walked up to the window. "Get in," he said.

As I hastily planted myself on the leather seat, a blast of warm air hit me from the vent. I didn't know where we were going, but he immediately pulled into a nearby parking space.

Bouck was wearing a light grey suit and tie; his white hair was thinning on top, and round-rimmed glasses sat just below the lines of distinction on his brow. "Christopher, nice to meet you." He put the car in park and stretched out his hand. "Robert Bouck." We shook hands and he got straight to the point. "You wanted to speak with me, so show me what you have."

I reached into the inside pocket of my overcoat, took out a copy of Evelyn Lincoln's letter and his own affidavit, and handed them to him. He read them to himself, then I handed him a small, inconspicuous box that held the president's wristwatch. He opened it, gently lifted out the watch, and held it in his hands. He stared at it, looking at the face and crystal, then turned it front to back and inspected JFK's initials inscribed on the case back. Becoming emotional, he cleared his throat. "This brings back so much; I haven't held this since 1963 when Robert Kennedy asked me to get it back to Jackie."

I searched for something to say, but came up short.

He let out a heavy sigh. "I've waited for this a long time . . . I guess you're it." He handed the watch and documents back to me and started the car. We drove out of the parking lot and headed towards the 495. "We'll take the beltway to the George Washington Parkway; nobody is tailing us, and the car is clean."

I felt like I was in an Ian Fleming novel, but this wasn't a book; this wasn't fiction.

"Christopher, if you're lucky to live as long as I have, you get to see how things really are; you get to see the truth behind all the cover-ups. I remember President Truman said, 'The only thing new in this world is the history you don't know about.'

"The men who gain power and play God don't gamble and roll the dice; they don't believe in fate or coincidences. The men who were responsible for President Kennedy's death stole power away from this country and forever changed the world we live in. I believed in what President Kennedy was trying to do, but it all collapsed when he was killed. He was far from perfect, but of the six presidents I served, I admired John Kennedy the most."

As Bouck spoke, I kept it clearly in my mind that he had been responsible for the physical protection of the presidents from Franklin Roosevelt to Richard Nixon, and was the founder and president of the organization for all retired Secret Service agents.

He went on, "If Kennedy had survived, the new world order you hear about these days would have died . . . instead, it's grown like a cancer." He paused again to catch his breath before continuing. "It was very difficult for Robert Kennedy to carry on in politics after what they did to his brother. For months after the assassination, he was literally wasting away. I thought he might never recover and fade away from public life entirely, but Robert and I were able to work together in secret to recover and secure evidence in his brother's death . . . but you already knew that."

I nodded silently to his riveting narrative.

"What I'm about to share with you I've never shared with anyone, not even my own family. The last time I spoke about any of this was to Robert Kennedy. You see, Christopher, I made Robert a promise to stand with him until he could reach the White House, take power, and give it back to the people. He intended to set the record straight. He would have told the world there *was* a conspiracy to force his brother into a corner, and there *was* a coup that stole the power in this country. Robert Kennedy was the only man who could have disclosed that, but they got to him first."

I looked out the window and saw the sign for Arlington National Cemetery, and noticed that the rain I predicted had started to fall. We pulled in, parked, and got out of the car. Bouck grabbed two umbrellas from the back seat and handed me one. "Come with me," he said, as he opened his umbrella and held it aloft.

We walked towards the eternal flame at JFK's grave; there was a line of people waiting to pay their respects, despite the weather. "Wait here," Bouck said. He walked up to a military honor guard who stood by the last resting place of JFK and Jackie. I watched him take out his credentials, show them to the guard, then beckon me forward. We stood in front of the president's grave while the guard solemnly stood between us and the line of waiting people. My father had brought me to this spot many times as a young child, before the reinterment; it looked different now.

Bouck nodded towards the grave. "All the other evidence is right there, just below us."

"I know," I said in quiet reverence.

Bouck took out a pill and swallowed it. "High blood pressure."

I could tell this was going to be difficult for him. As he regained his composure, we overheard a tourist talking about the Vietnam Veterans Memorial.

Bouck thought back to November 1963. "I remember the day before he went to Dallas; President Kennedy was upset with the reported number of our American boys dead in Vietnam. He said it was time for us to get out; there was no reason for us to lose another man over there. Vietnam was not worth another American life. When he got back from Texas, he was going to make that happen . . . instead, 58,000 of our boys never returned home alive from that country."

Bouck had a sad look in his eyes. "But first let me tell you about Cuba . . . . On October 2 in '62, President Kennedy called me, and five other Secret Service agents, into the Oval Office to discuss the island. That was weeks before history remembers his being aware of any missile problem; he was ahead of the intelligence agencies."

I thought about the secret Oval Office recordings, and the call that came into Evelyn Lincoln in September to warn the president about Cuba.

Bouck continued, "The Pentagon had planned to conduct terrorist activities within the United States using our own military and intelligence.

They would do anything to justify an armed invasion of Cuba: assassinations, bombings, shooting down American airlines, killing our own citizens, but President Kennedy aggressively and permanently rejected and dismissed all such proposals.

"There was a plan if *Mercury* astronaut John Glenn died in his attempt to orbit the Earth in 1962. The Pentagon was going to plant fake evidence of sabotage to implicate the Cuban Government. It would have ensured public pressure on President Kennedy to finally take action against Cuba. No amount of time, effort, manpower, or money was spared to overthrow the communist regime on that island. The Cuban problem was our government's top priority.

"The director of the CIA, Allen Dulles, wanted to take Cuba militarily, and nuke Russia in the process. Since 1947, it was believed that if Moscow was taken out, the chain of power in Russia would crumble. When President Kennedy came into office, General Curtis Lemay wanted to utilize our nuclear weapons to destroy communism anywhere on the globe . . . President Kennedy said Dulles and Lemay were insane lunatics who were out of control with power.

"It was a closely guarded secret that President Kennedy was very sick with Addison's Disease and probably wouldn't live past 1962. Not only did he survive and thrive, but it seemed certain that he would win a second term, and his brothers would be his successors to the Oval Office. Without a Vietnam War to deter the communist threat, or a military action to seize Cuba, the U.S. Government was terrified that a nuclear war with Russia was inevitable, and we needed to be the country to make the first strike.

"The CIA and the Pentagon fully backed the Bay of Pigs invasion, an operation planned by Eisenhower and Nixon which President Kennedy inherited. Secretly, the Agency promised President Kennedy they would kill Castro the day of the invasion, and the numbers of the landing force wouldn't matter, because a popular uprising would take place. Castro would be gone and U.S. involvement would be concealed. When the president found out the Agency had failed to kill Castro and men were dying on the beach, he lost all faith in the CIA's super-covert tactics.

"He and his brother stood alone in their refusal to commit the U.S. military. Following that decision, both Kennedy brothers were targeted as serious problems for national security. It became an all-out war between the Kennedys, the intelligence community, and the Pentagon over Cuba and our position with Russia. President Kennedy needed to keep everything and everyone on record. I know because I was the man he trusted to bug the White House for him.

"During the CIA's failed invasion of Cuba, President Kennedy did what he did for damn good reasons. He was able to keep his promise to Eisenhower and Khrushchev and keep us out of World War III, but the CIA's failure was placed squarely on him anyway. He took responsibility publicly, but privately he was both furious and devastated. He was so deeply upset by the bungle that cost all those lives that at one point I thought he might resign. He often called his father for guidance during that period, but Joseph Kennedy was brutal to him. Despite his disillusionment and the enormous pressures put upon him, he persevered.

"The CIA and the Pentagon believed invading Cuba was essential; they were convinced that Castro was willing to sacrifice himself and his island in nuclear fire for the cause of communism. At that time other countries watched Castro's stand against the United States with great interest . . . that was when North Korea began their own nuclear program.

"A general in the Pentagon said that even if there was only one American left standing, but no Russians, then we win. President Kennedy felt that once nuclear war started, there would be *no* winners. He knew that an aggressive act, beyond his orders, could easily take us to World War III. He had prepared a speech to the American public in case of that eventuality. Robert Kennedy devastatingly calculated that a first strike by the United States would cost forty-two million American lives, but not striking first would cost ninety million. It was unacceptable; both brothers were prepared to give their own lives to stop that from happening. In the end, that's exactly what they did."

Bouck paused for a moment to reflect. "On D-Day President Eisenhower found God, and from then on he feared that WWIII would be around the corner. He pleaded for President Kennedy to prevent that war at any cost, to make it his top priority. President Kennedy prepared programs of conflict resolution for the United States, and began working with Khrushchev to end the damn Cold War altogether, but his actions were considered seditious. The CIA and the Pentagon viewed him as a traitor and evaded and stalled his orders; they even went so far as to keep Khrushchev's correspondence from him. President Kennedy said the men surrounding him all had a collective death wish for the world."

We moved and stood to the far left of the grave, allowing the line of waiting tourists to recommence their viewing of the eternal flame. "He knew he was the most watched and recorded man in history," Bouck said.

"He couldn't make a move without the agencies knowing exactly what he was doing . . . he was forced to operate in secret. People make a big deal about his infidelity, how he always flew off to Lawford's house in California to meet with movie actresses. But what they don't understand is that he created his own covert network of spies outside the White House, civilians who would allow him to communicate with world leaders in private, people he knew and trusted, from journalistic backgrounds, the diplomatic corps, and Hollywood. He was able to gain secret intelligence that he couldn't have gotten any other way; our services didn't have access to it. His spies were many of the women he purportedly had romantic trysts with.

"The most famous was Marilyn Monroe; her Russian codename was Masha. She helped with secret communications regarding the president's efforts to end the Cold War, and she ultimately paid for it with her life, as did others. The CIA, the Pentagon, and Washington's powerful were outraged when they were forced to endure President Kennedy's choosing civilians, especially women, to operate on the highest levels of national security. The code had always been 'no outsiders' . . . but the president's methods were working."

It was single-minded and brilliant! I thought of how George Washington had set up a spy ring that included housewives; they helped him win the Revolutionary War and found this country. In the mid-1800s, Kate Warne also understood how women could get access to information that no man could. She uncovered a plot to assassinate President Abraham Lincoln and then protected him on his journey to Washington, D.C., for his inauguration. Perhaps President Kennedy went a step further, living his life as the James Bond character he identified with. The intimacy of the women who loved him provided a strong connection that he could trust more than the intelligence community. He did whatever was necessary for the betterment of his country and the world. I realized with surprise that Jackie Kennedy must have been his greatest asset in this regard. Together they could justify it. She knew what he was doing and why . . . she was a partner in it! They used these methods to keep control when the U.S. Government was planning nuclear war. They were in a battle against the government to understand our rivals and cultivate a peaceful future.

"Things were beginning to go the way the brothers had planned," Bouck stated. "President Kennedy had gained the cooperation of Khrushchev to degrade cold-war tactics. He ordered NASA to share information and cooperate with Russia in the attempt to land on the moon. He hoped it would end the competition of missile construction between the two superpowers and encourage the efforts to create peace. It would lessen the chances of extreme government officials pushing a war of annihilation that nobody could win. But the Kennedy brothers couldn't sustain being at odds with their own government indefinitely; they had to reform the power structure.

"The joint chiefs and the CIA were furious over President Kennedy's negotiations with Khrushchev on détente and mutual nuclear disarmament in '61. They were overjoyed when the summit failed. Six weeks later President Kennedy was shown a proposal for a preemptive thermonuclear attack on the Soviet Union, to be launched in late 1963. He left the meeting in total disgust.

"He kept the text of his American University speech completely secret from the Pentagon, the CIA, and the State Department. That speech was meant to convey the president's intentions to Khrushchev, that he was still serious about ending the Cold War. It shocked the national security state, and they quickly mobilized to try to derail his nuclear test ban treaty. But the president was determined to get that treaty passed, even if it cost him the election in '64 . . . He told me it was the most important thing he had ever done.

"In November of his final year, President Kennedy's goal was to have a free and democratically elected Cuba, with no nuclear concerns, by December 1, 1963. The president and his brother were running out of time, and were forced to act quickly. Castro was becoming more unreceptive, and Russia was finding him more difficult to deal with. The brothers were secretly trying to make peace with Castro, which would ease their concerns with Russia. But if they couldn't, they would be forced to use Robert's last resort: secretly having the Cuban Government overthrown from the inside with the cooperation of Castro's military commander, Almeida.

"Despite the president's secrecy, the NSA was aware of the brothers' plan to try and make peace. President Kennedy would not allow a future U.S. President to go through a missile crisis with Cuba again, risking the security of all Americans and the world. He expected his brothers to be in the Oval Office after him, and would not leave them with a more advanced version of the same threat. President Kennedy was going to put an end to the Cuban problem once and for all, and he was going to do it without the CIA or the Mafia.

"The president knew Castro had top-notch intelligence, clearly proven by the Bay of Pigs fiasco. That although the CIA had failed to solve the problem, he was confident he could secure Castro's cooperation before the December 1 deadline. But as a safeguard, the morning of November 22, 1963, Juan Almeida was paid for the Cuban coup with money sanctioned by the Kennedys. Agreements were in place for Almeida's family to fall under our government's protection. Following Castro's murder by his own military leader, the U.S. Government would be invited into Cuba to take control and stabilize the island.

"The trip to Dallas began a ten-day countdown; on November 22, we were just nine days from the Cuban coup, and the CIA and Mob would be out of world-staging events for good. The Dallas trip was President Kennedy's last public appearance before that deadline. He was going to announce his plans for major government restructuring at the Trade Mart in Fort Worth, using the coded message 'government reform, we are going forward' to let Khrushchev know his intentions regarding Cuba."

Jesus! Those were the words written on the *Air Force One* note I had seen at Robert's, the last thing JFK had scribbled down before departing the plane in Dallas!

Bouck looked down at the grave. "President Kennedy wouldn't be pushed around, so there was a plan to force him on board. When the CIA failed to assassinate Castro, the Cuban leader made a public statement to the Associated Press in September 1963. He said: 'I know the Americans are trying to kill me, and if this continues, there will be retribution.' That quote, on record in the international press, was used to create a false flag assassination attempt on the president—a U.S.-fabricated Cuban retaliation. The idea behind it was to induce public outrage, which would turn the screws on the president to invade Cuba. After the public and clearly-communist attempt, President Kennedy would be left with no choice but to invade. But he knew about their plans and desperately tried to avoid being placed in that compromised position. The irony is that the intelligence community misunderstood Castro's words; Robert told me Castro was actually trying to warn President Kennedy of the dangers of the CIA's uncontrolled attempts."

As we walked away from Kennedy's grave, Bouck turned his eyes to the horizon. "Dallas's mayor, Earle Cabell, and Sheriff Bill Decker were both CIA assets. They told the Dallas police to stand down from their protection of President Kennedy by order of the Secret Service. At the same time, several key men in the president's Secret Service detail were told that there would be a test of the president's security in Dallas, and that there could be a staged event that would lead to the door of the pro-Castro Cubans, and to stand down. The men following that order thought they were doing the right thing for their country. It's how the loyal Secret Service men were made part of the plan and played a role in the assassination. I remember debriefing a CIA man who had been sent to Dallas to abort the false flag assassination attempt; he was shocked and horrified when he saw the president shot in the head."

"So, who turned the false flag into the real assassination?" I asked.

Bouck looked at me. "Lyndon Johnson."

NOVEMBER 22, 1963, 7:40 A.M.

Vice President Johnson's Secret Service Agent, Mitchell J. Sharron, walked into suite number 850. "George, I'm here to collect all the President's personal items for a radiation check." George Thomas, the president's valet, was obliged to hand over anything containing metal that Kennedy might wear that day.

The president wore two medals of the Catholic faith around his neck: a St. Jude and a St. Christopher. George knocked on the bathroom door. "Radiation check, sir."

"Damn it," exclaimed Kennedy, "can't it wait until I finish my shower? I'll leave my necklace on the shower head; it can be picked up when I leave."

Sharron overheard the conversation, told George he would return for the items after the Chamber of Commerce breakfast, and left the room.

George began to gather the items the Secret Service would require for the check: the president's wallet that had a large gold St. Christopher money clip fastened into it, sunglasses, his box of cufflinks . . . he didn't wear rings, so his wedding ring wasn't there. George replaced the French cuff dress shirt he had already laid out for the president with a button cuff version; JFK would be disappointed he couldn't wear the Texas cufflinks he had brought especially for his trip to Dallas.

After JFK finished showering, George helped the president into his cloth back brace and said, "The agent is coming back to collect everything after the breakfast." When he finished dressing Kennedy he said, "It's raining this morning, Mr. President."

JFK wanted to see the crowds, but didn't have a view from his windows so he walked into Jackie's adjacent room. He was surprised to see her still in bed. "Jackie it's time to get up. Where's Mary?" Mary was Jackie Kennedy's personal assistant, but she had not shown up that morning. She was supposed to help Jackie get dressed. JFK told his wife what he wanted her to wear that day; it was the first time he had ever dictated her dress. He knew the iconic pink Chanel outfit would illuminate her presence and clearly define her from a distance. Jackie hadn't planned on wearing that ensemble, and it took her more time than she had to get ready.

JFK peered out the window in Jackie's room to see that thousands of people had gathered in the rain outside the hotel. He headed back to his room and grabbed a quick bite before going down to greet the crowd. After he addressed the throng of onlookers, JFK entered the grand ballroom of the Hotel Texas for the Fort Worth Chamber of Commerce formal breakfast. Jackie Kennedy arrived late.

***

After the meal, the president and his wife returned to suite 850. For the first time, they noticed the artistic masterpieces that adorned their rooms: a Monet, a Picasso, a Van Gogh, and thirteen other paintings and bronzes. A great deal of effort had been taken to make their time in Texas pleasantly memorable, so Jackie looked up the phone number of the woman who was responsible for the welcome surprise, and had the president thank her personally. It was the last phone call he ever made.

Taking advantage of the lull in the schedule, Lyndon Johnson came into the suite with his sister and brother-in-law to introduce them to the president. The meeting reminded Kennedy why he desperately needed to heal the party's differences in Texas. He had to appear respectful of Connally and Johnson so the party would not be split when Johnson got the axe in '64 and Kennedy took on a new vice president.

Bobby Kennedy had ensured a *Life* magazine article would come out on December 1 that would finish Johnson's political career. It had been tricky; Johnson had tried to attach his wrongdoings to the Kennedys. Both brothers were eagerly anticipating office without Johnson in '64. When Johnson went, the president would also retire Hoover; two thorns in his side, gone.

Johnson was accompanied by his Secret Service Agent, Sharron, who had requested the president's personal effects earlier that morning. While JFK changed into a lightweight suit in preparation for the forecasted warmer weather, he handed over his Omega watch, which had been set to local time the day before. George gave the agent everything he had gathered, forgetting about the necklace in the bathroom. Shortly after, the president left for the airport.

***

Agent Sharron now thought he had every item he needed from the president, but he didn't take them to a radiation check; instead he left the Hotel Texas, got into a car in the parking lot, and waited. A few moments later, another of Johnson's Secret Service Agents, Rufus Youngblood, code-named Dagger, walked up and said, "Did you get everything?"

"Yes," Sharron said, and handed him a brown paper bag containing the President's effects. Sharron closed the car door and drove; he drove for four hours.

***

Secret Service Agent Ron Pontius found the president's medal necklace hanging in the shower and put it in his pocket.

AUGUST 1997

"Why did Johnson's agents withhold all of the president's belongings?"

"Christopher," Bouck stopped to look at me, "in the White House we routinely gathered the president's metal possessions that would have prolonged contact with his skin, and ran a Geiger counter over them to ensure no miniscule capsule of uranium had been concealed there. There was no radiation check in Fort Worth. Lyndon Johnson's agents removed anything metal that might have been on the president's person during the motorcade, anything that could deflect a bullet from its course: the large St. Christopher money clip the president had always kept in his breast pocket, his cufflinks, his Catholic medal necklace, his watch . . . It left President Kennedy totally vulnerable to gunfire. Those agents' orders came directly from Johnson."

With a jolt, I realized that the letters Evelyn Lincoln had written for the St. Christopher and the watch, for Robert White's museum, described both objects using identical words: "Discarded by the president." She didn't want to address the artifacts' involvement in the assassination, to avoid controversy for the museum and for the continued safety of the Kennedy family.

There was anguish in Bouck's voice, anguish, remorse, and despair. "I was the head of the Protective Research Section in Washington; it was my responsibility to protect President Kennedy. He trusted me, and I missed it . . . agents of the Secret Service betrayed me, they betrayed their president, and they betrayed their country."

NOVEMBER 22, 1963

Aboard *Air Force One*, on the thirteen-minute flight to Love Field, President Kennedy was anxious to resolve the in-fighting of who would be riding in what car; there could be no division visible during the motorcade.

The president combed his hair and changed his shirt in preparation for his appearance before the Dallas public. Once his shirt was buttoned, he pulled back his sleeve to check the time and remembered he had given up his watch. He turned to Jackie. "What time is it?"

"Where's your watch?" she asked.

"Secret Service took everything for a radiation check."

"Well, that's what you get for talking to Ian Fleming," she said light-heartedly.

Some time ago, Fleming had spoken to the president about assassinating Fidel Castro by irradiating something he came in contact with. When President Kennedy shared the anecdote with his Secret Service, they took it as a possible threat to Kennedy as well, and started doing random radiation checks.

"Come here," Jackie said gently. "When I went to Cartier to get your St. Christopher clip replaced, after . . . Patrick," her voice still choked on his name, "I wanted to get your watch serviced." She pulled a round, gold Cartier wristwatch from her bag, wound it, set the time, and fastened it around her husband's wrist. She had given it to him for their fourth wedding anniversary. "I've always hoped you would wear this again," she said. "You wore it while you were campaigning to be president, and now you can wear it while you're campaigning for your second term." She smiled, but there was worry behind her eyes.

Jackie didn't want the pressure anymore; she needed her family safe. She thought of the relief she had experienced a month before while abroad, and wished Jack could just walk away from it all. But she knew her husband was the only man to stand against the tide and make a difference. "You know it doesn't matter what I wear," JFK said, trying not to notice the truth written on his wife's face. "They're all waiting to see you."

"Jack, I'm scared," she said. "Evelyn told me what her husband heard."

JFK cut her off. "I know, I know, don't worry; I've been assured everything is ok. Like I told Congressman Gonzales yesterday, there is nothing to worry about."

He positioned the watch high on his wrist, as he always did, and pulled his shirt sleeve over it as the plane began its descent to Love Field.

***

Agent Sharron drove to Lyndon Johnson's ranch—JFK's scheduled destination for later that day. The jewelry box containing the president's cufflinks sat on the car seat beside Sharron. The box was the only item intentionally not included in the brown paper bag he had given to Young-blood.

***

President Kennedy arrived in Dallas at Love Field on *Air Force One*, and Vice President Johnson arrived on *Air Force Two*. Once the president had taken five minutes to greet his admirers gathered in the warm Texas sunshine, he and Johnson continued to argue loudly, for the first time in public, over who should ride in the presidential limousine. Johnson said, "Senator Yarborough should sit with you." Johnson had never liked Kennedy's man. "No," Kennedy said, "Connally is the Governor of Texas; he should be in the car with me." But Johnson kept pushing, even suggesting that Jackie might like to ride with him and his wife in the V.P. car. The suggestion both angered and troubled Kennedy. He wanted the Connallys in the car with him and Jackie. He put his foot down and, almost yelling, said, "That's it; Connally, get in the car, *now!*" Governor Connally didn't look happy as he sidled into the open vehicle with his wife. Connally tried to squeeze into the rear left-hand side of the limousine, the same seat he had occupied the previous day and earlier that morning. President Kennedy ordered him into the jump seat instead; JFK wanted Jackie on his far left, and Connally in front of him.

Jackie turned to her husband. "I'd like Clint with us, too." Kennedy gave the order to have Secret Service Agent Clint Hill placed in the car directly behind them.

These were last-minute changes that were not pre-planned.

***

The motorcade was delayed as the driver of the presidential limousine, Secret Service Agent Bill Greer, was ordered to pull over so President Kennedy could greet a group of nuns and a Boy Scout troop that were waiting to see the president pass.

***

Agent Sharron looked at the clock on his dash. He was anxious as the seconds ticked by: 12:15.

***

It was a beautiful sunny afternoon in Dallas as the limousine drove along the motorcade route. Everyone cheered as the president and his wife waved to the onlookers.

***

12:26: Sharron waited, almost holding his breath. Surely, history had now changed.

***

The shooters were frustrated. The timing was off; everything was delayed.

***

Greer awkwardly swung the Lincoln convertible wide onto Elm. He stopped to reposition the vehicle before continuing.

***

The limo crept though Dealey Plaza. Lyndon Johnson leaned down in the VP car, out of sight. Shots were fired; they sounded like firecrackers. They came from behind the limousine. President Kennedy looked to his right. Suddenly he felt a bullet punch him in the back and he rose in his seat. His elbows swung up into the air. "My God!" he said desperately, "I've been hit!"

"God, oh God! *No!*" Jackie panicked.

The President could feel the lead mass nestled beneath his skin; he knew the bullet had not gone through him. It was a half-load, low-impact round, targeted at the area of the human torso with the thickest skin and fewest nerve endings.

The president tried to bend forward and down, but he was restrained by his back brace. This had to be the false flag assassination attempt he had been dreading. *Christ . . . now I will have to invade*, he thought; *those bastards trapped me . . . I have to get out of here now!*

The limo slowed, allowing the shooters precision. Again, shots rang out from behind, almost on top of each other. A bullet missed the president's head just high and to the right. Governor Connally was hit; he cried out for mercy, "God . . . they're gonna kill us all!" His words were very telling; JFK noted them with alarm.

Secret Service Agent John Ready leapt from the right running board of the follow-up car to try to protect the president. He was immediately called back by Emory Roberts, the Secret Service agent in charge of the Presidential Protection Detail. Secret Service Agent Kellerman was riding in the front passenger seat of the presidential limousine; he turned to Greer. "We are hit." Greer turned his head to the right to evaluate the situation; he slowed the limo down even further.

The president could have leaned hard towards Jackie to protect himself, but he would not put his wife in further jeopardy. *Why in God's name wasn't the Secret Service doing their job?* He prayed Jackie's bright pink attire would keep her safe, a clear target *not* to be hit. As President Kennedy bowed his head down, Jackie grabbed hold of his left arm, screaming, "Jack, what are they *doing* to you?!" His gold Cartier watch revealed itself from beneath his sleeve, gleaming as it caught the brilliant Texas sun. Jackie tried to look into her husband's eyes. The expression on his face was the same she had seen a thousand times before; it was one he wore whenever he was deeply troubled or concerned, when he was trying to figure something out.

The president whispered his last words to Jackie. "Get me to a hospital!"

The limousine stopped. One second. Two seconds . . .

The shooter from behind hesitated; Jackie was too close. She wasn't even supposed to be in Dallas, but she had decided to accompany her husband last-minute. At the eleventh hour, the shooter had been given strict instructions not to hit the First Lady under any circumstances, but he was running out of time. He squeezed the trigger.

***

The shooter from the front had already waited as long as he could; he took his shot.

***

A deafening report shook the plaza. The president was shot in the back of his head as a mercury-filled frangible round impacted him above his right temple.

The shot to the front was the fail-safe shot to ensure a wounded president would not return to Washington with even more power and support than he'd had before. The round disintegrated as it hit his temple and exploded upon entry. It did not track like a normal bullet; it never entered or exited Kennedy's skull as a solid projectile. Small metal fragments and liquid mercury were forced through the president's cranium and caused the bullet from behind to break apart. Kennedy's skull plates violently separated from the pressure. A cloud of atomized blood and brain rose up in a plume. The dispersion of metal fragments created a shotgun effect that left a gaping hole in the back of the president's head, strewing his blood, bone, and brain matter all over Jackie, onto the trunk of the limousine, and onto the windshield of the car behind them.

So much gore landed on the police motorcycle escort to the left rear of the limo that the officer briefly thought he had been hit as well.

Dust-like particles of metal embedded themselves in the president's skull, several fragments embedded in his cheek, and another ricocheted out through his throat. His Cartier watch was less than five inches away from the explosion; it was the closest material evidence to his mortal head wounds.

No matter where the mercury round had hit the president, the toxic contents would have killed him, but that didn't matter: the round did so much damage on impact that the president would not survive.

***

The planned cover-up would now become the most convoluted conspiracy in history.

***

Jackie scrambled to retrieve part of her husband's brain from the trunk of the limousine. Clint Hill jumped forwards to protect her. He was not stopped; the president was already fatally wounded. Jackie was exposed to the liquid metal and fumes from the mercury throughout her hair, face, and mouth. As the limo sped to Parkland Hospital, Jackie, in shock, pushed her husband upright and desperately tried to put his fragmented brain and skull back together. Her efforts were futile. "Oh, no, no, no!" she cried out. "Oh my God, they've shot my husband! They've killed my husband!" She was shaking. "I have his brain in my hand."

***

Lyndon Johnson was now in control.

***

One of President Kennedy's closest friends, Dave Powers, had been in the car just behind JFK. He smelled the gunpowder and saw smoke to the right and felt sure they had been led into an ambush.

As the president's limousine came to a screeching halt outside Parkland Hospital, Powers frantically ran up to see him. The president's eyes were open, and Powers half expected him to say, "I'm ok, Dave." But it became shockingly apparent that the president was not going to be ok. Powers noticed a metal fragment lodged in Kennedy's right temple, and saw that the back of his head was missing.

***

Nurse Diana Bowron tried to convince Jackie Kennedy to let her husband go. "Please, you have to let go, you have to let him go." But Bowron couldn't get the First Lady to loosen her embrace.

Agent Clint Hill interceded and gently pulled Jackie from her husband. "We've got him; I'll put my jacket over him," he said. As the president was placed on a gurney, Jackie tenderly supported her husband's head. As he was rushed into the hospital, a three-inch piece of the back of his head remained in the right rear corner of the back seat of the presidential limousine.

***

Blood pooled on the gurney and dripped onto the floor as they wheeled him to Trauma Room One. Bowron watched as a small piece of Kennedy's brain fell out the back of his skull. There were red roses all around his head—the remnants of the bouquet that Jackie had held in her lap during the motorcade. Nurse Hinchcliffe grabbed the flowers and threw them in the trash, initially unaware that the man on the gurney was the President of the United States.

An intern immediately began efforts to save the president's life, but he was quickly pushed away by the Secret Service who demanded a senior doctor be called. Dr. Ronald Jones arrived and started a cutdown on the president's left arm to insert an IV. Nurse Bowron saw the President's watch, splattered with gore, slipping from his wrist. She reached out to grab it before it fell to the floor, and put it in her pocket for safekeeping.

***

The seconds were stretched by horror and despair. Then at 1 P.M., Central Standard Time, the doctor in charge made it official: the President of the United States was pronounced dead.

Jackie stood in the trauma room, more alone in that moment than the world would ever be allowed to know. She silently placed her own wedding band on his bare ring finger. Through her unimaginable anguish, she secretly prayed she had conceived the day before; if not, she would never have a chance to bear another child by her late husband.

***

Orderly Joe Sanders mopped up the mess of blood and fluid, and Nurse Bowron used cotton swabs to clean the clotted blood from the president's hair. Government agents swarmed over the scene. They seized anything that had come in contact with the president or his blood: sheets, tubes, scissors, gauze. They jammed everything into plastic bags and hauled them away. Not a trace was left, except for the casket that now held the president's nude and lifeless form wrapped in sheets.

***

A ruckus broke out as the Secret Service forcibly removed the president's remains from the hospital before an autopsy could be conducted, and boarded *Air Force One* for immediate takeoff to Washington.

Agent Youngblood sat on the plane holding two brown paper bags. One contained the president's clothes that had been removed in Trauma Room One; the other contained his personal effects that had been retrieved from his hotel suite that morning. The president's Omega watch and wallet would be logged as evidence back in Washington, making it appear they had been removed from Kennedy's body in the hospital room. They would claim both items were found in the president's right front pants pocket, to account for the lack of bloodstains.

***

Nurse Bowron stood alone in the hospital hallway to collect herself. She held her hands at her waist, then ran them down her sides trying to process what had just happened. She felt something, and put her hand in her pocket: the watch. She had forgotten all about it. She looked everywhere for a Secret Service agent to give it to, but they were all gone. She held it in her hand, and began to cry.

AUGUST 1997

Bouck's recounting of the story had an immediate effect on me. Something happened to me physically; my head was spinning and I felt a loss of presence. Despite my discomfort, Bouck continued to reveal the country's secrets to me.

"Nurse Bowron relinquished the president's watch to the Hospital's head of security, O.P. Wright. Shortly before that, Wright had turned over a bullet to the Service that had been found on a stretcher by a hospital employee. That bullet—along with others recovered on the twenty-second—was given to the FBI on November 23. These materials were manipulated on the grounds of national security, and the bullet logged as 'evidence from Parkland' became the keystone of the government's case, the foundation of the biggest lie in the word.

"You see, Christopher, by the evening of the twenty-second, enough evidence had been secured to prove multiple shooters, a conspiracy, and a false flag operation, but every shred of evidence from the assassination—including the autopsy materials from Bethesda—was gathered by the Secret Service and secured back in Washington within fifteen hours of the shots in Dallas . . . all of it, except President Kennedy's Cartier watch. The Secret Service didn't know about it; they hadn't considered the possibility. That's why it wasn't collected that day; that's why they didn't know they'd left it behind at Parkland . . . not until Forrest Sorrels was contacted by O.P. Wright.

"That watch changed everything: it foiled the plan to log the president's wallet and Omega watch as evidence. Robert Kennedy knew it proved that Johnson's agents, and Johnson himself, were part of the operational stage of the assassination. It was key evidence of the exploding mercury round to the front of the president's head. Robert refused to turn it over to Johnson and the FBI.

"People have always wondered why Jackie Kennedy sued William Manchester over his book that was based on his interviews with her. The fact is, she recalled events too vividly, and Robert Kennedy was upset she had discussed details about her wedding ring and what was on the president's person when he was assassinated. Jackie made a formal request to have the president's gold St. Christopher money clip placed with him in his coffin. Robert refused because he wanted to keep it as evidence; that clip was withheld from President Kennedy the day of his murder. Jackie had to sue Manchester to keep all of those specifics from the public."

I recalled a letter I had read in Robert White's basement, that he had written to Evelyn Lincoln back in '93, in which he thanked her for the most insightful and informative letter he had ever received from her. It shared details about President Kennedy's gold money clip. He said her information had cleared up the mystery that Manchester's book had created, and he thanked her for setting the record straight.

Bouck and I continued to walk down the path, away from Kennedy's last resting place. "How did it come to that?" I asked. "How could it all have been allowed to happen?"

"In the '50's, President Eisenhower and the CIA came to a top-secret agreement: no CIA agent was to report a criminal act that involved CIA personnel or CIA assets. It was so secret that nobody in President Kennedy's administration knew about it, not even President Kennedy. . . The U.S. Secret Service relied heavily on the CIA's instructions in Dallas, and because the false flag operation was already planned, Johnson easily manipulated it.

"As vice president, Johnson pressured President Kennedy for more and more power. Johnson had blackmailed his way into the position of V.P. from the start, at the 1960 Democratic Convention in Los Angeles. He got help from his next-door neighbor and best friend of twenty-plus years, J. Edgar Hoover. Either Kennedy would run for the White House with Johnson in tow, or everything would have ended right there at the convention.

"Johnson pressed President Kennedy to sign an executive order giving him supervision over all matters of national security, with all government agencies reporting to him. The president compromised; he let Johnson review national security policy and sit in on executive committee meetings of the National Security Council. President Kennedy was also blackmailed into giving Johnson full presidential power of appointments in Texas—the pipeline for fat military contracts. Johnson had been a chairman of the Naval Affairs Committee since the 1940s and coerced President Kennedy to appoint his friend John Connally (whom the president despised) to Secretary of the Navy in 1961.

"Despite the power that Johnson siphoned away, his past was catching up to him. His maneuvers had kindled Robert Kennedy's intense hate for him, and had fueled Robert's crusade to bury him once and for all. Robert's investigators had gathered enough evidence to prove that Johnson was deeply involved in corrupt schemes of bribes and kickbacks that Johnson's protégé, Bobby Baker, used to land lucrative government contracts. Robert had Johnson's fate sealed.

"Johnson was on the verge of a breakdown; he hid away at his ranch in Texas whenever possible. President Kennedy and his brother had pushed Johnson into a corner with only one way out. Johnson knew he was about to be indicted and sent to prison for his part in the schemes; his political future was finished . . . unless President Kennedy was taken out of the picture.

"Johnson used Connally to bring the president to Texas, and one of Johnson's aides, Bill Moyers, was in charge of the entire trip. Connally told the president's Secret Service advance man in Dallas that either the president would follow their plans for the trip, or he was not welcome in Texas. Just hours before the motorcade, Moyers forwarded Johnson's demand to the Secret Service: "Get that goddamned bubble off unless it's pouring rain." If the bubble top had remained on the limousine, the assassination was off.

"Johnson knew about the false flag plot; Hoover had told him. If it appeared that the covert operation got its wires crossed, made a mistake which led to President Kennedy's death, Johnson knew he had the power to ensure the murder could be covered up. With help from Hoover, he would protect the interests of all parties involved. As the new president, Johnson would be a hero and approve the Pentagon's pre-planned ten-year war in Vietnam to deter the Russian resolve and the domino effect of the spread of communism throughout Asia.

"That day in Dallas, all the evidence against Johnson went away, and any further investigation or legal action against him ended. It wasn't the first time Johnson had used murder to climb to the next rung on the political ladder, then used that new power to cover up the crimes that got him there. He was a man who could be bought, a man who was used to being rewarded for his treachery. His participation in Kennedy's assassination awarded him the ultimate prize: the office of the President of the United States—along with three quarters of a billion dollars, in today's money, of taxpayer funds for him and his friends— and the extreme pressure built up between the Kennedys, the CIA, the Pentagon, and the Mafia was resolved. In the aftermath, President Kennedy's plans to end the Cold War were simply swept away.

"It's hard to believe, but at that time, killing a president was not a federal crime, not unless there was a provable conspiracy that crossed state lines. Upon his arrival back in Washington, Johnson's aid, Cliff Carter, made several phone calls from the White House to law enforcement officials in Dallas, and to the Attorney General of Texas, ordering them not to file any charges of conspiracy, or release any statement that referred to more than one shooter.

"President Kennedy's murder should have remained in the jurisdiction of the state of Texas, both to investigate and to prosecute. Johnson pulled all the evidence from Dallas, except what Robert Kennedy secured, and gave it to the FBI in Washington where Hoover ran the entire investigation. Hoover reported directly to Johnson, effectively cutting Robert off from any power he had as Hoover's boss."

The revelations were shocking; I was surprised to find they were hurtful on a personal level. These events had happened just over a year before I was born, but I had seen the shockwave ripple through the decades.

"People don't know it was Robert Kennedy who controlled the autopsy of his brother," Bouck said. "The watch, the remains of the president's brain, the blood samples, and the x-rays—he had all the evidence he needed to prove there was more than one shooter in Dallas."

"Why he didn't pursue his brother's murder investigation with more vigor?"

"Because there was so much more at stake: the fate of the country, the entire world hung in the balance. If Robert had attempted to expose the truth to the public, the Unites States Government would have taken the position that any conspiracy surrounding the murder of President Kennedy involved Cuba and ultimately Russia, and Russia was ready and preparing for war. Robert could either overthrow the current U.S. Government, or work within it to effect change. I can't imagine how difficult it was for him. In the end, he concluded that what mattered most was the future of the country, not personal vengeance. The truth needed to be protected and remain secret . . . Those were the directions Robert Kennedy gave Evelyn Lincoln and me, and we followed them, even after his death."

We stopped walking and stood over Robert Kennedy's grave. The flat marble headstone lay flush against the grass: "Robert Francis Kennedy 1925 1968."

"I retired from the Secret Service shortly after Robert was assassinated," Bouck said. "He was one of the most straightforward and honest men I had ever met in Government; I just couldn't see the sense anymore . . ."

NOVEMBER 22, 1963

Bobby Kennedy received the telephone call informing him that his brother had been shot in Dallas; he knew he had to act quickly. He couldn't trust the CIA, the Secret Service or Hoover's FBI, so he ordered federal marshals to surround his estate. Every marshal on duty in Washington requested to be placed on that detail. Robert called John McCone, the new director of the CIA appointed to help the Kennedys identify and flush out rogue agents, and demanded he come to his home in McLean, Virginia, immediately.

It was late afternoon when McCone arrived at Hickory Hill. Bobby was angry and blunt. "Did the CIA kill my brother? Don't lie to me, John. As a good Catholic, don't you lie to me."

McCone thought carefully about his response and replied as calmly as he could. "We know there were at least two shooters firing at the limousine, but at this time, I don't believe the Agency was directly involved." Unfortunately, McCone had recently turned his loyalty away from President Kennedy. Either his statement was covering for the Agency, or he legitimately didn't have the answer.

McCone was the man Bobby's brother had used to replace Allen Dulles, the head of the snake at the CIA. Despite being fired by the president, Dulles retained power and had his subordinates report to him in Georgetown. Dulles felt he was above elected law and that subverting presidents, targeting leaders for assassination, and overthrowing foreign governments was his duty.

AUGUST 1997

Bouck coughed into a handkerchief and cleared his throat. "Ten hours after the president's murder, Chief Rowley informed Robert Kennedy that there were at least three, maybe four, shooters in Dallas, but Rowley added that those facts would *not* be part of the official story. He also notified Forrest Sorrels in Dallas. Sorrels knew the truth; that's why he gave you my phone number.

"Robert's first priority was to ensure the country wasn't thrown into World War III; he contacted everyone he could, both directly and secretly. He contacted Fidel Castro. The Cuban leader adamantly denied any association with President Kennedy's death. In fact, Castro challenged Robert to send his best investigative team to interview him off the shore of Cuba, and that's what Robert did. At its conclusion, he was fully convinced Castro didn't have a hand in his brother's assassination."

A gust of wind caught our umbrellas and we braced against the chill. "Robert knew who Oswald was. The CIA had funded 'The Oswald Project,' the plot to assassinate Fidel Castro."

What? "Oswald worked for the CIA?"

"My superior, Chief Rowley, found out from the Agency that Oswald was trained by them and was working under the Office of Naval Intelligence. They thought he was their ticket to kill Castro. The CIA created a false Cuban file on Oswald to fool Cuban counterintelligence. A lot of the information on Oswald, in the FBI files and elsewhere, was planted there to get him close to Castro.

"He was supposed to be the CIA's dream assassin for Castro, not President Kennedy, but when the president was fatally shot in Dallas, Oswald was looking at a very different scenario. Everything was in place beforehand for him to take the blame. I was briefed by Chief Rowley that there were two prior plans to shoot at President Kennedy just before Dallas, one in Chicago and one in Tampa, but both times they never got close. I was ordered not to say anything to the Warren Commission about the other plots."

The idea that Oswald was one of the good guys was a hard pill to swallow; for decades his name had been held in the same contempt as Benedict Arnold's. "So Oswald should have been heralded as a hero, but he died one of the most hated men in America?"

"Yes," Bouck said, "a scapegoat who would never be recognized for his service. He tried to make contact with his government controller while he was locked up in the Dallas jail, but Johnson's agents made sure the call never went through. After Oswald was shot, Johnson's men pushed on his body so he would bleed out on the way to the hospital. When he was in the operating room, Johnson made a call to the attending physician, pressuring him to confirm a deathbed confession, but the doctor wouldn't do it. Oswald's death was pronounced at 1:07 P.M. on November 24 from hemorrhage. Johnson was the first to be notified." Bouck paused. "I thought on Truman's words many times in those days: 'Nothing happens in politics by chance.'"

I needed time to process everything Bouck was telling me, but the river of information continued to flow from him. I had so many questions, but I was swept up in the torrent.

"After I retrieved the president's Cartier watch from Dallas, I delivered it to Robert Kennedy and told him it was the closest material evidence to the fatal head shots. He knew those wounds were the key to unlocking the truth behind the assassination. I told him the watch was still encrusted with the president's blood. I couldn't bring myself to say *brain matter*, it was just too personal. It hurt to think it was all that was physically left of the best man I had ever known; I was still trying to come to terms with the fact that President Kennedy was actually gone.

"I was supposed to take the watch to the FBI for testing, but Robert insisted I didn't. He wanted to keep control over the forensic tests himself. Then he told me the Secret Service was banned from any investigation due to what the FBI had determined was a conflict of interest, and that my job title was about to be changed. I would become the head of the Secret Service's new intelligence division. Even though it meant a promotion, it also meant I would be reporting to the intelligence community; I would be part of the cover-up.

"I had to choose between law and loyalty. I ruled my life by law, but in the same breath I was fiercely loyal to the last president I served. That day loyalty won out, and for the first time in my life, my allegiance stayed with the previous president instead of the newly sworn-in Lyndon Johnson." Bouck paused a moment to catch his breath. He wasn't physically exerting himself, but I could tell that vividly revisiting the past in his mind was taking its toll on him.

"Robert said he would give me a receipt, but not to talk about it or show it to anyone. I knew then that, as Attorney General, he had also chosen loyalty over law. I left the watch in his hands and took his receipt . . . I still have it."

"What happened to the watch after that?"

"Robert kept it for six days. He removed the band soaked in his brother's blood and replaced it with a new strap, cleaned the biological material from the watch, and had everything forensically tested; he took photos to record the entire process. After that, he returned the watch to me, told me to give it to Clint Hill to return to Jackie, and to log my receipt, from Hill, in the Secret Service's records as 'worn on November 22.' The result was twofold: without that record, nobody would have ever know the watch was actually evidence, and, once it was in Jackie's possession, Robert knew Lyndon Johnson would never request it back.

"Robert said the whole process—documenting the results, and keeping them suppressed—was the hardest thing he'd ever had to do."

"What did the results show?" I asked.

"The watch was only inches away from the explosive impact to the front of the president's head; fine striations in the crystal of the watch were caused by the shock wave. Mercury and other particles the size of dust were embedded in the crystal, as well as on and inside the watch itself. The mercury was consistent with top-grade U.S. military munitions. A doctor explained to Robert that the x-rays showed fuzzy grey-clouded areas that were not caused by the minute bullet fragments, but rather by mercury dispersion.

Startled, I recalled a passage from *The Day of the Jackal*, a book by Frederick Forsyth that had come out in the summer of '63:

> As the bullet struck flesh, gristle, or bone, it would experience a sudden deceleration. The effect on the mercury would be to hurl the droplet forwards toward the plugged front of the bullet. Here its onward rush would rip away the tip of the slug, splaying the lead

outwards like the fingers of an open hand or petals of a blossoming flower. In this shape the leaded projectile would tear through nerve and tissue, ripping, cutting, slicing, leaving fragments of itself over an area the size of a teasaucer. Hitting the head, such a bullet would not emerge, but would demolish everything inside the cranium, forcing the bone-shell to fragments.

Without comprehending the revelation that had just taken place in my mind, Bouck went on, "Johnson's Secret Service had already attempted to log the Omega watch as 'removed from the president's wrist at Parkland Hospital,' which showed they were complicit. Once the president's Cartier watch appeared at Parkland, the planted evidence had to be pulled. Robert knew that if he had exposed those facts he could have taken control of the investigation, but there was so much more at stake, so he continued to gather information quietly."

Bouck turned to look at me with an even more serious expression. "Robert Kennedy took it upon himself to share the burden of knowing what had happened to his brother with the Russian Government. He did it in absolute secrecy. He assured the Russians, through covert channels, that he knew they were not involved, and that they would not be blamed by our government; he said he would make sure of it personally. Johnson's administration would have considered it an act of treason, but Robert knew it was essential for the Russians to be shown evidence of a domestic coup to relieve their national security alert, so the world could remain out of conflict.

"At one point Robert's emotions got the better of him. Just outside the White House, following a press conference, he confronted Johnson face to face, banged a pillar with his right fist, and held the watch in his left hand for Johnson to see, demanding to know why Johnson had killed his brother.

"Johnson was so shaken by the confrontation and its implications that he had the U.S. House of Representatives pass a bill: all evidence in the assassination of President John F. Kennedy had to be turned over to the government to be secured and classified. Robert was threatened legally, with one year to comply. He decided he would never give up all the physical specimen evidence related to his brother's murder until he got what he wanted: the Senate and then the White House.

"Robert shared some of what he knew with Jackie Kennedy, and implored her to go along with his plans. At his request, she resisted placing the St. Christopher money clip in her husband's coffin. Jackie had never trusted or liked Lyndon Johnson. After President Kennedy's funeral, she secretly met with the presidents of France, Ireland, and Ethiopia to ask their advice on how to handle the situation. She also asked the French intelligence services to do an investigation on who was responsible for the death of her husband. At its conclusion, they told her Johnson was involved . . . the French Government threatened to cut diplomatic ties with America's new administration, but Johnson threatened them with war reparations; France had no recourse."

Bouck was like an open book, and it was the most incredible book I had ever read.

"It was such a mess; Johnson and Hoover were running everything, and Robert Kennedy was trying to hold on to whatever power he had left, which wasn't much. Johnson created an investigative commission to head off any genuine fact-finding by the U.S. Senate or Congress. He tried to get the impeccable Chief Justice Earl Warren to head up his commission, but Warren wanted nothing to do with it. Then Johnson told him enough of the truth that Warren felt he had no choice but to play along with the lone-assassin fiction in order to hold the country together and avert WWIII. The need to present a farce as truth to the American people had Warren in tears and deeply wounded his sense of integrity."

"But Warren couldn't have convinced the world by himself," I said.

"No, there were many people involved in the charade after the fact—some because they thought it would keep the country out of war, others for personal or political gain. Gerald Ford was the FBI's man in Congress. He was placed on the commission to ensure everything lined up with the FBI's evidence of a single shooter; that bought his ticket to the White House. Robert Kennedy knew the commission's report would be a fabrication; he wanted to keep the real evidence disassociated from it. The commission was hanging itself with the one-shooter premise.

"On June 12, in '64, Earl Warren personally wrote to Robert Kennedy notifying him that he was formally requested to testify before the commission, and would have to provide any and all information he had regarding a domestic or foreign conspiracy in the murder of his brother. This was done on Johnson's orders.

"Robert forwarded that letter to a trusted lawyer, Nicholas Katzenbach, with a note that asked: 'Nick, what do I do?' Robert stalled for two months while Katzenbach worked out the best deal he could. On August 4, '64, Robert was forced to sign a letter stating that he didn't know of any credible evidence to support allegations that the assassination of President Kennedy was caused by a domestic or foreign conspiracy.

"In effect, that letter handed Robert the power he needed to reach the Senate quickly and got him one step closer to the Oval Office. On August 22, '64—just eighteen days after signing the letter—Robert announced his candidacy for the U.S. Senate. With help from President Johnson, Robert became the next Senator for New York.

"Johnson agreed that Robert would remain a U.S. Senator, but demanded he turn over the original autopsy photos and x-rays. The Kennedy family attorney came up with a deed of gift which turned over Robert's rights, title, and interest in his collected assassination materials to the U.S. Government. It also contained a clause that Johnson had insisted upon. That clause stipulated that Robert's access would be completely restricted for five years; it was a long-term showdown to ensure Johnson's re-election in '68. Robert then gave the evidence he had collected—his brother's brain, the Oval Office recordings, the Cartier watch, and copies of the autopsy photos and x-rays—to Evelyn Lincoln so Johnson couldn't completely pin him down.

"Johnson continued to try to align himself with Jackie and Robert, allowing Robert some power in the Senate in the hopes it would keep him in line. But with the never-ending Vietnam war and the domestic troubles across the nation, Robert knew just how much the country desperately needed to return to the course his brother had set it on.

"He would use the evidence he had gathered to obtain the Oval Office and facilitate a course correction, and instill new policies for the benefit of the American people. When Robert told Johnson he was going to run for president, they struck one of the most secret and significant deals in American history, intended to pave the way for Robert in 1968."

FEBRUARY 1967

Senator Robert Kennedy walked into Lyndon Johnson's Oval Office Johnson welcomed him with a sticky smile that had cold steel beneath it.

"Let's cut the bullshit," Bobby said. "You had a hand in Jack's death."

Johnson kept his mouth glued in the same grin. "I am sick and tired of these cockamamie allegations. Vietnam had to happen; I did what I had to do to keep us out of war with Russia. I got you the Senate. You said we'd all get through."

Bobby's voice was unwavering. "I'm not holding you accountable for the Warren Commission and what came after my brother's death; I'm holding you accountable for having knowledge before the fact and ordering your agents to assist in his murder."

Johnson's eyes narrowed to slits and his voice seethed with venom. "I gave you the Senate, you ungrateful little . . . You'll be dead, politically, in six months." The volume of his voice increased dramatically. For the first time, Johnson felt his second term slipping away, but he almost welcomed it; the stress of Vietnam and JFK's assassination had weakened him.

Through Johnson's political past, blackmail had been one of his favorite weapons to get what he wanted; now Bobby was using that same ruthless tactic against him. "The Secret Service has cooperated with me," Bobby stated calmly, his voice resonating with the power of having the upper hand. "We've been documenting evidence in Jack's assassination since day one. If the curtain falls, everyone will see what you've done."

"You little son of a bitch," Johnson thundered. "You'd let us all go down?"

"No, just you, Lyndon," Bobby said evenly. "I know what your Secret Service agents did in Dallas under your direct orders, I have the draft of your memorandum reversing Jack's policy on the withdrawal from Vietnam dated the day before his death, and I will testify that I never gave you instruction to take the oath of office on *Air Force One*."

In a fit of rage, Johnson picked up a glass from his desk and smashed it against the wall. The shattering pieces reverberated outside the office, but no one dared come in to see what had happened. In 1967, these two men were the most powerful lions in the political jungle. This battle had been brewing under the surface for years and it would be to the death: one would gain all the power, and the other would be laid waste.

Johnson had everything he wanted, everything he had worked for, secretly killed for . . . but Bobby Kennedy was the one man who could make it all disappear, and Johnson knew it. He reigned in his temper; getting physical wouldn't get him anywhere. He turned back to face Bobby. "Suppose you can convince someone that what you say is true . . . let's just suppose . . . What do you want?"

"I want what was my brother's, I want should be mine: this office, and I want it in '68. I'm going to stop your God-damned war."

Johnson's voice was low and angry. "You goddamned Kennedys, you think you can change the world?"

Bobby knew he had Johnson by the balls, but Johnson knew something Bobby didn't . . .

"What assurances can you give me?" Johnson asked. "If you run, you will have to cooperate..." Now it was Johnson's turn to direct the conversation. "Let go of the evidence in your brother's assassination, put it to rest permanently, and accept the Warren Commission's findings. Otherwise, I guarantee you will never be allowed to make it."

Despite what he said, Johnson knew Bobby Kennedy would never be allowed to reach the White House. He also knew he couldn't run against Bobby; if he did, the death of another Kennedy would fall on his doorstep. Bobby trained his eyes on Johnson. "With you as a witness, I'll take the evidence I have in my custody and place it with Jack's remains in Arlington. The evidence will stay there permanently. I'll continue to accept the findings of the Warren Commission, and I won't expose you, or anyone else; your legacy will be left without a blemish."

Johnson turned, stoic and silent, and stood with his back to Bobby. He looked out the massive windows and pressed his hands against his Oval Office desk. He'd had enough. Without another word spoken, he nodded his head. He never looked back at Bobby.

After that meeting, Robert Kennedy thought his future was set; he would run for president, and he would win.

MARCH 16, 1968

Robert Kennedy gave a brilliant speech in his opening bid for the presidency:

> "I am today announcing my candidacy for the presidency of the United States.
>
> "I do not run for the presidency merely to oppose any man but to propose new policies. I run because I am convinced that this country is on a perilous course and because I have such strong feelings about what must be done, and I feel that I'm obliged to do all that I can.
>
> "I run to seek new policies—policies to end the bloodshed in Vietnam and in our cities, policies to close the gaps that now exist between black and white, between rich and poor, between young and old, in this country and around the rest of the world.
>
> "I run for the presidency because I want the Democratic Party and the United States of America to stand for hope instead of despair, for reconciliation of men instead of the growing risk of world war.
>
> "I run because it is now unmistakably clear that we can change these disastrous, divisive policies only by changing the men who

are now making them. For the reality of recent events in Vietnam has been glossed over with illusions. [...]

"No one knows what I know about the extraordinary demands of the presidency can be certain that any mortal can adequately fill that position.

"But my service in the National Security Council during the Cuban Missile Crisis, the Berlin crisis of 1961 and 1962, and later the negotiations on Laos and on the Nuclear Test Ban Treaty have taught me something about both the uses and limitations of military power, about the opportunities and the dangers which await our nation in many corners of the globe in which I have traveled. [...]

"I have traveled and I have listened to the young people of our nation and felt their anger about the war that they are sent to fight and about the world they are about to inherit.

"In private talks and in public, I have tried in vain to alter our course in Vietnam before it further saps our spirit and our manpower, further raises the risks of wider war, and further destroys the country and the people it was meant to save.

"I cannot stand aside from the contest that will decide our nation's future and our children's future. [...]

"But now that the fight is on and over policies which I have long been challenging, I must enter the race. The fight is just beginning and I believe that I can win...

"Finally, my decision reflects no personal animosity or disrespect toward President Johnson. He served President Kennedy with the utmost loyalty and was extremely kind to me and members of my family in the difficult months which followed the events of November of 1963. [...]

"But the issue is not personal. It is our profound differences over where we are heading and what we want to accomplish.

"I do not lightly dismiss the dangers and the difficulties of challenging an incumbent President. But these are not ordinary times and this is not an ordinary election.

"At stake is not simply the leadership of our party and even our country. It is our right to moral leadership of this planet."

MARCH 25, 1968, SAN FERNANDO VALLEY STATE COLLEGE

A reporter did his best to describe the scene. "It's undoubtedly the largest crowd that's ever been here, there could be 10,000 or more people... He is mounting the podium in preparation for his speech in his attempt to take the democratic nomination away from President Johnson, a feat, which of course if accomplished would be a remarkable one, because it almost never happened in American political history. But the senator is attempting it; he's staking his political life on his attempt to oust President Johnson and take the nomination away from him."

The excitement was palpable as a hush fell over the crowd. As RFK prepared himself for the speech, he opened his eyes to the sun shining through the cloudless azure sky and recalled the events following his brother's murder . . . He was pulled back into the present when the cheering crowds reached a fevered pitch. He breathed deep and took a moment to center himself before he approached the platform.

He wore a perfectly fitted grey suit, a white collared shirt, and a burgundy and navy tie with a gold pinstripe. He stood at the podium with half a dozen microphones poised, waiting for his words. "I am very pleased to be here with all of you," Kennedy said.

With strong rhetoric and flashes of humor, he addressed the crowds of supporters and non-supporters alike. "I thought that I had a bright future, but when I came back from my speech at the University of Kansas about Vietnam, a reporter came to me and asked me if I would take the vice presidency under Lyndon Johnson. And I said, 'Evidently they didn't understand my remarks; I said that a coalition government was possible in Saigon, but not here.'" Everyone laughed, but there was a sharp edge underlying his statement.

He continued, "We need, most of all, leadership which puts the power to change in the hands of those who are willing to change, leadership which will put the resources and control, not in remote offices, but in the towns and communities of America. These are the kinds of things that I think need to be done in the United States, and I think all of us have a role to play. I don't think it should be left just to Washington; I don't think it should be left just to those who are public officials in Washington. I think the problems are too great, and I think all of us have a great stake in the future." With a profound projection of that future, he said, "What we are going to do in the year 1968 is going to determine the future of this county for decades and decades ahead." He finished his speech, and the masses cheered.

Then out of the crowd came a woman's pleading cry. "Who killed John Kennedy? We want to *know*!" Her statement rang above the roar of the crowd, and the hearts of the supporters paused and collapsed in silence, awaiting an answer.

Caught up in the moment, Bobby Kennedy, who had publicly supported the Warren Commission up to that point, spontaneously addressed
the question. His once strong and sure oration became pensive and halting: "Can I just say that, and I haven't answered this question before, but
there would be nobody that would be more interested in all of these matters as to who was responsible for the death of President Kennedy than
I would [. . .] the archives will be available at the appropriate time." That
answer weighed heavily on his fate; it was in direct opposition to what
he had promised Johnson. In that one unguarded moment, Bobby Kennedy's emotions, and all the secrets he was harboring, got the better of
him. There on the campus of that state college he publicly undermined
the Warren Commission.

Bobby instantly knew he shouldn't have answered the question. He
closed his eyes and felt a tightness in his chest and thought, *Many years
will pass before the truth of my brother's murder is revealed, but until then, I
will do everything within my power to make things better now.*

***

Six days later, Johnson sat in the White House before a television
camera to deliver what would become known as his "Sherman speech":
"I shall not seek, and I will not accept, the nomination of my party for
another term as your president."

After Johnson's unexpected announcement to a shocked nation, a
close friend asked him who he thought would be the next president.

"I don't know," Johnson replied, "but it will not be Bobby Kennedy."

AUGUST 1997

Bouck stared at the ground through decades of sorrow. "It was less than
three months later, in the Ambassador hotel . . ." His voice trailed off;
his cut narrative echoed the end of the Kennedy dynasty of that era. "Robert Kennedy believed he would be successful, the whole country did. We
all thought once he got into the Oval Office a healing would take place,
but after his assassination, there was simply a great silence; it was like the
heartbeat of the country had stopped. We were all stranded on a mighty
ship in the middle of the ocean with no compass and no power to get
anywhere . . .

"The brothers had so much strength; not only did each man fight physically for their lives despite wounds that should have killed them instantly,

but they kept fighting one after another to keep the White House, to keep the country. They had great strength and intelligence, but they couldn't adapt fast enough to deal with the overwhelming powers that wanted them gone; the odds were stacked too high against them." Bouck's shoulders sank under the weight of the history.

With each new revelation he shared with me, my perception of everything shifted. I'd always trusted and respected information from people who had actually lived it, had actually been there, and this man certainly had. But I sensed great danger in what he told me; secrets are secrets for a reason. The men who gained power and won the day are the men who have the most to lose now. I felt a wave in time; I felt the past catching up with the present.

"We have one more person we need to pay our respects to," Bouck said as we stopped at Columbarium Court Four.

"Who?"

He pointed to Niche Three in Stack Sixteen of Section A and said, "Evelyn Lincoln."

A small insignificant plaque bore her name. I tried to fathom the person it was meant to represent.

"Evelyn Lincoln was steadfast through the years; she devoted her whole life to President Kennedy and his brother, to the very end. She kept her promises, but it's obvious you're one of the only people she shared her secrets with; that's the reason I agreed to see you today."

Robert Kennedy's evidence and Evelyn Lincoln's affidavit had led me here. I was determined to honor the task that had been inadvertently bestowed upon me.

"Evelyn, and Robert's secretary, Angela, never caved under the pressure when the government demanded answers regarding Robert Kennedy's intentions. Those two courageous women never divulged what happened to the evidence from the president's assassination.

"When Robert was collecting evidence, he asked Jackie to get the pink suit she wore in Dallas back from the government, but she was too afraid to request it—after Dallas she was solely concerned with the protection of her children—so she asked Evelyn Lincoln to make the call on her behalf. Evelyn did what she could, but Jackie's clothes, purse, and shoes had already been secured by the National Archives. They flatly told her, 'No.' They said, 'No' to a request from Jackie Kennedy, the grieving widow. The things Jackie wore that day were considered so sensitive that the Archives didn't even have a record of how they had received them. Now, nobody gets to see those clothes until 2103, and they will never be subject to public display or research."

Bouck sat on the stone bench in the middle of the court. "Robert said if anything happened to him during his bid for presidency, everything he had collected should remain secret and silent in Evelyn's keeping for the rest of her life, for the safety of the Kennedy family. That pledge of silence was Robert's last request of her, and she kept it. It must have been an incredible burden to carry her whole life. She held true for all those years; she was so fiercely loyal.

"Without Evelyn Lincoln and Angela Novello, the little remaining assassination evidence, that the government was so determined to gather up and cover up, would have disappeared, or been doctored or lost forever. Believe me, this country owes those women a great debt. When the truth about John F. Kennedy's assassination is revealed, it will be because of their faithful dedication.

"So many things have gone in a different direction now," Bouck continued. "I have no doubt that after Evelyn's passing, President Kennedy's son, John Jr., has learned a lot about his father's death, and is struggling with some of the same issues Robert Kennedy faced. But that's why you contacted me, isn't it? As far as the public is aware, there is no evidence that can prove conspiracy in Dallas. Well, you have that evidence in your possession now. I hope my helping you initiates a positive change; I hope it aids the efforts of another Kennedy to return to Washington. Tell him if he wants me to testify, I will."

I don't know why I didn't see it before—Bouck believed I was working for John F. Kennedy Jr. After all the time he had spent with me and all the things he had disclosed, I didn't want to distress him with the knowledge that I was not there at the request of President Kennedy's son.

The rain that had threatened on and off all day started to fall in earnest, and with it our conversation ended. Bouck's energy had dissipated and we walked back to the parking lot in silence.

When we reached the car, the rain was cascading off of our umbrellas. Bouck looked at me through little evenly-spaced waterfalls. "I have one last thing for you," he said, and clicked open the trunk. He took out a manila envelope, and passed it to me. "This is my notarized and signed affidavit."

I watched as raindrops hit the envelope like tears.

"It details everything we discussed today. I'm glad I was able to pass it on in person and talk about it while I'm still here; it's weighed on my mind for so many years. I'm keeping the receipt that Robert Kennedy gave me for the watch. I've held onto it for so long, it reminds me of everything, but if John Jr. needs it for any reason, have him contact me. Please, Christopher, do everything you can to help this country get back on track; it's a great country and worth every effort, but I am too old and tired now."

"I'll try, sir," I said, as I returned his umbrella. I felt the weight of an enormous pendulum desperate to swing towards its amplitude, but I wasn't the one who was supposed to set it in motion.

"Where do you need to go?" he asked.

I took a moment to really look at him. I could see that our conversation, and his emotions, had exhausted him. I just wanted to let him go, let him get home to find some peace from the ghosts of our country's past.

"Leave me here," I said. "It's been an honor, sir."

He nodded and shook my hand, then drove off in the Hertz rental car.

The rain poured down but I couldn't move. I was rooted to that ground. I had been given a glance through a solitary window in time, and it had changed me. The Kennedys' sacrifices had been so great that without them, I doubt I would have even been standing there, that any of us would have survived. I was left motionless, trying to find my way back to the present, and figure out what it all meant for the future of the country.

An incredible account had been shared with me straight from the man who had lived it, and I had the material evidence to corroborate his verbal and written statements. The reality of the monumental ramifications of what I was doing struck me: I was documenting what Robert Kennedy had done in 1963, but this information wouldn't be buried in Arlington. I had unequivocal proof in my possession, proof that confirmed the truth.

I was headed down a very dangerous road, but what I felt was only a fraction of what Evelyn Lincoln must have endured every day of her life after President Kennedy had been killed. Her courage and dedication to this country were indisputable. She reminded me of Kate Warne. Warne had protected President Abraham Lincoln from assassination at the beginning of his presidency, and Mrs. Evelyn Lincoln had protected everything President Kennedy had stood for, even after his death. They were unsung, load-bearing pillars of strength; if they had cracked the world would have turned differently.

When I regained mobility, I headed straight to McRobie & Shaw's law office and delivered Bouck's affidavit into Henry's custody. I retained a copy, and he promised me he would keep the original with the other affidavit and letter until the time came when I could find their place in history.

17

BROKEN PROMISE

LATE 1997

Richard Curtis, the literary agent for the photo book, called me with news, but it wasn't the news I wanted. "Christopher, I think we are pigeonholed here. The responses from potential publishers seem to be uniform. They all say they're interested, but none of them is willing to take on the project without the consent of the Kennedy family. Let me read the turn-down letter from Little, Brown and Company:

> Thank you very much for giving us the opportunity to review The Evelyn Lincoln Collection. The material is certainly fascinating, but we had to conclude a book on this subject is too far outside our territory. Regards, Chris Lyn, Senior Editor.
>
> There is a written note at the bottom that said:
>
> Have you made any progress in contacting Caroline Kennedy to write bridge material?

I knew what the postscript meant, but the editor couldn't come out and say it directly: they would proceed with the project if we could get Caroline Kennedy's permission, otherwise, we were dead in the water. I had nothing to do with the feud between Robert and Caroline, but now the impasse between them was burying the project. I could understand Caroline's position; I, myself didn't trust Robert White's discretion. It didn't matter that I was at the helm of the book; it still wasn't going to fly. When I told Robert the news, he sounded more disappointed than I was. He confirmed that Caroline wouldn't have anything to do with him, or any project she knew he was affiliated with. In fact, he said she had done nothing but threaten him ever since his inheritance. We both understood we were stuck; Robert was desperate to find another way to fund his museum, and without any return on the book, my savings were sunk and Shauna and I were in financial trouble.

***

Robert was beside himself; he could feel his dream slipping away. He had to think of some other way to finance his museum. Just as he sat down to deliberate, the phone rang again.

"Mr. White, this is Arlan Ettinger, from Guernsey's Auction House in New York. I'm sorry to disturb you, but I'm calling to see if you've changed your mind; have you reconsidered my proposal for an auction?"

Robert vividly remembered how he had been questioned before the Assassination Records Review Board, and wondered where it would all end. He didn't want to spend the rest of his life being hounded to death by the government or Caroline Kennedy.

He had promised Evelyn Lincoln that the items she had entrusted to him would be kept in his possession, and that provisions would be made for the materials to stay together even after his death . . . but the prospect of actually having the resources to open his museum was too tempting. He felt a mix of elation and nausea; the thought of giving up part of his inheritance made him sick, but the siren song of wealth and realized dreams galvanized him into action. "Yes," Robert said, "I'm interested."

LATE 1997

Robert's wife called to him from the other room, "The phone's for you." "Who's calling me this late?" he yelled back. "Mr. Ettinger, from New York."

He picked up the receiver. "Hello?"

"Hi, Robert, this is Arlan, sorry to call so late. I wanted to let you know that at Donald Trump's suggestion, we've arranged for some of your items to be on display in Trump Tower; it will be the starting point for the promotion of the sale. The first time Evelyn Lincoln's collection will be unveiled to the public will be in the atrium of Trump's tower."

"That's wonderful, when?"

"December 23. Things are going well, Robert. There's going to be heavy press coverage before the sale. Be prepared to do interviews, but don't get political, just talk about your museum and your relationship with Evelyn Lincoln."

"Yes, of course."

"Thanks Robert, this is going to be one for the history books. I'm glad you decided to do it; I know it's a difficult emotional step for you."

"Yes, it is. Thank you, Arlan."

18

THE DEVIL CUT IN

LATE 1997

Philip Adder sat in his office on Pennsylvania Avenue, a few blocks down from the White House. He worked for a conservative law firm that handled difficult and delicate matters. Adder had received a dossier with numerous commentaries, articles, a personal history on Robert L. White, and the current undertakings of Caroline Kennedy and the John F. Kennedy Presidential Library: Operation Bobwhite. After reading an interview that outlined the inheritance from Evelyn Lincoln, Adder dialed White's home phone number.

"Hello, my name is Philip Adder. I'm an attorney in Washington, and I just finished reading another article about you and your amazing collection."

"Hello, yes, thank you!" Robert White responded. "It is rather amazing, and I'll be sharing it with everyone when I open a museum. I have been very blessed with all of this."

"That's the reason I'm calling you, Mr. White; I also am a true lover of history and I very much appreciate what you are trying to do and what you have accomplished thus far. Like you, I'm a great admirer of President Kennedy and I feel that history should be preserved and shared, not only for this generation, but for future generations as well. But more to the point, Mr. White, I heard that you were questioned in a preliminary meeting with the Assassination Records Review Board, and they were a little heavy-handed because of their concerns about what you have in your possession, and that you'll likely be subpoenaed in the near future."

"Where did you hear that?" Robert exclaimed.

"Mr. White, I'm well connected in Washington. Now, it seems to me you're going to require very competent legal representation. I can assure you I am extremely competent, and though some may claim my fees are exorbitant, I would be willing to waive them for you, especially if you find yourself in need of assistance in defending yourself and your property."

"Wow," Robert said, "that's very generous of you, but I already have a lawyer."

"That's fine. Forgive me for not being modest, but this is just beginning; very soon you're going to require someone with extremely advanced abilities . . . So much good has come to me through the years, this will be my gesture of good will to you and the American people. I can ensure your rights are protected.

"I think we should have a meeting in my office as soon as possible so we can get a handle on things before you get subpoenaed, or the FBI shows up at your home. I can't stress this enough, Mr. White: prevention is everything."

"Ok, yes," Robert said, "I can come in this week."

"That would be fine. Please bring any legal documents you have signed involving the items in your inheritance. Now, if a government agent does make contact with you before we meet, say you will not speak to them without my counsel, but cooperate with them so they won't have to arrest you. Don't worry, Mr. White, I've got your back. My secretary will give you my address and contact information; please don't hesitate to call my personal number if anything comes up."

"Thank you, Mr. Adder, sir," Robert said gratefully. "I can't thank you enough."

Adder smiled into the phone. "Thank *you*, Mr. White. You have a nice day."

***

Later that week, Robert sat in Adder's waiting room. The surroundings were uncomfortable for him: marble, cold, formal. The office reeked of old Washington and the power structure. The secretary spoke without looking up. "Mr. White, Mr. Adder will see you now."

Robert stood and adjusted his ill-fitted suit; its extra length made him look podgy, but it was the best he had.

Adder was polished and smiling; he exuded confidence, lots of it. "Come in, Mr. White. How are you this morning? Can we get you anything? Coffee? Tea?"

"No, Mr. Adder, I'm fine, thank you."

"Did you bring all your documents?"

"Yes," Robert said, and handed the lawyer his will, the contract for the book deal, and a contract with Guernsey's Auction House.

"Thank you." Adder took a moment to peruse the papers as Robert sat down. "So let's get to it, shall we?" Adder said as he took a seat opposite Robert. "These are the provisions for the Lincoln items in your will?"

"Yes."

"Uh-huh, and this is a publishing contract to put the inheritance in a picture book?"

"Yes."

"Tell me about that."

"I signed the contract with my friend Christopher Fulton; he lives in Canada."

"Has the entire inheritance been photographed already?"

"Yes, well, most of it, just what will be on display in my museum."

"And Mr. Fulton has the photographs?"

"Yes."

"Are you tied to him in any other way . . . other than the book?"

"Yes. He has the only full set of Oval Office recordings."

"Uh-huh," Adder said again, keeping his face expressionless. "Are the recordings originals or copies?"

"I thought they were all copies from the original dictabelts, but after Chris left I realized two were original Dictaphone analog cassettes." As an afterthought, White added, "I also sold Christopher an item from Mrs. Lincoln that was assassination evidence." He immediately felt foolish and quickly added, "But I didn't know that at the time."

If Adder had been transparent his eyes would have widened and his mouth dropped open, but Adder was not transparent; he merely said, "Are these items presently in Canada with Mr. Fulton?"

"Yes."

"Is he aware that you gave him two original cassettes?"

"No."

"Good, keep it that way. It says here that Mr. Fulton funded the book project and will negotiate its publishing on your behalf, is that correct?"

"Yes."

"Ok. When is the book scheduled to be released?"

"We have a problem with that; Christopher told me the publishers aren't willing to take it on without the consent of Caroline Kennedy."

Excellent, Adder thought. "Now tell me about this most recent contract with Guernsey's."

"Arlan Ettinger, the owner of Guernsey's, has been calling me since I inherited. He wanted me to put some of my collection up for public auction. When Christopher and I ran into trouble with the book, I finally agreed, and signed the auction contract."

"I see specific items are defined in the contract," Adder said. "When is this sale scheduled to become public?"

"My consignments have been in New York for a while, and Arlan tells me the catalogue for the sale is already in development; he plans to announce the auction date publicly sometime in December, with Donald Trump in New York."

Adder realized it was too late to get White out of the Guernsey's sale. The preparations were too far advanced; a retraction now would cause public blowback and serious legal problems. He also knew attacking Fulton in Canada to obtain the assassination evidence and recordings would cause an international stir. One way or another, Fulton's items would have to be brought back to the United States to be secured. Adder quickly weighed which lever he would pull on White: fear, greed, or self-preservation.

He smiled kindly at Robert and said, "What I'm going to say may be uncomfortable for you, even difficult, but remember it is in your best interests. You have to trust me on this, Mr. White; most people without a practical understanding of Washington politics and a law degree from a prestigious school would never anticipate the moves necessary to win this game."

Robert's face was ashen.

Adder took a dramatic breath and leaned back in his chair. "This is the beginning, Mr. White; it's just starting, but I can help you navigate through the shark-infested waters."

"Just tell me what to do," Robert said, alarmed by Adder's words.

Adder leaned forward. "I know you hope to open a museum, but if you don't find a way to appease these government agencies, they will come down on you very hard and you will never, and I mean *never*, get the chance to display your inheritance." Adder spoke with courtroom precision. "What you need to do—as quickly as possible—is cancel the book contract with Mr. Fulton and get him to consign the evidence with Guernsey's."

Robert didn't understand. "Why do we have to kill the book deal?"

Adder stood up; he spoke like a school principal. "Robert, you are standing on a blind curve on a superhighway; I am in a helicopter above you and can see what's coming. I am asking you to change your position. Your question should not be 'Why?' but instead a quick 'Where to?' . . . It will eliminate the government's concern for any further leaks, so when and if we have to negotiate an agreement with them—which in my opinion we will, when this sale goes public—we will be in a better position. If you can get Mr. Fulton to agree to be in the auction, it would greatly negate the possibility of his suing you for breach of contract. We don't want to compete with him if he decides to sell what he has; it's in your best interests to have the pieces up for sale at the same time. After this auction, you won't need money from any book; you can just open your museum. So have your other attorney terminate the book contract, and have him gently request that all the recordings be returned to you. Just make sure you don't talk to Mr. Fulton about any of our plans or conversations."

"Alright," Robert said weakly, "if you think this is the only way."

"I know it is," Adder said, as he put his hand on White's shoulder. "Believe me when I tell you, this is your next step: contact Christopher Fulton and get him in the sale."

"Alright." Robert gave him an appreciative look before he turned to leave the office.

Before Robert reached the door, Adder said, "One more thing."

"Yes?" Robert asked, stopping mid-stride.

"You must get Mr. Fulton to return the Oval Office recordings to you personally. Don't allow those recordings to end up in the sale under any circumstances or I may not be able to protect you."

"What if he decides to takes legal action against me?"

"Just let me worry about that," came Adder's calm and assured response. Robert agreed and continued out the door.

19

WINGS OF WAX

LATE 1997

The next time Robert called me on the phone, I was surprised to hear him so buoyant, considering the subject of our last conversation. "Hi, Chris. I wanted to let you know I decided to put a part of my collection up for sale in New York to fund my museum."

"What?" I said, shocked; this was a total reversal of the man I thought I knew. It was hard to believe he would willingly part with any portion of his inheritance. "What about your promise to Evelyn?"

"What can I say? Life goes on," he said, with a notable twinge in his voice.

It seemed he had also forgotten about the photo book, completely. All I could think to say was, "When is it happening?"

"March 18 and 19 of next year; I want to invite you to put your items in the sale, too." He was insistent. "This is your shot, Christopher; if you don't take this opportunity, I doubt you'll get another one . . . and when you come to New York, you can bring the recordings back."

"Whoa, wait a minute," I said, "you gave me the recordings. What are you talking about?"

"Well, I can't really say . . ." he fumbled for the right words. "My lawyer told me to get the recordings back. They're the only copies; if something happened to them . . ."

I cut him short. "That's not what we agreed to, Robert."

"I know, I know, but my lawyer says . . ."

"I don't care what your lawyer says; you and I are going to stick to our agreement." I felt very uneasy; Robert wasn't acting like his normal self.

He was clearly being pushed in a direction contrary to the one we had been travelling along together.

"Just think about putting your items in the sale," he said. "Especially the Cartier; it would draw a lot of attention. This is the time to do it, Christopher. Deirdre Henderson is a consignor, and there are Kennedy consignors and bidders too! The auction house president is Arlan Ettinger; just give him a call. I know that *CNN* and *Entertainment Tonight* will want to interview you if you consign the watch; it would really add to the promotion."

Taken aback by Robert's sudden transformation and requests, I said, "I'll call you later."

I assumed Robert understood that by allowing a public auction catalog to display materials he had inherited from Evelyn Lincoln, that I had already paid to photograph, he would be in breach of our contract. I would have a legal right to stop the sale, but he never brought any of that up.

One week after Robert's phone call, I received a letter from someone I didn't recognize, a Mr. Jarrod Glazier, attorney-at-law:

> Please be advised that I represent Robert L. White.
>
> Upon careful review of the "contract" executed on May 1, 1997, Mr. White has elected to terminate in full the referenced agreement and any further participation with you on a book project. You are directed to cease any and all activities on his behalf. Further, in accordance with the terms of this termination, the Oval Office recordings must be returned, and Mr. White does not consent for you or anyone acting on your behalf to use, display, exhibit and or utilize for any purpose whatsoever the photographs taken of his collection during the week of April 26 through May 2, 1997.
>
> Pursuant to Mr. White's request, please direct all further inquiries regarding this matter directly to my attention.

The letter disturbed me far more than the phone call. It seemed the actions of Robert White and Caroline Kennedy had left me with little choice; I was being directed into a situation I would not have chosen for myself. Robert said the Kennedys would be bidding at the sale. Maybe Caroline was just representing herself and not the family when she went to Sotheby's. Maybe the watch could still find its proper home ... After a lot of thought, and long conversations with Shauna, we realized our options were getting narrower; we would agree to be in the sale.

I called Arlan Ettinger. He knew who I was and what I had. He told me he couldn't think of a more historically significant item in the last hundred years, and offered me a million-dollar reserve; it seemed I was already in. Copies of a contract were quickly faxed and signed, and I was told I would receive a hard copy in the mail within the week.

I received the contract and a specific insurance rider from Harrison Dillon Bond & Williams LLC for $1,150,000 from Guernsey's, and was given assurances the items would be placed in a secured bank vault, only to be taken out the day of the sale. I arranged for the transport of President Kennedy's watch and sunglasses, accompanied by a copy of my book of provenance, to New York in a Brink's armored truck. I did not send the recordings.

DECEMBER 23, 1997

Shauna and I went to New York for the announcement of the Guernsey's sale. JFK's sailboat, *Flash II*, stood in the center of the floor of the atrium of Trump Tower. Surrounding it were historical items from Camelot: a cigar humidor, Deirdre Henderson's diary from JFK's European trip, one of his famous rocking chairs, and the desk that sat alongside the Oval Office desk on which the president signed the establishment of the Peace Corps, the Nuclear Test Ban Treaty, and most other major legislation. The backdrop for the display was a large photograph of President Kennedy sitting at his desk in the Oval Office, with Evelyn Lincoln assisting him in the foreground.

Donald Trump stood at the podium and leaned into the microphone. "This is a great opportunity for Trump Tower to really be a focus of a very important display. The items you see here were some of the personal belongings of former President John F. Kennedy that will be auctioned off by Guernsey's Auction House of New York." The crowd applauded.

"This is all so exciting," Shauna exclaimed. "It's a shame the Cartier couldn't be part of the preview."

"At least we're in the sale," I said, "and we get to spend Christmas in New York."

I watched Donald Trump sit in Kennedy's rocking chair for a photo op. I wondered if he imagined himself as president one day. Robert materialized out of the crowd. "Christopher," he said, walking up to Shauna and me, "I'm glad you made it. Look, I know you're still upset about the book, but this will work out. I'm really happy Donald Trump opened the promotion. I spoke to him earlier; he really seems to believe in what I'm trying to do."

As soon as he stopped to take a breath, I said, "Robert, I'd like to introduce my fiancée, Shauna."

Robert brightened. "Hi, hello!" he said with a smile and shook her hand. "*Again*, I'm sorry about everything, but I have a very good feeling about this sale."

"It's nice to meet you, Mr. White. I've heard a lot about you," Shauna said flatly.

I took my cue and ended the conversation. "Well, Robert, we have a busy day planned," I said, and Shauna and I turned to walk away.

Considering my passion for construction, there was no way I was going walk out of the building without introducing myself to Donald Trump. We found a break in the crowd and I took my opportunity. "Hello, Mr. Trump, my name is Christopher Fulton, this is my fiancée, Shauna; we are consigners in the sale."

"Glad to meet you," Trump said. "You know, I think this is great; it's good for New York, and it's good for the country . . ." But before he could say anything else, someone pulled his attention away.

Shauna looked at me and smiled. "What? Did you think we were going to have dinner with the man?"

"Well," I said, "maybe next time."

We spent the rest of the Christmas holiday in New York doing all the things that tourists do: we went skating in Wollman Rink, admired the Christmas tree in Rockefeller Center, went to the top of the Empire State building—the setting for two of Shauna's favorite movies, *An Affair to Remember* and *Sleepless in Seattle*—and we took the ferry to Ellis Island to take a tour of the Statue of Liberty. It was an incredible trip that we would remember for the rest of our lives.

EARLY JANUARY 1998

Once back home, I called Jacques Lowe to arrange the purchase of the rights to his photos for the promotion of the auction. I also told him I had a small print that had originally come from President Kennedy's personal photograph files. It showed Jacques holding a camera around his neck, standing just behind President Kennedy, who took up most of the foreground. Jacques told me how much he would like to have a copy. He had always taken the photos, so he seldom had one of the president and himself together. I offered to gift it to him when I could make a copy. As he thanked me, a hint of emotion began to bleed through his firm dialogue.

"It's hard for me to talk about the past. I was friends with both the Kennedy brothers. When Jack was assassinated I became deeply depressed. I didn't think much of Bobby at the time; I didn't believe he could instill hope for America's survival.

"I actually met Bobby before Jack, and found him angry and brash . . . I wouldn't have voted for him to be a school superintendent. But over time Jack rubbed off on him; Jack's murder left him considerably changed. In the end we all tied our hopes to Bobby to win the presidential election in '68 . . . After his assassination, I moved to France. I just couldn't take the tragedy anymore; I had to get out." Jacques said it took him eighteen years to decide to move back to New York.

I noticed the pattern. In 1968, Jackie Kennedy said, "If they're killing Kennedys, then my children are targets . . . I want to get out of the country." Evelyn Lincoln had left altogether as well.

Just when I thought the conversation with Jacques was winding down, he brought up an unexpected topic, one that I had little reference to.

"You know," he said, "Nostradamus predicted the Kennedy brothers' assassinations. I used to think that sort of stuff was silly, but I've come to believe in prophecy, in fate. It should be taken seriously. I'm telling you this because of what you have; the evidence in Jack's death connects you to the sequence of events. You have to be careful, Christopher."

On that strange note, we ended our conversation. It prompted me to think back to January 1, 1996. I had never discussed that unusual meeting in depth with anyone; I had tried to forget it. Cable had advised me that Sasha was a female shaman, one of very few recognized and utilized by CSIS for remote viewing.

Before Sasha had left my house, she grabbed me by the wrist. "You have worn the watch!" she whispered.

"Yes, I put it on right after I got it." I said, uncomfortable in her strong grip.

"There is death associated with this, there are agendas associated with this. Your life has changed now; you have to be careful."

20

A Matter Of National Security

January 10, 1998

Robert White held the federal subpoena on the table in front of him:

U.S. Department of Justice

SUBPEONA DUCES TECUM
FOR THE PRODUCTION OF DOCUMENTS AND APPEAR-
ANCE FOR TESTIMONY BEFORE THE ASSASSINATION
RECORDS AND REVIEW BOARD

Mr. Robert White
YOU ARE HEREBY REQUIRED AND DIRECTED, PURSU-
ANT TO 44 U.S.C. § 2107, TO APPEAR BEFORE:

T. Jeremy Gunn, Executive Director and General Counsel of the
Assassination Records Review Board at 600 E Street, N.W., Washington, D.C., on the 12th day of February 1998, at 9:30 A.M., and
at the same time each day thereafter until the taking of testimony
is complete, to testify under oath regarding any records or objects
relating to President John. F. Kennedy. [. . .]

Issued at Washington, D.C. This 9th day of January 1998
By: Frank W. Hunger Assistant Attorney General

He scanned the next three pages:

Attachment A Definitions and Instructions
• "You" means Mr. Robert White, any of Mr. White's agents,
representatives, partners, or any other person who may have pos-

session, custody or control of Mr. White's records and objects that are identified in this subpoena. [...]

• "Records" should be understood broadly to include, without limitation, handwritten notes, drawings, photographs, electronic recordings, dictabelts, tape recordings, agreements and legal instruments. [...]

• To the extent that it is impossible to comply with any of these requests, you should comply fully with all remaining requests and be prepared to explain the reasons why you cannot comply with any request.

• To the extent that you are unable to make available one or more records and/or objects that would otherwise be responsive to the subpoena, provide a list that identifies (for each record and/or object that is not produced): (a) a description of the record and/or object; (b) the source from whom you obtained the record and/or object; (c) the date that you obtained the record and/or object: and (d) the reason why you were unable to make the record and/or object available. [...]

• All correspondence with other individuals, institutions, or organizations, regarding the terms of Evelyn Lincoln's and/or Harold Lincoln's will.

• All records pertaining to the sale, transfer, gift, or bequest of any objects or records that relate to President John F. Kennedy, by yourself to any other individual and/or institution.

• Any records reflecting the names and addresses of persons or institutions other than yourself with whom you have stored or currently store any objects and/or records that relate directly to President John F. Kennedy.

• All records reflecting the disposition of President John F. Kennedy objects or records from the estate of Evelyn and/or Harold Lincoln.

You are required to bring with you all of the above-described objects and records, including, without limitation, any objects and/or records that you have in your possession, custody, or control that may presently be on loan to another party or in the physical possession of another party. [...]

Jesus, he thought, *when is this going to end?* His hand fell to his side, still clutching the papers.

JANUARY 22, 1998

Assassination Records Review Board Meeting:

A closed meeting on CIA/NSA issues, review of classified memoranda, designation of Secret Service records, and Joint Chiefs of Staff histories.

Executive briefing:

Medical Experts

Public Affairs Issues

NARA Fragment Testing

Other issues of concern to the board: Robert White

FEBRUARY 4, 1998

A RRB internal memo to Kim Herd from Deputy Director Tom Samoluk:

Subject: Questions for Robert White

I have learned that given the admission by White that he does, in fact, have dictabelts, a relevant question is does he possess any analog tapes. Based on what the JFK Library told me, there are analog tapes of meetings that they believe exist, but do not possess. Thus, the possibility that Evelyn Lincoln took some analog tapes, as well as dictabelts. An additional question is does White possess any logs or other records relevant to the dictabelts or analog tapes. You may recall that I asked him about logs related to the dictabelts when we interviewed him. He said that he did not. I want to make sure that we get him on record about this whole area.

Thanks.

FEBRUARY 6, 1998

A RRB internal memo to Kim Herd from Tom Samoluk:

Subject: Additional Information Regarding Potential White Holdings

An anonymous person called the JFK Library last week, and advised Frank Rigg, of the JFK Library staff that White had dictabelt recordings of President Kennedy's telephone conversations ([...] the source has good information), in addition to other materials.

Perhaps most important of what the caller claimed was the following: Among the textual materials is a file on the Dallas trip containing seating plans for the various events and motorcade arrangements for the various locations. One of these documents bears a handwritten reference to a "bubble top." This description appears to match what we have heard from other sources and is obviously very important to us.

The caller made other claims that we can talk about at some point, but I was very interested in the additional information provided above.

FEBRUARY 12, 1998

Robert White found himself sitting in front of the Assassination Records Review Board with his attorney Philip Adder at his side. After swearing him in, Federal Judge Tunheim said, "Be aware, Mr. White, anything discussed here today is to be treated as sensitive to the security of the United States, not to be discussed outside of this room. Do you understand?"

"Yes, sir."

"Mr. White, I have in front of me copies of letters from attorney Nicole Seligman, who is representing JFK Jr. and Caroline Kennedy, to you, dated January of this year, addressing the Kennedys' concerns about items that came to you from Evelyn Lincoln. I ask you on behalf of this panel, Mr. White, are you now, or have you ever been, in the possession of items or documents or any other materials relating to the assassination of President John F. Kennedy or the government's position on Cuba?"

Adder encouraged White, and he timidly responded, "Yes."

"Speak up," Tunhiem demanded.

"Yes," Robert said again, louder, leaning into the microphone; it sounded like the word had been punched out of him.

"That is in direct contradiction to your last testimony before members of this board. I warn you, the full weight of the United States Government is about to fall on you. Do you know what I mean when I say that?"

"No, sir."

"At this time, the board is in full cooperation and coordination with the Justice Department, the FBI, the CIA, the White House, the Kennedy family and their attorneys, the Security Oversight Office, and the President of the United States of America. That is what I mean, Mr. White . . . Are you aware that lying to a federal official is a felony that can result in your imprisonment?"

Adder wrote on a legal pad and slid it in front of Robert. It read "Answer: NO, nothing else." Robert did what he was told.

Tunheim continued, "If I were you, I would be very focused on answering all the questions we put to you without any deception or reservation so that we may resolve this matter as quickly as possible."

Adder stood and stated, "I have advised Mr. White as such, Your Honor.

"Very well, counselor." Tunheim nodded. "The majority of the parties aforementioned will be reviewing your client's materials that are scheduled for auction in New York next month to determine their security status. The Justice Department requires Mr. White's full cooperation and signature on an agreement so he won't have to spend any time in prison."

Adder stood again. "I am confident that by end of the deposition the board will be completely satisfied."

"Then let's proceed."

Over the course of the next two days, Robert White was forced into submission.

***

The subpoena was clear and all encompassing; there was no room for interpretation during Robert's testimony. The intelligence community wanted this matter locked down. Adder knew what his strategy would be, what it would take to get the chess pieces into position. Christopher Fulton was the knight that would be sacrificed to win the game.

***

Tunheim's voice filled the room. "I have before me documents from the House Select Committee on Assassinations. Listed is the clothing President Kennedy was wearing during the assassination; after the assassination, those clothes were given to the Protective Research Section of the Secret Service and Orrin Bartlett of the FBI for forensic testing by Secret Service Agents Robert Bouck and William Greer. Just below that, President Kennedy's Cartier wristwatch is listed. There is no record of who the watch went to, or who it came from. I must assume that information was classified and not available to the HSCA as of 1978.

"That same watch is now in Guernsey's auction catalog; however, Guernsey's inventory list shows that you, Mr. White, are not the consigner . . . Did the watch originally come to you from Mrs. Evelyn Lincoln?"

"Yes. She gave it to me in 1992."

"How did it transfer out of your possession?"

"I sold it to Christopher Fulton in 1994."

"Have you submitted Mr. Fulton's contact information as per the terms of your subpoena?"

Adder spoke for his client, "Yes, Your Honor."

"Did Evelyn Lincoln provide you with any documentation for the watch?"

"Yes," Robert answered, "I got a routine letter from her, like the others she had given me, but after the Lincolns died there was something else..."

"What was that, Mr. White?"

"A letter came through the will; it went directly to Christopher Fulton's attorney."

"What did it say?"

"I don't know; I asked him, but he never told me."

An ARRB attorney taking notes on the proceeding scribbled down: "Pres. Clinton requested. Fulton has original letter on Cartier Watch."

Judge Tunheim continued, "You and the other direct beneficiaries of the will made agreements and had a judge seal the information, is that correct?"

"Yes."

"That is very unusual," he mused.

White didn't respond, and Tunheim didn't pursue it further. "Mr. White, what else did you transfer to Mr. Fulton?"

"I gave him some photographs, a pair of sunglasses, and four cassettes that were the only copies of President Kennedy's dictabelt recordings from the Oval Office." Adder had specifically told him not to mention the two original Dictaphone analog cassettes. Adder wanted those tapes back to relinquish to the CIA. If it was known that Fulton had two original tapes it would reduce his chances of accomplishing that.

Adder stood up. "Your Honor, Mr. White entered into a book agreement with Fulton with the intent of publishing President Kennedy's recorded memoirs in a supplemental CD meant to accompany the book of photographs. He quashed their contract shortly thereafter."

Tunheim nodded. "Thank you, Counselor. Mr. White, did you attempt to contact Mr. Fulton in reference to your subpoena and compel him to come here to testify about the Cartier wristwatch?"

As the judge spoke, Adder wrote on the legal pad again: "Say yes, and only yes." He slid it in front of Robert.

Robert spoke: "Yes, Your Honor." The waver in his voice was barely audible. The knight had been pushed into position.

MARCH 3, 1998

ARRB internal memo to Mr. Steven Garfinkel, Director of the Information Security Oversight Office, from T. Jeremy Gunn:

-SECRET-

HAND DELIVERY BY NATIONAL SECURITY CLEARED COURIER

Re: Possible National Security Classified Records in the Possession of Robert L. White

As the Security Officer of the Assassination Records Review Board, I am transmitting herewith four sets of records that contain national security classified information. We obtained these records during the course of our deposition of Robert L. White, who appeared with the records at our offices pursuant to a subpoena duces tecum that was issued by the United States Department of Justice. It is our understanding that Mr. White obtained these records from the late Evelyn Lincoln, the personal secretary to President John F. Kennedy. Mr. White intends to sell these records at a public auction in New York City at the firm of Guernsey's later this month. The enclosed records are copies made from the records brought to the deposition by Mr. White. [. . .]

Given the circumstances of his acquisition of these records, and other testimony he provided, we perceive it is highly likely that Mr. White may have additional national security classified records at his home in Baltimore.

21

UNAMERICAN

MARCH 8, 1998

At President Bill Clinton's request, JFK Jr. met with him at the White House. It was the first time the young Kennedy had been back in the upper level private residences since his father was president in 1963. It was a cathartic meeting for Kennedy; President Clinton shared his personal collection of JFK memorabilia. They discussed the assassination evidence and other items of possible national security concern that were in the upcoming Guernsey's sale in New York. The auction was just ten days away. They had some decisions to make. Clinton requested that JFK Jr. take a private meeting with Attorney General Janet Reno to talk about the auction further.

MARCH 9, 1998

The Oval Office doors were still open; Senior Attorney and Analyst for the Assassination Records Review Board, Kim A. Herd, was ready to take the minutes for the meeting:

CLASSIFIED
No name meeting, Oval Office: President Bill Clinton, All agencies
Purpose: Sharing information concerning the Evelyn Lincoln Project by all agencies and the ARRB reporting to the President.
When everyone was present, the doors closed.

***

Following the meeting, Attorney General Janet Reno called FBI Agent Callahan and IRS Agent Mancini to her office in the White House. "Take a seat," she said brusquely. "I have a job for you both."

Agent Joe Callahan, the Bureau's man at Evelyn Lincoln's will hearing, was in his early fifties; he was intelligent and level headed. His father had been a highly respected, long-standing agent in the Bureau who had retired with honors. Joe's reputation for unprecedented investigative and research skills had seen him all the way to the White House. President Reagan, whom Joe had met on several occasions, was his inspiration for staying in the Bureau for so long. But now he didn't want to be a part of it any more. After turning fifty he had requested retirement from the Bureau several times, but was turned down; his skills were still deemed an asset.

Clara Mancini, on the other hand, was a hammer. At thirty years old, she was a special agent for the IRS involved with investigations that dealt with national security. She had a reputation for using severe scare tactics, anything it took to obtain a goal. She acted like a gun for hire with something to prove, which established her as useful tool for the White House and subsequently landed her a position there.

Janet Reno turned and grabbed two folders off her desk labeled "United States Justice Department: Evelyn Lincoln Project." She handed the identical dossiers to the agents to examine. They contained background information on Robert White, Guernsey's Auction House, Christopher Fulton, Donald Trump and a list of media promotions for the auction, current legal correspondence, public and private statements made by JFK Jr. and Caroline Kennedy, a memorandum from Senator Edward Kennedy, and the legalities of the Kennedy family's deed of gift to the government from 1965.

"Evelyn Lincoln was the custodian of the most secure information from the Kennedy presidency," Reno said. "She bequeathed the items she held for Robert Kennedy to Robert White, both while she was alive and through her will after her passing in 1995. Those materials are concerns for national security, and must be repatriated for deposit and classification. The CIA briefed President Clinton, who contacted all former presidents and put the ARRB on it.

"Robert White testified in front of the ARRB; they found him to be less than honest about what he has in his possession. They had to subpoena him for deposition. We need him to sign an agreement that will allow us to secure his materials. Start by serving a warrant on the residence of Robert White's mother; his collection is housed there. Take whatever experts you may need, and search everything.

"Through the Evelyn Lincoln inheritance, White is in possession of Oval Office recordings that are non-security reviewed. The only copies of those recordings are in the possession of Christopher Fulton. Fulton also acquired the wristwatch President Kennedy was wearing when he was assassinated; he bought it from Robert White in 1994. That watch is material evidence that was held by Robert Kennedy; it needs to be secured and classified.

"Robert White and Christopher Fulton have both consigned their materials to Guernsey's Auction House for public sale in New York. I want White to sign that agreement before the auction takes place so if we need to, we can crucify him. Fulton currently resides in Vancouver, Canada. He is dual national, but still a U.S. citizen and subject to U.S. law. White and his attorney told us Fulton will not be cooperative; we have a sealed warrant for him. After we've secured the evidence from him, you two will be making the arrest.

"Members of my department at Justice, federal officials from the NARA and Information Security Oversight Office, and representatives of the Kennedy family will be reviewing the materials White and Fulton have slated for auction in New York. We've missed our window for an entire media blackout, but we are prepared to place an injunction on the auction to stop it if necessary. If need be, everything will be placed under seal. You will report back to my office, and I will inform the President. I want this done as quietly as possible. Do you understand?"

"Yes, ma'am," Mancini and Callahan said in unison.

"I feel confident we can reel in White; he needs this auction, he has a family, and his attorney is a trusted man on the inside. I am not, on the other hand, sure about Fulton: as a dual national with no wife and no children, he'll be less predictable. His mother is a close friend and neighbor of Linda Tripp. I shouldn't have to remind you that Tripp worked for the State Department and is the woman who persuaded Monica Lewinsky to save the blue dress and go public. We know from wiretaps that Fulton's mother has been giving advice to Tripp on what to say to the press. We are looking into the possibility that this might be a family plot to influence or embarrass the White House, but so far Fulton has not sought any media attention."

Agent Callahan thought it didn't make sense. *Why would Fulton offer assassination evidence for sale, but refuse any publicity?* He spoke up. "Why not subpoena him and give him the chance to come in?"

The attorney general was frustrated at the senior agent's question, but answered him. "By serving a subpoena in Canada, we would have to expose this situation to a foreign government; we are not going to do that.

We will bring Fulton in under criminal tax code to keep the situation secured."

"Where is the watch now?" Callahan asked.

"It's currently in New York awaiting the sale. We have been asked to stand down regarding that item for the moment."

"What agreements are in place between the White House, the Kennedy family, and the U.S. Government as far as these materials are concerned?" Callahan continued to probe.

"The White House and Congress agree that my department retains jurisdiction over the entire Kennedy matter. The Secret Service is totally out. However, I am concerned about Texas state law; it's up to the Kennedy family whether or not we re-open an investigation based on new evidence from the Evelyn Lincoln inheritance. At this moment, federal law, and our job, is clear: gather and secure the necessary materials for classification."

"How much do you want on Fulton?" Mancini asked.

"I want to know who he knows and how he thinks; I want to know what he had for breakfast and how many times a day he goes to the bathroom. Get surveillance on him in Vancouver. Inform the Royal Canadian Mounted Police we're there, but only tell them he's a person of interest. It's too risky to make contact with him before the auction; we don't want to spook him."

"Yes, ma'am," Mancini said stiffly.

"Drop everything else you have, this is all you're working on now. The warrants for White's residence and a wiretap for Fulton are in your dossiers, get on it right away."

"Yes, ma'am," both agents said again, and walked out of the office.

In the hall, Agent Callahan opened the file and flipped through the pages, stopping on the initial brief for Christopher Fulton, and scanned the information:

> Name: Christopher Fulton
> Nationality: Dual National, United States and Canada (Made Canadian National by order of Secretary of State of Canada, Francis Fox, at Canadian Embassy, Washington D.C., 1979)
> Occupation: Owner/Operator of Twelve Global Ltd.–Maryland, USA; Vancouver, Canada; Turks and Caicos, British West Indies; Moscow, Russia;
> Has a legally-acquired second name used for permission to enter Russia.

There was a list of information about his extended family members and their careers:

> Pentagon and NSA, Classified ... McDonald Douglas Aircraft ... Black Watch ... honored by King of Holland ... Civil War General ... all the way to an ancestor who fought in the American Revolution.

Agent Callahan noted the family's rich military history and that Fulton had worked in Russia. *Who was this man? And who was he working for?*

JULY 1964

Joe Callahan was eighteen years old. His father had asked him to mow the lawn. He would use the John Deere that was his father's pride and joy. It was a warm summer morning and the sun was shining through the branches of the oak tree in the back yard.

"Let me show you, Son: here's the throttle, the gas pedal, the brake."

"Dad, I know how it works."

"Well ..." His father looked like there was something more he wanted to say. "Just be sure you don't drive over any fallen branches or the garden hose."

"Alright, alright," Joe said, but as he turned the key in the ignition his father reached out and grabbed his shoulder.

"Son, you're growing up. Someday if you follow in my footsteps ..." Joe turned the motor off as his father continued, "something important could be up to your discretion, and if it is, I want you to make a difference where I failed. Remember what I told you before, what you promised me."

"Yeah, Dad, I know. I promise."

MARCH 9, 1998

Callahan and Mancini didn't waste any time; they reached out to New Haven, Connecticut-based FBI Agent James Margolin via conference call. "We want you to go to Danbury to interview former mayor James Dyer," Callahan said. "Find out what he knows about Evelyn Lincoln in regards to the items she kept from JFK's presidency. Dyer was a close friend and confidant of Lincoln's for thirty years. We want to know what she had, and we want you to confirm her actions from a firsthand source."

"Yes, sir," said Margolin, thinking, *Why am I being asked to do this? Hell, that was thirty-five years ago!*

Mancini was cold and to the point. "Take this seriously; make sure your interview is by the book and your report is concise."

Agent Margolin thought, *You know a lot more than you're telling me,* but he only asked, "Is there anything more you can share with me before I go to Danbury?"

Mancini snapped back, "Stop asking questions; do what you're told."

***

When Agent Margolin met with James Dyer, he flashed his credentials and said, "Please tell me everything you can about Evelyn Lincoln and her possessions belonging to President Kennedy."

Dyer was confused. "Aren't you a little cold on the trail on this?"

Margolin thought, *It's heating up pretty good now,* but responded, "The information I need is for a current investigation. Please tell me what you know about Evelyn Lincoln passing items of national security concern through her will."

"If she did anything like that, I don't think she would have done it with malice. Whatever she did, it was out of love and affection for the man she worked for and adored." Dyer paused a moment and decided it was his turn to ask a question: "Where are the orders for you to speak to me coming from?"

"Sir, I don't even know," Margolin replied, "but it's coming from very high up . . ."

MARCH 10, 1998

Arlan Ettinger received a letter by courier:

> To: Arlan Ettinger, President/CEO Guernsey's Auction House, New York from: Christopher M. Runkel, Acting General Counsel for the National Archives Records Administration.
>
> Reference: JFK auction March 18 and 19, 1998
>
> Dear Sir,
> We have reason to believe that some of the items listed for auction belong to the United States Government, and may contain information that is classified for national security reasons. We are requesting that these items be removed from your catalogue and

placed in a government repository, under appropriate security, until they can be reviewed for declassification. If you attempt to sell any of the aforementioned items we will file suit.

Arlan immediately showed the letter to his wife. As she read it, worry visibly creased her brow. "What have we gotten ourselves into?"

Guernsey's response letter simply stated: "It seems only fair and appropriate that you supply us with a complete list of the items in question so that this matter can be promptly resolved."

FRIDAY THE 13ᵀᴴ, MARCH, 1998

Like the coordination of the assassins of the Knights Templar on Friday 13, 1307, the government agencies descended upon Robert White and his inheritance, forcing him into submission.

A knock came at the front door of Robert's mother's brick home in Baltimore. She opened it wondering who would be calling so early in the morning.

There on her front porch stood a man and woman, both in grey suits. The man already had his credentials in hand, open for her to see. "Good morning, ma'am, I'm Agent Joe Callahan of the FBI; this is my partner, Agent Clara Mancini."

"Good morning," she responded. She poked her head around the doorframe and saw another twenty FBI agents standing in her yard; one of them waved.

***

Attorney Philip Adder stood in the quiet hall of New York's great Historical Society on Central Park West. The doors would not open to the public until eleven A.M., but a large group of official-looking people were already inside; this was a very important review. The bulk of Robert White's consigned items lined the display cases arranged for potential buyers to view before the upcoming Guernsey's Auction. The president of the auction house stood apart from the main group with an anguished look on his face.

As Robert White nervously walked towards the gathering, he could just make out part of what Adder was saying: ". . . a good citizen, he's not going to challenge a national security claim." Adder heard Robert's footsteps, turned, and stretched out his hand. "Good to see you this morning, Mr. White. These are the people who have been tasked with reviewing your material," he said, gesturing to the intimidating group of nameless faces. He made introductions to the members of the NARA, the Kennedy family attorney, members of the Justice Department, and the people from the Information Security Oversight Office.

White started in with a million concerned questions, chattering almost incoherently to everyone present. Adder smiled at them, put his hand on Robert's shoulder, turned him around, and quietly said, "Don't worry, I'll ensure your best interests; just let them do their jobs."

"I need the auction to go ahead," Robert pleaded. "I need the money for . . ."

"I know what you want, Robert; I know you're nervous . . . How long has the FBI been at your mother's home now?"

"My wife said they served the warrant at six this morning. They told her they don't intend to leave until well into this evening, but it could take several days."

"Has she been fully cooperative with them?"

"Yes, of course; she baked them cookies."

"That's good, Robert. I've received a list. You've already turned over Evelyn Lincoln's diaries, the Secret Service trip records from Dallas, Robert Kennedy's documents from 1963 to '65 including his signed copy of Dr. George Burkley's original autopsy report, and the letter between President Kennedy and his wife dated just before the Dallas trip; that's good. They also want the president's Cartier watch, which you no longer own; that's also good . . . But, you gave an interview to the press and stated that a St. Christopher money clip, a wallet, and a Hermes briefcase were with the president in Dallas; those have all been requested and have to go, as well as a two-page letter between Evelyn Lincoln and Jacqueline Kennedy dated 1963."

Robert was distraught. "I'll give up the wallet and money clip, the letter too, but I can't give up the briefcase; it's the most valuable item I have in the sale."

"Was it in the limousine on November 22?"

"No, Mrs. Lincoln had it."

"Ok, let me work on that. The recordings you gave to Mr. Fulton also need to be turned over and placed in the care of the NARA before the auction. Mr. George of the National Archives said that if the recordings and other materials are not surrendered at once, the matter will be turned over to the Attorney General for legal action. Have you heard anything from Mr. Fulton regarding the letter your other lawyer sent?"

"I asked him over the phone," Robert said, "but he still insisted it would breach our contract. I told him to bring the recordings when he comes to New York. What else can I do?"

"Remember what I told you, Robert, you cannot continue with this book; it will disrupt the agreement we sign today. They've been quite specific about it; there is no room for negotiation. I'll try to get the items and documents they've requested down to a minimum, but when it's all over, you *will* be giving more up."

Robert opened his mouth as if to protest, but Adder continued, "Believe me, Robert, even in my experience, this is an overwhelming government presence to deal with. So what we will do is try to appease them before the sale, then you'll make your money, get your museum, and get on with your life. The fact that the president's watch and the recordings in Mr. Fulton's possession are two of the government's biggest concerns, and that Mr. Fulton has not cooperated with our requests to return the tapes and release you from the book, means we need to disassociate ourselves with him to keep you clear. He is a liability for you . . . a big one. I have it on good authority that the attorney general has been given permission to arrest both of you under sealed indictments and procure your items by force. I'm prepared to give them Fulton . . . do you understand what I'm saying to you?"

"Yes," Robert said quietly.

"Listen." Adder tried to educate Robert. "Under the umbrella of national security the Justice Department can indict a ham sandwich. If they arrest you, you will never go to trial. They will stick you in their version of hell until you crack and agree to plead guilty to any charge they bring against you. What is working in your favor here is that it is in the government's best interests to keep this matter as quiet as possible. We can use that; we just need to cooperate with them now and sign their agreement today."

***

Later that afternoon, Adder accompanied Robert White to the Department of Justice.

After the agreement had been signed, Adder's phone rang. The caller praised him: "You're doing a good job, Adder. The only loose end now is Fulton. The DOJ is on top of that, but we need you to file a temporary restraining order in federal court to secure Fulton's White House audio tapes when he gets arrested on sealed indictment."

"Yes, sir," Adder responded.

Adder was pleased with himself; he would keep Robert White out of jail, rope in the recordings, and the secrets would be kept secret. But something was bothering him: JFK Jr. was stalling on signing his part of the agreement. Adder was unsure what the former president's son's true intentions were concerning this matter.

The following Monday, just two days before the sale, a number of items and documents were removed from Robert White's inheritance by federal officials under provisions of national security.

22

IT'S NOT THE FALL, IT'S THE STOP

MARCH 17, 1998

Shauna and I travelled to New York to attend the auction. My anxiety over flying had gotten worse, so I decided to stop flying altogether. I would travel by boat, train, horse, or camel, anything but a plane, so we bought Amtrak tickets.

When we first arrived, I dropped Shauna off at my aunt's house to get settled, and headed out for my scheduled meeting with Arlan Ettinger at 108 E Seventy-third St.

Arlan sat me down in his private office and started talking at me a mile a minute, while doing twenty other things in preparation for the auction. I found him to be intelligent and carefully spoken, as if used to the idea of the constant possibility of litigation.

"So, Mr. Fulton," he said, "Guernsey's expects this to be a very exciting auction. My assistant, Lorie, spoke to you before you came to New York about doing interviews. Robert has already done a few pieces. The president's Cartier has been featured on *CNN*, *Entertainment Tonight*, *Dateline*, *Good Morning America*, the *Today* show, and a few of the local New York stations, and I have been asked if you would appear for interviews. Katie Couric also asked about you, but as per our contract, I haven't given anyone your name."

"I would like to remain anonymous," I stated. "I don't want to do any interviews."

Arlan studied me for a moment. I could see he understood my position, but he still wanted me to do the interviews; it would be priceless, and costless, promotion. To his credit, he let it go. "Have you been watching the coverage on TV?"

I'd seen the Cartier on several programs, but they always said the same thing: "President Kennedy wore it the day he died." I was relieved there were no more details than that. "I did watch the piece where Katy Couric interviewed you," I said. "She made it quite clear she thought this sale was not a good idea."

"I didn't get that," Arlan said quickly, looking defensive.

He sounded like I had bruised his ego, so I added, "I thought you handled it well."

"I ran into Jacques Lowe yesterday." Arlan artfully changed the subject. "He asked about you."

"Did he consign as well?" I asked.

"No, he just stopped by to check things out." Arlan got up to close the door to his office. "Christopher, let's talk seriously; we've had some very interesting events take place concerning your consignment. I can't tell you everything, and I don't want to get ahead of myself, but I will tell you we've had an offer for six million dollars. The interested party actually said they didn't care what it would cost to procure the watch."

I was left speechless . . . eventually my curiosity moved me to ask, "Who was it?"

"That's not something I would usually divulge," Arlan replied, "but under these circumstances I can tell you it's someone representing England's Royal Family."

I was quite concerned that another foreign government was so interested and willing to pay so much.

Arlan tried to read my reaction, then abruptly said, "Let's get something to eat."

We walked outside to a little kiosk just down the street from Arlan's office. The air was cool, and the spring breeze was brisk. "This is my favorite place," he said, and ordered a burger and fries; I ordered a turkey sandwich. I assumed we would find somewhere to sit and eat, and continue talking, but Arlan demonstrated to me how literally they take the phrase "Time is money" in New York. Not bothering to sit at all, Arlan stood there and voraciously attacked the greasy, dripping burger while I still waited on my order.

He had practically devoured his entire meal before I had even taken my first bite. In that moment I could see Arlan was not concerned with pleasantries or politeness, it was all bottom line. He was about money, and seemed to have little interest in the history behind the items he was selling. I wondered what he would do while he waited for me to finish my lunch; perhaps he wouldn't wait at all, and just get back to the all-important business at hand. I let him off the hook and wrapped my sandwich to go.

During the cab ride back to my aunt's house in New Jersey, I noticed that a grey, late-model Ford had been behind me since I left Guernsey's. I had been looking around at the bustling city when it caught my eye. I didn't think much of it at first, but the longer it stayed glued to the bumper, the more interested I became. I decided to veer off route; I leaned up to the cabby and said, "Make a right here." The driver signaled and hung a right without question. We travelled another three blocks before I asked him to make a left. He did, and the grey Ford stayed with us. Then I asked the driver to get us back on course; he made the next left and another right and proceeded on the road we were on originally. The grey Ford was still on our bumper. *I was being followed! Maybe my name had been leaked to the press?*

When I got out of the cab at my aunt's, the grey Ford took a turn before it reached the house. Now whoever had been following me knew where I was staying.

As soon as I walked through the front door, Shauna wanted to know how the meeting went. I shared my impression of Arlan, and the weighty projection for the sale. I think she went into shock; she stood in front of me blinking and wordless as she tried to come up with something to say.

Shauna had grown up with an understanding and respect for money, and for the hard work it took to earn it. She was an elementary school music teacher, and her salary was modest. Never in her wildest dreams did she picture herself a multi-millionaire. As the reality of it began to sink in, she started to giggle, then laugh. She flung her arms around me; suddenly all of life's possibilities opened up before her. "We can buy our house, we can start having children!" She paused. "I'd still like to teach, though; you know I love what I do."

"Of course," I said, "you can do whatever you want. This will just make everything easier; it doesn't have to change who we are as people."

That night we stayed up late watching old films. We tried to calm the anticipation that had us both wired. When we finally went to bed, I could tell Shauna wasn't able to sleep a wink, because I couldn't, either.

***

It was the first day of the sale. The auction wouldn't start until two P.M.; Shauna and I turned on the TV to see what coverage the auction was getting. Ted Sorensen was being interviewed on the *Today* show. I remembered from my conversation with Deirdre Henderson that he was

JFK's speechwriter, now a New York lawyer, who had lied about penning one of Kennedy's speeches. He was saying, "I am outraged that some of President Kennedy's own personal material and proper belongings of the government are being auctioned off for someone's own personal profit. "I feel sorry for Mrs. Lincoln, who was a devoted secretary of the president's. I don't think she knew what she was doing when she took property that belonged to the family, belonged to the estate, and belonged to the government. The property was misappropriated; it was taken by someone who had no right to it.

"With all due respect, it's too bad for Mr. White that he's let his greed outrun his devotion to the Kennedys, because those who do not have good title cannot pass on good title. Mrs. Lincoln did not have good title, and Mr. White, I think, knew that when he, I think, purchased or induced her to give or bequeath those items to him."

Shauna let out a gasp, but I understood what he was trying to do. This was, at least, the second time the media was being used to shine a bad light on the sale. I felt even more compromised than I had before.

We decided we'd had enough television, so we got ready to head into the city for the sale. We caught a cab to the Seventh Regiment Armory on Park Avenue. As we entered, *Flash II*, the president's sailboat, was again prominently displayed to draw attention. Shauna took my picture standing next to it. There were hundreds of empty chairs waiting for bidders to arrive, but the press corps was already there in force. There were at least seventy reporters, cameramen, and technicians gathered like vultures swarming a fresh carcass.

I noticed Robert White sitting in one of the chairs nearest the podium. Shauna and I walked up to say hello. He seemed very anxious. Without saying hello back, he asked, "Did you bring the tapes?" His voice was harsh and his manner abrasive, a far cry from the amiable attitude he'd had at the promotion.

"No," I said simply. "Don't you remember our last conversation on the topic?"

He glared at me.

I still wanted to find someone willing to publish the photo book; maybe after the sale I would have the money to self-publish and see the contract through. I had put so much time, money, and effort into the project; I didn't want to give up on it completely.

I tried to change the subject. "I wish you well with the sale, Robert; if the amount of press present is any indication, something pretty big is going to happen." It didn't seem to make him feel any better; he was clearly under a lot of stress and wasn't dealing with it well.

People began trickling through the doors as the starting time of the auction drew near. My items wouldn't be on the auction block until the following day, so this was my chance to see firsthand what the front line looked like. The hall should have been packed with thousands of people; instead, a meager 150 arrived. Feeling a distinct lack of buzz and excitement, I walked up to a group of the press and asked what they thought about the small turnout. "Everyone's afraid the Kennedys will take legal action," a cameraman said. "That's why nobody's here and nobody's going to bid. We're hoping the Kennedy kids come storming in to stop the whole thing." His response was alarming, but before I could ask him anything else, Arlan took the podium and presented Robert White.

The noise in the hall suddenly fell silent. All cameras were pointed at Robert as he spoke to the bidders and the press: "I have reached an agreement with the Kennedy family and the National Archives; this sale will go forward." With that, the few people in attendance clapped, and the media looked disappointed. I didn't know what Robert was talking about, and I didn't know what he had agreed to; all I knew was that I was on the outside. As Robert stepped off the podium he was swarmed by the press corps. "Mr. White, Mr. White, tell us about the agreement that allowed this auction to go on." A dozen microphones were thrust in his face.

"No, sorry, I can't say anything about that."

"Mr. White, what do you think about the Kennedy children's comments about Evelyn Lincoln?"

"I think it's terrible the Kennedy children had to criticize her in that way. I'll go to my grave defending that woman."

On the other side of the room, the rest of the press corps gathered to get their sound bite from Arlan Ettinger. "Mr. Ettinger, we have reports that certain members of the Kennedy family have instructed you that they want no ceiling on their bids for particular items, is that correct?"

"No comment."

"What is your response to Caroline and JFK Jr.'s statements in the press?"

"It is disappointing that the Kennedy children have chosen unnecessarily to sully the name and image of a woman like Evelyn Lincoln, who was so dedicated to their father."

"How do you respond to the children's statements that some of the items in this sale are, in their words, 'intensely personal and never meant for Evelyn Lincoln's possession'?"

"Look," Arlan spoke clearly, "this is a celebration of the president's life; these items are of great historical importance, and we are proud to take them to pubic sale."

"Mr. Ettinger, Mr. White just stated he signed an agreement so the auction could go forward; what was that agreement?"

"I cannot comment on that." He paused. "But I will say this: it's nice that it's over. We never could have imagined the controversy; it's not what we bargained for." He turned to walk away, but stopped and faced the press again to make one final statement: "A lot of misinformation was generated from one side to achieve a goal. When this is all over, maybe I'll be inclined to say what really went on here." With that he turned, and left the press hanging on his words.

As the auction began, Shauna and I took our seats near Andy Rooney from CBS's *60 Minutes*. The first few lots came and went without much interest. Then lot 8 came up, the antique drop-leaf signing table that President Kennedy had adjacent to the Oval Office desk for signing important bills and drafting legislation. I remembered seeing it in Robert's basement and at the Trump Tower promotion. The auctioneer said, "This item will be passed." Incredibly, and without explanation, the historic table was taken out of the auction entirely. I wondered if Robert's agreement included removing the table from the sale.

I waited for the next items of significance to be offered: lots 21 and 22, the Oval Office flags. The bidding quickly shot up to $175,000. Then it was announced that these two items were also out of the sale, and they were passed. The auctioneer was embarrassed, and apologized for his mistake.

What the hell is going on? I excused myself from Shauna's company and found the restroom.

There was a man in the bathroom talking on the phone by the sinks; he was pacing and obviously distressed. As I washed my hands I couldn't help but overhear his conversation: he was disappointed with how the sale was going and was worried that the presidential yacht, *Honey Fitz*, wouldn't sell, even thought it had nothing to do with the controversial collection of Evelyn Lincoln. He said if he could just get someone to cover his expenses of $150,000 he would sell it for that. My ears perked. When he hung up the phone I introduced myself. I told him I had inadvertently caught part of his conversation, and asked, "Do you own *Honey Fitz*, or represent her owners?"

"Yes," he replied.

"And you'd be willing to get out for $150,000?"

The man's face flickered and he asked if I would be willing to purchase it.

"I would love to," I said, but before I could say anything else he jumped in: "I'll draw up a contract, and sell it to you for $150,000 right now."

I told him I wished I could, but I wasn't in a position to buy it, and I bid him luck in the sale.

As I was heading back to my seat, Robert walked up and barred my way. He started talking about the photo book and the necessity of cancelling our contract. He told me there were important reasons behind his decision, but he didn't enlighten me about any of them. Essentially, he said I should just lie down and say goodbye to the money and time I had invested in our project. It was a frustrating, one-sided conversation. I listened as well as I could, but I had no good response to his pleas because nothing he said made any sense.

It was looking more and more like I would have to sue Robert; I didn't want it to come to that because we were friends, or at least I thought we were. "Robert," I said, "I believe it's time for us to talk more frankly: you are getting what you want from this auction, while all my money and all my efforts on our book were thrown over for it because of your issues with Caroline Kennedy."

For the first time, I could see Robert heard the threat in my voice. He became flustered, and stammered for a moment before blurting out, "It's not just me you know, you're in this too; ask Arlan about the letters!"

"Letters?" A wave of apprehension washed over me. "What letters? What are you talking about?"

Robert hurriedly said, "Nothing . . . nothing. More of my items are coming up on the block, I need to go."

An uncomfortable feeling crept up my spine. Before Shauna and I left for New York, I had become more and more concerned about Robert's erratic behavior. Then when he announced he had reached a settlement, literally hours before the start of the auction, it was obvious that much more was going on than I was privy to. And now he was saying I was in it too? If I was in it, how come I didn't know what *it* was? I was anxious to speak with Arlan and start filling in the blanks.

I sat back down with Shauna and waited for *Honey Fitz* to come up. The auctioneer opened the bidding at five million, but the room fell silent. In a quick two-step, he lowered the initial price to two million, and the phones began ringing with bids. After that, the bidding took hold: it rushed and waned, stopped and started, but always kept climbing. I wondered where it would end. The hammer fell: "Sold, 5.4 million dollars." The crowd collectively gasped, the media took note, and I turned to Shauna and said, "We just lost 5.25 million dollars." The delight drifted from her face. "Oh God, what happened?" she asked, looking very concerned.

"Nothing happened," I said, "that's the trouble."

My cell phone rang, so I excused myself again. Shauna remained to follow the auction's progress as I answered the phone: "Hello? . . . Yes, speaking . . . Pardon me? . . . But it's up for auction tomorrow . . . Why? . . . Yes, I would agree to that . . . I understand . . . Where? . . . Yes, Ok, I'll be there. Very nice speaking with you." I grabbed a pen and paper and wrote down the instructions I had been given.

"What was that all about?" Shauna asked when I sat back down.

"That was the most amazing phone call I've ever received . . . You're not going to believe who it was." I whispered the name in her ear; she jolted back in her seat and stared at me, wide-eyed and speechless.

MARCH 19, 1998

On the second day of the auction, I felt detached from the proceedings. Arlan made sure to greet Shauna and me when we first arrived. I wanted to bring up the letters Robert had mentioned the day before, but it wasn't the right time or place. The three of us were standing behind the rows upon rows of empty seats when a man approached. He introduced himself to Arlan as the President of Cartier; Arlan did not introduce Shauna or me, nor did the gentleman ask who we were.

"I want to talk to you about the Cartier piece coming up for auction today," he said. "We want it; what do we need to do to get it?"

Shauna squeezed my hand. I waited to see what Arlan would say. He made an excuse that he had to go take care of some other business and would get back to him later. I just watched as the owner of an auction house walked away from a powerful and important buyer with an open pocketbook without so much as a dalliance. Shauna and I were left alone standing next to Cartier's president, and we couldn't say a word.

We made our way to the front row of seats just before the auction began. Some people sat quietly in anticipation; others talked loudly even after the bidding was underway. Shortly before the Cartier hit the block, I heard two men behind us speaking about it. "The assassination piece is coming up," one said.

"I know," the other responded, "it belongs to a Mr. Fulton."

My name was familiar to bidders? Who had released my name?

As it was wheeled onto the stage, the Cartier was the center of attention. I had personally designed the five-foot-tall display frame; it had a silver plaque with an inscription and presidential seal, numerous photographs of Kennedy wearing the watch, and a unique, custom-made rotating glass cylinder with sterling silver ends that housed the watch itself, all set against red walnut and royal blue silk.

CNN's cameraman moved in to get a close-up; he asked to have the glass case turned to get a shot of the front and back of the watch. The rest of the media took note and tried to get their own coverage.

The auctioneer waited for the room to hush before saying, "Up next is the much-anticipated lot 153: John F. Kennedy's gold Cartier wristwatch, worn by him in Dallas on November 22, 1963." The bidding began with a frenzy: low six figures, mid six figures, higher and higher, then $800,000. Shauna looked at me, bewildered. Then the auctioneer announced that the next high bidder on the telephone had been accidentally disconnected and the lot would have to be passed. They hadn't let it meet reserve; whoever was on the phone was cut off . . . on purpose.

The hordes of hungry press had waited with bated breath, hoping the bidding on the assassination evidence would provide the fireworks of Kennedy drama they all wanted to see. When the bidding halted, and my lot was passed for failure to meet reserve, they lost their enthusiasm.

When President Kennedy's tortoiseshell sunglasses sold for $46,000, the auctioneer announced it made a new world record by beating out Elvis Presley's sunglasses, which had sold four years earlier for $26,450. Now JFK's sunglasses held a spot in the *Guinness Book of World Records*; Shauna delighted at the novelty of it.

23

LETTERS TO NO ONE

MARCH 20, 1998

The next day I went to the office of Guernsey's Auction House for the last time. After signing a release, Arlan returned President Kennedy's watch to me. "Mr. Fulton, I'm sure you can appreciate there was a lot going on with this auction; I don't want you to be upset that the Cartier watch was passed. I'm sure I'll be calling you in the next few days with an offer."

Before I had a chance to respond, I heard two of Guernsey's employees talking about the sale in the hall: "Is it true that several Kennedy family members had winning bids?" one asked.

"Yes, Maria Shriver spent $51,000 on two diaries; Robert White got $1,500,000 at the end of the day!"

Arlan turned his head abruptly and said, "Excuse me a moment, Christopher." He walked over to the employees with the loose lips and spoke, almost inaudibly. "Unless you are looking for another job, I suggest you stop talking openly about the sale; there are confidentiality agreements in place. Understood?"

Arlan walked back to me, shaking his head. "I'm sorry about that. Is there anything else I can do for you, Christopher?"

"As a matter of fact, Arlan, I still need a few minutes of your time."

"Of course, what's on your mind?"

We walked down the hall to his office. As Arlan closed the door, I noticed a pile of newspaper articles on his desk. The topmost was from the *Boston Globe*, dated Sunday, January 11, 1998: "The Kennedys had been long aware that Lincoln had accumulated many of the president's personal belongings after his death, some with the approval of Mrs. Kennedy and Robert F. Kennedy."

I cut to the chase. "Has Guernsey's received any legal letters in reference to my consignments?"

Arlan looked over the top of his glasses at me. "Yes, we received a letter on the sixteenth of this month, we responded on the seventeenth, and sent you copies that same day."

"Why didn't you just give them to me when I was here on the seventeenth? Didn't you think it was pertinent to inform me right away?"

"I didn't want to concern you; our attorney had resolved the issue."

"Resolved the issue? I saw Ted Sorensen on TV yesterday morning and was very upset by what he had to say."

"I didn't see that," Arlan said. "I was too busy with the auction."

I couldn't imagine that this man would not be aware of all the publicity out there regarding the sale. "Arlan, I need copies of whatever correspondence you have that concerns my consignments."

"Yes, of course. My wife will get them for you." Arlan picked up the phone and got his wife on the line. A few minutes later Barbara Mitnz, who was both Arlan's wife and Guernsey's vice president, walked into the office and placed three letters in my hand. I read each one silently in sequence of date.

The first letter was from Nicole Seligman from the law offices of Williams & Connolly in Washington, D.C., addressed to Molly Sherden, Esquire, Guernsey's attorney in Boston.

Dear Mrs. Sherden,

As I believe you are aware, on February 6, 1998, I wrote to Philip Adder, Esquire, attorney for Robert White, with regard to the ownership of items in Mr. White's possession that he had received from Evelyn and/or Harold Lincoln. The items whose ownership my clients contest, and whose return they have demanded, include items in your client's scheduled auction, as we understand you and your client have been advised.

I write now with regard to an additional item in your client's auction which I now understand was not consigned by Mr. White: Item No. 153, the Cartier Wristwatch. Mrs. Kennedy sought to gather the possessions her husband had with him on November 22, 1963. If your description is accurate, the watch was never given to Mrs. Lincoln for her personal ownership.

Please advise me as soon as possible as to the consigner of this watch, so that we may directly demand its return. If you cannot disclose the consigner's identity, please inform him or her immediately of this claim by Caroline and John Kennedy, and their demand that the watch be returned immediately to them.

Thank you for your assistance.
Very Truly Yours, Nicole Seligman

The next letter was the response from Molly Sherden to Nicole Seligman on March 17.

I am responding to your letter of yesterday concerning your clients' demand for the Cartier wristwatch, which is designated as Lot No. 153 in the Guernsey's auction catalog. As you have requested, I have put the consigner on notice of this demand and have given the consigner a copy of your letter.

I have reviewed the provenance of this item that was provided to Guernsey's. The watch was removed from President Kennedy's wrist at Parkland hospital in Dallas on November 22, 1963. According to sources and the provenance of this watch, this item was too vivid a reminder to Mrs. Kennedy of her late husband and, therefore, she gave it as a special gift to Evelyn Lincoln when she moved from the White House to Georgetown in 1964. I have spoken personally with an individual who was in the service of the Kennedys at the time in question and who has substantiated this account.

I am just now leaving for New York so that if you should need to reach me after you receive this letter, I can be contacted though Guernsey's office.

Very Truly Yours,
Molly Sherden

The final letter, also dated the seventeenth, was from Molly Sherden to me, CEO of Twelve Global Ltd, West Vancouver, Canada.

Dear Mr. Fulton:

I represent Guernsey's Auction House in connection with the auction of JFK documents and artifacts that will take place tomorrow in New York. I received this morning a copy of the enclosed letter from Nicole Seligman, who is the attorney for John and Caroline Kennedy.

I have already written a response to this letter on behalf of Guernsey's, which I also enclose. I have not disclosed your identity or provided any other information to Ms. Seligman besides what is contained in the letter. I do not believe there is any merit in the Kennedy children's claim to ownership of the Cartier wristwatch. They have taken no legal action and all government agencies have reached a final resolution with Mr. White.

Should you feel that any additional response to Ms. Seligman is required, I would be happy to assist you or your counsel in any way.

I am leaving just now for New York and can be reached through Guernsey's office there.

Very Truly Yours, Molly Sherden

I took the three letters and the watch and went to meet Shauna at the train station. Shauna took the watch with her back to Vancouver, and I caught a train south.

24

DESTINY OR DESTRUCTION

MARCH 21, 1998

I liked traveling by train; it freed me from obligation, forced me to slow down and reflect. Many of the passengers were consumed with the news out of New York. I caught glimpses of newspaper headings: AUCTION INFLAMES PASSIONS OVER KENNEDY MEMORA-BILIA, JFK SALE A BUST, KENNEDYS SECRETLY BID ON JFK ITEMS. The couple next to me was engaged in conversation about the auction. "The yacht got 5.4 million!" the man said.

"People with all that money are ridiculous," his wife responded. "They have too much leisure time, they don't live in the real world."

It was a pleasant enough train ride, but long. I was able to relax and admire the scenery as I travelled through the countryside. At last the announcer's voice came over the speakers: "Miami." I collected my bag, got off the train, and hailed a cab.

"Where to, sir?" the driver asked.

"A decent but economical hotel near the Delano in South Beach." It was late. After I arrived and checked in, I went straight to bed.

MARCH 22, 1998

I woke early, freshened up, ate a light breakfast, then hailed a cab and headed to the Delano Hotel. I asked the concierge for directions, then walked to room number 915 and knocked on the door.

"Just a minute."

I recognized his voice.

"Come on in, I've just got to grab something," he said.

There are single moments in life that can transform who you were into who you are destined to be. I pushed the door open and walked into the room. I saw his unmistakable profile in the back of the room. He turned, walked towards me, and held out his hand. "Hi, Mr. Fulton? Nice to meet you; I'm John Kennedy."

How could I not know who you are; you've been famous since you were born! We shook hands. "Hi, yes, Christopher; it's a pleasure to meet you."

"Please, Christopher, take a seat."

I sat on a sofa and he sat opposite me. With an easy, unpretentious air he said, "First let me say thank you for taking this meeting. Did you bring it with you?"

Right down to business. I felt the photocopies of the affidavits and letter in my pocket, but I'd asked Shauna keep the watch on the chance that Caroline Kennedy might intercede at the meeting.

"No," I said, "my fiancée took it back to Vancouver with her."

I couldn't tell if he was disappointed by my response, but he didn't skip a beat. "I can appreciate you were told by Guernsey's there was a high offer from the British Government, but as I told you, that transfer would not have been allowed to complete.

"When this auction was announced, I was placed in a delicate position with a deadline. I informed the attorney general I would make the purchase and place it in the custody of the National Archives. Caroline and I had Nicole Seligman write letters to Robert White and Guernsey's in the beginning of February to inform them they could not sell or transfer any items of national security concern. I hoped I would get a response through Guernsey's about your position, but I didn't. So, just before the sale, Nicole sent you a letter through Guernsey's. It kept your anonymity intact and demanded the return of my father's watch; I was sure it would prompt a response from you. I wanted this transfer to happen quietly, quickly, and privately. Were you made aware of that letter?"

"Yes," I said, "but not until after the sale; Arlan had Guernsey's attorney handle the matter on my behalf without my knowledge or consent. I was kept in the dark." I handed John copies of the legal letters that had I received in Arlan's office following the auction.

John took a moment to read them. "OK," he said, "that makes sense; White and Ettinger wanted the auction to go forward without fear of being shut down by us or the Justice Department. When I didn't hear from you through my attorney, I called you . . . We have a mutual friend, Jacques Lowe."

Now I knew how John had gotten my number and had known exactly where I was.

John went on, "Due to all the press coverage, Robert White was investigated by the FBI, the Assassination Records Review Board, and the Security Oversight Office through the White House. That made arranging a private transfer with you more complicated."

"What?" I said, mostly to myself. "The FBI investigated Robert? . . . I'm sorry, I'm not familiar with all of this. Could you explain to me what the Security Oversight Office is?"

"They classify items of national security for disclosure or non-disclosure in collaboration with President Clinton. White signed an agreement with the Department of Justice and Caroline and me, then turned over what he had that was involved in my father's assassination and Cuba to the National Archives to avoid any problems."

I tried to keep myself composed, a difficult feat. The Cartier was certainly the most sensitive and contentious item in the sale. That is what Robert was talking about when he said I was in it too.

Now I knew why the bastard didn't tell me what was going on: he was covering himself and leaving me to twist in the wind.

John continued, "I held out signing the agreement with the agencies until two hours before the auction was scheduled to begin; that's the only reason the Justice Department withdrew their injunction to stop the sale. I signed reluctantly; I didn't want to be tied to their agenda. I originally thought any evidence in my father's murder would have fallen under the deed of gift that our family lawyer drew up with the government in 1965. Nicole assured me the deed stated that all rights, title, and interest, of all the clothing and personal effects worn by my father during his assassination, which was in the possession of the United States Government in 1965, as well as the x-rays and photographs of the autopsy, reverted to their custody for deposit and security. Because my uncle kept the Cartier, the government cannot legally claim it . . . and that opens up a window of opportunity that didn't exist before. However, the DOJ is overlooking the legalities on this; they just want the watch turned over to the Security Oversight Office."

He reflected for a moment. "I wrote Evelyn Lincoln in 1992 to thank her for her service to my family and asked if she wanted to donate any of the papers in her collection to the library; I had no idea what she had at that time. I didn't realize any direct evidence in my father's murder still existed that had not already been given over to the government, secured or destroyed . . . What compelled you to sell it publicly?"

176

"My lawyer recommended I sell it, then Robert White urged me to be in the Guernsey's sale. How did you know I was the owner of the watch?"

"I read your book of provenance that my sister acquired through Sotheby's."

I thought about the word *acquired*; I wondered if John knew she had taken it. "Your sister never contacted Sotheby's back about a private sale," I said. "I figured you had no interest in the watch."

"That was Caroline's decision, not mine; she only recently showed me your information. I've stayed out of this until now, but you've accomplished some impressive research; getting a Secret Service agent to sign an affidavit couldn't have been easy. You *must* know more about this than you shared with Sotheby's."

I thought back to everything Bouck had told me. The letter and affidavits in my pocket needed to be given to the man who was sitting right in front of me; he was the only person I could give them to. It's what Bouck believed I was going to do all along. Fate had led me here; it seemed obvious. I pulled out the only copies of the original letter from Lincoln and affidavits from Bouck, and handed them to John. "The originals are at my lawyer's in Maryland," I said. "I was never going to put them in the public sale."

John read them quietly for several minutes, then looked them over a second time. "How did you get these?"

"Following Evelyn Lincoln's death, Robert White forwarded the Lincoln letter and Bouck affidavit to my attorney, who transferred them to me. The other affidavit was given to me in person by Mr. Bouck when I met him."

"Secret Service Agent Robert Bouck met with you?" John said with surprise, realizing my knowledge about his father's murder went much deeper than he had assumed.

"Yes," I said, "Mr. Bouck and I talked at great length, and he told me if you ever needed him to testify, he would, for you alone." Then I admitted to John, "Because I had the evidence in my possession, Mr. Bouck thought I was working for you, everybody did; they all just assumed . . ."

John breathed a sigh of relief, or maybe it was a sigh of preparation. When he spoke again, it was with restrained excitement. "My Uncle Ted told me a lot about Uncle Bobby securing this evidence. It's true; this is all tangible," he said, holding the documents tightly. He was quiet for a few moments. I could see his cogs turning. Then he looked at me and said, "I have a question to ask you and I need an honest answer . . . I was informed that you have been to Russia. I was warned to stay away from you because you attempted to sell what you have while you were there. What happened?"

I was very surprised by what John had been told; I needed to set the record straight. "I took a construction consultation job in Moscow from a client I worked with in Vancouver. I realized later that I had been manipulated; the real intention of the trip was for me to meet General Alexander Lebed in the Kremlin."

"What did Lebed want from you?"

"He invited me to release information about the evidence through Russia. I told him I didn't know what he was talking about. I got out of the Kremlin as quickly as I could and left the country immediately."

John kept eye contact with me through my explanation. Once I was finished, he said, "You have something that belonged to my father; it's important to me, and before this meeting is over, I would like to come to an agreement between us concerning it. As I told you on the phone, I'm offering you your reserve price of one million dollars for the watch, but I also want you to do an interview for my magazine."

Again, I was taken aback—*an interview?*

"Keep all of this confidential for now," John said, not waiting for me to respond. "Because you didn't release anything through Russia or capitalize from the media attention in New York, you've paved the way for us to do an important exclusive interview." He leaned forward, ready to hear my answer.

George was the most widely read political magazine in the United States. "Mr. Kennedy, with all due respect, I knew I wanted to make this deal with you, that's why I'm here, but I'm not entirely sure about why you want to interview me."

"Because, Christopher, you are part of the chain of custody of material evidence in my father's assassination . . . Let me share something with you: I recently interviewed Fidel Castro. I told him I realized his association with my father's death was crafted by more sinister people here at home." He reached over and took a paper from a stack he had on the table and put it in front of me. "Read this."

I picked it up and scanned the page; it was a transcription of Castro's words:

It was Vice President Nixon who planned to have me killed in 1960. The CIA paid Johnny Roselli, a mobster from Chicago $150,000 to take my life. When Nixon became president he would take credit for my death; a great victory for the Republican Party, but Kennedy won. I liked your father, and I feel the same way now as I did just before he was assassinated. I believed Kennedy was sincere, I also believed that the expression of that sincerity could have had political significance. But, I felt Kennedy inherited a difficult situation; I don't think a President of the United States is ever really free, and I believe that Kennedy felt the impact of that lack of freedom. I also believed he understood the extent to which he had been misled, especially, for example, on Cuban reaction at the time of the attempted Bay of Pigs invasion. I cannot help hoping that a leader will come to the fore in North America who will be willing to brave unpopularity, fight the corporations, tell the truth, and, most important, let the various nations act as they see fit. I thought your father might have been that man. He had the possibility of becoming, in the eyes of history, the greatest President of the United States, an even greater president than Lincoln.

After I finished reading, John said, "I'm going to publish the interview, and I'm going to show the American people that they were lied to for all these years. It's going to be a turning point for me, my family, the magazine, and the country; I want to incorporate your information into that exposé. If it gets the reaction I hope it will, I'll use it as a platform to run for office."

Every fiber in my being lit up; John was going to run! This was an opportunity for everything I had discovered to be shared with the American people, by a Kennedy! John would reach out and shine a light on what had really happened in 1963.

He continued, "I can give you my personal promise that your hard work will not be in vain."

Shauna and I had discussed John's phone call back in New York, and agreed this was the best thing to do. Now I knew we had made the right decision. I felt truth and power in what John told me. I had watched him many times on documentaries and televised interviews. They always tried to initiate a response as to when or if he would run for public office, but all he ever said was, "I am happy with what I am doing right now."

John went on, "I've always felt like the citizens of this country expected me to heal the wounds caused by my father's murder. Before I was born, my father said that if he had a boy, he hoped he would take some responsibility for what goes on in the world. That's why one of the main focal points of my magazine is to make the truth in politics accessible to every-one. My mother was rightly terrified, and tried to keep Caroline and me safe. I loved her with all my heart, but it's been said that we all must follow our destiny, or be destroyed by it."

I couldn't believe he was saying all of this to me. "I'm sure you would win," I said, "but I think it will be dangerous."

"My family has suffered so much in their efforts of public service," he said solemnly, "but I don't want my children growing up in an America I no longer recognize. I want to resolve this tension and pressure.

"When I run, I will have to hire my own private security team, and I will need to show the American people my reasons for doing so. That's why your interview is so important. Uncle Bobby opened a clandestine investigation into the Secret Service and their role in my father's assassi-nation; not one shot was fired to protect my father. They knew what was about to happen, and they not only allowed it, they participated."

I remembered talking to the widow of Bill Greer, JFK's limousine driv-er in Dallas. She said her husband had testified that there had been more than three shots fired, then laughed when he said, "But we didn't do any of the shooting."

"I have real concerns that the U.S. Secret Service would not protect me," John said. "When my father was president, key members of the de-tail were corrupted, they subverted his protection, and the rest followed orders to stand down. I always believed that certain Secret Service agents had to be complicit in his murder, so did my mother; now I know for sure. The research and the documentation you obtained will help me show that the men sworn to protect my father betrayed and abandoned him at the time he needed them most.

"When I run, my goal will be to reach the White House. I will, in a modern way, recreate the ideas of my father. I will empower and rally ev-ery American to restore our freedoms and end the trail of lies and deceit regarding the need for superfluous secrecy and security, continued arms buildup, and false propaganda about foreign enemies. The United States needs foreign policies built on mutual respect and understanding; it's go-ing to become ever more critical for the nation's prosperity."

His rhetoric was stirring, just as his uncle's and father's before him. I thought of John in the White House; it felt like freedom, a pride in the present and an unshakable positivity for the future. The legacy started by his father alive again, and pushing to enhance the greatest country in the world.

I would never have expected John to be so open with me, but it seemed it was in his nature. I reached out my hand. "You have a deal, John." It felt right: alive with promise and energy. Everything had fallen into place. This was a cornerstone for a new movement in the United States.

"Good," he said, and we shook on it. "If anything leaks I cannot comment; I want to keep this under wraps until late next year. We'll go ahead and use Guernsey's for the transfer; they'll have to get their commission. They will contact you with an offer and the transfer will be handled by them in New York. Guernsey's will provide you with a cashier's check. I would ask that you put it in a private bank abroad; it's safer for both of us that way. You can have your lawyer courier me the original documents."

"Alright," I agreed, but I still had a burning question. "When do you want me to do the interview?"

"Right now."

I was there for several hours. When we were done, I signed a release and we shook hands again. I stood up to leave, but I didn't want to go. Our deal surpassed any business agreement or legal contract: it was a personal promise. During my time with John, I got a clear sense that our country was going to experience a substantial transformation.

From that moment on, I was tied to what people termed the "Kennedy curse," which was little more than the hatred and opposition the Kennedys attracted by their ability to inspire and lead the nation toward change . . . which made all of this very real and very dangerous.

25

SLIPPING THE SNARE

LATE MARCH 1998

O n the train home to Vancouver, my cell phone rang. "Mr. Fulton, this is Arlan. We have an important offer on the Cartier watch."

"Good news," I said.

"We have a guaranteed, non-negotiable offer at $650,000 minus our commission and insurance, which makes $604,000 net to you.

"Really?" I said, confused by the figure. "Are you sure that's as high as the buyer is willing to go?" I wasn't going to mention John's name.

"Yes; if you agree to that amount, you will sell it to a division of Guernsey's that will deliver it to the buyer, whose name I cannot divulge . . . I need your decision immediately."

I furrowed my brow and tried to understand why I was being offered $350,000 less than what John and I had agreed to. *Was Arlan trying to cheat me?* I certainly didn't have enough time to look into it before giving my answer. I would accept, and once the dust settled, I could explore the discrepancy further. If Arlan *was* committing fraud, I would have to find out a way to recoup the stolen amount later.

While keeping my cool, I gave Arlan the go-ahead. My phone beeped a low-battery warning, but before it shut off, he told me the details of the transfer: it would take place at JFK Airport in New York.

I needed to call my father, but my cell phone had shut down just as my call with Arlan had ended. The lady in the seat next to me noticed my trouble and was kind enough to offer me the use of her phone.

***

Two days later, Agents Callahan and Mancini waited in the international terminal at JFK Airport. Mancini sat down. "Fulton should be coming in on this flight from Vancouver for the meeting with Ettinger."

The agents' orders were to execute a sealed warrant, arrest Fulton while on the federal property of the Airport, confiscate the Cartier wristwatch before any monetary exchange took place, and deposit it in the custody of a Fourth Circuit Federal Court.

"Let's just try and do this as quietly as possible," Callahan said. "The higher-ups don't want a scene. I'll approach Fulton myself, show my credentials, escort him out of the terminal, and we'll place him under arrest outside."

"Fine, whatever you want," Mancini mumbled.

They watched the passengers depart the anticipated flight and get in line at customs.

After a lengthy wait they got a nod from the customs officer on the far right. The traveler at the customs window had grey hair and looked to be in his sixties; he didn't match the profile of Christopher Fulton at all. Mancini kept eyes on the grey-haired man as he walked through to collect his luggage. Callahan walked up to the customs officer. "What have we got?" he asked quietly. The officer tilted his computer screen to reveal an image of the traveler's passport:

Surname: Fulton
Given name: John
Place of birth: Virginia.

Callahan walked back to Mancini. "It's his dad; the fox bought the ticket with his credit card but sent his father to do the exchange." Callahan was impressed; Fulton had outsmarted the FBI wiretaps.

Mancini was angry. "We don't have a warrant for his father." It meant she would have to make all traces of the transaction disappear.

"We don't have the time to do anything about it now," Callahan said. "This deal is going to go through."

Mancini immediately dialed Janet Reno's direct line. "Ma'am, we have a problem."

***

Once I arrived home, my father told me the transaction at JFK Airport had gone through without concern; Arlan was there to meet him personally. I was very thankful to the woman who had offered me her phone on the train. It was integral that my father complete the sale for me, as I was still in transit on Amtrak and Shauna had to work. It was my thirty-third birthday when my dad handed me the check numbered 1412 from a holding company for $604 000. I immediately had it couriered to open an account in Credit Suisse in Zurich. The check cleared and all was well.

I called Henry McRobie and told him I had taken his advice. "I sold it, it's all taken care of," I said, and asked him to send the original letter and two affidavits to John F. Kennedy Jr.

"Jesus Christ, Christopher," he said, "I told you to get rid of it, not bury yourself with it." I appreciated Henry's concern, but I was confident I had done the right thing. I told him to make sure there were no copies made, and gave him the address John had given me. Henry said he would send them out that day.

***

Guernsey's website showed the Cartier wristwatch had sold for one million dollars, just as John and I had discussed. But that statement was in contrast to the $604k I had received. I called Arlan to query him about it; I wanted to see what his side of the story was. When I got him on the line, I asked, "What happened with the Cartier sale?"

"What? Who wants to know? Is the press on this?" Arlan seemed overly nervous and agitated by my question.

"Relax," I said, "it's just me; I want to know."

"Well, you know I can't tell you who the watch went to. The whole sale was very stressful; there was a lot of pressure to achieve certain outcomes which I had little or no control over. I'd like to tell you what happened, but not now," he said, and abruptly hung up.

Arlan had not instilled me with any confidence. It seemed probable that he had pocketed $350,000 of John's money which was owed to me. I sent the information to Henry and asked him to start building a case against Arlan and Guernsey's, but not to file anything until I said so. I was worried the press might grab it, and I didn't want to cause a public problem for John.

184

26

Best Interests

March 28, 1998

Dave Powers, President Kennedy's closest friend, and protector of the JFK image, died at his home in Arlington, Virginia. JFK Jr. made a statement to the press: "He was the link between the past and the present."

Soon after, President Bill Clinton received a letter that was sent to his private fax in the Oval Office; it was from JFK Jr. Clinton expected it to be light and comical, likely in reference to a previous fax he had received from the former president's son regarding the Monica Lewinsky affair, but it was something that caused him concern.

> I know both you, and the new generation in our nation, are still very much interested in the truths behind my father's murder being released to the public. I feel we should now allow the legal process, established by the Constitution, to function as it should; therefore, permitting a proper forensic autopsy of President John F. Kennedy. I believe it is important at this time, not only for my family, but for the best interests of our nation. I am asking your cooperation in this matter.
>
> Sincerely,
> John F. Kennedy Jr.

After reading the letter, the President requested that Janet Reno meet him in the Oval Office to get him up to speed on the Evelyn Lincoln Project. As Reno entered, Clinton clasped his hands in his lap and leaned back in his chair. "Tell me everything," he said.

Reno took a deep breath. "Evidence in JFK's assassination transferred to JFK Jr. It's our belief he's prepared to publish information in his magazine relating to his father's assassination sometime in the coming year. It will likely include his interview with Castro."

"Well hell, Janet, I thought you at Justice were going to stop the sale."

"We didn't put an injunction on the auction because Robert White, the main consigner, cooperated with us, signed our agreement, and relinquished the items we requested," Reno explained, "and JFK Jr. told us he would secure Fulton's evidence for the National Archives."

"Yes, I know . . . but?" Clinton pressed.

"Ted Kennedy was concerned about JFK Jr.'s involvement, so we had a sealed indictment and warrant ready for Fulton when he came into the country; we were going to arrest him at the airport in New York before his transaction with JFK Jr. took place."

"So what the hell happened?"

"We were ready to arrest him, but Fulton's father showed up in his place; we weren't prepared for that contingency."

"Jesus, Janet! That's one more nail in the coffin," Clinton said unhappily.

27

CROSSING THE THRESHOLD

LATE MARCH 1998

Shauna was over the moon that we could finally move forward and buy a house of our own. As soon as the check cleared, she confessed she already had a number of houses in mind she wanted to show me. Unfortunately, our timing wasn't the best; Vancouver's housing market had exploded and was steadily climbing.

The house we eventually set our hearts on was in Lions Bay. We were both attracted to its privacy, seclusion, and price. It would be a bit of a commute, but it was an enjoyable drive. The papers were signed, and Shauna and I were ready to move in by the end of April. I took Shauna out to celebrate the new chapter in our lives: we had a home, some money in the bank, and were going to get married in June.

Over dinner we began planning our future together. "What about starting a family?" she said coyly.

I wanted children, but had always imagined them in my distant future. With surprise, I realized I was already there: we had the dogs, the house, the wedding, and a financial cushion, and my company was going full bore again. All the proverbial ducks were in a row. The thought of it gave me an unexpected jolt of excitement and nervousness, as well as a tremendous sense of fulfillment and contentment I had never experienced before. "Yes!" I said, and Shauna beamed.

AUGUST 9, 1998

Shauna and I were enjoying settling into married life together. It was a sunny morning. I was reflecting on how grateful I was that everything had turned out so well, when Shauna kissed me goodbye and headed out to get some groceries. I had half an hour to relax and read the paper before I needed to leave for work. I was sitting at the kitchen table with my dogs curled at my feet when the phone rang. It didn't ring differently than usual; there was no hint this call was going to change my life. People talk in retrospect about their phones ringing with a certain urgency when a loved one has been taken to the hospital, or it rings joyously when there's good news on the other end. There was no urgency, no danger signal, no warning of any kind; it was just my normal phone ringing normally.

I picked up, expecting to hear Shauna asking me what I wanted for dinner, but a man with an authoritative voice barked, "Surrender yourself."

"Excuse me?"

"This is Captain Richards of the Royal Canadian Mounted Police; your house is surrounded, do not force us to breach."

A prank call? Maybe a wrong number? I heard the Captain's words, but couldn't place any real meaning to the seriousness they represented. "I think you have the wrong…"

He cut me off, and demanded, "Don't think! Put down the receiver, go to the front door; exit with your hands above your head . . . Do it now."

I'd heard a house in the area had once been used for a meth lab; it had been raided and gutted. *Was this a drug raid? They got the wrong place!* I hated drugs, stayed away from them my whole life. "You've got the wrong number," I said, "the wrong house!"

"If you don't surrender yourself now, we will be forced to come in; we will shoot your dogs. This is your last chance," the Captain stated with finality.

The tone in his voice told me if I didn't comply, the consequences would be terrible. I told my dogs to stay as I stepped out the front door; I closed it quickly behind me so they couldn't follow. I put both my hands in the air, turned away from the front door, and turned towards the enormity of what was happening.

Two helicopters hovered high overhead and all access roads around my house were blocked by police vehicles. Two officers, dressed in black with *RCMP* printed in white across their flak jackets, approached me quickly from left and right with their guns drawn.

"Get on your knees, interlock your fingers behind your head," one ordered. I had no choice; I did what I was told.

The officer on my right holstered his weapon, placed his hands over mine, and forcefully pulled them down behind my back one at a time, snapping them in cuffs. The other officer kept his weapon trained on me.

"Don't hurt my dogs!" I pleaded.

As they placed me in the back of a police car, I caught a glimpse of a man and woman dressed in grey suits. She had a coffee in her hand as if this was just another day at the office. They stood apart from the other officers, more like observers than part of the team that surrounded my home. Before the car door slammed shut I heard the woman in the suit call out, "Stay out of the residence; there's no search warrant, just a warrant for his arrest."

As the RCMP officers slid into the front seats, I said, "You've made an error, you must have the wrong house."

The officer in the passenger seat turned around. "Christopher Fulton?" he asked.

"Yes," I said, realizing with shock that he wouldn't have known my name if this was a mistake.

"This is the biggest warrant we get in Canada. I'm notifying you that I'm required to write down everything you say. I've already recorded that you've stated we made an error and we must have the wrong house, but I assure you, there is no error. You're on the United States Top Ten Most Wanted list, considered armed and dangerous."

I tried to comprehend what was happening; my reality had just turned upside down.

***

At the police station they shackled my legs and transferred me to a secured transport vehicle. I slid onto the metal bench in the back; there were no windows. They must have driven me for over two hours; I had no idea where I was. When the vehicle stopped and the doors swung open, I found myself in an underground garage. The officers took me, shuffling in shackles, into a building where I was processed, fingerprinted, photographed, stripped naked, deloused, and thrown into an observation cell.

I don't know how long I was kept there, maybe a week or more; there was no clock and the lights never dimmed or went out. The hum from the fluorescent lighting was ever present, and the smell of disinfectant was overpowering. Three of the cell walls were glass. Nothing I had ever experienced could have prepared me for this. I was kept totally naked and exposed. It was base and animalistic. The room was excessively cold, the floor raw concrete; it was an icebox that numbed my body and soul.

Twice during my stay I was given a stiff canvas jumper with snaps up the front, one size fits all. Once dressed, I was cuffed by a guard through a slot in the door and taken to a room where a doctor asked me questions: "How do you feel?"

Cold, alone, frustrated, anxious, confused, uncomfortable, angry . . . but I answered her questions generically. I didn't appreciate being forced into the most stressful situation of my life, then scrutinized with a psychological evaluation.

"Do you ever have thoughts of suicide?"

Not until I was taken here. "No."

"Do you ever have violent tendencies?"

Only towards whoever is behind this. "No."

"Do you feel the need to circumvent authority?"

Not until a few days ago. "No."

"Do you feel like no one understands you?"

I've been placed in a zoo; taken away from my wife, my dogs, my home, and everything I love, to be stared at in a cell, stark naked, for over a week, with some crazy, mad-scientist bitch asking me stupid fucking questions . . . this experience was starting to change me; I didn't even recognize my own internal monologue anymore. "Why are you asking me these questions?" I demanded.

She didn't answer right away. "Mr. Fulton, this is standard procedure for extradition."

Standard procedure? Wait, what? "U.S. Extradition?"

"I'm sorry," the doctor said, "I can't discuss anything more with you." The uncomfortable session ended abruptly.

I knew extradition was a very expensive and complicated political undertaking, something that would make headlines. I was in a lot of trouble if the U.S. Government wanted me this badly. It *must* be about the evidence, and my meeting with John Kennedy Jr.

Back in my cell, food was delivered through the slot in the door; when I finished eating, I put the empty tray back through the slot. There was no opportunity to speak to a guard, or anybody. Other than the doctor, I had contact with only one other person: a young woman. I had to get up routinely to keep the circulation going in my legs. It was during this exercise that I noticed her, just standing there, fully dressed, outside my cell; she appeared frightened. "It's alright," I said jokingly, "This sort of thing happens to me all the time. My name is Christopher."

"Rebecca," she said.

"What are you doing here, Rebecca?"

"I don't know, they arrested me and brought me here. I think I'm supposed to be going somewhere else, but they just left me here."

"Did they arrest you because you hurt somebody?"

"No," she said.

"Then I'm sure everything will be fine, try not to be upset."

I wasn't thinking about myself; I just wanted to help her. Although she was clothed and I was completely naked, we spoke normally. There was nothing sexual about it; we were just trying to figure things out: base humanity reaching out to each other looking for something to hold onto. It seemed this was the only real conversation I'd had since I'd been arrested, but it wasn't long before a female officer came and escorted her away. I would never know for sure if our chance meeting had been just that, or a manufactured psychological test.

When they finished observing me anatomically and psychologically, I was released from the glass walls and placed in a maximum security immigration holding facility. It was overcrowded, with up to six people stuffed in a cell. I had just gone from a twisted deserted island to a miserable busy downtown street.

There were two tiers on two adjacent walls, a shower on each tier, and a group of metal tables in the center of the ground floor. Opposite the tiers was a front desk, constantly manned by an unarmed immigration officer. Above him, raised on a second level, was a tinted glass control room where several other immigration officers, alongside video cameras trained on the cells, monitored everything, all day, every day.

I was taken to the first cell on the right side of the upper tier. One of my cellmates was a European named Dietrich. He told me he was in for a drug-related offense, but I never asked any specifics. My other cellmate was a meth junkie named James.

The place was crazy; every day officers brought in methamphetamine pills to keep the addicted detainees from crashing and becoming violent. That meant James was always high. He never stopped talking, and he never slept, so I couldn't sleep either.

During one of his incessant rants, he confessed to a murder the authorities didn't know about. He told me that when his drug boss died, he inherited the territory. His boss had owed a lot of money to another drug dealer, so James also inherited that debt. Rather than pay, he put on a hoodie, went to the bar where the dealer hung out, walked up, rapidly stabbed him in the neck numerous times, and simply walked out the back of the bar. Apparently it was the perfect murder, because they never got him for it.

This facility was supposed to be for people with immigration problems only, but because the Canadian prison system was so overloaded, they also used it to hold drug offenders and murderers for pretrial. Most of the men didn't care about anybody but themselves; they had no remorse for what they had done, and given the opportunity, they would gladly do it over.

One of the guys was called Little Capone, in for multiple murders, armed robbery, kidnapping, and assault. He told me he killed someone with a baseball bat, just because he enjoyed the sport of it. He was merciless; when he got out he would kill again. Two other men, in for first-degree murder, shared Little Capone's mentality. I watched all three of them sentenced to only two years in prison for their crimes.

A few men stood out from the rest. One had flown into Canada to find work so he could send money home to his family. When customs agents discovered he lacked the proper documentation, the authorities brought him here. Good-hearted people should never have to cohabitate with drug hounds who never thought twice about taking another's life; it lacked all sense and reason. Officer Jacob, a senior immigration officer who was about to retire, seemed to feel bad about that man's situation, as well as my own.

Every detainee was given a specific job: wash the laundry, serve the food, clean the floors. My job was scrubbing the showers. A week into my new career, a supervising officer called me over to his desk and handed me a different chemical in an unlabeled jug. "Make sure you use this," he ordered. "We're phasing out the other stuff."

I took the jug, turned the hot water on, and started to scrub, but when the hot water hit the new cleaner, the mixture instantly turned caustic. It only took a second for the pain to overwhelm me; the searing in my eyes brought me to my knees. I reached out for a cloth or cold water, anything that might assuage the burning pain, but there was nothing. I crawled out of the shower on my hands and knees, coughing, trying to hold my arm against my face.

Once free from the vapors, I tried to open my eyes; the officer who had given me the chemical cleaner was no longer at his desk. I felt my eyes swell shut, then I couldn't see anything.

I heard Officer Jacob call my name. "Christopher, what happened to you?"

I tried to make my way towards him. "It was a new chemical for the showers; I don't know what it was, it didn't have a label. As soon as I turned on the hot water it started burning."

"Who gave it to you? Taft?" he asked. I didn't say anything.

"That stuff wasn't for cleaning showers," he said, "you're going to need to see a doctor; I'll put in a request."

Since I couldn't see, Dietrich brought me food so I could stay in the cell. After three days, two officers escorted me out of the secured block. Being unable to see put me in a very vulnerable position. One of the officers must have seen my concern. "Don't worry," he said, "we're not going to beat you; this isn't the United States." I heard a car pull up, and I was helped inside.

At the doctor's office I was ordered to sign a waiver releasing the immigration facility from any liability because "the swelling and damage to my eyes was in no way related to the cleaning chemicals I was given."

"What happens if I don't sign?" I asked.

"I won't be able to give you anything to reduce the swelling or help you regain your eyesight," the doctor said.

I didn't have much of a choice, so I signed the paper and prayed the damage was temporary. I knew I might not survive immigration hold if I was permanently blind. I was issued drops that would hopefully help my vision come back once the swelling went down; then I was returned to the holding facility. I stayed in my cell, waiting for any signs of improvement.

***

The holding facility had many unwritten rules, particularly about who got to use the phones, and when. A lot of the guys were habitual, and the phones were a direct link to their lawyers, or the police, so they could snitch on other detainees or pretrial inmates. When new guys came in, the regulars would play it cool, get close, and instill a bond of friendship in the harsh environment. Undoubtedly the newcomer would share details of their case with their newfound confidants. Then the regulars would head directly to the phones, offering up details of what they had just been told in hopes of reducing their own sentences.

I was sitting in my cell, still unable to see, when I heard a scream emanate from the phone bank. The block was immediately put on twenty-four-hour lockdown. James asked me if I saw anything. "No," I said, gesturing to my severely swollen eyes. A detainee in an adjoining cell said he saw one of the prisoners dart out and head to the phones. "I saw it," said Dietrich, "Malcolm went to use the phones; I don't know why he did it, he knew better. Then another guy, I think his name is Jerry, came up and threw a cup of boiling sugar in his face."

"What?" I said, morbidly curious. "How did he get boiling sugar?"

"Jerry works in the kitchens," Dietrich stated. "He must have been stockpiling sugar packets. Do you know what happens when you get boiling sugar thrown at you?"

"No."

"You reflexively put your hands up to your face, but they stick, and when you try and pull them away, the skin comes off."

I never heard what happened to Malcolm after that, but his wounds would have been treated by some butcher doctor, and he probably lived out the rest of his sentence, and life, disfigured and in pain.

***

As the days passed, the swelling in my eyes went down until I was able to open them again. I kept using the drops from the doctor, and my sight did improve, but I would never see the way I did before. It was like looking through a muddy windshield with bad wipers, but it was better than nothing.

When I was able to work again, I was placed in food service. It was alright; I was able to keep to myself and stay away from trouble. The food was awful stuff, unrecognizable mush that was ninety percent filler. The cook told me they put additives in the food in every max security facility to keep the detainees calmer; I didn't want to eat what I was serving. On occasion I was able to acquire chocolate bars, prepackaged and un-tampered with. I ate those as often as I could. Not only did it keep me from having to eat the prison food, but I also put on a substantial amount of weight, which was a plus in a place like this.

One detainee was vegan; he refused to eat altogether. There were no natural foods: no greens, no vegetables. I literally watched him start to waste away. I was amazed at his tenacity, his sheer strength of will. The authorities eventually gave in and served him something he would eat, but there was no doubt in my mind: if they hadn't, he would have let himself die. On another day of many, the officer at the front desk stood up with a clipboard in his hand and said in a loud voice, "Someone's tested positive for tuberculosis, you've all been exposed; you'll all have to be quarantined and tested."

Things just kept getting better.

28

Red White and Bars

Prison Time

Finally the day came when I would be told something about my situation. A guard took me out of the block, down a corridor, and into a long room of booths; each had an uncomfortable metal stool behind a window. I was told to sit.

The window was a thick, bulletproof piece of glass positioned between me and a man sitting in front of me; it had a circular vent in the center to speak through. As I sat, the man began speaking. "I'm Larry Schumer, from the public defender's office in Washington State. I was asked to come here to speak with you today in regards to your case, and to ensure that you have U.S. legal counsel. I am required to go over everything with you, so please, let me get through it before you ask any questions."

Mr. Schumer retrieved a heavy pile of documents from his briefcase before continuing. "Mr. Fulton, you're being charged with multiple counts of three different felonies. The first is structuring to avoid tax reporting requirements: the IRS claims you moved your funds within the United States in such a way as to avoid the federal reporting requirement of $10,000 or more per transaction."

I couldn't hold my tongue. "You're telling me that any time I legally took my own money out of the bank, or moved it from one account to another, in any amount under $10,000, it was a crime?"

"Yes," he replied, "if the IRS feels you did so in an effort to avoid reporting the funds."

"What about the times I took twenty dollars of my own money out of my own bank account? Was that a crime?"

"It's not up to me. If the IRS wants to charge you with that, they can."

What a load of bullshit. I had never heard anything like it before in my life. Beside me, the other detainees talked to their own legal counsel; could they hear this crap? A Middle Eastern man sat in the booth directly to my left; I wondered what he was dealing with: was it warranted? I heard his counsel say, "Large donations . . . you won't have to testify . . . State Department . . . you'll be released very soon." It seemed he was in a far better position than I was.

"Please let me continue, Mr. Fulton," Mr. Schumer said. "The second felony is bank fraud, which derives from a federal guarantee letter you signed at Riggs Bank. They claim you falsified your income in the United States at the time you signed the letter, and therefore committed bank fraud."

It was true; ten years before, I had fudged my income, when I first took out a loan to start up my business in Potomac, Maryland. A close friend of mine told me he had done it to start up his successful business and convinced me to do the same. He never faced prison time.

"What's a federal guarantee letter?" I asked. "I was under the impression I just took out a regular loan."

"It's a guarantee that allows the government to step in and assume your loan, so you owe the government, not the bank. The third felony derives directly from the second; it's called access device fraud. The credit cards issued to you in the United States were based on your falsified income statement signed at Riggs Bank; therefore, anytime you used any of those credit cards, you committed counts of access device fraud."

For the first time I truly understood the phrase "making a federal case out of it." If I wasn't living it, I wouldn't have believed it. I knew there was more to this than what I was being told.

Schumer went on, "Each count and charge goes towards a federal point system called 'the federal guidelines for sentencing.' I'm not an expert at interpreting all the variables, it's very complicated, but I can tell you, you are looking at decades in prison."

Decades? I thought I must have misheard him.

"The Federal Government wants you back in Washington D.C., but I've been instructed to inform you that you have a legal choice to make: you can either waive your extradition rights, be transferred to Washington State, plead guilty to all of the counts and charges against you, and you'll be looking at a maximum of fifty years by statute, or you can waive your extradition rights and be transported to Washington D.C., where you can request a trial and fight the allegations. Your last option is to fight extradition and become a fugitive from U.S. justice. I'll need your decision as soon as possible." He gave me two minutes to think about it.

Two minutes . . . how could I come up with an answer in two minutes? *Fifty years?* My mind was crowded with thoughts of escape. I was a caged animal, cornered and harried, overcome by a primal urge to break out of my snare.

The public defender returned with a cold distance between what he was saying and my life; he would be going home to his wife, his children. "What do you want me to tell them, Mr. Fulton?"

I couldn't break away in a frenzy, or silently sneak out of custody and somehow get back to the way things were; I was paralyzed. "I'll give you my answer after I speak with my Canadian attorney," I said, "he's here to see me now. Please give him your contact information before you leave; his name is Roger Stein."

I trusted Roger; I was desperate to speak with him. It comforted me to know he had come; I needed someone on my side. Roger took a seat where U.S. Public Defender Schumer had just been. "Christopher, how are you?"

Without much effort to hide my confusion, disgust, and frustration, I said, "What the *fuck* is going on?"

Roger looked at me pityingly and cut to the chase. "They're stonewalling me; nobody is telling me anything. From what I can tell, your warrant and indictment are sealed; they definitely want you back in Washington D.C."

"They're charging me with structuring to evade reporting requirements for income tax in the States, and bank fraud," I said. "I've never tried to dodge paying income tax in my life. I file in Canada . . ."

Roger saw my panic and said, "You've been told more about this than I have."

"Can't you help me?! I'm looking at fifty years in prison!" Hearing myself say it aloud curdled my blood and stopped my heart . . . this was insane. "I'm your business attorney in Canada; I can't practice in federal court in the States," Roger said. "God, Christopher, I'm so sorry."

I thought I should tell Roger everything, just in case he could think of some way to assist me. "Look," I said, "I sold something in New York a few months ago, I'm not supposed to talk about it, but you're my lawyer . . ." I hesitated. Roger looked lost. "I sold physical and documentary evidence in JFK's assassination, evidence Bobby Kennedy had collected and with-held from the government in the '60's. I gave a private interview to John F. Kennedy Jr. in Florida for an exposé about it. It's going to run in *George* magazine. These U.S. Federal charges must be the government's way of controlling the situation."

Roger's eyes grew wide, as if I were telling him a strange joke and choosing a strange time to tell it. He half smiled and said, "Are you serious?"

I tried not to yell. "Roger you know me, look at where I am . . . Do I look like I'm *not* fucking serious?"

"God, I'm sorry," he said, instantly recognizing his mistake.

I spoke as calmly as I could. "I had a photo book deal with a man named Robert White. While I was in Florida with John Jr., he told me White had been under investigation by the FBI for obtaining items of national security that were willed to him by President Kennedy's personal secretary, Evelyn Lincoln, and that he was forced into signing an agreement with the United States Justice Department to avoid prosecution. My charges must be directly related to all of this. What should I do?"

"Jesus, Chris, Jesus Christ! You're going to have to hire a top U.S. criminal attorney to do the federal casework. That means tons of money, but your assets are all frozen. Canada is cooperating with the U.S. Government fully on this through the U.S. Embassy and State Department; they're all over your case. I can't even think of an attorney to recommend to you; just try and get someone who is local where your court case will be held so they'll be familiar with the judge and court prosecutor's office. This is going to be a very rough ride, Chris. From what I hear, the federal system in the States turns very slowly, and once you're indicted they have a ninety-eight percent conviction rate. You're going up against the whole United States Government: the best lawyers in the world!"

"What do I do, Roger? I need *real* advice."

"Right, sorry . . . You could force the government to hold a hearing in Canada, fight them taking you back to the United States, fight extradition. It could take up to five years, and they won't like it; they'll hit you as hard as they possibly can. Your main problem with fighting extradition is that you're a U.S. national. With this much pressure you won't be granted bail; the Canadian Government will fold. It won't matter that you're a Canadian citizen in good standing, the U.S. will push it through anyway. This is way over my head, Christopher . . . God, I'm sorry I can't be of more help."

It sounded like there was no way to escape my frightening circumstance. I was a fly in a web, waiting for the spider to decide what to do with me: kill me right then and there, or wrap me up and save me for later. I had no real choices.

Roger said if I got a trial I could fight. I slowly started to breathe again. There was logic in what he said; I liked logic. I just had to keep breathing. Going to Washington, D.C. would at least get me the hell out of here, although not the way I wanted.

"What do you want me to tell Shauna?" he asked.

I hung my head with the weight of the question.

"She told me to tell you she's going crazy," Roger continued. "She needs to know what's going on. She knows where you are and wants to come see you as soon as possible."

I was silent. I equated everything I had just learned to being told I had a terminal disease. This was all bad, it would not resolve quickly; my business and reputation would certainly fail . . . I might not even live through it. But above all were Shauna and the dogs, they were most important. Once I really started to comprehend my situation, what seemed like a rational decision reversed.

I couldn't make eye contact with Roger. "Tell her I love her very much . . . Tell her what's going on, but that I can't see her now . . . There's still some money in our joint account; do whatever you can to get it released for her."

"Of course." Then he said goodbye, but it looked like he was saying it at my funeral.

It was clear he couldn't help me at all; maybe no one could.

29

KNOCKING AT THE DOOR

PRISON TIME

I was approached by the Middle Eastern detainee I had sat beside while talking to the lawyers. He had cropped grey hair, a neatly trimmed beard, and a British accent. "Hello, my name is Amir, nice to make your acquaintance. Christopher, isn't it?"

Over the next week, Amir and I spoke often and developed a trust. He was a worldly man of means and had been given the best formal education. When we spoke, I felt I had stepped out of my surroundings; I wasn't locked up in a nightmare. Amir didn't belong here, like I didn't belong here, and that helped me keep my sanity.

My cellmate Dietrich and I had also become friends; close quarters tend to make you friends or bitter enemies, and becoming enemies with a cellmate is very dangerous. Dietrich possessed a moral compass, and was easy to get along with. I can't say we were friends in the traditional sense; we watched each other's backs. It was strength over isolation.

One day, as Dietrich and I sat at one of the metal tables on the ground floor, a man in his fifties walked over to us and sat down. I had seen him before; I'd heard he was dangerous. He had a reputation as a psychopath's psychopath; everyone feared him and kept their distance. He looked at Dietrich and said, "Take off," with authority. Dietrich looked at me before he moved a muscle; I gave him a nod that said I would be alright, so he got up and left.

"What do you want?" I said.

"Do you know who I am?" he asked.

"No."

"They call me the Baker. I'm a professional problem solver; I take care of people for the right price."

"You murder people," I said, with neither malice nor acceptance.

"No, no, that's too harsh," he said with a smile. "I make them disappear, like magic, for a fee. I'm very good at it."

"I'm sure you are, Mr. Baker, but I have no interest in your line of work."

"Listen," he said, his smile gone. "I know you're smart; I need you to do me a favor."

I didn't want anything to do with him, but I thought in this place doing him a favor might not leave me in a bad position, whereas not doing him one might.

"What do you want from me?" I asked.

"Not much, I just want you to write a letter."

"Ok? Can't you write your own letter?"

"I want you to ask for a typewriter; if you ask they'll give it to you, and I know you'll use the words I need to get what I want."

"Fine," I said, "I'll help you." I would word it and type it, and then he would be indebted to me.

"Good," he said, "it's good to have friends here, and later when you get out…"

Jesus. This was the last man I wanted to see if I ever got out. "Look," I said, "I'll do this for you now, but that's it."

I put in a request for a typewriter and paper for legal communication, and true to the Baker's assurance, I was granted permission to use a private, all-glass secured room within the facility.

As I sat at the table, I positioned myself to make sure the Baker was in front of me, not behind. I typed out the date and asked, "Who am I addressing this to?"

"The Attorney General of Canada, in Ottawa."

Shit. I knew I shouldn't have had anything to do with it, but I reminded myself I was, in essence, just a typist; I wasn't the one sending the damned thing.

The Baker dictated: "You've got me in this shithole place again, you motherfucker."

I looked him, then back at the white paper, and typed: *Dear Sir, I am now detained at the maximum security immigration holding facility in British Columbia.*

It was difficult to read the keys; I couldn't see the way I did before. I had taken that for granted … Hell, I had taken *everything* for granted.

Baker said, "You put me in here every time, but there will never be a trial, because you never find a body."

Your sustained efforts to prosecute me in a murder trial have been futile, as no evidence has come forth to convict me.

Before he went on, he turned to me and said, "If you ever have to kill anyone and get rid of the body, put it in a plastic bag, and take it out on a private boat at night, at least twenty miles out from shore. Stab the body and punch holes in the bag before you dump it in the ocean; that way the blood can drain out into the water and it's bon appetite for the fishes."

I thanked him for his insight before he continued his dictation.

"You stupid goddamn motherfucker, if you don't stop this fucking harassment . . ." he paused for me to type.

Sir, if you do not cease and desist in your attempt to incarcerate me . . . I looked at the Baker and waited for him to continue.

"I will kill your family. I will find out where you live, and murder every last one of the people you love."

I will visit you upon my release to discuss these matters in person, to the great detriment of you and your family.

"Fuck you, from the Baker," he concluded.

Sincerely, Mr. Baker

I took the paper out of the typewriter and handed it to the Baker. He read the letter then looked at me expressionless. "You see," he said, "I knew you would be better at this than me," and he broke into a smile.

***

I later mentioned to Amir what I had been cornered into doing for the Baker.

"That man is an animal," Amir said. "Try to avoid him at all costs." He looked at me poignantly. "Christopher, what he had you write doesn't carry a penalty here in Canada, but in the United States, a threatening letter like that to the U.S. Attorney General carries a penalty of life imprisonment. The American extradition you are facing is far more serious than what that Canadian man will ever come up against here, even though he is a murderer. Never get yourself in that kind of position again."

I took his advice to heart.

"Allah commands that I, as a Muslim, should do right for other people as if they were my own family. I couldn't help hearing your conversation with your lawyer before we first met; I overheard everything about your case, but I wanted to know you better before I spoke openly with you. I think I can help."

Any hope in this place was a rare and precious commodity. I was hungry for hope.

"I am close friends with Bill and Hilary Clinton," Amir continued. "With your permission, I can contact them on your behalf and see if they would be willing to speak to you, and perhaps help you. I would have to share your situation with them; would that be acceptable?"

Amir's words triggered an instant surge of optimism that I might somehow be reunited with Shauna and my dogs. The feeling was overwhelming. Could Amir possibly be my ticket out? I couldn't speak the words fast enough. "Yes," I said, "of course, you have my permission."

A few days later Amir told me his lawyer had been successful in contacting the president and the First Lady, and I had permission to write to them. Amir provided the personal address I would need to get my letter to them directly; he also gave me their private phone numbers.

Again I requested a typewriter and found myself in the glass room, only this time I was doing something for myself, something I hoped would lead to my release.

Dear Mr. President and Mrs. Clinton,

I am an American and Canadian citizen. I am incarcerated in an immigration hold in British Columbia, Canada, at the request of the United States Attorney General's office. The U.S. State Department and U.S. Embassy are in full cooperation with the request for my extradition back to Washington, D.C., on criminal tax charges.

These proceedings hide their true motivation; they are, in fact, in an effort to gain control of non-secured and non-classified materials and information regarding the assassination of President John F. Kennedy. As the members of the Assassination Records Review Board were appointed by you, and report to you directly, I know you are familiar with the situation. I ask that you contact President Ronald Reagan if you require further clarification.

I am offering to place all materials in my possession related to the JFK assassination in your custody, with your commitment for their full disclosure to the American public. Please intervene on my behalf for mediation and/or relief in this matter. I respectfully await your reply.

Sincerely,
Christopher Fulton

30

MOST WANTED

PRISON TIME

It was hard adjusting to being locked up; it was so different from life as a free man. Human nature was still human nature, but everything was under pressure, a focused spotlight that intensified everything. When one man confronted another behind bars, there was no neutral corner. After names were called and challenges issued, the precarious balance of everyday life was upset, and in the plainest terms, something had to give. That's how it was when Mark called Dietrich out.

Mark was big and heavy set, 250 pounds of trouble; he had a big attitude and a big mouth to match. He would constantly brush his long greasy brown hair behind his ears as he ran his mouth to anyone who listened, but ninety percent of what came out of his mouth was a load of shit.

Mark was playing cards with other detainees on the ground floor. I was sitting at my own table when Mark started loudly spouting about Dietrich, who was still on the upper tier. Mark yelled out and called him a pussy. To a free man, a comment like that would be shrugged off, or at most, settled with a fist in the face, but not here. In here, the rules were different, everything was about survival.

I didn't understand why someone would take a step down a path that they knew would ultimately lead to an all-or-nothing situation, especially when all-or-nothing meant life itself. Maybe it was the effect that captivity had on people—anything to break the monotony and despair of the menial day-to-day living; it really wasn't living at all. Sometimes it was necessary to shake things up, just to shock yourself into realizing you were still alive, even if that meant staring death in the face.

It was a public humiliation in the cell block. When Dietrich gave no immediate response, Mark sneered, and turned back to his card game. Dietrich looked down at me. We both knew if he did nothing, his once-passable existence would become a living nightmare. Mark had made him a target; whatever his motivation, it would not end well for one of them. Dietrich's look told me he wasn't about to let his life get any worse than it already was. I knew what was coming; Dietrich had to rise to Mark's comments, he needed to show everyone he would not be fucked with.

Dietrich was a volunteer trustee who served food to the other inmates when we were on twenty-three-hour-a-day lockdown. Today an immigration officer had allowed him to take a coffee pot to our cell, so he could have coffee throughout the day. He used his opportunity, grabbed the metal pot, and quickly darted down the stairs to the ground floor where Mark was still playing cards. When he hit the floor he looked at me one more time and nodded his head. I nodded back; we said goodbye in the slightest of gestures.

Dietrich stopped just behind Mark, lifted the coffee pot, and brought it down on his head with thunderous power. He followed through on the downstroke, like a machine that suffered no loss of momentum. Two blows and Mark tried to stand up. He should have been dead already; his head was bashed in, his blood pumped and spattered over the coffee pot and Dietrich's face. Mark's fellow card players scrambled out of the way; this was Mark's own doing, he would pay for his words alone. The block reverberated as the alarm sounded. Dietrich hammered the pot down into Mark's head another four times to snuff out his life. His adrenaline exhausted, he looked at me, bewildered at his inability to put Mark down.

Dietrich stepped back out of the blood that pooled under Mark's chair and watched, everybody watched. Mark stood up, blood streaming down his greasy brown hair, his head a mess of flesh and skull. He was a walking dead man. Every detainee was silent as the sound of the siren bounced off the cement walls. Mark took several painfully slow steps and collapsed before reaching the shower. I had never seen a man die like that; I had never seen murder before. It was not like in the movies. Mark had to wait for his brain to get the message, and send it to the rest of his body: that he was, in fact, dead.

Institutional murder in Canada was an automatic two years. I never saw Dietrich again.

***

After that experience, I found the courage to call Shauna; I needed to hear her voice. I had to get preapproved to contact her, so I submitted a request form and waited. Days later, I was granted permission to call my wife. I picked up the phone and followed the recorded instructions. It rang.

"Hello?" Shauna said.

I heard her voice but I wasn't connected yet. A recorded voice answered: "You are receiving a call from the Port Coquitlam Detention Center from: Christopher Fulton" (my name was said by my own pre-recorded voice). "This call will be recorded and logged. Do you want to receive this call? Press nine for yes, press seven for no."

I heard the tone of a number pressed; if she accidently hit the wrong one, I would never be able to call her again. But the recording ended and Shauna and I spoke for the first time since my arrest.

"I needed to see you," she said, "I tried to come, they told me you declined any visitors." The words spilled out of her so quickly; she spoke in emotions.

Hearing the sadness and distress in her voice was one of the hardest things I've ever had to endure. What do you tell someone you love, someone you were supposed to have forever with, when you know your life may be over? I asked Shauna if Roger had talked to her after visiting me.

"Yes," she said.

"Good. I love you so much, Shauna, but you can't take this ride with me; it could ruin your life too, and I can't let that happen."

Shauna sat silent and trembling on this other end of the impossible phone call. I hadn't been able to tell her before; it had been too painful to even admit to myself.

"I won't call you again until I know what my probable outcome will be . . . the pressure will just be too much. I need you to be ok, I need to know you and the dogs are alright or I won't make it through this."

Shauna couldn't hold back. "Roger told me the U.S. Government wants you in Washington D.C. to stand trial for evading tax reporting requirements and fraud?"

"Yes, that's what's happening on the surface," I said, burdened, "but I believe there is a lot more to this than what we're being told."

"You mean . . ."

"We can't discuss it on the phone; everything we say is recorded."

"Christopher, I'm your wife, give me something, I need something. What are we going to do!?"

I hesitated. I just had to tell her, recording or no. "Shauna, I've written to President Clinton. I should hear back sometime soon, but until then,

I just need you to know that I love you and I'm doing everything I can to fix this."

We only had fifteen minutes to speak; we used every second of it, but in the end nothing changed: I would return to my cell, and she would continue worrying in her own private hell at home.

I was allowed one more call; I used it to phone my Canadian attorney. "Roger, I wanted to let you know I've made a move to help myself, but until I hear back, is there anything else I can do? I just got off the phone with Shauna and my heart is breaking."

"You should have the extradition hearing as soon as possible," Roger said, "the U.S. expects it. You should answer them now; the longer you delay, the more they're going to think you're fighting them."

"Fine," I said, "set it up."

"Good, it won't take long."

"Will you be there?"

"I'm almost positive I won't be; I'm stuck with another client, and I'm sure your hearing will take place in the next few days. But just do it, Christopher, get it done."

"Fine," I said, feeling like I was digging my own grave; I would be cooperative in my own demise.

***

Roger was right; it only took a day before I was taken to the Supreme Court of British Columbia for an extradition hearing.

"Hear ye, hear ye, all rise for the Supreme Court Justice Wallach in the matter of United States v. Fulton extradition hearing." Chief Justice Wallach entered and sat behind the bench. "Please be seated."

A slick-looking attorney with a pompous attitude stood up and addressed the judge. "Chief Justice Wallach, I am representing the United States in this matter; I am here under direct request from U.S. Attorney General Janet Reno. My name is William Trotter."

"Counselor Trotter," said Justice Wallach, "I see I have jurisdiction over this matter. It states here that the United States is requesting that Christopher Fulton, a natural-born citizen of the United States, also a citizen and resident of Canada, be extradited from British Columbia to the United States for the purpose of enforcing charges of structuring to evade U.S. tax reporting requirements, and bank and credit card fraud within its borders, and to obtain justice in this matter. Is that correct?"

"Yes."

"There is a matter of congruency here that I am concerned about, counselor. I am responsible for the Canadian equivalence of sentence time and charges."

Trotter interrupted. "Yes, I'm aware of that, but let me stress that our government deems this extradition a matter of the utmost importance; I have the backing of the Attorney General and the Justice Department, the State Department, and the U.S. Embassy . . . If you'll read the letters before you."

The judge put on his glasses to review the documents.

Trotter continued, "Mr. Fulton is a natural-born U.S. citizen, and my government wants this handled as soon as possible."

Chief Justice Wallach looked over his glasses at Trotter. "There are procedures in Canada, sir."

"Then let's address them, and get this resolved."

The U.S. attorney was talking down to the Canadian judge, and the judge did not take kindly to it. "I see here that you have placed Mr. Fulton, who has been audited by Revenue Canada with an exemplary record, and who has no priors at all in Canada, on the FBI's Top Ten Most Wanted list: considered armed and dangerous, yet you did not ask for, nor execute, a search warrant for weapons at Mr. Fulton's residence?"

"Yes," Trotter fumbled with some of his papers, "we contacted the U.S. Marshal Service about that; it appears the FBI placed Mr. Fulton on that list by mistake."

"By mistake? I see. It was my understanding that the Top Ten Most Wanted list had to be approved by the director of the FBI. I would hate to think, Counselor Trotter, that this was a tactic used to speed up the diplomatic request to have Mr. Fulton arrested and held without bail."

Chief Justice Wallach looked at me sitting in the back of the courtroom and raised his voice. "Mr. Fulton, do you understand it is your right to fight this extradition, and fight it on several different matters of Canadian law?"

I stood and spoke clearly, "Yes, sir, I understand that. But may I ask the U.S. representative to define more clearly their intentions in seeking this extradition?"

There was an uncomfortable pause as Trotter turned to look at me for the first time. I continued my plea to the Canadian judge. "With all due respect, I'm certain I've never been armed and dangerous, but I am very uncertain about the actual reasons behind the U.S. Government's request for my extradition."

Trotter's look turned to contempt. Who was I to dare interfere with the proceedings and requests of the U.S. Government? Who was I to interfere with his job to bring me back as a trophy in chains?

Chief Justice Wallach said, "Counselor Trotter, please define the parameters of the extradition to Mr. Fulton."

Trotter, in continued aggravation, said, "Judge Wallach, you have all the documentation you require, and then some. You understand . . ."

Wallach stopped him mid-sentence: "Counselor Trotter, it is by Canadian law necessary to turn, face Mr. Fulton, and explain to him the charges against him and the reasons for the request of his extradition."

"Your Honor . . ." Trotter continued to object.

But Wallach held firm. "You will do as I request, now please."

I could see Trotter was fuming, but he held his tongue. He turned, walked the rows of empty benches to where I was, and held his face within inches of mine. I could smell coffee on his breath. Trotter spoke quietly so only I could hear, "Listen to me, you little son of a bitch. The U.S. Government wants you, and I am going to deliver you. We can play these games all day long, but it won't change a goddamned thing; in the end I *will* get you. Is that clear enough for you?" Then Trotter spoke aloud for the judge to hear. "Do you understand, Mr. Fulton?"

"Yes," I said, "I understand."

Chief Justice Wallach was satisfied it was on the record, and Trotter smirked as he walked back to his place before the bench.

Wallach continued, "Now with that understanding, Mr. Fulton, what is your decision? Will you contest the U.S. Government's request for your extradition on matters of Canadian law, or will you waive those rights and concede to their extradition request?"

This was it: turn left, turn right, or stagnate at the crossroad. I loved the United States, but here was a man representing its government, telling me in no uncertain terms that I was going to be broken under the yolk of their resolve, yet my home, my dogs, and the woman I loved were in Canada. I had just written the President of the United States requesting his assistance, but I was not about to share that information in this courtroom. I couldn't give my answer until I got a response from the White House.

"Your Lordship, am I able to think on this matter?" I asked.

"No, Mr. Fulton, I'm sorry, you will have to decide now."

Trotter looked back at me again, expecting me to waive my rights and expedite the extradition. I looked him dead in the eye: "Your Lordship, I'll contest."

The gavel hammered down. Trotter's grin turned into a flat, thin line of malcontent. I knew he would report the decision back to Janet Reno's office, and I knew it would not go over well.

31

FALSE FLAG

PRISON TIME

"Fulton!" My name rang out from the front control desk of the immigration hold. It was Officer Taft; Officer Jacob was there too. I assumed it had something to do with my eyes. "I have to give this to you personally," Jacob said. "It came through the Attorney General of Canada from the President of the United States." Officer Taft looked up, shocked.

"Thank you," I said, and headed back to my cell to open and read it privately.

This was it: the president had agreed to communicate with me, and his response was going to be my ticket back to the real world. My hand shook as I tore open the envelope. Inside I found a standard embossed greeting from the president and a personal letter addressed to me from the White House. The letter was to the point:

> Dear Mr. Fulton,
> We have received your request for assistance regarding your case. We appreciate the trust and confidence that your request represents; however, we are unable to offer assistance in this matter due to the fact that you are outside the borders of the United States of America.
>
> Please be assured that your request received a thorough review, and it is my hope that your matter can be resolved to your satisfaction as soon as possible.
>
> Sincerely yours,
> Hillary Rodham Clinton

The president hadn't addressed me personally, but the First Lady had. *What did it mean?* I knew they understood who I was and what was happening. The First Lady's letter seemed to be pulling me back to the United States, which was exactly what the U.S. Government was already going to great lengths to accomplish. I'd hoped the president would intercede on my behalf, at least confer with the attorney general's office, but he removed himself from the situation almost entirely.

I wondered if Amir had truly attempted to help me or if he had taken my information to the White House simply to help himself. I couldn't ask him, he had gone home; he wasn't stuck in this place anymore.

The whole U.S. Government wasn't after me for a matter of bank fraud; it was a spiteful and vicious attack in response to what happened in New York and Miami. But in the end, it was like Counselor Trotter said: it didn't matter what I did, it wouldn't change a goddamned thing.

I would have to call Shauna and tell her about my failed rescue and my decision to fight the extradition. I would plead with her not to visit me; I couldn't stand the thought of her seeing me like this. I would tell her it could take years, but I would come home to her . . . But this moment felt like my forever, and I wanted to die.

***

New detainees came in all the time, and there was always an adjustment process involved. Like a new animal being introduced to the pack, they would either be welcomed in, or torn apart. One of the new guys was much older than most of us, in his late 60's. He was scared and everyone could see it like a bull's-eye.

I was sitting at a table on the ground floor when he came up to me looking like he might collapse with fear. "What's the matter with you?" I snapped. I couldn't show the normal concern or care I would have on the outside. This was a different world: compassion was weakness, and weakness made you a target.

"I, I shit in the shower," he stammered. "I just, I just, I can't stay here, I'm not going to make it."

"Listen to me, you're fine," I said sternly, looking around. "Nobody's been in the shower since you came out. Don't say a word, just go back and clean up your mess. Do it quickly. You have to be a different person in here and you are off to a bad start."

He nodded his head and turned back to the shower.

Another new detainee became very significant in my situation. He was a bruiser, a sledgehammer of a man: 6′6, and at least 300 pounds. There had been rumors that the most aggressive inmate in the whole facility was being transferred to our block; this had to be him.

After checking in with the guard at the front desk, he walked directly up to me. He just stood there, at the edge of the table, and scowled down at me. Then his voice thundered throughout the block: "What do you mean by that, you disrespectful FUCK?"

I didn't say a word. Everyone took notice, and I quickly realized what was happening. I thought of Dietrich; I'd just been pushed into the arena at the Colosseum. I had been surprised by his theatrics, but they were effective. The hulk of a man kept yelling at me, "I'm gunna kill you for that." He made like he was going to break my arms off. The alarm sounded for lockdown, and I could see the guards were already outside the only entrance, waiting for the door to be released by the guards in the upper control room. Had they anticipated something kicking off with the transfer? Apparently, and I was at the center of it.

The door opened. I didn't resist as the guards pushed me to the floor, but the bad-ass did. It took about six guards with batons to get him to his knees. The whole damn time he yelled, "You're dead, I'm gunna get you, you fuck; I'm gunna *kill* you."

The two of us were taken to our respective cells: mine on the top tier, his the opposite corner on the bottom. I decided, although trumped-up, the threat was real: it was this guy's task to either force me to comply with extradition, or kill me. Since Dietrich had been taken away I had no one to watch my back; I was totally alone . . . even James had been transferred. A guard was sent to speak to me and the bruiser separately. Luckily for me, it was Jacob; he came to my cell first. He stood outside my door and loudly said, "Detainee Fulton, what's the story?" Then he called to the control room, "Pop this cell." The lock chinked, the door slid open and he came in.

He walked over to the bunk where I sat pensively. "What happened down there?" he asked.

"I have no idea," I said, not able to give him my whole story. "I was sitting there when this side of a barn came up to me issuing threats in retort to an insult I never made; I never said a word to the guy."

"Listen, Chris, that asshole's been trying to get in this cell block since you arrived. He's an enforcer for a gang on the outside and he's extremely violent. Yesterday he put a guy in the infirmary and was finally transferred here."

"Do you know what he wants with me?" I asked.

Jacob looked at me as if to say, *You expect me to know?* but said, "I'm going to try and get you relocated before I retire. Maybe I can convince them they can't afford to have a problem with you, but it could take a few days." He sat down on the bunk beside me. "I know this guy; do what you have to do to protect yourself. If it comes down to it, it'll be just you and him, and one of you will die." When he stood up, a Bic pen was sitting on my mattress.

I stayed in my cell with the pen in my hand for the next twelve hours, waiting for the enforcer to cross my threshold. He would likely come just before the last lockdown of the day, slip in right before the cell door closed, and we'd be locked in together, trying to kill each other before anyone could reach us. I didn't want it to come to that; he was a mammoth, and although I could move quickly, I didn't think I would stand much of a chance in such close quarters. I prayed. The last lockdown of the day came and my cell door closed and secured. I had one more night to be myself: not a murderer, and not dead.

I felt bad for myself, but I felt worse for Shauna; her life had been put on hold with no answers, no understanding, and I had caused it. It was gross overkill, but that didn't matter; this was how things were now. Maybe it would be better if I was killed, then Shauna could get on with her life. It was eating me alive, but I wasn't ready to give up; I still longed for my life with her and the dogs, and the future we had planned together. Fifteen minutes later my cell door popped, and Jacob walked in. "You're being transferred."

"Where to?" I asked.

"A regular prison."

I knew that was illegal; I hadn't been sentenced or even charged in Canada.

"The U.S. wants you bad. If you waive your extradition rights, you'll be transferred immediately out of here to a regular prison, then extradited to the States. You could leave in the morning."

My heart sank. Where there's a will there's a way; just like Trotter said, in the end he did get me.

"Thank you, I'll waive my rights. I'm still going to fight, but I'll do it back in D.C."

"I won't see you again," Jacob said. "Good luck."

***

The regular Canadian prison was overcrowded with asshole criminals: obnoxious, opinionated, and stupid. Amir had told me hell was the absence of reason; so now I was in hell. There was a plethora of meth heads and crack junkies that flooded the place, and the Canadian Government, in their infinite wisdom, deemed it easier, or cheaper, to continue to feed the addicted inmates their drug of choice to keep them level, rather than to employ a detox program and actually get the crazed, half-baked idiots some help.

The noise was maddening: screaming, jeering, abhorrent profanities, and the intolerable continual ramblings of total nut jobs. It never quit, there was no escape, and I thought if I had to spend too long in this place, I would soon become one of the drooling, yammering, mentally dead zombies that raised the unholy cacophony to begin with.

32

EXTRADITION

PRISON TIME

Two U.S. Marshals were tasked with taking me on a flight from Vancouver International Airport to Washington State to deliver me into the jaws of the United States Federal Justice system.

I wasn't wearing an orange jumpsuit, and I had no visible chains around my ankles and waist. I was in my civilian clothes, the ones I had on at the time of my arrest. The marshals didn't want to cause a stir in public, draw any attention, or distress other passengers; they wanted it all nice, quiet, and normal.

I actually looked a little bit like my old self: clean shaven, wearing grey slacks with a light blue dress shirt and a dark blue tie. They instructed me to hold my blazer over my cuffed hands so no one could tell I was a prisoner. My situation was so close to normal, I felt disoriented, out of balance. I was being hidden in plain sight from the rest of the world.

A little boy watched me. He must have been about six years old; I envied him, his whole life stretched out before him with endless opportunity. He must have seen a glint of silver from beneath my blazer, maybe even some bracelet and chain. Recognition dawned on his face and he tugged on his mother's jacket sleeve, but she shook him off. "Just a moment, honey," she said, with an audible level of irritation in her voice.

Part of me, the part that was ashamed I was in cuffs, hoped she wouldn't pay any attention to the boy, and I would pass by unnoticed. The other part, the part that was angry about the injustice I was going through, wanted the attention. I wanted her to see exactly what her son saw. I wanted to cause a stir, have the people all around me see how unfair reality can be. I wanted to break their illusion of safety; show them you can think you are prepared, think you have it all, think you have rights, but there is always a secret machine turning out of view that can grind those illusions to dust. There are always men behind the curtain pulling strings and pressing buttons that can easily shatter lives on a whim. If you never cross their agenda, you'll never know they exist, and you'll live happy and oblivious. But God forbid you take a wrong turn and accidently cross the road at the wrong time, you'll find yourself living in a story you don't recognize, and you can kiss all you know and love goodbye.

The boy continued to tug on his mother's sleeve. She abruptly turned to him with mommy words pouring out of her mouth until he was firmly subdued. The mother turned away again to attend to whatever incredibly important conversation her son had distracted her from, as I walked by, unnoticed, someone the U.S. Government had declared a fugitive, a most wanted criminal considered armed and dangerous, bound for their same flight.

As the marshals flashed their credentials, every airport official instantly bowed to them.

We swiftly bypassed every security check and customs procedure before boarding the plane. Walking on to the hunk of metal, that would soon be hurtling through the air at 500 miles an hour, made me start to sweat and my hands involuntarily shake. I knew this time I wouldn't be able to drink myself into oblivion to numb the fear that was gnawing at my guts. The senior marshal from Baltimore told me he knew everything about me from my file; he knew I was a political embarrassment who was getting sucked down by the Justice Department. Shortly after the plane took off, he removed my cuffs, allowing me to feel slightly more at ease for a few brief moments. As we landed, he wished me luck.

On the ground, Agent Clara Mancini and Agent Joe Callahan were waiting to collect me.

I recognized them as the two officials in grey suits who had observed my arrest in Canada.

When Mancini saw I wasn't in cuffs, she roared at the senior marshal, "What the hell is this? Who's running this operation, you or him?"

I felt bad he received such flack for showing me a little kindness and comfort.

I was transferred into the custody of the two agents, and fell a little further down the rabbit hole.

As I rode in the back seat of a government car, Mancini turned to Callahan. "I'm going to call the head of the marshal service and report him for taking Fulton's cuffs off." I could hear everything despite the thick plexiglass and metal grate that divided the front seats from the back.

Callahan tried to talk her out of it. "He's a good man; he's been with the service a long time. If he made that decision, it was for a reason; he knows what he's doing."

"Bullshit," Mancini snapped, "it was improper procedure."

After about ten minutes, we pulled up to the curb in front of a large facility. They had me exit on the street side and took me through the building's front door. Callahan turned to me. "You are at SeaTac Federal Detention Center; this is where you will be processed into U.S. Federal custody." They took me into an empty agency locker room. I could hear other agents talking and laughing through an open door. Callahan told me to sit, and Mancini started hammering me with blunt questions. She became angry when my answers didn't match her expectations. Callahan stepped in when her professional façade began to crack. "Is there anything you want to share with us before you're processed?" he asked.

I wanted to test their knowledge. "What do you think about the Clintons' letter?"

Agent Callahan made a mental note of my question but stayed quiet while Mancini answered angrily, "I'm not talking to you about our boss, but know this: we can do anything we want with you." She abruptly stood and walked out of the room. I had frustrated her. It seemed like she would have rather put me up against a wall and shot me in the head rather than keep questioning me . . . I figured the only thing stopping her was not having received the order to do so.

Agent Callahan looked at me and said, "Stay here," and calmly followed her.

***

Mancini had given something away. She wasn't speaking in generalizations; she was a White House agent, reporting directly to President Clinton, or at to least the attorney general.

With both of them out of the locker room, I could clearly hear the agents in the adjoining room. Their tone wasn't somber, it was more humorous, like they were telling a comedic anecdote. One federal officer said, "He had access to military shredders, had the bright idea of putting them at the border. He said he wanted to see what would happen."

"What did happen?" came another voice. "He was working for border control in Texas, right?"

"Yeah, I guess he wanted to take things into his own hands. When the wetbacks got close enough, the things detonated. About eight families were massacred: wives, children . . . they were literally in pieces, all over the place."

"Oh shit! What happened to him?"

"They dismissed him, but that was it."

"No charges?"

"Nah, they kept it quiet; you know how it is, like nothing ever happened." The room filled with laughter.

I got the distinct feeling this kind of sadistic horror story was not out of the ordinary. Before I heard any more, Mancini and Callahan came back and took me to begin my processing in earnest.

***

I was put through hours of medical questions, medical examinations, shots, psychological questions, finger printing, eye scans, and photographing. My blood was taken and sent to the FBI, and I was given a federal BOP number and told it would be part of my identity for the rest of my life. Everyone who becomes a federal detainee gets one, guilty or not. One of the agents processing me said, "Oh this guy . . . I'd say, forty to fifty years, easy!" I tried not to show any expression on my face, but his words sent a jolt through me; my fate was already sealed. This processing officer was joking around like the agents in the locker room, but this wasn't a joke either; he was guessing how many years of my life I would lose, and they were all taking bets. It was the first time I had experienced a federal employee throwing out years of someone's life with such routine abandon, but it certainly wouldn't be the last.

After being deloused with powder and shower, I was placed in a holding cell with sixteen other inmates, and one toilet. I tried to find a place to sit. While locked up in Canada I learned that you find a spot against a wall and claim it as your territory. I wouldn't move from that spot, no matter how long I had to be there: three hours, five, eight, it didn't matter. The only space left in this holding cell was next to the toilet. I had to sit there while another inmate defecated, my face parallel to the bowl. I couldn't stand up; hovering over him while he did his business would be construed as an invasion of privacy, so I just stayed put. Extreme rules manifest in extreme places. The other fourteen guys yelled at him: "Put some water on that shit." "Motherfucker, you stink." I was starting to lose the memory of who I used to be.

I don't know how much time passed before I was taken out of the holding cell. A guard escorted me to a separate room and handed me a shallow grey tub, the kind you put your possessions in when you go through an airport metal detector. He ordered me to put in a pair of underwear, an orange jumpsuit, a toothbrush and toothpaste, a white washcloth, a bar of soap, and a pair of rubber flip-flops. After that, I was put in an elevator with four guards—one on either side of me, one in front, and one behind—and delivered to the eighth floor. The doors slid open to reveal an expansive floor that was white and stark. The perimeter was lined with two tiers of cells, and heavy metal doors were controlled by a guard in a bulletproof booth. There were octagonal steel tables with stools bolted to the floor in the center of the room, same as the facility in Canada.

Inmates watched me as I made my entrance and one spoke as I walked by. "You're lucky, this is the best floor."

I couldn't see how anything about this place could be considered *lucky* or *the best*.

"Look there," he said with a grin, pointing to a slit of bulletproof glass at the far end of his cell. "We can see the women's wing from here. Sometimes they put on a show for us and strip."

This is what I had to look forward to now? I gave him a knowing smile, and continued to my own cell.

There was an inmate sitting on the lower bunk, nervously bouncing his knee up and down. He looked up at me with keen intensity. He fancied himself an intellectual and engaged me in conversation all night long; his mouth moved endlessly telling me about life and philosophy and the way things worked.

Prison was not a place where you could choose who to spend your time with, twenty-four hours a day, in the same closet space. I learned that a cellmate could be likened to a gun: if he was a good mate, he could help you survive; his conversation and companionship could keep you going. But if he was bad, the opposite was true; he could get you hurt, or killed, or put you in a very dangerous state of mind.

I was held in SeaTac for three weeks. During my first week, I got a taste of what was in store for me on the very long road ahead. Every day at mealtime, one of the toughest-looking guys in the place deliberately stared me down. His stare was not something you would see in normal society, it was a stare that cut through, blatantly with no apology; it was a challenge that had to be responded to. I got the sense that he didn't care about the outcome of what would happen, just that something *would* happen.

The first few times I ignored him, but he didn't quit. Every mealtime it was the same: an unpleasant, purposeful stare that followed my every move. Whatever this guy's problem was, I wasn't going to cower, so I stared back. When his gaze trained on me, I locked eyes on him, and glared back with the same intensity.

After a week of this silent showdown, I'd had it. The constant pressure in this place was already high enough without these unwavering staring matches every time I was allowed to eat. I walked up to the guy, forcing the other shoe to drop. As I approached, his stare softened slightly and he said, "You're all right." It turned out he had been testing me, measuring my character against a bar of cowardice and strength. Apparently, approaching him regardless of consequence was my best move.

Despite his messed-up personality test he was able to shed light on many of the dark and confusing corners of the federal penal system. I told him I would be going back to Washington D.C. but I feared flying. I asked if he thought there might be another way to get there. He laughed hard and said, "You don't think the feds know you don't like to fly? Of course they do; they love that shit. You'll fly alright, you'll fly and fly and fly. They call it diesel therapy, it's one of the ways they'll try to break you."

I had been trapped into going to Washington D.C., but now, like a cow corralled for slaughter, a nightmare of proportions I could never have imagined was about to unfold.

33

DIESEL THERAPY

PRISON TIME

While chained to other inmates, I was forced onto an unmarked plane that would take off, hit cruising altitude for ten minutes, then steeply descend. We would land, take off, climb high, descend quickly, then land and take off again, over and over, all day long. At the end of each day we were removed from the plane, strip searched, and left in holding cells in the care of a new facility where we would be processed, deloused, and subjected to other such miseries until around eleven P.M. In the mornings we were woken up at four A.M., processed out by eight, and taken on the same joy ride as the days before.

I flew all over the country like that for a month, never being told where we were landing, or going next, never told anything. I learned that an important foundation of my sanity and my emotional and mental well-being was simply to know where I was. Without that basic awareness, I became disoriented, apart from myself. I had no relation to anything: my home, my dogs, my wife; the panic ate away at me.

Sometimes to get to the plane, the guards would order us onto the runway. With our legs shackled, we'd shuffle and waddle like penguins. Federal marshals, with shotguns at the ready, stood over us as we waited, shivering for hours, to board the plane. The marshals needed to take away any illusion of power they thought we still possessed, beat into us an understanding of our own insignificance. At other facilities, we would never leave the building at all. We would be walked down the hall and through a gangway that led directly on to the plane. They had this kind of torture down to a science.

At one prison facility along the indiscriminate route, where we spent the night, the guards thought it would be entertaining to put me in a cell with a bevy of huge angry black guys they had pissed off by withholding dinner. They wanted to watch the shit get beaten out of me.

As I was pushed into the cell, the guard said, "We expect a show," then glanced up at the security camera. Several large unhappy men crowded me into a corner. Luckily the first thing to hit me was not a fist but a question: "You like fucking black chicks?"

I looked at the hulking inmate standing over me. *Damned if I do, damned if I don't.* I held my ground, answered honestly, and prepared myself to take whatever was coming. "Depends on the girl," I said.

He laughed, they all laughed; my answer amused them. But in a flash I heard a crack and felt an intense burning radiate from my nose; blood squirted everywhere.

"Don't worry, I won't hit you again," he said as I wiped the blood from my face. "Yeah, you're all right," another chimed in, "but we're still gunna take your shoes, motherfucker."

My answer to a yes or no question had awarded me a broken nose and the loss of my shoes, but it had saved me a severe beating that could have left me hospitalized, or dead. I bet the guards were pissed they were cheated out of their entertainment for the evening.

The next morning on the plane I heard the marshals talking about the new pilot: he was young, and a novice at flying con air. During takeoff he turned the plane so the wingtip wanted to kiss the ground. I don't know if he was nervous due to lack of experience, or just incompetent. Either way, we were lucky we weren't all burned up in a fiery crash, charred corpses in chains, where a coroner would joke that they would need to have a mass grave because they couldn't tell which pieces belonged where.

For a man who valued being in control, I was in absolute hell. My very life was in the hands of children, assholes, and idiots. I couldn't eat when I was hungry, I sure as hell couldn't save my life if it was threatened, I couldn't even shit when I had to shit.

If you had to use the bathroom, and you were lucky enough to get acknowledged, you had to wait until the plane reached an altitude of 10,000 feet. The guard would keep you shackled, but unlock you from your prison pals. You would be led to the bathroom by a male, or female, marshal. On a good day they would uncuff one hand and watch as you did your business; on a bad day, if the marshal had an attitude, both hands would remain shackled to the black box at your waist and they would chuckle as you tried not to piss all over yourself. This, of course, brought the discomfort of being chained back up to the other prisoners wet and stinking of piss.

The plane transported both men and women prisoners and detainees, but they were separated—women in the front quarter, men in the back. The women's wailing echoed through the whole plane. They cried and they screamed over their lost lives: the children they would never see again, their lovers that were gone forever. But they were the ones who were gone forever, swallowed alive into a heartless, hopeless system. I'm glad their loved ones were spared the hysterical cacophony that perpetually emanated from them. That sound will forever be etched into my brain. I could practically taste the agony in their cries, the absolute heartbreak that could only manifest itself in endless sobbing.

These women were often the casualties of their husbands' less-than-stellar business ethics or job choices, which were usually drug related. They would be charged with hiding an asset in their name, falsifying records, or obstruction of justice because they were trying to protect their family. They were fed into America's federal machinery, swallowed and forgotten. Maybe I'm old school, but I'm still of the belief that women should be loved and protected, not used as shields, and certainly not used as leverage.

I felt a great pity for these broken women. Some hardwiring in my brain clicked; an age-old instinct fired in me, and I felt a need to defend them. All of this was just wrong. My thoughts of self-preservation dissipated as I imagined myself free of my chains: in a flash of ultimate masculine heroism I incapacitated every air marshal, took the plane and granted freedom, ending the misery that suffocated the fuselage. But despite the burning sensation in every muscle to take action, I could do nothing but sit motionless, chained in place, forcefully paralyzed, unable to effect any change.

***

For one day I sat next to a man named Kyle. We would eventually end up in different places so we had no fear or distrust of each other and were able to strike up conversation. Kyle told me a lot about himself, but instantly caught my attention when he said he and his brother had gone to New York to auction off three exceptionally documented saxophones from the 1930's that had been played by some of the best jazz musicians of all time. The New York auction house told them the most they could expect for the three instruments was $15,000 to $30,000.

New York was still claiming to be the number one financial center of the world, where all the money was spent, and where everyone worldwide, made their acquisitions. "We weren't the Rockefellers," Kyle said, "we weren't going to be repeat customers, so they treated us like we were fools, like what we had was worthless, so someone on the inside could buy the instruments for nothing and sell them two years later and make a fortune."

He told me he and his brother decided to take their saxophones to Japan. "My brother and I know a lot of Americans who moved there and burned their passports."

"Why would they do that?" I asked, having never heard of people burning their passports before.

"They realized the U.S. Government no longer represented their best interests, or the best interests of their families. Anyway, like them, my brother and I moved to Japan for good."

"How could you live there with no citizenship and no passport?"

"The Japanese don't mind as long as we don't break any of their laws or traditions. They never try to force anything on us; they treat us with respect and dignity."

"So what happened with the saxophones?" I wanted to know how his story ended.

"The Japanese loved them; they were welcomed with admiration. The Japanese worship history, even American history, even more than Americans do. For the Japanese, it was never about trying to put us down or keeping us in our place, it was about celebrating the wonderful things we had brought to their country. We sold the saxes for 300,000 U.S. dollars."

"So why are you on con air; why aren't you still in Japan?"

"I had to visit my mother before she died. My brother stayed, but I had to come; I had to see her one last time." Kyle's voice waivered with the emotion he couldn't hide. "They're locking me up for multiple counts of tax evasion, but it was worth it to see her again."

"How long are you looking at?" I asked. I was curious to see how his fate compared to mine.

"Five to ten years."

When the plane landed at the end of the day, Kyle was delivered to another facility, and I never saw him again.

That was my life every day for a month: process out, take off, ascend, descend, ascend, descend, learn another's life history and tragedy in a brief moment, then process into a new detention center for the night. We were all being broken against the government's resolve.

I was taken off the plane for good somewhere in New Jersey. From there I was transported by secured van from prison to prison until I ended up in Washington, D.C. They were awful places, places I never would have imagined existed on American soil.

34

THE GAUNTLET

PRISON TIME

Those of us relegated to ground travel were transported in windowless vans. We were always chained together and ordered to slide down the metal benches until we were squeezed in so tightly it was impossible to be a stranger to the man next to you. As the doors shut, the air quickly became stifling. The government drivers found it entertaining to speed down the roadways at eighty miles an hour and stop or switch lanes abruptly.

I reached a turning point; I was having trouble coping with the abuse. I needed to change my personality to survive, at least for the time being. I tried on the persona of a tougher, back-talking, cursing inmate; I told the guards to fuck themselves and I spat at their feet. I caused disorder when I could, and made enough noise for the guards to pull over and give everyone some water. Funny, becoming more of an asshole created a positive effect in this shit existence. An older wise guy I was chained to, named Dino, thought my brazen defiance was entertaining.

We were delivered to a prison in New Jersey and I was kept there for a month. It wasn't like the SeaTac Facility, or any of the prisons I had been in while on diesel therapy, it was the Grand Central Station of East Coast prisons. It was privately run and leased out for both federal and state prisoners. It was so overcrowded there weren't enough bunks for the inmates. I was forced to sleep in a military transport coffin. I would get into it at night, and slide underneath a bottom bunk. I would lay there and think, *This is what it felt like for our young military men and women killed overseas taking their last trip home: perpetual silence sealed in a box.*

But I still had the chance to wake up. Through that experience, I felt for every one of them. In the morning, I would have to stick my fingers out of the crack between the top of the coffin and the bottom of the lower bunk, and slide my way out.

Dino was in the same block as me; he was in for second-degree murder but on his way home after decades of incarceration. He was left completely bedless, didn't even get a coffin. Dino told me he was a connected man in Vegas; he was Steve Wynn's best friend. He was in his 60's, and although he clearly had a checkered past, I couldn't stand the thought of him sleeping on the cold concrete floor, so I berated the guards endlessly until it became easier for them just to give in to me rather than put up with my big mouth . . . so Dino got a bed. He told me to look him up if I ever went to Vegas; he said he'd take care of me. I never took him up on his offer.

One of my cellmates was a young militant Muslim who demanded to know what my faith was. I told him I was raised Methodist. "You either convert to Islam, or it will be my duty to kill you," he said with conviction. With that he held up a copy of the Koran, pointed to it, and growled, "The truth is in *this* book." I had no intention of starting a holy war in an overcrowded prison cell so I told him I would read the book; that seemed to mollify him and he handed it to me. When I read it, I couldn't help but wonder if my bunky had actually read it himself. His murderous threats seemed to be in stark contrast to many of the peaceful teachings I read on its pages.

Halfway through my stay at the New Jersey facility, a riot broke out. One of my cellmates informed me I could choose to stay out of it, stay in the cell and be branded a traitor by the other inmates, and if the guards used tear gas, I would die of suffocation in the cramped room with the door locked down. Or, I could disregard the orders of the guards, stay outside the cell and fight; the only real danger there was being shot by a guard, or beaten or stabbed by another inmate in the confusion. I figured I might survive a gunshot, or heal from other wounds, but the thought of choking to death in a cell was enough to make up my mind for me. The prisoners took over the cell block, and the guards were forced outside. I stayed outside my cell, but remained as neutral as I could. The National Guard was called in. In the end, better living conditions were negotiated without violence. The situation ended abruptly.

When it came time for me to be transferred from that facility I was chained to a line of men. I didn't see what happened, but one of them must have provoked a guard and was promptly maced. The guard didn't care who he hit, and every man in the line was affected. I had to fight hard just to keep the air moving in and out of my lungs. Guards weren't worried about collateral damage; we were not valued cargo.

Next I was taken to the inner-city prison in Baltimore; it made my stay in New Jersey seem like the Ritz. I had been transported back into the 1800's, and not in a good way. The prison was constructed of old masonry with cobbled floors; the cells were small and uneven. Piss and shit ran between the stones, making the nights I was forced to sleep on the floor horrendous. Necessities weren't always provided. The best underwear we had were the communal pairs with the least amount of staining, and they all had stains. When we used up our allotted roll of toilet paper, we were told to use our hands.

I was brought in by a big bull captain. His only words to me were, "Keep your mouth shut; we *will* beat you here." This place was run by inner-city cops, not the feds, and they enjoyed dishing out a good beating, often.

At first I couldn't figure out why my cellmate smothered himself with his own excrement. Not just his arms and legs, but over his entire face and in his hair. It was impossible to keep downwind from him in a six by eight cell. I first thought he must have been insane, and should have been given psychiatric help, but the truth was simpler and his actions smarter than I expected: guards don't like feces.

One guard had taken a special liking to beating him, but after much trial and error, he discovered the best way to keep the officer at bay was to cover himself in shit. Although the guard no longer beat him, I bet he still got enjoyment out of watching a man suffer through covering himself in filth day after day. Forget toilet paper being a necessity–for this guy, *not* using toilet paper was a necessity.

One day a guard stopped at our cell, looked at me, and gestured to a huge smear of crap on the stone wall.

"Did you do that?" he demanded.

Did I do that? I'm a historian, and a goddamned international builder who's overseen hundreds of millions of dollars in high-rise construction; I had a home and a wife and a future, and you are asking me if I smeared shit on the wall of this God-forsaken cell? I wanted to state that perhaps it was the man who was always covered in feculence himself that might be the perpetrator of such a crime, but I didn't. Luckily, and most likely due to my shitty friend, the guard felt no need to come in and discipline me for staining the walls of his fine establishment anyhow.

229

They continued to move me from prison to prison for another month. It's hard to describe the kind of hell I was living; words aren't powerful enough to convey the exhaustion, stress, fear, filth, and absolute unending misery of being stuck in those places. Then they sent me to Charles County Detention Center, CCDC, in La Plata, Maryland.

35

TEMPORARY BODIES

PRISON TIME

Iarrived at CCDC, where the government had wanted me from the beginning. It was the fourth circuit, the toughest federal prosecution district in the country; this was where my sealed warrant and indictment had originated.

I was delivered in chains attached to rows of other damned men. Once processed into CCDC, I was afforded a meeting with a lawyer. I was taken to a private room where a fit, grey-haired man in a tailored suit stood behind a white table. "Hello, Christopher, I'm your attorney, Stephen Salvin," he said as he shook my hand. "I'm here to help you. Here is a copy of your case." He handed me a thick stack of papers. "Read it through," he said, "but don't share it with anyone. If you have any questions, ask only me."

His greasy grin told me a lot about his character, but I didn't know Stephen Salvin. My mother had searched for someone to represent me while I was being transferred across the country, but this man, from one of the most prestigious law firms in Washington, had magically appeared to offer his assistance.

"First of all, Mr. Salvin," I said, "I don't have any money to retain your services, so how is it you wound up representing me, and I'm not stuck with a public defender?"

Salvin sat down with a lipless smile. "Mr. Fulton, be assured my firm is one of the top in the country for federal litigation. Senator Edward Kennedy is amongst our many retained clients; does that make things more clear?"

Was John trying to help me? "Ok," I said, happy to think someone was on my side, "do you have a copy of my warrant?"

"No, the government has that sealed; we will not be getting a copy."

"So what's your plan?"

"They've got you in a pretty tight knit here; there are a lot of counts to deal with. You and I both know it's built on mud, but it will stick. I propose we try to circumvent it entirely. I will present a request to the attorney general to have the charges dropped in lieu of some concessions on your part. I need information from you so we can figure out how to best whet their appetite."

I spent the next two hours answering Salvin's questions. Once he was finished with me, I asked him to contact my father and find out how Shauna and the dogs were doing, and to tell them I loved them. At the conclusion of the exchange, I was taken to a two-tiered, maximum security block. Unlike the Canadian immigration holding facility, this block had two walls of glass for observation, one wall of cells, and one wall of phone banks. There were no guards inside, only inmates. German shepherds and their handlers were positioned outside both walls of glass. Again I was given a plastic tub to hold my shower flops and underwear, but now my personal effects included the private transcript of my case with the government.

I was unlocked from my chains and ordered to enter alone. A tall black prisoner with his hair in corn rows stood by the stairs with a handful of inmates crowded around him. I kept to myself, and walked up the stairs to my assigned cell.

My cellmate stood up from the lower bunk and towered above me. "My name's Leonard," he said, "but they call me Big Len."

I looked up at him, shook his hand, and said, "I can't imagine why." Len couldn't have been more than twenty years old, but he was 6'5 and 280 pounds.

"You look like you've been around," he said, "like you've been through it. Maybe you could teach me a few things?"

Now I was an old-head, a seasoned prison veteran? Big Len must have just arrived; he still bore the unbroken friendliness of a free man. But nobody would ever peg him as a target; he was just too damn big.

Our concrete bunks were covered by an inch-thick green mattress, a blanket, and a small plastic pillow. It became a necessity to wake up every fifteen minutes and turn to relieve the aching pain that bore into our hips from the cold, inflexible, concrete bunk. This was the perpetual endeavor, every night. The lights dimmed in the evening, but never went out. The passage of time was a controlled illusion.

At six in the morning a Correctional Officer, CO, yelled through a slot in the only door to the cell block: "Razors!" It was the only time we'd be allowed to shave that day. I liked the routine of shaving; it reminded me of what it felt like to be civilized. The inmates were asked their BOP numbers before being issued a disposable razor. The CO ordered us to bring them back as soon as we were done shaving. "Don't make me come in there," he warned.

I stood in front of the sink in my cell and looked intently into the polished metal that was a poor substitute for a mirror. I could make out that my head was oval, so I could estimate where the razor should go to get the job done.

I stayed to myself, but noticed that the guy with corn rows had been watching me; I wasn't sure why, but I knew it would only be a matter of time before I found out. It was a small block of only fourteen inmates.

There was a daily inspection. In the early morning we had to make our beds, then present ourselves outside the cells. Our orange jumpsuits had our names written on them in black ink.

Some jumpsuits retained names crossed out with new ones added, a reminder that we were just temporary bodies to be sorted and shipped on. Each bunkmate stood at attention to the left and right of their cell as the COs came into the block from the only entrance in the glass wall. They inspected us from the bottom left of the ground floor to the top right of the tier. I don't know what they expected to find—the place was airtight, contraband was impossible.

During the cell inspections we would be called down for individual shower inspections. Some of the guards found that job distasteful; they'd ask you to lift your junk so they could examine you, then instruct you to turn around and bend over. If you were lucky, that would be it; you could pick up a towel and leave. Other guards enjoyed the process and got physical. If you didn't cooperate, they'd discipline you right away, or they'd call the goon squad, the riot guys, to come in later and beat the shit out of you.

As I entered the shower area, a gloved guard stood in front of me. This CO didn't show any signs of disgust or anger, just anticipation. "Raise your hands over your head," he ordered. Once I did he ran his fingers through my hair, then he got down on one knee as he lifted my cock and balls to inspect them, his face directly in front of my manhood. I watched in anguish as he started to stroke himself through his pants. Fortunately for me he couldn't linger, as other inmates were waiting their turn. "Turn around and bend over," he barked, "spread your cheeks." I did what I was instructed but was gripped with overwhelming anger as I felt his fingers probe my asshole. "Fuck you," I said. I recoiled, not knowing what was coming next, but the CO simply chuckled and said, "Get your towel . . . Next." I had to go through that same process every week.

I began to observe the pretrial inmates with whom I shared my close confines. They were entirely different from the individuals I had met in Canada: harder and tougher, with strong codes of honor. I felt a kinship with the American prisoners; I respected them more.

The man with cornrows eventually walked into my cell to introduce himself. Big Len respectfully said, "Mr. Wilson," then got up off his bunk and walked out. Respect was all-important within these walls. Mr. Wilson smiled. "My name's Lamar, but call me Cutter."

I jumped to the conclusion he was in the habit of cutting or stabbing other inmates, but he read the expression on my face and said, "C'mon man, I cut people's hair in here; I'm the last person you need to worry about."

"Christopher Fulton," I said, and reached out my hand.

"I'm a bank robber," Cutter said, "I make no bones about it; it's what I do, it's what I know. The banks are more criminal than I am anyway. I never took from an individual man; I ain't a criminal like that. I've been in and out of all the best jails my whole life; I understand this kind of life real good. But you, you're something different; what's your story, man? Did you catch your wife with a lover and kill him? Or embezzle from a corporate scheme? You can tell me, I've heard it all." Cutter sat down and leaned back on Big Len's bunk.

"From the way I've been treated, you'd think I did all that and more," I said.

"But those aren't your stories, are they?" He said knowingly.

"No," I said, "I've got a White House problem."

Cutter didn't ask me any more questions, he simply said, "While I'm in your neighborhood, let me introduce you around." He got up off the bunk and walked out onto the tier and hung his arms over the rail. He pointed down to an inmate on the ground floor and said, "The skinny kid down there playing chess, we call him Skinny. He doesn't talk much; you think he be talking his head off considering he's not gunna have a voice much longer. Skinny's waitin' to get the needle for killing three girls. He stuffed them in his trunk, leaving them there to rot while he drove cross country. What was telling for the judge was that he forgot they were in there. I heard the smell was so bad that the arresting officer threw up. Anyway, that boy's time is almost up . . . sure can play chess, though." Cutter looked at me. "Do you think life is like a game of chess, Christopher?" He turned back to the floor. "Some people think so."

He scoured the block before pointing out another inmate. "See the young bull giving the finger to the camera? Be careful with him, he likes to think he runs this place, his name is Roe. On the streets, he's what we call a shooter. He rather let his gun talk for him; shoot you sooner than speak to you. He's basically a thug, but he's strong. I don't think anyone in this place could kill him; the motherfucker got six bullets in his back when he was on the street and it didn't finish him. If I ever have to go to war with these pig COs, he's the guy I'd want in front of me.

"The white kid sitting at the table to the left, that's Tech. He's in here for hacking every federal communication in the world. He'll tell you he's the smartest person you'll ever meet in your life. I've seen this bullshit since Nam; the government has a bad habit of destroying, killing, or locking up the best and brightest in the country, and this kid is one of them. Two cells down from you is Dougie; dumbass white kid tried to rob a bank, amateur.

"The first cell by the shower on the top tier, that's the Jew, Yusuf, but we call him Spielberg. He's murdered so many people that you'll never read about him; law enforcement doesn't want *that* kind of publicity."

I wondered how that correlated to the name Spielberg.

"Man," Cutter said, "of all the time I've spent in all the different prisons, he's the only Jew I've ever seen locked on the inside. You know he had to be really bad for the judges and prosecutors to put away one of their own. Once a week the FBI come in and take him out for the day so he can show them where another body is buried; it gives the families of his victims some closure. I would have bet Roe would have killed him a long time ago, but Spielberg keeps to himself; never speaks to anybody, and doesn't leave his cell until the FBI come to get him.

"Your bunky, Big Len, he's a good kid, but the feds are really fucking him. He barely dealt any weight on the street, just stuck to his own neighborhood, just did enough business to support his family. But others were trying to save their own skin and gave Len up to the feds, makin' him out to be the heavy on the street. They're sticking him with a kingpin charge; kid's gunna get life. Believe me I've seen it before . . . No way he deserves it though.

"Now, that's Toni Rigoletti." Cutter pointed to an inmate who had torn his t-shirt into a wifebeater against regulation. He was on the phone.

"We call him Meatball, Italian guy, drug dealer from Queens. I like to say his name: *Rigoletti*, but he's another dumbass, so we call him Meatball. Everybody gets a name man, I just haven't figured out what yours is yet. Anyway, the feds wanted Meatball for life; he moved a lot of snow. I've come back to this hell hole twice, both times he's still here. He's in the cell closest to the phone bank; that's not by accident. Man, stay off the phones if you can, and stay away from Meatball.

"These prosecutors play their fucked-up games with us. They give a guy life, but keep the sentence pending while he sits in these pretrial shit holes, finding out whatever information he can by being a friend, then transferring the info back to the feds. Some of these dumbasses take that sucker deal, like Meatball."

"How can he be a rat and still survive?"

"Normal rules don't apply in here. This is a small block, man, and Meatball is valuable to the feds; the goons would kill you if you laid a finger on him."

"Who else is ratting?" I asked.

"Don't worry about that man, I've told you all you need to know."

THE COLOR RED

PRISON TIME

Over the next few days I got to know Dougie. He made himself friendly to me because I was one of the five white guys in the block. Actions mattered to me, not color, but racial segregation was a code in prison. As for the other three: Tech wouldn't talk to Dougie, Dougie wouldn't talk to Meatball, and Spielberg didn't talk to anybody.

Dougie was a GQ-looking kid; if he was wearing a blazer instead of an orange jumpsuit I would have taken him for a Wall Street type. He looked clean-cut, from a good family. He would come to my cell to talk, but he was by no means a great conversationalist.

"I hate my bunky," Dougie said, "he's such an asshole; I can't stand being in the same fucking cell as him. I'm glad I can talk to you, though."

"Sure," I said . . . I guess I wasn't much of a conversationalist anymore, either.

"Hey," he said, "do you remember that song 'Brandy?' I love that song; do you remember how it goes?"

I started to sing quietly, trying to remember the words:

There's a port on a western bay
And it serves a hundred ships a day
Lonely sailors pass the time away
And talk about their homes.

I used to be big into music when I was a kid. I started playing the guitar when I was twelve, and was in a band that played at nightclubs when I was in high school. But I hadn't thought about music much since then; funny I would find it again in a place like this.

Dougie and I spent the next few days fumbling through the rest of the lyrics until we had them all down, then we sat in my cell snapping our fingers, singing "Brandy" to ourselves. It took Dougie back to a moment in time before he ever got into drugs and lost his life to them. I thought about all the soulful songs I had heard over the years; they took on new meaning for me now.

If you can't find the depths of your soul in a place like CCDC, you'll never understand what it means to be happy in a moment, just because you are allowed to live, even if everything else is gone. It was like seeing the color red all the time, but never knowing what it meant until feeling the heat of it; from that point on whenever there was red, there was also the depth of understanding how it felt.

**

Legal mail, being the only kind of mail we could receive, was delivered like the razors. The next day as I was issued a razor I also had to sign for a letter. I went back to my cell before reading it; it was from my attorney.

> Attorney General Janet Reno received our request for your dismissal, and was considering it, but responded that everything has proceeded too far, and your prosecution will be seen through. I believe the Justice Department's decision is based on their need to interrogate you.
>
> Considering their agenda, our best course of action is to stall for as long as possible. I know that's the last thing you want to hear, but my ability to make the best deal for you, with the shortest amount of jail time, will be accomplished by holding out until they are forced to concede in order to keep to their timetable. If you have any questions or concerns, please feel free to contact me to arrange a meeting.
>
> Stephen N. Salvin

Nothing about Shauna.

I wondered what the government's timetable was. I recalled Roger saying everything in the federal system moved very slowly. Salvin's letter gave me no indication if we were talking weeks, months, or years. I felt the sword of Damocles hanging over my head, but that's what this place was all about.

I hadn't communicated with Shauna by phone since Canada. I couldn't; this was my war. The attack on me had been so great I needed to separate

238

myself from everyone I loved to prevent them from incurring any of the devastating blowback by proximity. The best thing I could do was survive, let the wounds heal, and limp back to life if I ever got the chance.

Maybe it was the tremendous amount of stress I was under, or maybe it was the amount of time that had gone by under that stress, but I was beginning to forget what the people I cared about looked like. I felt a desperate need to see Shauna's face again, before I lost the essence of her completely. I wanted to draw her while I still retained some memory, but the only guy I knew with a pencil and paper was Spielberg. Fuck it, I thought, I like his movies, I'll just ask to borrow a pencil and some paper. I didn't need courage, I didn't care anymore; I was forced into feeling nothing. I didn't want to be this way; my mind was in a battle for its survival.

When I walked into Spielberg's cell, I didn't use his jail name. "Yusuf, I would like to have some of your paper and borrow one of your pencils."

He had greying hair, wore reading glasses, and had no features that stood out as threatening, dangerous, or even slightly psychopathic; now I knew why Cutter had given him the name Spielberg. He didn't look up from his writing. "What do you want them for?" he asked without emotion.

"I want to draw a picture of my wife's face before I forget it."

"Do you know why I get pencils?" He asked, still looking down at his notes.

"No."

"Because I'm cooperating; I'm helping them with their ongoing investigation of me. They keep me preoccupied with my pencils and paper, but I think I'm wasting my time, no one will ever see or read what I've written. I'd much rather use my pencils to kill some of these inmates; their snores aggravate me. I could just drive it up their nose and into their brain while they sleep, then there would be no more snoring."

I paused for a moment. "Is that a yes?"

My persistence must have intrigued him because he looked directly at me and said, "You may have the paper and borrow the pencil, but only if you sit down with me for a moment."

Spielberg didn't talk to anybody, but now he was talking to me. I wondered if the security cameras would catch my image going into his cell but not coming out, and they would find my dead body on the floor in a pool of blood with a pencil up my nose. But I had made up my mind.

"The FBI considers me one of the most dangerous serial killers that ever existed, and you are sitting here alone with me; how does that make you feel?"

"I don't know any details about your situation," I said.

"Then you need details." A look of fond memory crossed his face before he started to tell me his story. "I was in a grocery store and I noticed a man buying groceries for one; he had no family, no partner, but I could tell by what he purchased that he had means. I had never seen him before; I had no association with him at all, but I could visualize his home and his neighborhood, his habits and lifestyle, and I wanted it, I wanted them to be mine, Christopher. Do you know why that happens?"

"No," I said.

"When we are born, our parents give us everything, but in the world, as an adult, power is not given, it's taken. So I took it, Christopher, I took everything that man ever had or would have.

"I followed him to his house; he never noticed me, why would he? He went in the front door, and soon after came out the back door to work in his garden. It was a well-tended garden; I could tell he put a great deal of effort into it.

"He looked so puzzled when I shot him in the chest for the third time with my silenced 357 magnum. He shit himself before he fell to his knees. I was just doing what God would have done eventually, but I spared him the indignity of the frailty and failings of old age. I buried him under his roses; I knew it would please him to nourish his garden in death.

"I showered in my new home, put on my new clothes, and ate the food my friend had purchased for dinner; I was now him, so it was my dinner. "I saw this all in an instant in the grocery store, and then I made it real. I'd done it many, many times, Christopher. Don't believe them when they tell you they're super sleuths, like you see on television; the reality is you can do anything you want, and no one can stop you if you're smart enough. That's what they are afraid of, that people will realize it, realize that justice can't protect anyone." His eyes went passive; he looked back down at his papers. "Please enjoy the use of your pencil and paper, Christopher; don't forget to return the pencil to me when you are done."

I walked back to my cell, and sat on my bunk. I put Yusuf's rendering out of my mind and tried to remember Shauna. She was good and pure, a dwindling spark of light, a memory of a candle in this darkness. I started to sketch her eyes; I needed to capture their kindness, their life . . . I tried, but she was too far removed from where I was now. I dragged the lead heavily across the echo of her features, scratching out my inability to portray her. I tore the paper and crumpled it, and let the mess fall to the floor. I began to draw again, not really thinking about what my hand was doing. When I stopped, I looked at my sketch: a Degas dancer on point, partially dissected.

What was happening to me?

I retreated and lay my head on my pillow. I was like Icarus, banished from freedom, plummeting into a cold and dark reality. I knew life went on—children still played, oblivious to anything but their own play; people bought groceries and ran their errands. Their lives still whirred and hummed like a well-oiled machine: so much to do, all the time, every day, so much to do. But I had nothing; my life had stopped. What's the use of a machine once it's stopped running? This was the landscape: *The Fall of Icarus*. In the background, my world was falling apart as I tumbled to Earth to drown in a bottomless sea, my descent not even so much as to make anyone look up from what they were doing. I was already invisible, already dead, a ghost walking through a world I could no longer have an effect on.

Someone walked into my cell, picked up the pieces of paper and started smoothing them out. I turned to see Big Len, but it wasn't him, it was Tech. "I wanted to see what was so important for you to go into Spielberg's cell," he said. "You raised my curiosity, and I have nothing better to do."

"So now you know," I said, and looked back up at the ceiling.

"It was a valid attempt. Who is she?"

"My wife."

"The head and the heart really collide in here, don't they? You're going to have to take some pressure off, believe me; it's obvious you're in a dangerous state of mind. This is your life now; it doesn't matter what's going on outside, to the rest of the world you are dead. For all intents and purposes, they're right: your actions no longer have any effect on that world, no ripples in the pond, so you have to let it all go."

"Great, thanks," I said, wishing he would get out of my cell.

"When you experience sudden and traumatic loss, your deepest ingrained subconscious self usually decides it is too far beyond repair; it is no longer fit to be functional in this life, and must make way for fresh, undamaged individuals. It's a trick of nature. You have little control of it; once that switch is flipped, you'll start making mistakes, get careless and irrational, put yourself in harm's way. That shift will either lead to your demise, or you will draw such a conclusion to yourself. But if you can overcome nature: understand the trick, you can begin the processes necessary to take control, and be reborn."

I wasn't interested in his preaching. He could easily sense that, but it didn't stop him.

"Listen," he said, "I want you to think of your intelligence and mine, then think of your federal prosecutor, and the people that put you here. Would you be able to do their job?"

"No."

"Do you know why that is?" he asked.

I stared back at him. "Because I couldn't live with myself."

"Right; their mental illness, their lack of development as human beings, gives them the perfect ability to do what they do and flourish. Their negative effect on us is not our fault. You can't make yourself less-than, and mentally submit because you find yourself in the slaughter house. The butcher doesn't care how smart a pig you are, how hard you've studied, or what you've experienced, you're just there for slaughter . . . but it doesn't mean you deserve to be. *Dum spiro spero*, whilst I breathe, I hope: you have to stick it out until you can get out.

"Once you know the truth of it you'll get angry, because the fed lawyers are evil and they tricked you into believing you deserve to be slaughtered. Then comes sadness, a severe sadness at the condition of humanity, that's where you're headed now. After that is forgiveness and love, if you make it that far. In the end, all we want to do is live out our lives in peace and joy, with the fulfillment of accomplishment.

"You know, it's a trick of nature and humanity; if the gov says something long enough, with the power to enforce it, people's resolve weakens, then the gov's words become truth. Individually, most men in our gov are nothing; they should be digging ditches and pumping gas at best, not controlling other people's futures.

"Of course that can't be said of the men who wrote the Declaration of Independence and the Constitution, the original idea of it all; I would have trusted those men with my fate. The founders wrote the Constitution with the foresight to give us the right to impeach the government or any president that takes away our liberties. That's why constitutional arguments are banned from federal criminal court, banned by the rules of engagement. We are now at a junction. Our founders' ideas have been made limited to the point of obscurity."

"I hear you're the smartest guy I'll ever meet," I said.

"When you hear it from two more different sources, you'll know it to be true. 'If I can see further than most mortal men, it's because I'm standing on the shoulders of giants.' Those are Isaac Newton's words, but I embody them. I was a preemie, but I was born being able to use a higher percentage of my brain than most people. My name's Jonathan."

"Christopher," I said, sitting up, but not getting down from my bunk. Jonathan proceeded to take off one of his blue, rubber-soled slippers, the federal prison issued footwear, and remove his sock. He stepped onto the steel toilet bowl and used the sock to muffle the intercom speaker that was high on the wall. It was difficult to accomplish, but he was able to cover most of it.

"What are you doing?" I asked.

"Those aren't just for the COs to speak into the cells you know, it goes both ways; they can listen in whenever they want to.

"I'm in here because they consider me a national security threat; I'm better at playing with their toys than they are, and they hate anyone who messes with their monopoly. The truth is, when you learn how stupid these people really are, you become fearful for humanity, and a desperate need to intervene and do something about it comes over you, but that's against the rules. Now the White House is run like a private corporation with no accountability. It's really just a PR firm. They want to have private companies cover their communication, ditching the NSA to have them spy on the rest of the country, so they can operate in total secrecy for pure profit using the entire gov's resources and tax money."

"You hacked private government communications?"

"That's right, amongst other things. The gov has gone to such trouble to keep their secrets. If people knew the truth they'd realize there's no need for them, or all the rules and regulations and pressures they put on us. They are dumbing down humanity through our food, inoculations, education, religion, false information, pollution; the list is endless. Our protectors control and manipulate the masses. Most of our problems are created for the sole purpose of our gov to fix said problems, so they can write the history books where they are the heroes, and shouldn't we be grateful. Do you feel grateful, Christopher?

"Our Constitution says it's our duty and obligation to remove men and women in high office if they become tyrannical, and replace them with better guardians of our safety.

"The funny thing is, the tools they are using against us, the technological pacifiers that everyone will become addicted to, are their weakest link. Like the Internet: it will eventually become the chink in the armor of the dominant and powerful. Sure, they will use it to surveil and hoard personal information for whenever they need it, but we can use it as a tool as well. The World Wide Web will become a superhighway where everyone has a voice, and if you sift through the buildup of bogus material, you'll find the truth will actually make it out into the public domain. We all just need to open our eyes to see it, and be discerning enough to cancel out all the trash. George Orwell said, 'During times of universal deceit, telling the truth becomes a revolutionary act.' Winston Churchill said, 'Truth is so precious that she should always be attended by a bodyguard of lies.' Most people think in terms of the great change of light and dark coming from a physical battle, but that's not the entire story. The truth is information, and not all the misinformation in the world will be able to scrub it from people's minds once they see it and understand it, things will start to change for the better . . . a union of awakening, a real revolution of the mind; that's what I'm waiting for.

"Unfortunately, until then, this country is going to keep changing for the worse. We have always needed an enemy; peace isn't good business. 'Of course, the people don't want war. But after all, it is the leaders of the country who determine the policy and it is always a simple matter to drag the people along, whether it is a democracy or a fascist dictatorship or a Parliament or a Communist dictatorship. Voice or no voice, the people can always be brought to the bidding of the leaders. That is easy, all you have to do is tell them they are being attacked and denounce the pacifists for lack of patriotism and exposing the country to danger. It works the same in any country.' Do you know who said that?"

"No."

"Hermann Göring. War has always been a bizarre perversion for the global elite. Put your guy in the White House, find a pretext for war, wage said war, make massive profits, repeat. After the atomic age, the elite realized they might not survive an uncontrolled thermonuclear war. Now, with advanced technology linking all of us, they need a new agenda; not just a war against an outside aggressor, but an internal war of secrecy for the few and no privacy for the many. Scary thing is, those people in power don't think like you or me, or most of the people on the planet. There is no humanity left in them. They have their inner circle, their elite programming from birth to control the rest of the world, and they see everyone else as insects, as a threat. Most people find it easy to stomp on an ant, or squish a mosquito, and that's all it is to them, obliterating a pest.

"I spent some time in a super max prison before I came here. They debriefed me numerous times, then told me I'd never be a part of society again, unless I worked for them. But I don't follow orders well, especially from small-minded gov types. Anyway, the FBI's so-called most brilliant guy was sent to interrogate me. We got into this mind-fucking repartee. I played on his ego, and he spilled that he had interrogated the bomb maker who attempted to blow up the World Trade Center, but blew the garages out instead. The FBI had the option of replacing the explosive with useless powder before it blew, but they didn't do it . . . Now the elite are banking on the Twin Towers coming all the way down in the future. They're going to use it as a catalyst to change everything and fund their growth for decades. I'm telling you this so when it happens, you'll know the truth, and once you know the truth, Christopher, nobody can take it from you."

Tech seemed to be in a situation similar to mine, but way farther down the road.

"I've got you pegged as a problem with the White House," he said waiting, to see my reaction.

"You've been talking to Cutter," I responded.

"It's a small block," he smiled. "You haven't seen your warrant, have you?"

"No."

"So you're a national security concern."

"I'm formally being charged with evading tax reporting requirements."

"Classic White House bullshit," he spat. "They've been sweating me in here for a while, but won't take me to trial; they want to make a deal and find out everything I know. They'd prefer to lobotomize me, but then they'd miss out on how I outsmart their technology. Luckily, my family is all living in New Zealand, out of the circus, so the gov can't use them as leverage. Were you arrested in the District?"

"No," I said, "they extradited me from British Columbia, Canada."

"Wow, in the sixties you would've had it made; now they have FBI offices right in Vancouver . . . If you want to show me your paperwork I'll give you my best advice; it'll be worth far more than what your lawyer will give you."

"How do you figure that?" I asked, and thought of the letter I had received that morning.

"You're funny," he laughed. "Any attorney practicing federal law is required to give an adequate defense only; they are expected to bend over for the federal investigation and not cause waves in court. If you could find a lawyer to give you a great defense in the federal system it would be a one-time show. The gov would find a way to ban them from court for life, destroy their career. There's a reason the federal courts have a ninety-eight percent conviction rate. I'm confident the other two percent are either turned to work for them, or terminated."

I was very impressed with Jonathan. I got off my bunk and handed him my transcript and added all the behind-the-scene details I could think of.

He listened to me intently as he scanned my paperwork. "Wow, this *is* interesting," he mumbled. "Your case is ancient history; have you ever heard of the green lion?"

"The green lion?" I asked.

"The jealous green lion that devours the golden sun: it's an image from as early as the twelfth century. One drawing was found in Sir Isaac Newton's papers. The lion is a symbol for mercury; he's got the sun secured in his jaws and the sun has blood pouring from the right side of his face. Sound familiar?"

"I've heard of that, isn't it called the philosopher's stone, the alchemist's formula to create gold?"

"Think about it like a prophecy rather than a formula: jealous, green, powerful lion; mercury, destroying a golden *son* . . . who is bleeding from his right temple . . ."

"JFK is the sun?"

"That specific transference of power in the political structure was prophesied many times before; the green lion isn't the only one. But it clearly shows that the event would take place and the chemistry of the world would change forever. There is another depiction of the same image with a second sun in the water, close to shore, witnessing the reaction. Strange thing is, the sun in the sky isn't bleeding, and the lion has seven red stars that run the length of his body.

"After everything you've told me," Tech paused to read a segment of my transcript again, "I think those seven stars are the seven presidents that came after JFK . . . That brings us to the present day, to your meeting with his progeny." He looked at me poignantly, "Maybe that's why there's no blood from the sun's temple; it's not about that moment in time anymore. As for the sun in the water . . . maybe it represents JFK Jr., but I don't know what it means, I don't know why he's in the water, but it's not a good sign."

I was left speechless, with an unsettling concern for John Jr. I felt like doors had been opening all through history, and the human race was filing through without asking any questions. Is this the right way to go? Could there be a better path? I wasn't just an individual being unwaveringly led down a road of destruction; according to Tech, the whole human race was being funneled in the same way, driven in a specific direction, but to what end?

Tech broke my train of thought. "I'll need to look this over for a few more days before I can give you a real strategy . . . Can I take the pencil?"

"Sure."

"You're in a unique and dangerous position. You need someone like me, with centuries of historical perspective, to tell you the truth about what's *really* happening."

"Thank you," I responded. I couldn't help but feel unsettled by Tech's revelations. I was being sucked into a black hole and my perception of everything was distorted and uncertain. I didn't want a role in this cosmic disruption. Was I going to lose my life over it?

Before Tech left, he said, "Listen to me, don't let yourself get weak. Because evil is attacking you with such vigor, you also have the equal and opposite force to meet it. Bad is attracted to good, but good has the ability to overcome.

"Do you think John F. Kennedy just came out of nowhere, was able to attain the White House against everyone's agenda, at the exact moment in history needed to stop a nuclear holocaust? Do you think if JFK had lost in 1960, President Nixon would *not* have gone to war with Russia? We were on a path of nuclear confrontation, but JFK's and RFK's resistance, and ultimate cognizant sacrifice delayed everything long enough to allow the agenda to change. So, can you really believe there isn't a broader plan?

"I believe your incarceration could actually be protecting you; I think you have a good chance of making it through this . . ."

He left my cell just before lockdown.

Jonathon seemed to have answers to questions I didn't even know to ask. I had never met another person like him. I was encouraged; he was going to help me. Then I realized what I had done: I had given Tech the pencil I promised I would return to a murderer the feds considered one of the most cold-blooded serial killers in history. I would have to see Spielberg first thing in the morning, explain my situation, ask to keep the pencil a little longer, and hope he wouldn't kill me for the inconvenience. That night I thought long and carefully about what I would say to him.

The next day I returned to Spielberg's cell without the pencil, my palms open and empty.

He looked directly at me as I barely entered his sanctum. His eyes scanned me like a computer and said, "Don't worry about the pencil."

He could tell something had changed in me; I didn't brazenly walk right up to him, today I actually had hope. I decided to leave my prepared speech unheard, and turned to leave.

"Christopher," he said, and I stopped in my tracks. While still engrossed in his work, he advised me, "Do not participate, sit idle, or bear false witness to what you have experienced."

37

LIFE

PRISON TIME

Big Len talked lovingly about his family; they were his main priority. Anyone who got to know him could see what a big heart he had, what a good person he was. Selling drugs in his neighborhood wasn't the definition of him as a person; it was the motivation behind the action that spoke to who he truly was. I can't imagine he was ever very good at selling drugs; it just didn't match his personality. That's probably why he was rolled on and left to take the rap as a kingpin.

Len and I stayed up all night discussing what he wanted his life to be like when he got out. He wanted a beautiful home where his family could be safe; maybe they could travel a little. He wanted to give his daughter a better life than he had: a good education, a safe and happy place to grow up, out of the reach of people that could lead her down a bad path. He asked me where a nice place to live would be, because the only place he had ever known was the inner city of Baltimore.

He told me that when he got there, to his dream life, he would invite me to visit and meet his family, and we could celebrate our survival and freedom together. I didn't want to bring up the obvious truth and take away his lovely delusion; I enjoyed hearing it as much as he enjoyed telling me about it. Maybe he was aware it might never happen, but in that moment, it was the only thing he had to hold on to.

Big Len was processed out at four the next morning to go to court for his sentencing. I said a prayer for him. After razors, Dougie came into my cell. "I guess it's Big Len's day," he said. "I can't wait to get sentenced, get out of CCDC, out of limbo. I want to get to a regular facility where I can have some sort of existence. This, in here, this isn't even existing; we're ghosts. You know, I didn't use a gun in the robbery, only a note, but the feds still considered it a threat of life. I wouldn't have hurt anybody; I was just jonesing so bad I had to get money from somewhere, anywhere, to get a fix. My lawyer says I'll probably get a medium security prison for maybe six to eight years."

I thought of the remorseless first-degree murderers in Canada who would get no more than two years in prison. It was a grave contrast to Dougie's six to eight years for a foolish, drug-fueled mistake. Taking human life was far less of a crime than having the audacity to break the rules in a federal building; life is cheap, it's the institutions that matter.

"I just want to know," Dougie said, "I just want the waiting to be over. What I did was stupid, but it was the drugs; I made a big fucking mistake and I'll pay for it, but I just want to know how I'm going to pay for it, and get it done."

I'd seen this many times now; it didn't matter what someone was facing, they just wanted to know where they stood, and get on with it. It was the waiting in purgatory that took away a person's foundation, and eventually their sanity. I wondered how Meatball could hold on so long.

That night, after dinner, there was still no sign of Big Len. I needed to know what had happened to him. When you spend twenty-four hours a day with a person, you become a part of their life, and they become a part of yours; there is no separating it, especially if the person is as admirable as Len. An inmate who had been at court that day came back into the block, but Len wasn't with him. "What happened?" I asked. "What happened to Len?"

"Oh, they fucked him man, they put a shock belt on him before he even got to the courtroom; you know that's no good."

"Why did they put a shock belt on him?" That was new to me.

"They do that to the guys that are about to hear something that might make 'em go berserk, so the officers in the court can drop 'em to their knees if they go nuts."

"So what did they give him?" I asked, feeling a pit in my stomach.

"Life, man, they gave him life; he's gunna to do it all in a penitentiary and leave in a body bag."

I was devastated. "Was his family there?"

"I think so." The inmate walked off, and I went back to my cell. I hated this! Len would come back before he transferred, but what do you say to someone who just lost their life? "Gee, I'm sorry"? or, "Better luck next time"? I felt a burning hate grab hold of me; it came from the presence of pure malevolence, from being subjected to irreversible and senseless loss.

Eventually, Big Len came through the secured door and walked quietly to our cell. I could hear a few guys yell out, "Hey, what d'you get?" and, "How'd you do?"

Quietly and calmly Len responded, "Life, I got life." He tried to smile. I knew he didn't want to discourage anyone else in the block; we were all facing similar fates.

"I heard what happened," I said when he walked into our cell.

"Yeah, they took it from me." He handed me a piece of paper.

It said: "Date of release: Deceased." I was holding his federal death certificate. "I heard your family was there; you got to see them, right?"

"Yeah, that was good, until they read out the sentence. The marshals told me they would put me down if I said anything, but I turned to my family and told them not to cry, not to give them the satisfaction; the marshals didn't shock me, though. Christopher, do you think I'll be ok in the penitentiary?"

"You'll be fine; it's going to be better than here, Len."

He lay quietly on his bunk; he didn't have anything else to say and neither did I. As I lay staring at the ceiling, I realized that when Len left I would never see him again, and for as long as I was alive, he would be in prison . . . but I would always consider him my friend.

38

FIGHTING THE GREEN LION

PRISON TIME

Big Len left. It wasn't long before a Middle Eastern man in his late thirties came into my cell and sat on the bottom bunk, Len's bunk.

He wasn't particularly talkative, just the opposite of Len, but no words were better than threatening ones. He kept to himself, and I was fine with that.

I settled into the comfort of routine, knowing that any routine could easily be broken by the actions of fellow inmates. But one day, it was broken by the actions of the guards. I was sitting at a table on the ground floor when I heard a loud buzzer. I had never heard the sound before; it noisily blared on and off: a warning signal. A voice from the control room came through the main intercom system; it was unforgiving: "Place both your hands against the wall above your head. Do not turn around."

Every inmate followed the command, and turned to face whichever wall they were closest to. The red lights on the surveillance cameras blinked off; now no one was watching what they would do to us. I feared for everyone's safety.

We were ordered to keep our noses against the concrete wall, effectively cutting our field of vision, but I covertly disobeyed and turned my head slightly to the right. Being at the farthest left-hand corner of the block, I had a better view of what was happening than the other inmates.

The steel door slid open and they swarmed in like bees, individual-less, black body armor from head to toe, visored helmets, and batons at the ready. This was the goon squad, the federal prison's version of Special Forces. I could hear the German shepherds ready to be let loose on anyone who got in the way. The squad synchronized and converged on a cell on the far right bottom tier near the shower, but I couldn't see around the wall of men in armor; I couldn't see whose cell it was.

I heard a struggle; it sounded like one of the thin mattresses was being used as a makeshift shield. The thuds of batons against the foam pad sounded like a downpour of heavy rain on a skylight. "Stop! Stop!" Sharp cries rang out as it changed to a sickening harmony of weapons on flesh, and cracks when they missed and hit the wall or bunk. I hoped it would be over quick, but it wasn't; I listened to an endless reign of blows, falling with abandon, and without lull. I heard more screams: "Oh God, my God!" and then there was silence. I watched a black man stumble past the circle of officers, but I couldn't recognize him for the swelling mess of his face; his bare feet left prints of blood behind him as he staggered out.

Then I saw the body; it had no life left in it. The guy was white. *Oh my God it was Jonathan!* I was going to throw up. They pulled him by his feet so his face dragged along the concrete floor. I tasted bile and tried to breathe. There was no respect for life, no respect for the soul, or the body. The goon squad had cracked his head open. The wound was gaping and massive; they had literally split his skull in half. There was too much gore and mess left in his wake, so two other guards picked up an arm each to get his body off the floor. Tech's head swung limply between his shoulders as they carried his lifeless form through the large metal door. His physical remains in no way reflected the enlightened man I knew.

He was a young man, maybe the smartest man I would ever meet, and the goons had destroyed him, his brain and his life, twenty against one, with thunderous blows that should have been reserved for defending life, not taking it. I went into shock. My thoughts were numb and delayed; I couldn't get a rational grasp on what had just happened or what it meant.

Once we were all back in our cells, the COs blacked out our small slit windows while the mess that used to be Tech was cleaned up. That night the mattresses were removed from our bunks, cold air was blown into the block, the lights were kept at full brightness, and the dogs were made to bark continually. It was punishment, but we didn't know what we were being punished for.

The next morning at razors, I was handed a legal manila envelope. When I opened it I found my blood-splattered transcript; the red marks were the last of Jonathan I would ever see. He had written notes with the pencil on the inside pages . . . pages he knew they couldn't destroy:

A few scattered persons which God hath chosen can set themselves sincerely and honestly to search after truth – Sir Isaac Newton.

Christopher, you are a part of what prophets have predicted centuries before our birth. I know the wheels are turning. Have faith in your part.

I knew they were meant to be words of encouragement, but they just stained my soul.

While I was fighting through my own inner turmoil at the loss of Jonathan and Big Len, my new bunky came back from razors with his own envelope. After opening it and reading the contents, he collapsed on the floor and convulsed silently before letting out the most heart-wrenching sob I had ever heard uttered from another man.

I had never seen a man break, reduced to nothing but raw emotion with nothing to hold onto, and nothing to keep their façade intact. It was a disturbing transition to witness.

He knelt and beat his fists and head against the concrete bunk, wailing as tears streaked down his reddening face. His cries echoed the feeling in my heart; I lay on my back and let the sound wash over me. Usually when men cried in here, they cried for themselves, but today my new bunky was crying for me too.

It was the sound of ultimate anguish; it was not to be interrupted. Without knowing what prompted it, all I could do was wait until it subsided to see if he would talk to me, see if I could offer him any solace. He finally exhausted himself and fell asleep. Finding unconsciousness was a blessing. When he woke from his comatose slumber we were already locked down for the night. "Christopher," he said quietly, his voice hoarse from grief, "are you awake?"

"Yes, do you need to talk?"

"It's my wife," he started, "she's younger than me, nineteen, but in my culture age isn't so important; you marry and are married for life and have many children together."

"What happened?" I asked.

"I own many high-end stores in Tyson's corner, in Virginia, but I was brought here because they suspect I have terrorist connections; they charged me with money laundering. My lawyer says it could be many years before I can rejoin my wife; it has been very difficult. I don't talk to anyone about this, my lawyer said I shouldn't.

"The letter was from my lawyer. My wife requested to come visit me many times, but she is not from this country and didn't have the proper identification, so they denied her. The last time she tried to visit me one of the officers told her she would never see me again, that I would get thirty or forty years in prison. But it wasn't true, Christopher, it was just a problem with her getting ID, it would just take a little longer. Why would he do that? It was not correct information."

I remembered how I had been treated by the federal intake officers when I first arrived. They were all petty assholes, coming up with shitty ways to keep themselves entertained at the expense of their new charges.

My bunky continued, "My wife thought it was true; she wrote a note to me, then hung herself with her own scarf." He started sobbing again and said, "She wrote she could not go on living without me, and she wished that I would not hate her for what she did. My lawyer says they discovered she was pregnant with my son; I did not know this, Christopher. My heart is broken; I have nothing left. What do I do?" He completely broke down again.

What can any of us do? I put my hand on his shoulder.

During my transport from Sea Tac to CCDC I had witnessed inmates commit suicide. One man hung himself from a basketball net; the hoops remained netless after that. Another ripped up his bed sheet and hung himself from a door handle. It couldn't have been easy; his despair must have been tremendous to have the tenacity to end his life in such a way. It would have required consistent struggle to complete the task. Many inmates were condemned knowing they would never have a chance at life again, and this was understandably too much to take. The insurmountable pain had led my bunky's wife to kill herself while pregnant. I could think of nothing more sad.

The night was full of torment; I heard another inmate on the lower tier start to yell out; I closed my eyes and hoped he would stop. If God was merciful, I would fall asleep and leave this day behind. I wished I could leave all of these days behind.

***

I could smell the grass and I felt a cool breeze against my face. It was winter, no, earlier, September maybe, the leaves were just starting to turn. As I lowered my gaze I saw them, the endless rows of white stones. They were uniform, without individuality, except for the motion of color that waved in the wind. Placed with care at the base of each mini-monument was an American flag; hundreds, no hundreds of thousands of them.

I woke with a jolt. I felt like the oxygen had been sucked from my lungs. I swung my bare feet onto the cold cement floor and tried to catch my breath.

39

WISDOM

PRISON TIME

I wasn't scheduled to be sentenced yet, but one morning I was called for court anyway. Tech had been murdered before he could give me his advice, so my lawyer's counsel was all I had. It seemed to be a battle of wills and time: unless I conceded to make a deal, or forced them to trial, I would linger in purgatory. I was aching for it to be over.

I was ordered from my cell at four in the morning. The cold and lack of sleep made me ill; I silently wretched in the toilet. As I exited through the steel door at the front of the block with the other inmates bound for court that day, a CO yelled out, "Chains." One by one we were fitted with shackles around our ankles and wrists, secured to a lock box at our waists. "Chains," and the line shuffled forwards as the next inmate was outfitted in steel. Anytime an inmate left the matrix of super security blocks they were chained to somebody else. We were told when to move, and when to stop. We were taken to a holding cell and left to wait. Three hours later, we shuffled into an armored transport vehicle parked in the garage below ground. This was the beginning of the long day's agonizing process.

We slid onto the cold metal benches of the van until we were sardine-packed. The doors were closed and locked. The air quickly became thick and foul as sweat bled through our orange jumpsuits. We were transported to the courthouse by a driver who drove at stupidly fast speeds, stopping and turning abruptly, shaking us around like grasshoppers in a tin can. Did every driver get the same directive, or was it just the common personality type that this job attracted? Sadistic motherfuckers.

We made one stop to pick up another person, a woman. She was ushered into a part of the van that was partitioned off, but each compartment was verbally accessible to the next. It was obvious how nervous she was. Slightly wild eyed, her lip quivered as she slid along the seat, only an inch away from men whom she envisioned as brutal murderers . . . well, some of them were.

The guy sitting next to me was a terrorist, an explosives expert: Kaddafi. His face was deformed, an early acquired mark of his trade. He flashed the girl a lascivious grin as she glanced through the window to the back of the van where we sat. He sucked a breath of air in through his teeth, licked his bottom lip, and said, "Girl, I'm going to knock you out, nut in your mouth, suck it out and spit it in your cunt, and baby, you're having my baby." He laughed, they all laughed. She trembled as every muscle in her body tightened in fear, but she never made a sound.

I spoke up over the other men, silencing their jeers at the novelty that had been placed in front of them. I understood their side: they had been repressed for years, and this was their one awkward moment to fraternize. I also understood the view of the prey: one moment she was a private citizen, next she was locked beside men who had been turned into base predators.

"Listen to me," I said, "nobody can get to you, we're all locked up in chains back here; you're perfectly safe where you are." She began to breathe a little easier and relax, and the men muttered their displeasure at my ending their fun. "What are you here for?" I asked. She opened up and said she had written a few checks that bounced, and the feds picked it up. It wasn't long before the van pulled into a concrete underground parking garage, and we were led to another holding cell in the courthouse. We were never given the opportunity to see daylight, not even a glimpse of the outside world. I missed the simplest things: fresh air, a breeze, a glimmer of sunshine.

The holding cells at court were cold and sterile; the overpowering smell of cleaner made it hard for everyone to breathe. Even though we were in it together, it was weak to show how you were affected; no one wanted to be a target for everyone else's frustration, anger, and despair.

The only bench in the holding cell was curved and made of plastic, a masterpiece of engineering to provide no comfort. We hadn't been given food or water, we were tired, disheveled, ill, our brains only firing on half cylinders: perfect to go to court to try and defend ourselves. One by one, we were sorted like cattle and taken to whatever fate awaited us. Most would be sentenced; I saw one guy get a shock belt put on him before he was taken out of sight.

Some guys in the holding cell wouldn't make it into court, and would have to go through the same process day after day until they were called up. I wasn't being sentenced, but they came to get me just the same. Most cases didn't involve an inmate talking with the assistant district attorney, the ADA, but because the government wanted information from me, I was taken to him. Unfortunately that put me in danger of being labeled a rat, even though, at worst, I would only be ratting on myself. When the feds came to see an inmate for a short period of time, ratting was generally the reason. There were a lot of rats in this place; the feds loved to breed them.

Two marshals escorted me to a room and sat me down at a table. The ADA sat directly in front of me, with an agent on either side of him, the same agents who had initially questioned me at SeaTac, the same agents I had seen at my home in Vancouver. The ADA motioned for the marshals to take my handcuffs off. Once they did, they moved away from me but remained in the room.

"Mr. Fulton, I am Assistant District Attorney Stewart Barman from the U.S. Attorney's Office. To my left is Special Agent Mancini of the IRS; to my right is Special Agent Callahan of the FBI." Barman placed an ice cold can of Coca Cola in front of me. "Is there anything you'd like to speak about to us today?" he asked, watching me intently.

Coca Cola? What was this? It was a manipulative tactic: they could gauge my mental state of weakness and agreeability, and try to initiate a conversation without my attorney present. It was a good ploy; after all this time being silenced and tortured, persecuted and threatened, there was nothing I wanted more than to open my mouth and begin negotiations for my own life. I thought of Evelyn Lincoln, Agent Bouck, JFK Jr., and Shauna to try and quiet my mind. They were all strong; I had to be, too. I showed no expression, said nothing, and made no move to drink the Coke.

The four of us sat there in silence, staring at each other waiting for someone to say something. It was Barman who broke the silence; he began talking to the two agents about nothing in particular, I guess to see if that would affect me in some way. But I was determined; I had held out under the worst and I wasn't prepared to let it be for naught. Barman eventually motioned for the marshal to take me out of the room. It was hard not to open my mouth, not to yell at the top of my lungs. I had to tell myself that by not speaking up, I was acting in my own best interests for preservation, that I might see home again.

After the whole routine of chains, processing, transport, and reverse, I got back to CCDC late that evening.

**

The next day a CO's voice came over the intercom in my cell: "Inmate Fulton, you have a call. Pick up phone one."

I didn't want to use the phones; Cutter had warned me, but I didn't have a choice, so I walked down to the phone bank and picked up the line.

"Mr. Fulton?"

"Yes."

"My name is Phillip Adder; I'm an attorney representing Robert White."

How did he know where I was?

"Mr. Fulton?"

"I have nothing to say to you."

Adder went on, "Your attorney will inform you there has been a TRO, a temporary restraining order, filed against you in the fourth circuit. You must immediately place the Oval Office recordings in your possession into the custody of the court. You are not to alter them in any way or destroy them." He waited for me to say something.

"I have nothing to say to you." I hung up the phone. As I did, I heard someone call to me. "Hey, you, come 'ere." I looked up to see Meatball motioning me over to his cell. As I walked in he sat on the lower bunk and stretched his arms over his head, grabbing the top bunk. Meatball had a beat-up looking face; it was obvious his nose had been broken many times before. His hair was short, like a two-day growth of beard. He reminded me of the legendary fighter Rocky Marciano. I guessed he was about twenty-eight years old; he had a habit of rubbing his hand over his head as he spoke. "I heard you were only out for fifteen minutes at court yesterday," he said, "and you weren't sentenced; are you ratting?" Before I could answer, he continued, "That's what I do; I hate myself for it, but I just want to be a part of my kids' lives again. I've got life, but my sentence keeps gettin' postponed; the more I can help the feds with their other cases in here, the more time they'll take off my sentence. I hope to get it down to twenty years; it'll take a while, but maybe I can get out and be a father to my kids before I die." He looked at me with conviction. "In my old neighborhood, I'd be shot for what I'm doing here, but I'll stay in this God damned hell hole and be a rat for as long as it takes."

I thought about spending twenty years in this place; hell is real. "Why are you telling me this?" I asked.

"I don't know," Meatball said, "I just needed someone to talk to. If you're ratting too, I thought you'd understand."

He was caught in an impossibly miserable position. I had to keep my distance, but the human side of me, the part that was looking into his eyes as he poured out his guts, felt sorry for him. I had to remain strong, not be a sucker. "The only person they want me to rat on is myself," I said, and walked out.

As soon as I emerged from Meatball's cell, Cutter called me over. "What did he want with you?"

"He wanted to know if I was in the same boat as him; I told him I wasn't."

"I saw you on the phone. You didn't give 'em anything, did you?"

"No."

"Good. You don't want to be another Meatball, man. That rat'd cut your heart out and eat it in front of you if he thought it would get him closer to home."

I took Cutter's warning seriously; I understand how a man could be ruthless in here, do anything, just for a chance to see his family again.

"Listen," I said, "I've been meaning to ask you something. I've been in here long enough to recognize patterns: most guys end up losing their wives and families one way or another, but your girlfriend still comes to visit you all the time. What makes you different?"

Cutter smiled and said, "Most guys you see come through here aren't seasoned. The federal system is different than state, man. The feds use a heavy hand. Even on a first offense, guys will get fifteen, twenty, thirty years; they don't come back over and over, they just lose chunks of their life, gone, the first time.

"What they don't understand about their relationships is that everything is about being together. When you have a wife, you have a relationship because you are together. When you're not together everything stops. "For us in here, all the feelings and memories are embedded in our heads and don't change from how things were. But to them out there, it's like we died. Their lives move forward, they move on, they experience everything without us. As time goes by their memories of us fade. How do you have a relationship with a ghost? Women don't want that, man, they want someone to hold them close and tell them everything will be all right. "The women don't want to hurt their men, so they make their relationship more like a friendship, even though they're still married. Some dumb motherfucker will get out of prison, not tell his wife his release date to try and surprise her, and come home to find his replacement, the 'sport coat,' now the father to his children, fucking his wife; he'll lose his head, kill the guy, and go back to prison for the rest of his life.

"Can you imagine leaving your house for thirty years, then coming back and expecting everything to be the same as it was before you left: perfect lawn, and your car still in the garage?" Cutter laughed. "The best thing you can do is tell your wife or girlfriend you love her but she should move on; just end it right there and don't think about it again. If you go home and she's still around, you have a chance of starting a new relationship with her from that point on."

Even though Cutter's life was involved with the dirty and dangerous, he had a sense of humor and intelligence. Every time his girlfriend came to visit, which she did religiously, Cutter told me she would profess her absolute loyalty to him while the women next to her were all leaving their men. She had the loyalty of a soldier; she would stick with him until death, whether he won or lost. I found it amazing for someone like Cutter, who would be serving a sentence of twenty-five years to life, to maintain such a strong connection. This young beautiful woman chose to stay with him, even though all she had left were short and very public conversations, and shadows of their old relationship.

Cutter continued, "Christopher, it's a simple thing that seems to be missed by everyone else. Look around at the guys you see in here; some of their experiences vary, but the pattern stays the same. When they escape poverty, make something of themselves, gain respect, and have a few dollars to control their environment, they take a woman and control her too, keep her down. They act the same way they would in a business deal; they use their money to have power over her and make sure she only does what he wants. That's not love, man, and it certainly isn't anything like mature love. These guys have never been loved; they don't know what it is.

"My experience wasn't so different from theirs. I became an independent man, starting from nothing. I didn't know love either, but I knew there must be more than what I could see, and I wanted to find it. When I first met Sharize she acted like all the other girls, but instead of keeping her down, I taught her everything I knew, told her she had as much value as me and anyone else that was ever born. I taught her to find strength in herself whether I was with her or not, prepared her to take care of herself. I keep telling her I'm looking at twenty-five years or more, that she needs to move on and find somebody to spend her life with, but no matter what I say, she never leaves me. If and when she decides to move on I won't ask about it, I don't want to know. I just take the time I have with her now.

"You know, Christopher," he spoke with quiet intensity, "you've got to be careful about your family. These fuckin' feds will take whatever you love and use it to hurt you. They'll haul members of your family in for questioning, they'll charge them with obstruction; then it's not just you in here, you have to worry about your family living this life too. If you love them, man, let them go; your punishment is not for them. Stay off those phones."

I had made the right decision from the beginning not to involve Shauna in this hell. But I still clung to the hope that I would somehow be able to go back and rekindle what we had. Until then, I wouldn't make her life more difficult by involving myself in it from a distance. It was the hardest God damned thing I ever had to do.

I believe the nature of a good man is to want to fix a problem and make everything right, or die trying. I was neither dead nor able to make things right, I wasn't even given the chance to fight for it; it was unnatural.

The corners of Cutter's mouth turned down, and his voice was laced with sadness. "I heard a little about your case from Tech before . . . you know. Normally I wouldn't say anything about that, but he's gone. He said your situation is unusual; you're dealing with issues from thirty-five years ago. Man, that's back when I was in Vietnam; you think there would be a statute of limitations on that shit, but it just never ends with the feds.

"Tech said that guys high up have rolled a pretty big ball of string, and you're dangling at the end of it; if you pull hard enough it might start to unravel. It's one thing if you were on the inside, but you're not, so they've branded you an enemy. Anyway, that's what he told me, I just thought you should know . . . I think I'm gunna call you Wisdom, because by the time you're through with all of this shit, you're certainly gunna have a lot of it." Cutter smiled again.

***

The following day I heard someone call me by my new name for the first time. "Wisdom, come here." *That didn't take long to catch on.* I turned to see Roe standing behind me; he had never spoken to me before, but maybe getting a prison name validated my presence.

"What's a white-collar, white-bread boy like you doing in here? Shouldn't you be running some bank somewhere, fucking people over?"

There were no parallels between us: he was a street thug, and I hadn't killed anyone or been through the shit my whole life; in his eyes, I hadn't earned the right to be here.

I said the only thing that came to my mind. "I heard you took six shots and didn't go down."

"You heard that, huh?" He widened his eyes and stepped up into my face. I didn't move. He responded to the fact that I didn't buckle on his approach. He gestured to the other men in the block with disgust and spoke loudly. "What would these motherfuckers know anything about that!" He looked back at me and said, "You wanna see what being shot looks like?" and pulled up his shirt. I saw the six circular puckered scars that decorated his lower lumbar. "You know what that feels like?" he said.

"No."

"That's the right answer, motherfucker!"

"What happened?" I asked. He was the second man I had met who had been shot six times and survived.

He smiled at me. "You wanna know what happened? You're curious, right? It was Christmas Eve. I was with my crew and these motherfuckers were driving around in our neighborhood. I ordered my crew to pull on them; we started firing, emptied everything we had into that car. But my own boys, dumb motherfuckers, pumped six bullets into my back because it was dark and they couldn't shoot straight." Roe got close to me again but spoke quieter. "Everything inside told me it was time to let go, but I said, 'No! Roe's not going now. Nothin's gunna tell me when my time is.' I told my boys to take me to the hospital. Some white-bread motherfucker like you dug the bullets out of my back. That's how I spent *my* Christmas; Merry Christmas, motherfucker."

Since Roe had initiated conversation with me, I wanted to ask him about something I had noticed shortly after arriving at CCDC. "I've seen the guards take you out at least once a week, and you come back looking like they gave you bad news…" I quickly found out it was the wrong thing to ask.

"Boy, you must be some kind of dumb motherfucker; you look smart, but you don't know shit. Cutter can call you whatever he wants, but you ain't got no wisdom." I tried to back it up, but he said, "Nah, nah, I'll tell you, otherwise you'll never get it, dumb motherfucker. You see, I'm the only real man in here; I've never lived by anybody else's rules. Because I'm a strong black man who refuses to bend like a house nigger, the guards take turns beating me with a phone book; they put me in cuffs, so I can't fight back. It makes them feel like bigger men when they go home and fuck their wives. But they know if they took my cuffs off I'd kill 'em with my bare hands."

He wouldn't let anyone take his pride from him; it was the only thing he had left. There was a big division of our life experiences, but now I understood why Cutter said he would put Roe in the front line of battle; I would too.

40

HOLY SIN

FEBRUARY 1999

The doorbell rang at a quiet family residence in Chicago. As the door opened, Agent Callahan held out his credentials. "Mr. Sean Waters?"

"Yes."

"I'm Special Agent Callahan of the FBI, and this is my partner Clara Mancini of the IRS. We have a few questions to ask you regarding your friend, Mr. Christopher Fulton.

TWO DAYS LATER

A government car pulled up the gravel drive to a small rural farm in southern Virginia. Christopher Fulton's grandparents had just sat down to a late lunch when Callahan and Mancini walked up and stopped outside their screen door. "Ma'am, we're federal agents from Washington D.C.," Callahan said. "May we come inside?"

"Yes, of course." Mrs. Fulton replied.

Mr. Fulton rose from his chair and shook both the agents' hands. "What can we do for you?"

Mancini stood, cold and silent; she had yet to remove her sunglasses.

"Nothing, sir," Callahan said calmly.

Mancini was blatantly surveying the Fultons' property and its contents when she joined in. "We just needed to stop by to . . ."

Agent Callahan strongly disliked their orders. He interrupted her and addressed Mr. Fulton. "I understand you served in the Navy in WWII and later became a police sergeant in Baltimore."

"Yes, that's right." Mr. Fulton was confused, *Why would two agents have driven five hours from D.C. to talk about his career? Could it be about his confidential work for President Nixon?*

"We won't take up any more of your time," Callahan said respectfully. "It was nice to meet you, sir."

TWO DAYS LATER

Christopher's mother was at the office when a young woman approached her. "Mrs. Wendy Fulton?"

"Yes?"

"You have been served." The woman handed her a federal subpoena, then left as abruptly as she had arrived.

Moments later, a man and women walked up and identified themselves as Special Agents Callahan of the FBI and Mancini of the IRS.

"I have nothing to say to you." Mrs. Fulton took a strong offensive position. "If you want to arrest me, read me my rights."

Mancini immediately took over the conversation. "Your son is liable to die where he is; he's being treated as an enemy of the United States. I would like nothing more than for you to join him. When you testify, you *will* lie to protect your son—I know you will—and when you do, I'm going to make your life a living hell."

Callahan had to step in, but he could see a great deal of damage had already been done. He couldn't tell whether Mrs. Fulton was about to explode in a fit of rage or grief. "Mrs. Fulton, you do not have to talk with us; that is your choice. Please have a very competent federal attorney with you when you testify."

The confrontation and attack by Agent Mancini had left Mrs. Fulton so terribly shaken that she had to leave work immediately. In a daze of worry, fear, anger, and frustration, she lost control of her car and totaled it when she crashed through a fence. A few days later she was let go from her job; her employer didn't want the FBI and IRS making repeated public visits to the office. Fired up by her conflict with Mrs. Fulton, Agent Mancini followed Barman's instructions and called Christopher Fulton's father. He was living in Vancouver, Canada. She called his cell phone. "Mr. John Fulton?"

"Yes?"

"This is Agent Clara Mancini of the IRS. I wanted to let you know that as an American citizen you can't hide up there forever."

PRISON TIME

My Middle Eastern bunky had been broken; I knew he would never heal from his wounds. He had been sentenced and was moving on. He just left me with a blessing of peace from God and I never saw him again.

That same day, I saw a Catholic priest and two nuns being escorted along the corridor outside the block's glass wall. The priest had short grey hair parted to the side, and a short grey beard and glasses; the two nuns were dressed in their habits. I assumed they were requested to give last rights to Skinny before he got the needle. That seemed odd though, Skinny requesting something like that; he wasn't exactly the religious type. Maybe they were coming in at someone else's request.

Later that day the secured door to our block opened, and two men walked in. One was a short Chinese kid, around twenty-eight or twenty-nine, the other was the priest I had seen before. He was in an orange jumper; *he was an inmate!* He was assigned to Jonathan's old cell, and the Chinese kid, Zao, became my new cellmate. I didn't have time to talk to the priest before lockdown. His arrival bothered me. Why was he here? I would have asked Zao, but he didn't speak a word of English.

The next morning I introduced myself to the priest and shook his hand; he said his name was Father McKinnon. I asked him how he came to be here. He told me that he, and many others, felt that nuclear weapons stockpiled by Russia and the United States were the most dangerous threat to humanity. He wanted them dismantled before it was too late, so he had dedicated his life to that cause. He, and the two nuns I'd seen the day before, had entered a military air force base and threw red paint, to symbolize blood, on an aircraft that would be used to deploy atomic weapons. All three were arrested without trouble and sentenced to six months each. Because their sentencing was the shortest that could be given by the Federal Government, they would do their time in pretrial lockup.

I was disappointed to hear that the government had decided to give a priest and sisters jail time for protesting the annihilation of the human race.

"Don't be sad, my son," McKinnon said. "This is exactly where I belong. I can see I am needed here; I can do good. My job is to save souls, so what better place could I be in?"

It was a peaceful perspective.

"Are there any Bibles here?" he asked.

"No."

"Well, let's see what we can do about that, shall we?" Father McKinnon walked to the front entrance and spoke through the porthole. "Excuse me, I'd like to speak to someone in charge."

"What do you want?" came the CO's flat response.

"We'd like some Bibles, please."

"Fill out a request."

Father McKinnon wrote down what he wanted, then looked at me and shrugged with an open-minded enthusiasm that only a free man would have, and said, "Let's see what happens."

Sure enough, two days later the slider opened and a CO placed fourteen Bibles on the cement floor. Father McKinnon picked up one for himself, handed one to me, and said, "Let's pass these out to anyone who would like them." Almost everyone accepted.

The next day Father McKinnon led a small prayer group on the top tier. He began by asking each man to share something of himself. I listened to the different stories; they were horrific. When it was my turn, my mind went blank, except for a seemingly unrelated blink of an eye from my previous life. I hesitated. McKinnon said, "Don't hold back Christopher, it's alright."

"It was my wedding day. Now it seems more like looking back in someone else's memory, rather than my own. I was making a toast, and what I thought I was going to say just disappeared; I raised my glass and said, 'God, please make me a better man.'" My anecdote was worlds away from the others' experiences, and it only cast me further from them.

After the rest of the inmates shared their respective stories, McKinnon said, "You men sitting here with me today share more in common with the Disciples of Christ than the men of my church who are free on the outside. Regardless of your sins, you have been removed from your loved ones, are being persecuted, and have your very lives threatened in this harsh environment. With all the hate that is perpetrated against you, you still find yourselves sitting here with me of your own free will, to pray and study God's word."

His message carried some comfort in a place where there was none. McKinnon was the first person, other than Tech, to help me find acceptance of what was happening, rather than condemnation.

After a few of our Bible studies, one of the men openly confessed to us who he was and his situation was. "My name's Tyrone, I know Roe from back home; we're kind of in the same business. I end people, for hire, dealers that've crossed a line. I'm in here 'cause some rat motherfucker saw me do my business; he's the whole case against me. I want all us to pray together; I want us to pray for him to die so I can get out of here."

Father McKinnon had told us that two or more voices raised in prayer had an exponential effect, so we all had requests when the group prayed. Usually it was for the safeguarding of families or loved ones, but Tyrone was a confessed murderer asking us to pray to God for the death of another human being.

Father McKinnon said, "We will all pray at the end of the study, and each man can decide what is most important to pray for."

Tyron said, "Yeah, well, if anyone can join me in my prayer, that's my way out of here; it's what I need."

Father McKinnon prayed aloud: "Father, we must live life as if ordained by you, for being born made it so. We are the much-loved prodigy of every man and woman that came before us in this world that you created. Every great work of art, every act of bravery, every achievement of mankind, is ours to claim as the inheritance of your divine provenance. We are all part of the past and destined for the future you have planned for us. Keeping that in the forefront of our minds is a powerful shield against the evil in our midst which these men now face. Amen."

When the group left the tier, Father McKinnon turned to me. "You share your cell with a young man who doesn't know any English. He's having a hard time in here. I'd like you to teach him to read and write; I think you'll find it rewarding."

"I'll try," I said.

I spent the next few months teaching Zao one word at a time: *mirror, toilet, bed*. At first it seemed like an overwhelming task, but he was extremely bright. We were in a unique position, able to devote most of our time to the lessons. He was reading and speaking fluently within six months. Father McKinnon was right: not only was it rewarding, but it helped keep my mind out of depths of despair. I had been able to change Zao's life for the better, and that made me feel better than I had in a very long time.

41

The Deal I Had To Make

February 1999

Agent Callahan stepped into the elevator with prosecutor Barman. As Callahan turned around he saw Fulton's mother walking towards them. The stress of the situation was clearly written on her features and in her body language. She had hired a federal attorney, and it probably depleted her life savings.

"Hold the elevator, please," she said. Callahan noted that Barman made no motion to do so, so he held out his own arm to stop the door from closing. Mrs. Fulton thanked him as she walked in. She was likely meeting with her attorney before going into the grand jury, where she had been subpoenaed by Barman to testify against her son. Callahan knew Barman had used this ploy to upend Christopher, show him that his family could be toyed with. But Barman's ultimate goal was to catch Mrs. Fulton in a lie to protect her son, and he would use that as very powerful leverage.

Callahan hoped the ride would be silent, considering the tension between Barman and Mrs. Fulton, but she turned to the prosecutor and said, "I think what you are doing is despicable. You had my son in chains on a plane for over a month, then transferred him from prison to prison; I never knew where he was!"

Oh God, Callahan knew that would open the door for Barman, who immediately snapped back, "Mrs. Fulton, I think your family is the worst kind of scum; I think you should all be placed in prison, and if I have anything to do with it, you will never see your son again for the rest of your life."

Callahan could see the words cut Mrs. Fulton deeply. Any retort to Barman's poisonous response would have only escalated the situation until she was angered enough to assault him. If she had, Barman would have won. To her credit, and for the best possible outcome, she remained quiet and stony for the remainder of the elevator ride. Her son was counting on her. She must have had to fight every ounce of Scottish/Irish blood that coursed through her veins to keep from pummeling the black-hearted Barman to a pulp.

Upon Mrs. Fulton's departure, Agent Callahan found himself alone in the elevator with Barman, and was moved to speak. "Americans, great Americans, have died over all of this; you might want to…" but before he had a chance to say any more, Barman cut him off.

"Agent Callahan, I'm doing my job, and I do it well. If you have a problem, put it in a memo. Otherwise I would kindly ask you to shut your damn mouth and stay out of business that doesn't concern you." The division between the two men had just been cemented by Barman's cold and narrow-minded authority.

Prison Time

With the contentment I found in teaching Zao English, and with Father McKinnon among us, my spirituality grew; I felt a change in my heart and mind. The word of God became a beacon of stability through the upheaval of my trials and tribulations. I had found some peace within myself, so my surroundings didn't affect me as deeply on a day-to-day basis. It went on that way for some time until I was called in to court again.

After the physically and emotionally draining routines of processing, I was forced into the same chair, in the same room, with the same people as I was before.

"Mr. Fulton, do you have anything you want to discuss with us today?" Barman asked again.

I found it overwhelmingly difficult to keep my mouth shut, as I did before, but since Father McKinnon had arrived I felt less hate. I actually felt pity for these people, and that gave me strength.

Prosecutor Barman continued, "No? Still nothing to say?" There was a new harshness in his voice. "If you continue to refuse to speak to me, you will leave me no choice but make your time here less comfortable."

"God is watching over me," I said.

"You believe God is watching over you?" Barman smiled grimly. "Is he watching over your family, too? As you may or may not be aware, I subpoenaed your mother to testify before a grand jury; I have the transcript of her testimony right here in front of me." He placed his hand on the folder, as if to draw power from it. "I feel the need to make myself perfectly clear to you, Mr. Fulton; I am skilled at my job. When I review your mother's testimony I will find something, and I *will* arrest her for obstructing justice."

My heart jumped.

"Let me explain further," he continued. "If your mother said something was green, but the Justice Department feels it was more grey, that's obstruction. Am I getting through to you?"

This evil, inhuman being had subjected me to an infusion of horrors over time; he had no idea who he had forced me to become. In that moment I understood Roe . . . if my cuffs were removed I could have gladly taken Barman's life.

He slid a few documents in front of me. "Do you recognize these?"

I looked down and saw copies of the bank loan and deed to my grandparent's farm, the farm that had been in my family for over 150 years. I had spent much of my childhood there; it was ingrained in my fondest memories.

"Good, you recognize them," Barman sneered. "I can show that you wrote a check to your grandparents prior to your arrest that helped them pay down their mortgage. When I convict you, those monies will be considered proceeds of crime, and Special Agent Mancini here will take great pleasure in serving your grandparents a notice that says their property is no longer theirs. They will have you to thank for that."

His statement stuck into the base of my spine. I realized that whatever hope of hope I had of delaying this any further was gone. The world dissolved around me, but Barman wasn't done.

"Your father, well we haven't decided what to get him on yet. Agent Mancini, can you bring me a book of federal statutes? We can go through them together and see what fits best."

"You sick fuck!" I said, and Barman grinned again; he knew he had me. My fist hit the table, and a federal marshal moved forward to secure me, but Barman waived him back.

"We're finally communicating, Mr. Fulton. You've made me wait far too long; you're the one who's caused this. I'll be proposing the outline of a deal to your attorney; I expect your answer within a week. If I don't receive an answer, I will move forward on everything we have discussed here today." Barman waived for the marshal to take me out of his presence. It was his signal that he was done with me and that he had won.

*****

Agent Callahan hadn't said a word during the entire exchange; he kept his feelings to himself. He thought of his father's passing, two years earlier.

1997

Joe sat beside his father's bed; his father had become so frail in his old age.

Joe had just turned 50. He had never wanted to think about losing his father, but now that loss was imminent.

"Son," his father's voice cracked; his words were weaker than Joe had ever heard before, "I'm proud of you; I'm proud of the man you've become."

"I wanted to be like you, Dad. If it weren't for you, I never would have made it this far."

"Everything you accomplished you earned yourself."

"I never forgot what you told me, Dad; I'll keep my promise."

A smile creased his father's face and a tear ran down his cheek. Joe leaned forward one last time to kiss his father on the forehead.

1999

Callahan's investigation, of Fulton's case in particular, had opened some very dark doors to the Bureau's past. Good people had paid high prices for their knowledge of the Kennedy coup; some had paid with their lives. Callahan didn't want any part of the persecutions and cover-ups his father was forced to endure; he wanted out . . . but he couldn't leave yet. There was still something he needed to do.

PRISON TIME

The marshal escorted me to another room to meet with my lawyer. Stephen Salvin gave me his trademark smile. "How are you holding up?"

I thought for a moment. "No disrespect, but I don't believe we can have an honest conversation about what I've been through and how I'm feeling."

"Fair enough."

"Have you heard from Shauna?"

"I contacted your father as you requested, but I haven't heard anything back yet." He looked through his paperwork as he continued, "We have one more problem to hammer out. The election is coming up, and the Justice Department's main objective is to debrief you; that is where our leverage is. I've spoken at great lengths to Assistant District Attorney Barman about the Oval Office recordings still in your possession. There has been a temporary restraining order filed in court which makes it illegal for you to destroy or cause the destruction of the recordings, and compels you to deposit them, under seal, into the custody of the Fourth Circuit Federal District Court."

"No." There was no compromise in my voice.

"No?" Salvin was confused by my quick and certain response. He expected it to be another point for negotiation, from where he would lead me into capitulation . . . especially after Barman had threatened my family.

"No," I said again. I had kept looking for some last-minute insight from my supposedly genius attorney, but nothing was forthcoming. I had lost hope. "All of this has been collusion. I'm keeping the recordings because they are all I have to prove my involvement in the investigation of JFK's assassination and what has happened to me because of it."

"But you could simply . . ."

"No." I wasn't interested in hearing Salvin's advice anymore. "You tell Barman if they try to prosecute my family, everything on those recordings goes public."

Salvin took a moment to cogitate . . . "So if I can get a blanket immunity to cover your family and the Oval Office recordings, you will agree to be debriefed?"

For the only time during that meeting, I said, "Yes."

***

When I arrived back at CCDC, Tyrone was on the top tier shouting out to the whole block, "Hey, all you motherfuckers, God is good, God is good. Hallelujah, prayers work! That little cock shit that was gunna squeal on me, his body parts are strewn all the way from Baltimore to New Jersey." He laughed uproariously. "I'm getting out of here. I'm going home. I got God on my side, you motherfuckers." It was sickening. This shameless murderer was the only guy I ever heard of leaving CCDC without a sentence for his crimes.

***

The next day I received a legal letter from my attorney:

Mr. Fulton, as we expected, the government does have a timetable. I believe they are surprised that you have lasted as long as you have, and are baffled by it. My strategy was the correct one; they are offering you a deal.

Your sealed indictment will be quashed and replaced with superseding information. They will give the judge a recommendation of a greatly reduced sentence, with details to be discussed between the district attorney's office and myself based on the following: you plead guilty to structuring to avoid reporting requirements and to bank, and credit card fraud, and you give your full cooperation during a proffer session(s), (interrogation) conducted by the district attorney's office, where you will be required to answer truthfully any question posed to you without the ability to take the fifth amendment or enact any of your constitutional rights, which includes your right to an attorney; I cannot be present at the session(s). These session(s) may be classified and placed under seal.

The government will also agree to give you and your family blanket immunity for anything that occurred prior to or during the proffer session(s) including the Kennedy materials still in your possession, and will no longer seek any further prosecution or request any other government agency or foreign government to seek to prosecute you or your family.

You will also be required to sign over any and all monetary holdings and assets in your name; the government wishes you to have zero net worth. You will be giving up your rights to trial; the district attorney's office has threatened that if you force them into a trial they will recommend the highest possible jail time, which as you are aware is fifty years.

From your statements that the district attorney has threatened your family with prosecution, and the fact that you have told me your goal is to get the least amount of jail time, I highly recommend you take this deal.

If you have any questions or concerns please contact me as soon as possible.

Stephen N. Salvin

42

WHEN ALL THE STARS HAVE FALLEN, THERE'S NOTHING LEFT BUT BARS

MARCH 3, 1999

The intelligence panel and Mr. Barman stared at me waiting for my response. "Before I was arrested, the recordings were with me in Canada."

"Where are they now?"

"I don't know."

"I suggest you get very motivated to cooperate with me, Mr. Fulton. Why did you delay the matter of your extradition? Why didn't you submit to the request immediately?"

I wanted to say, *Because I wrote the President of the United States and was waiting to hear a response, you fucking asshole,* but instead I said, "I was told to submit and plead guilty or be marshaled to Washington D.C. to get a trial, or fight and become a fugitive because I was facing fifty years. I was overwhelmed; I couldn't believe I had been arrested."

"You mean you couldn't believe you'd been caught?"

"No."

"How many items did you get from Robert White?" Barman changed tack again. "Three."

"Being?"

"The watch, a pair of sunglasses, and dictabelt recordings."

"When did you acquire these items?"

"I purchased the watch in 1994, and I received the sunglasses and dictabelts in 1997."

"Were you named in Evelyn Lincoln's will?"

"No."

"Did you receive any other items from her inheritance?"

I hesitated; *if I answered incorrectly, if they already knew . . .* I was trapped, I didn't want to answer, but I had to. "Yes," I said.

"What did you receive?"

"A letter."

"A letter? Something President Kennedy wrote?"

"No, it was written by Evelyn Lincoln."

"What was the purpose of the letter?"

"It was written to accompany President Kennedy's Cartier watch."

"How did you receive the letter?"

"Through Robert White."

"Did Mr. White read the letter?"

"No. It was sealed; it was given to my lawyer."

"What are the contents of the letter?"

"Documentation of the president's watch." I hoped he wouldn't ask more, but Prosecutor Barman was relentless.

"What else?" he pushed. It sounded like he either knew about it, or needed to know about it; either way, he wasn't letting it go.

"It also contained an affidavit from Secret Service Agent Robert Bouck," I said. "I don't remember what they said verbatim."

"Do your best."

I tried to be as vague as I could, but specific enough to appease him. "They talked about the watch being assassination evidence, how it came to Evelyn Lincoln by Robert Kennedy, who got it from Agent Bouck. And that RFK was not going to turn it over to the government; instead he placed documentation of the evidence in President Kennedy's grave."

Everything stopped; Barman looked like the cat that ate the canary. The room had been quiet before, but after my statement the silence was palpable; I had just said something they didn't expect. They had been fishing for information they didn't already know, and I had just served it to them on a silver platter. For the first time during the proceeding I saw the prosecutor glance back at the panel, the men and women of the intelligence community.

***

Barman remembered the attorney general's instructions: on all court documentation, the federal allegations must appear to be a clear case of fraud. Fulton had to disclose everything during the interrogation. Barman was not to bring up JFK Jr.'s name, nor could he disclose what the Justice Department already knew about the situation. He could never take Fulton into an open courtroom; he had to force him into submission, full disclosure now, everything to be classified.

Barman's eyes zeroed in on the lapel pin on the man in the center of the back row. He knew the live feed was going somewhere, but that information was far above his pay grade.

***

It seemed to me as if the prosecutor had just lost his place in his script and had to wing it. He faced me dead on and spoke slowly and quietly. "Where are those documents now?"

"They were transferred to the new owner when the watch sold through Guernsey's." Just like that, the session was over, and I was returned to Charles County Detention Center.

***

The senior man was sitting behind his desk as the live video feed stopped. His hair was grey and his once-strong features were showing the wear of time and authority.

"They cut this short?" he asked curtly.

Williams, the only other man in the office, lifted his head from the report, closed the file stamped "Evelyn Lincoln Project," and said, "Yes, sir, they wanted you to be able to make a decision as soon as possible."

"Have you found out what his agenda is?"

"No, but he's had direct contact with President Clinton and his wife, as well as Soviet Leader Alexander Lebed and JFK Jr., and he may have had contact with President Reagan."

The senior man grimaced, then asked, "Well, who the hell is he working for? What does he want?"

"We just don't know." Williams was uncomfortable that he didn't have an answer for his chief, a man who had changed the course of history, and was continuing to do so. "He's either very good at what he does, or a very unlucky man. But so far the situation is contained."

"Who all was in the room?"

"We didn't I.D. everyone..."

The look Williams received was not good.

"Someone came over from the Pentagon, an Admiral from ONI, members from the Security Oversight Office, President Clinton had several of his people there, an agent from the IRS, part of the National Security Task Force, Federal Judge Harris and his stenographer, and the U.S. Assistant District Attorney reporting to Janet Reno did the questioning before the panel."

The senior man was losing his patience; he spoke sternly as he stood up and looked out the window. "If none of them have the answer, who does?" He was incensed. "I don't care what it takes, I want the documents and recordings found and secured. I want it done immediately and without a trace. Damn it, I don't want this to interfere with the election."

"Yes, sir."

MARCH 6, 1999

Two foreign female military officers approached the residence where Christopher Fulton had lived with his wife. They had entered Canada undercover as a couple visiting Vancouver on vacation. They were ordered to look for White House audio tape recordings and any affidavits from Evelyn Lincoln and Secret Service Agent Robert Bouck. If found, they were to remove those items and leave a calling card; it had to be something personal, something disturbing.

After picking the front door lock, they entered and began their search. They took inventory of everything in the residence. Before exhausting their time window, one officer said, "I've got something."

The other walked over. "What is it?"

"Legal letters from an attorney in Maryland referencing the sealed letter from Evelyn Lincoln. Have you found the tapes?"

"No, but here's something we can use." She held up two nude photographs of Shauna.

"Sexy pictures!"

"I found them in a box under the bed."

"Leave them on her pillow . . . Where are those fucking tapes!"

***

Shauna's best friend, Loretta, had a headache and didn't feel like going to the movie after dinner, so Shauna decided to go home early and busy herself with something, anything. It had been more than six months since Christopher had been mysteriously taken away. She didn't know where he was; all she knew was that he had waived his extradition rights and was somewhere in the United States. Her life was on hold and it was impossible to escape the anxiety and frustration; the unknown kept the pain of his absence fresh.

As Shauna drove up to her house, she saw a large, white, windowless van parked on the street beside her driveway. Not unusual, since most of the houses in the area had steep driveways and service repair men usually parked on the street. But as she rolled closer, Shauna caught sight of a woman standing on her front step, clearly pulling the front door closed. The woman turned around, looked at Shauna, and Shauna looked at her. She heard another woman in the driver's seat of the van call out, "Don't engage; just get in the van."

Shauna watched, stunned, as the first woman closed the door to her home, as if there was nothing strange about what was happening, walked up to the van and got inside. They began to drive away. Something inside of Shauna snapped. "No!" she said aloud, and began to follow the van. Her anger and frustration boiled to the surface; she couldn't take it anymore. She felt used and taken advantage of and she needed to know what was going on.

She saw the driver of the van look back at her through the mirror on the door. The van sped up. Shauna pressed her foot down hard on the gas pedal and kept on their tail. The van turned left onto the highway; Shauna followed. The Sea to Sky Highway had no streetlights, just sheer rock face on one side, and steep cliffs to the ocean on the other. They raced through the twilight along the famously narrow and serpentine road that stretched to Horseshoe Bay. The van barreled along at dangerous speeds; Shauna did her best to keep up. She had taken leave of her senses, but kept grip of her unshakable urge to dominate the situation. The driver of the van was a cool, trained professional; Shauna was simply a young woman fueled by pure adrenaline.

Shauna watched her speedometer hit 120km; she had never driven that fast before. It was beyond dangerous; she could hear her heart beating in her ears. As the needle climbed steadily, her right front wheel caught something. She looked up as her car crossed the road's outer line and quickly went airborne; she screamed as it flipped. Time slowed down. The car turned over and over and stopped, wheels in the air, just inches from tumbling over the cliff.

Shauna was in shock; her breath caught in her lungs and she tried to make sense of what had just happened. She was suspended upside down, still held by her seat belt. The numbness began to subside and gave way to throbbing pain: her head, her thigh, her arm. She tried to free herself; she let out a cry as a sharp pain shot through her shoulder.

It was pitch dark outside. *How long until the next car came by? Would they even see her? Would they help?* Shauna couldn't believe she had been so stupid. The pressure of the last few months had driven her to the brink. The thumping pain in her head drowned out any more thought; she worried her consciousness might slip away. Out of the corner of her eye she saw headlights. She attempted to call for help, but the sound that emerged was thin and feeble. She tried to focus as a pair of feet materialized out of the light and slowly walked towards her and the wreckage. Thank God she had been found; they would get her to a hospital. "Please help," she whispered, as the person crouched down beside her door.

She felt her arm being pulled out through the smashed window. There was a sharp pinch in the crook of her elbow and a warm sensation flooded her body. Shauna could no longer fight the heaviness and her eyelids involuntarily closed.

43

COURAGE RISES WITH DANGER

PRISON TIME

At the end of my proffer session, I'd hoped the government got what they wanted and I would be sentenced, but I was returned to CCDC to sit and wait. Four weeks later, I was called back for a second day of intense interrogation.

MARCH 31, 1999

From what had Salvin told me, this would be my second and final session in front of the tribunal; then the Justice Department would give a recommendation on my sentence.

As the time before, Agents Callahan and Mancini picked me up from CCDC. As always, I was deprived of sleep; I felt ill. After we parked in the underground lot, I was escorted out of the car, up the concrete stairs, and through a secured door. From there I was turned over to the federal marshals who took me down the hall to the holding cells. They removed the cuffs from my wrists and ankles; I could do nothing but wait until they came to get me for the day's session.

"Who's going to tell a story?" a muscle-bound marshal called out. "Who wants to make a deal? We're making deals today." He had a booming and boisterous voice like a barker at a carnival. He looked like "The Rock," and he had charisma, which was strange in a place like this, but unlike Dwayne Johnson, this guy was a total asshole. "Come on, we're makin' deals today." I ignored him and lay on the plastic bench with the curve that made it uncomfortable in any position.

I didn't know how long it would be before they came to get me; my time moved at the government's pace. After an hour or so, a young man was put in the cell with me. I could tell the kid was wrecked and under pressure, but he seemed to be holding it together pretty well.

Instead of the usual bullshit banter, the kid, who couldn't have been much more than eighteen years old, asked me a serious question. He was respectful. "Excuse me," he said, "I was hoping you could give me some advice."

"If I have any, I'll give it to you," I responded.

"I just had a meeting with my prosecutor and the agents in my case. The prosecutor put photographs of a guy in front of me and told me I knew him, and that I would identify him in an ongoing court case. He told me if I did, instead of getting life, my sentence would be reduced to twenty years. He told me I'd be able to see home, have a chance at a life on the outside, but if I didn't, I'd never get the opportunity again."

"Do you know the man in the photographs?" I asked.

"No, I've never seen him before in my life. What should I do?"

It was terrifyingly immoral. This frightened young man was being squeezed by the feds to commit perjury and bear false witness. Would he throw another man to the wolves to save himself? If the feds got their way, he'd become another Meatball. I looked at him sadly. "I'm sorry, I can't give you an answer to your question; it has to be between you and God. Pray about it." The boy nodded, sat down beside the bench and closed his eyes. "Hey" I said. The boy looked back at me. "Say one for me too."

***

Agent Callahan had poured cups of coffee for himself and Agent Mancini; he placed her mug on her desk. Mancini was standing, engaged in a phone conversation. She looked across the room at the clock on the wall. "Yes, ma'am. This is almost wrapped up . . . No, he won't be a problem much longer; he cooperated . . . Yes, but the recommendation to the judge will stay on the high side; he's going to be put away for a long time. He won't have access to the press, or anyone else for many years . . . Yes, ma'am, thank you. I appreciate you saying that . . . Ok, I will." She put down the receiver.

"Attorney general?" Callahan asked.

"Yep," she said, grabbing her coffee without saying thank you.

Callahan realized this was Fulton's last chance. Once he appeared in court for sentencing, he would be silenced, another casualty in the long line of past political and civilian tragedies. Fulton would disappear and the people in power would continue doing what they had always done, what they had become so good at. Callahan decided what his part in this case would be. It was time to keep his promise. "When will they be ready for him?" he asked Mancini.

"Ten."

Callahan looked at the clock. "I'll take care of it; you enjoy your coffee."

"Fine."

Before he left the office area, he searched another agent's desk drawers. "What *are* you looking for?" Mancini asked, annoyed.

Callahan thought quickly and didn't look up. "Oh, just a rubber band."

"Jesus, Joe, look in Graham's desk; he has stupid shit like that."

Callahan opened the top drawer in Agent Graham's desk . . . what he actually needed was a pencil. He found one at the back of the drawer. He tore a piece of paper from the legal pad on the desk and scribbled something down hastily before putting the pencil back where he had found it.

Looking up, he saw that no one had noticed what he'd done. He headed down to the holding cells.

***

The door to my cell popped and slid open and a marshal put my cuffs on. He walked me out of the holding area and delivered me into the custody of Agent Callahan. Once the marshal disappeared back through the door, Agent Callahan spoke quickly and quietly, "I know you thought you were doing the right thing, but they *will* make you pay for it. If you want to survive this, do exactly what I say." He put a small folded piece of paper in the breast pocket of my jumpsuit.

"What is . . ." I started to ask as I tried to see what it was.

He stopped me. "Not yet. Once the hammer falls, there will be no appeal. This is it; the rest of your life depends on that paper. Make sure before this proffer ends, you put it front of the judge. You'll have to walk quickly to the bench; you can't let anyone stop you."

"What's on it?" I asked.

"There's no time to explain, you're going to have to trust me; just confirm that it's coming from you."

I was confused. "Why would you . . ."

"You were just trying to right past wrongs and you don't deserve this. I can't fix the past either, but I *can* help you now. Covering for these sons of bitches isn't my job! My father told me courage rises with danger. Get that note to the judge."

We were almost at the secured door that led to the tribunal. Callahan stopped talking.

Could I really trust him? Could this help or hurt me? Could things really get any worse than they already were? I guess it was something in the way he told me, but I trusted him. Maybe he had discovered information about my case that would help me. I had to believe that; it was all I had.

Callahan handed me over to another marshal who escorted me through the secured door.

The second day of my interrogation started.

Prosecutor Stewart Barman began: "Mr. Fulton, for the record you are still sworn in from the previous proffer session, do you understand?"

"Yes."

"Why did you feel you needed a Swiss bank account?"

Here we go ... straight out of the gate. The account had been John's idea but I'd made him a promise to stay quiet, and I was going to keep it. I thought quickly and stated, "I did it to protect myself against lawsuit."

"Against lawsuit?" Barman's tone was snide and accusatory.

"Yes, in the business of commercial construction ..."

Barman interrupted. "You thought you required a bank account with ultra privacy laws to protect you?"

"Yes."

"We see this maneuver as an indicator that you were selling information to a foreign government and using it as a shield to protect your payment. You certainly had access and ..."

"As I stated before, I have not, nor would I ever, betray my country for any amount of money ... I signed over all my rights to that account; you know there was nothing like that going on."

Barman took offense; he hammered, "But you weren't so protective of the information you received through Evelyn Lincoln, were you?"

"Everyone in the press in New York wanted to interview me, but I spoke to no one!"

"Well, that's not true, is it Mr. Fulton?" Barman waited for me to answer.

I hesitated; was he was going to force me to talk about my meeting with John?

For some reason, he let me off the hook. "You placed material evidence in President Kennedy's assassination up for public sale in New York, which was televised. Who set up that sale with Guernsey's?" Barman asked.

"Robert White."

"Why did he do that for you?"

"He wanted to break the contract on our photo book; I assume he was trying to offer me a way to make my money back so I wouldn't sue him."

"Who did you contact to document the watch prior to its sale?"

"The John F. Kennedy Library."

"Who else? I mean everyone, Mr. Fulton."

There was no way around it. I began to list names, rambling in the hopes the members of Secret Service wouldn't stand out: "Robert Groden, Forrest Sorrels, Jacques Lowe . . . the Office of Protocol, Steve Landregan . . . C.J. Price, Roger Warner, Elizabeth L. Wright . . . William Greer's widow, Nurse Hinchcliffe's daughter, Robert Bouck, Dr. Ronald Jones, and Joe Hagen."

"Why did you contact the Secret Service agents?"

I didn't want to answer, but I had little choice. "To trace the watch's chain of custody after the assassination."

"Who gave you permission to contact them?"

Evelyn Lincoln. "I didn't know I needed permission."

"Did you do all the research yourself?"

"Yes."

"No one helped you?"

You mean besides Bobby Kennedy, Evelyn Lincoln, Secret Service Agents Bouck and Warner, and everyone I just mentioned? "No."

"Mr. Fulton, are you aware of law 89-318 enacted November 2, 1965?"

"I don't recall." I did remember what Evelyn Lincoln's letter and the affidavits said, but I wasn't going to share that.

"Let me refresh your memory," Barman stated. "The provisions of this law make it clear that all Kennedy materials directly related to President Kennedy's assassination are evidence, rightfully belonging to the U.S. Government. A federal order was issued that all such materials be turned over to the government within one year of the law's enactment. Thus, *you* are guilty of harboring assassination evidence, and the government considers you to be an accessory after the fact in the murder of President Kennedy."

I was astounded.

How clever. If you don't turn over evidence that proves there was a conspiracy to kill the President to the very people who are protecting that conspiracy, you will be the one accused of aiding and abetting. I had become the enemy of the lie.

"Mr. Fulton," Barman continued, "you made it public that this was assassination evidence in the New York auction. Did you notify the buyer of this watch of the government's position, that you had received this evidence illegally?"

"With all due respect, nobody notified me of that position when it was in my possession; my acquisition was legal and sound."

"Answer my question," he said.

"I could not make anybody aware of something I, myself, was not aware of."

My answer infuriated Barman and he spat back at me, "Who have you spoken with, or shared information with, in regards to the evidence in your possession?"

"Robert White, and my lawyer handled some arrangements, but that's privileged," I said respectfully.

"Not here," Barman declared loudly. "You were aware the watch would have been deemed a matter of national security, and it would never have been for public display, ownership, or examination."

"No, I was not," I said flatly.

"What did the buyer tell you about their motives, intentions, or reasons for the purchase of the assassination evidence?"

"I sold it through Guernsey's; they kept the buyer secret . . ."

"Mr. Fulton, I'll ask again, what were you told the future purpose of this evidence was?"

It was clear: they knew about my meeting with John. I couldn't answer; I tried to think.

Barman looked back at the panel, then walked directly up to me until his face was only a few inches from mine and repeated the question so only I could hear. "What are the intentions for the goddamned evidence?" he growled.

I responded quietly, quoting Evelyn Lincoln's letter: "The citizens of our country were denied information they had a right to know."

"WHAT?" Barman thundered. "YOU DON'T DECIDE . . ."

John had read those same words just twelve months before. At that time I thought it would be a headline for healing across the United States; now it was a just plea for my very existence inside a closed courtroom.

I stood up, holding the rails in front of me; I raised my voice across the room: "THE CITIZENS OF OUR COUNTRY WERE DENIED INFORMATION! THEY HAVE A RIGHT TO KNOW!"

Several members of the intelligence community stood from their chairs, including a high-ranking military admiral. Their demonstration communicated a clear separation of loyalty amongst the panel; it gave me courage.

This was it. I stepped out from behind the podium and headed towards the judge, moving as quickly as I could without appearing to be a threat.

Barman shouted, "Marshal, secure that man, secure that man!" I grabbed the note Agent Callahan had placed in my pocket and was almost within reach of putting it on the judge's bench when I felt the strong grip of the marshal stop me from behind, pinning my arms at my side.

I was frozen, and so was everyone else in the courtroom, except for Barman, who was still ordering the marshal to cuff me. I looked at the judge and spoke over Barman: "Your honor, I have a message for you, for your eyes only!" I struggled, "FOR YOUR EYES ONLY!"

Everything in the room went still, as if a photograph had been taken and we were all static in time. My words hung in the air until the judge spoke; it was the first time he had uttered a sound during the entire proceeding. "You have a document for me?"

"Yes, Your Honor."

"Does it pertain to the legal case before me?"

"Yes, Your Honor."

"I will allow it," the judge said.

Barman was infuriated. "Marshal, didn't you search this man?"

The judge didn't give him a chance to respond. "Marshal, please escort Mr. Fulton to the bench." He walked me forward, with a tight grip on my arms. He released his hold and I slowly reached forward to place the small, folded piece of paper in front of the judge. He looked down at the scrap, then up at the panel; each member watched him intently.

**

Judge Harris unfolded the paper. On the note was a single line, scribbled in pencil: "Working under executive order of Ronald Reagan, President of the United States."

He read the note silently, then looked back at me: "Is this true, Mr. Fulton?"

I didn't know what to say; Agent Callahan had never told me what was on the note. I had to believe in him, that he had kept the contents from me for a good reason. At that pivotal moment I thought of how John Lennon had first met Yoko Ono and changed his life. He was at an art exhibition and climbed a ladder that was part of a display. At the top was a magnifying glass and a word written on the ceiling. Lennon held up the magnifying glass and here in the courtroom that same word fell from of my mouth with decisiveness: "Yes."

Instantly, the judge declared the session over. He hammered down his gavel, leaving everyone in the room in a state of confusion. There was a possibility things could become more complicated now, or worse. But I didn't feel like that, I felt positive; something had changed.

The marshal handcuffed me, and escorted me out.

44

THE PROPHET'S CLOCK

APRIL 19, 1999

O n the day of my sentencing, I was anxious. Whatever my sentence, my life would never be the way it was. I just needed to know how long the predetermined routine of frightening illogic and senselessness would go on. The worst-case scenario was too devastating to even let enter my thoughts.

I would not be allowed to present myself as I used to be: clean cut, well dressed, healthy, intelligent; I was brought in stinking, sleepless, in pain, harassed, and already branded the loser of the day's battle. However, I was allowed to wear my own clothes. The last time I was afforded that luxury was when I boarded the plane in Canada for my extradition to the United States.

The marshals escorted me into the large, cold, marble room, the Fourth Circuit Federal District Court. I was placed at a table with my attorney, one of the best lawyers in the country, but there was little hope in that. What is the value of a great lawyer if they will only give you an adequate defense?

Mr. Stephen N. Salvin was all but wringing his hands; his face was pale. He had made the deal with Barman, and Barman expected him to keep me under control before the judge until the deal went through. If he didn't, Salvin's career would be in jeopardy, and that made him very, very nervous. To our right was a table with Agent Mancini and Prosecutor Barman. Agent Callahan was nowhere in sight. In front of us was the intimidating polished-wood bench where the judge would preside over my fate, and above her seat was the large ornate seal of the United States of America.

"All rise for Judge Chadawick," the bailiff's voice echoed through the great hall. I looked behind me; there was no audience in the gallery. As the judge took the bench, her black robes reminded me of an executioner's hood. "Be seated," the bailiff said.

Judge Chadawick began. "We are here for the sentencing of United States v. Christopher Fulton. I see here Mr. Fulton has pled guilty to the charges filed by the District Attorney's Office, and has cooperated with that office under a plea agreement for a recommended reduction in sentence under the federal guidelines. Is that correct?"

Salvin stood up. I noticed his hand trembling; the confidence I had originally seen in him had completely vanished. "Yes, Your Honor, that's correct." His voice was thin and weak.

"Mr. Barman, please proceed with your recommendation for the court."

"Your Honor, we placed Mr. Fulton on a fugitive status from the United States, and were forced to extradite him from Canada. Since his arrest he has been in the Charles County Detention Center maximum security facility. He has subsequently satisfied the requirements of this office under his plea agreement and we will be recommending a guideline sentence of 300 months."

Twenty-five years. I felt ill.

"I see," said Judge Chadawick.

***

She had received a pre-sentence memorandum that Judge Harris had obviously forced Barman to draft. It concerned Mr. Fulton's interrogation regarding his possession of JFK assassination evidence and non-security-reviewed Oval Office recordings. Harris had also confidentially informed her that Fulton had written him a note stating he was working under the executive orders of President Reagan.

This was a very tainted case. Fulton's guilty plea was undoubtedly obtained under duress. Judge Chadawick could either follow the guideline, which was clearly in response to Fulton being a national security concern, or she could use her seat to show mercy. She had worked hard her whole life and had overcome many obstacles to get where she was. The people in this room hadn't put her here; President Bill Clinton had put her here, because she was the best.

***

The judge took off her glasses and looked directly at me. "Mr. Fulton, I will allow you to speak at this time. Is there anything you would like to add to this proceeding?"

Barman visibly became anxious and interjected. "Your Honor, we have instructed Mr. Fulton that he is not to speak as part of his plea agreement; we respectfully ask for that to be honored."

"Mr. Fulton?" she said again, ignoring Barman.

I looked over at my lawyer, who seemed to be trembling more violently than before. A voice in my head said, *Speak up, defend yourself,* but the die had been cast. I couldn't speak, I had no voice; my future was being taken from me and my tongue had been cut out. I didn't know what Callahan's note had said, but I had to trust him. Saying something now could counter anything positive he had done for me; I would have to remain silent.

"No, Your Honor," I said, agonizing over whether I had done the right thing.

The judge looked down at me again. "Mr. Fulton, you understand that I am not bound by the District Attorney's recommendation, and that I can sentence you to up to fifty years for pleading guilty to these charges?"

"Yes, ma'am," I said. I was beyond fear; whatever she decided was what my life would be, and I was powerless to do anything about it.

The judge looked away from me and back to the documents on her bench and continued, "I have given this case very careful review, and I have familiarized myself with the government's terms of the plea. I am satisfied that Mr. Fulton has more than complied with those terms. Therefore, taking into account the district attorney's recommendations, I am allowing several downward departures, and sentencing Mr. Fulton to 102 months including time already served. I order the marshals to remand him into their custody and transfer him to Federal Prison Camp Loretto." She looked over at Barman's shocked and dismayed expression and asked, "Does the government wish me to state and publish my reasons?"

"No, Your Honor," he said, still trying to swallow the judge's ruling.

"Very well." Judge Chadawick's gavel hit the block before she stood and walked out of her courtroom.

Her words were slow to register: eight and a half years . . . I thought of Tech's limp body being removed from his cell. He had been right: I wouldn't spend the rest of my life in prison, I wouldn't die here . . . I would have another chance. It was more than I could have hoped for. Just then, I heard the door at the front entrance of the courtroom close. I looked back, but there was no one there.

***

Agent Callahan stood on the other side of the courtroom door and smiled. He had accomplished what his father had asked him to do. When

Joe was a young man his father had lost his best friend, Secret Service Agent Thomas Shipman, to a heart attack. He would never forget his father's words in the days following JFK's assassination: "Son, they killed Thomas. He was President Kennedy's limousine driver. He would have driven in Chicago, in Tampa, in Dallas, but they couldn't allow that . . . so they murdered him, just days before. He would have done his job; he never would have given those SOB's the chance to kill the President. Kennedy would still be alive.

"Agents Greer, who replaced Thomas, and Kellerman, who was the head of the Secret Service detail in Dallas, acted contrary to every foundation of the Secret Service, and allowed President Kennedy to be murdered. A weakened security force is critical for any coup to take place." His father looked the young Callahan in the eyes. "If you follow in my footsteps, Son, someday you will find yourself caught in this issue. Promise me you'll do the right thing, do it for Thomas."

Agent Joe Callahan had kept his promise.

***

I was returned to CCDC for the last time before being transferred. Father McKinnon had left the month before. The only inmate who acknowledged my departure was Roe, the most abrasive guy in the block, whom I had only spoken to the once before. He said, "Wisdom, when you can, let the world know Roe is still standing."

45

THE WOUNDS THAT NEVER HEAL

LATE JUNE 1999

Another meeting at the White House was over, and the officials in attendance made their way out of the Oval Office. Attorney General Janet Reno stayed behind.

"Mr. President, I need to give you our final report on the Evelyn Lincoln Project."

"Go ahead, Janet."

"As you are aware, the ARRB was successful in securing and containing any immediate national security problems. We were able to have Robert White sign a federal agreement. We were also successful in extraditing and convicting Christopher Fulton. We have effectively blocked him from any access to the press for almost eight more years."

Clinton listened intently.

"However, we have not been able to secure Fulton's copies of President Kennedy's Oval Office recordings. During Fulton's interrogation it was discovered that there are two affidavits and a letter that give direct testimony regarding Robert Kennedy's suppression and investigation of assassination evidence. We have been unsuccessful in obtaining those documents; we believe they are now in the possession of JFK Jr. As of this date, despite our requests to him, John Kennedy has not responded to us about this matter. We know he has spent money, time, and resources documenting his father's assassination. We believe it is his intention to publish that information in an exposé in his magazine . . . He has also been insisting that I do an interview for him regarding decisions made at Waco," she said uncomfortably.

Clinton cut her off. "Jesus, Janet, this puts me in a very tight spot. I thought we had an understanding with him about all of this. What changed his mind?"

"We believe the information that came to him from Evelyn Lincoln's estate is fueling his actions. We believe he will use *George* to disclose everything that he can now document."

Clinton leaned back in his chair. "I'll call a meeting in a few days; I want you there."

"Yes, sir."

***

A few days later Janet Reno, FBI Director Louis Freeh, former President George H.W. Bush, and Lawrence Rockefeller arrived at the White House without fanfare and entered the Oval Office. They joined President Bill Clinton, his wife, and three other parties who were waiting via teleconference . . .

By the time the meeting was over, everyone was in agreement about how to best utilize secret Directive 68 in a domestic capacity. The directive had been signed by President Clinton on April 30 that year to manage unified disclosure in the media. It roped in all agencies, together with the military, to control the press.

***

PRISON TIME

When I was transferred, the marshals didn't put me in an armored van; it was more like a school bus. Things were looking better already. There were windows on the bus, so I could see the blue sky and white clouds outside. We passed by parks, and homes, and people mowing their lawn; I was being exposed to daily life again. I could see it, and remembered it still existed.

Acting on Judge Chadawick's orders, the marshals transferred me into the custody of Prison Camp Loretto. It was the unfenced maintenance facility for the fenced in low security prison that was isolated on top of a mountain in Pennsylvania. Loretto was used to house family members of movie stars with drug offenses, ex-intelligence officers who had too much intelligence, and insiders from the White House who had received outside official favor—cases that the Federal Government deemed sensitive, and wanted handled with kid gloves. It had a small population of about 100 inmates.

There was one main housing building with upper and lower floors. The upper floor was the sleeping space, a big open hall filled with bunk beds and lockers. The lower floor was dominated by the mess hall. There was also a separate office building for the warden, and a number of small maintenance outbuildings that contained the facility's machinery and tools.

Following my dramatic change of surroundings, and now able to evaluate myself against the other camp inmates, I found I couldn't talk without stammering, and I shook badly. I couldn't write. I used to be rock steady, hands like a surgeon; now all I got when I put pen to paper was a mess of illegible scribbles. My harsh experiences in maximum security prison had clearly taken their toll on me, both emotionally and physically. I hoped some of the old me would come back once I adjusted.

The government was able to confiscate all my assets under the federal drug seizure law, which was part of my plea bargain. As a result I had to take drug counseling for the remainder of my sentence; it was an education I didn't want and didn't need. It was funny—I had always been disgusted by drugs, steered clear of them and people who used them, only to end up in a federal prison camp forced to take drug rehabilitation classes every day so the government could not only seize my life from me, but also all my worldly possessions. Hilarious.

On my first day I was instructed to move large rocks to keep me busy until I was assigned a permanent job. I was so appreciative of my new-found freedoms that I worked until I dropped from exhaustion; I wasn't used to physical activity anymore. An inmate came up to me after I regained strength and said, "Don't do that, we don't work like that here; if you work like that, they'll make sure the rest of us do too."

No inmates at this camp had a sentence over ten years; everyone knew they would be going home. I noticed the majority of the men had very different experiences from me; most had been able to self-report directly to camp—they drove themselves, or were taken by family, and just walked in. They were never subjected to diesel therapy, or inner-city prisons, or anything like CCDC. They had never been broken. They retained their arrogant attitudes, and I found I couldn't stand most of the obnoxious shits, but at least I didn't have to be concerned with my basic survival every minute of every waking day.

Each morning we were required to stand at attention at our bunks for the same sort of inspection as at CCDC, but the comparison was like a bull dozer to a child's sand shovel. The COs here had a quick routine; they just walked by us, no bunk tossing, and no cavity searches.

One morning, a guy in front of me on the opposite side wouldn't stop running his mouth before and after inspection. He was older, and most likely in for something drug related; he was cursing and jabbering non-sensically, like he was talking to somebody, but nobody was there. The sound of his voice was grating, but the guards paid no attention to him, so I supposed that was his normal state. Following inspection, as the guards exited, a wiry man in his forties walked with intention towards the yam-mering guy and hit him square in the jaw with enough force to knock his false teeth out. I watched as the teeth skidded along the waxed floor. He didn't retaliate, just went and picked up his teeth while everyone in the room jeered. I recognized the behavior; I went over to introduce myself to the man with the fist. "Hi, I'm Christopher."

"Tony," he said, "but call me Tone. What are you here for, Christopher?"

"It's a long story."

"It always is."

"The short version is bank fraud. I spent a year in max security, then I came here."

Tone's demeanor changed slightly. "I worked my way down from a twenty-five year bit in the pen; this is my last year. Still, I'm not going to put up with big-mouthed fools like Lucas, he's a fucking rat; I hate rats. He wouldn't last five minutes where I came from."

"I get it," I said, almost happy to find someone more hardened then me. "How did you work your way down?" I asked.

He laughed and said that was a long story too. "My father died on my eighteenth birthday; I was angry and hurt as hell. I fell in with a group of guys that convinced me to be the fourth in a bank robbery. All I was sup-posed to do was stand there and hold a gun, split the money four ways, and be set for life. I would finally be able to get away from my memories.

"We got away with the robbery; it was easy. The hard part was when one of the guys got caught and ratted the rest of us out to the FBI. At eighteen years old I was sentenced to twenty-five years and sent to a penitentiary. Those were my college years, the best education money can't buy. I took college courses while I was locked up, and did everything I could to lower my secu-rity level, but they kept turning me down. The change happened when I gave up and decided to get the rat; it took a lot of doing, but he's not breathing anymore. Funny thing is, the feds respected me after that, they lowered my security level. Trying to be good, and learn, and change, all that shit meant nothing, but I got the rat and they gave me what I wanted. I should have done it sooner; it would have been a lot less trouble and taken a lot less time."

***

Every night the COs walked through the rows of bunks, shining their flashlights in the inmates' faces. If they couldn't see a face or arm or foot sticking out they would say, "Skin," and the covered inmate would have to pull back their blanket. If they didn't, the guard would toss the blanket on the floor. This place beat the hell out of CCDC.

During the day, inmates were assigned jobs: dig large holes to move gas pumps, then be informed that the pumps would not be moved, and fill in the holes again; mow the expansive lawns, dig ditches, move rocks—anything to keep the grounds, or just keep the inmates busy. It was nice to be able to work outside; there were brief moments when I could imagine I was maintaining my own yard, at my own home, a free man.

As soon as I could, I wrote Shauna a letter. I had been locked up for so long with no answers, but I thought about her every day. I needed to know she was alright, and now I could tell her what my future held: seven and a half more years, then I could come home.

***

Not long after I arrived, a new inmate came in; he looked to be in his late sixties. He would just stand and stare off into space. "Are you alright?" I asked. This place wasn't so ruthless as supermax and CCDC; I could show concern or compassion and not be branded weak or vulnerable. Maybe I could help someone, have some sort of impact.

"I need my meds," he responded.

"What meds?"

"My heart pills. I told the judge, he said they would give them to me. I need them to live, but they haven't given them to me; nobody's helping me." He was overwhelmed.

"Ok, ok," I said, trying to calm him down, "we can figure this out, don't worry."

I spent my day making inquiries about what could be done to help him. The selfishness of the inmates was considerable; their responses were even across the board: "Stay out of other people's business," and, "If there's nothing in it for me, I don't give a shit."

I went to one of the COs and asked about the situation. He said, "I highly recommend you stay out of it. If you have a personal problem, put in a written request to the warden; otherwise, butt out. In fact, let me take it one step further: if you smell smoke and you wake up to find your bunky is on fire, let him burn; if you interfere, *you* will be charged."

I didn't know what the older inmate's story was, but someone had sent him here to die. It made me angry to still be so goddamned ineffectual.

The more I inquired into the man's well-being, the more I understood what a Federal Reserve was: what happens there, stays there, and any interference from the outside is shut down very quickly. After giving up for the day, but determined to try again the next, I met a man who became essential in helping me understand my case.

Argus Gregorios looked like a badass, silver-haired mobster in his sixties. It didn't matter what expression he had on his face, he always looked menacing, like he was going to bash your head in with a baseball bat. He was forward, but mannered, without a doubt a New Yorker. "Argus," he said, as he reached out his hand.

"Christopher, Christopher Fulton."

"Christopher, I hear you're trying to get medication for someone in here. Why?"

"He's scared. He says he needs his meds to live, and I believe him."

"Those motherfuckers, you think they care about him, or you, or any of us?" Argus said, gesturing to all the men in the barracks. "When you caught your case, did they treat you with any respect?"

"They extradited me," I said, "put me on diesel therapy, and stuck me in different max security facilities for a year. I wasn't sure I'd make it this far."

Argus's face changed; I don't think he expected that from someone in a camp.

"Then you understand my point," he said. "These motherfuckers don't care if we live or die. You better take care of yourself, don't get sick; the doctors that practice for the feds lost their licenses and have nowhere else to go." Argus had a great deal of contempt and anger that was fresh, unlike a man who had been dulled down by years of imprisonment, but his understanding of how the camp worked made me curious. I asked him what he used to do. "I was a lawyer and investigator in New York," Argus said. "I was good at it, but these motherfuckers stripped me; I can't practice anymore."

A lawyer, an angry lawyer! Maybe he could review my case and give me a real opinion, maybe fill in some blanks. But I would have to get to know him better before I would trust him to do that.

I was never able to get the older man his meds. A few days passed, and on the third day, he wasn't standing for inspection; his bunk was made, but he wasn't there. Nobody said anything about it. When the COs left, everyone went to get chow and go to work.

I was assigned a weed whacker and told to cut down the growth around the front of the low security institution. As I approached the front gate, I saw an ambulance outside. I stopped and pretended to thread the machine. I saw a stretcher with the old man's dead body on it. He needed his meds to live, and he never got them. Although it was an ambulance taking him away, it was being used as a hearse.

Nobody was trying to save his life, there were no lights or sirens. It looked more like they were taking out the garbage. They must have moved him to the low security prison to pronounce his death, discharge him, and put him on ice until he could be disposed of.

Somewhere that man had a family, maybe a daughter or a son. They should know what happened; they would need closure, but there would be none of that, not from what I could see.

Everyone had kept insisting it was none of my business, but it should have been someone's business. I had failed him. His death was senseless, and it made me angry.

***

When the mail was delivered there was a letter with my name on it. I assumed it was from Shauna, but when I read the envelope it was from my aunt in New Jersey:

> Dear Christopher,
> You know me, you know how I am, so I hope you can appreciate me writing to you. You are a strong individual, and you come from a long line of strong, independent people. Considering what you have been through, your family is concerned that any further negative news could drive you over an edge; they are too scared to tell you what has happened, but I feel you need to know, and by not telling you now, it will be far worse for you later.
> Darling Christopher, I am so sorry to tell you that your mother suffered a severe stroke and passed away. It was very sudden. The doctors said she should have died instantly, half of her brain function was destroyed; they didn't know how she even survived it. She was able to tell us she didn't want to live like that. Then she went quickly and without much pain within twenty-four hours.
> She loved you very much; she would want you to remain strong, get through this, and move on to a better future. I know she will always be watching over you. She once told me if she can help you from heaven, if it's allowed, she will.

Your grandparents in Virginia have also passed, your grandfather first, and your grandmother shortly after. I don't know all the details; you'll have to speak to your father. I'm sorry to be the one to tell you all of this, Christopher.

Your dad is still in Canada; the government threatened to indict him on charges of conspiracy, but they never made it official. He's afraid to come back to the States.

Know that we love you and think about you often. Sending you every bit of love we have to give.

Love,
Aunt Milly

The letter fell from my hands and slid to the floor. The noise as it hit should have thundered with the force of an atomic blast; instead it landed silently. The sounds in the hall enveloped me: coughing, shuffling, conversations of profane inmates endlessly complaining about insignificant bullshit. I quickly grabbed the letter from the floor; I didn't want it stained by this place. I put it in my Bible to keep it safe; it was a sacred piece of paper now, the only connection I had to losing my family. If it hadn't been for the letter, I would never have even known to grieve or say goodbye.

Their losses covered me in a blanket of memories that had faded into traced forms and impossibilities. My grandparents' passing was devastating. They deserved so much better than what they got. I deeply lamented never getting to see them again; I would miss them forever. The loss of my mother absolutely gutted me; it changed how I would see everything for the rest of my life. Friends who had lost their mothers had told me, "Until you experience it yourself, you can never anticipate what it really means." They were right. A part of me died, and a coldness entered my bones that would never leave. The pain was so great I couldn't process it. I locked it up, compartmentalized it, and hid it away. I had to, if I wanted to survive.

A new and overwhelming sense of despair gripped me; how was I perceived by my family at their end? I had caused them to suffer. They must have been tremendously disappointed in how my life had turned out. Their great love and hope they had for me had turned into a distant and agonizing torture. I thought about Tech and Cutter warning me to keep my family at a distance, to keep them safe, but evil had reached out and touched them anyway, and now they were gone forever. The agreements I had signed for their protection didn't matter. My family bore the strains of cruelty and died from the poison by proximity. I had signed a pact with the devil, but the deal didn't matter, my family and I still ended up the losers.

I generally stayed to myself after that. I threw myself into my daily work and routine, anything to drown out the blaring desolation of loss. I was an automaton living perpetual nothingness.

46

GOD TOOK A HOLIDAY

PRISON TIME

During a moment of regained awareness, I noticed an overweight, Italian-looking guy had been placed across from me. He would blink a lot, take off his coke-bottle glasses, clean them, and put them back on. He looked like an unassuming accountant. I needed a distraction, so I introduced myself. "What's your story?" I asked.

"I'm a musician."

"Really," I said, "me too; what do you play?"

"Drums."

"You any good?"

"Well, Frank Sinatra thought so; I used to play in his band in Vegas."

"I guess you've got some good stories, then," I said.

"Yeah," he said, with a far-off look in his eyes.

"So tell me!" I thought hearing about someone else's life might help me forget my own, but I could tell he didn't want to reminisce; maybe he didn't like to look back, either. It's hard to. In the past everything was so easy, but after tragic experiences and loss, it becomes clear: the combination of youthful energy, luck, and timing was everything. It would be impossible to live life like that again. It's like being pushed off a train going 150 miles an hour . . . try to catch up once you're off.

"Frank really loved my backbeat," he started. "I'd watch him all the time; if he needed more I gave it to him. He sang off the rhythm, it meant a lot to him that it was right. Man, I miss those days. And Frank was really great; we all loved him. He took care of us, treated us like family; if we had a problem, financial trouble or something, he'd privately take care of it without a second thought."

"Did he ever help you out?"

"Naw, I didn't need it, but once he asked me to entertain his wife, Mia Farrow, because he had something important to do; he wanted me to keep her company late into the night. I was scared as hell, not just because she was a young and beautiful movie actress I was supposed to keep amused, but because she was Frank's wife; I didn't want to mess up. I mean, he had a reputation; as great as he was, I'd never want to get on the wrong side of him. Anyway, it all went fine, and Frank was happy; I guess he trusted me, the dope that I am.

"There was one time Jayne Mansfield was hanging out with us. The gods must have been smiling on me, because I ended up with her that night."

"You slept with Jayne Mansfield?"

"Yeah."

I had to ask, "What was it like?"

"Not how I imagined."

We both sat silently for a moment; he was reminiscing about his sexual encounter with Miss Mansfield, and I was thinking about the encounter that I didn't have with her.

***

I felt renewed hope in my future when I received a letter from Shauna. She must have been staying at her parents' house in Nova Scotia because their address was on the envelope. I waited until I had a quiet moment on my bunk and carefully opened it. I didn't want to tear it open, it was something from the outside, from Shauna, it had to be cherished and protected, as if it were Shauna herself. I pulled out the letter, anticipating the words of my lovely wife; I had only been able to imagine them to this point. The note was surprisingly short. I recognized her mother's handwriting:

> Christopher, we are sorry to have to write this to you, but you need to know, Shauna has left you; it was all just too much for her to take. Please try to understand, and don't try to contact her again. We know you will make it through this and you will have another chance at life, just not with Shauna.

It was signed by her mother.

My body was empty, a thin shell that could crumple in on itself at any moment. Shauna had kept me going all this time, a force of good in this world that I could hold onto; now there was nothing for me. Cutter was right, but it didn't make it any less painful. I wanted to hold onto that pain. I knew when I let it go all my hopes of us together would end. The seconds of minutes of hours of days were impossible without her.

I hoped she would take care of Leo, Tao, Kelley, and Bear; I knew she would, she loved those dogs as much as I did. That was the one thing I could hold onto now: even though I had no future, Shauna and the dogs did. And really, what more could I ask for than to know the person and creatures I loved most in this world would have a happy life, even if it was without me. I didn't want to destroy myself with the hope of it, but maybe when I got out, if I could just see her again, there might be something left and we could start again, maybe it wouldn't be too late . . . but for now, and for years to come, I would have to let it all go.

It's a strange feeling not being a person anymore. No matter how hard you try not to plummet from a cliff, leaving all your loved ones on the edge to watch you fall, your will cannot stop the decent. There was no do-over, now it was just about surviving the stop.

***

There was a store in the camp where you could buy small luxuries: a battery-operated razor, food, a walkman radio. There were also tins of mackerel, called macks, which were used like cash; inmates would trade them for things they wanted, like a book or better food from the guys in the kitchen. You could have money put into an account for you, so you could purchase things from the store. When I was transferred to Loretto, my aunt put $150 from my mother into an account for me. I bought the walkman radio; it was a precious link to the outside world.

After getting the letter from Shauna's mum, I had to block out my despondency with something; my newly acquired radio was the only thing that could bring me any relief. I sat on my bunk and turned the knob to find some music that would take me away. Several stations crackled before I got a clear one, but it was a news broadcast:

> . . . to further report, the plane never made it to Martha's Vineyard and is now well overdue. It is presumed at this time that the plane may have crashed in the ocean just off the coast. John F. Kennedy Jr. was on his way to his cousin's wedding in Martha's Vineyard, along with his wife, Carolyn Bessette, and his sister in law, Lauren Bessette. We are currently awaiting an updated report, which we will convey to you as soon as it is made available to us.

The words pumped through the ear buds, and pumped through my veins.

Oh my God, John's dead!

I sat dazed; I couldn't believe it had come to this. I was still trying to come to terms with what the Federal Government had done to *my* life . . . I lamented the loss of John, for myself and for the country; we'd all had something precious stolen from us.

The next six days went by in a haze; I operated like a robot, performing my meaningless duties within the federal labor camp. I listened to the radio whenever I could. I understood there hadn't been a real search and rescue for days after they were reported missing. Then the military took over the investigation, and on the sixth day, the bodies were recovered. The whole United States Government and military had spearheaded the investigation, and it took six days to find the plane and recover the bodies just off the coast. Bullshit. The reports said John was incompetent, that it was pilot error and he was responsible for the crash and all their deaths. I knew it wasn't true.

I wondered if John had the evidence on him when he died. *My God, could my proffer sessions have been a part of this?* I heard excerpts of Ted Kennedy's eulogy for John; the words rang in my ears for days: "John F. Kennedy Jr. had only just begun, there was in him a great promise of things to come." Tech was right: the watery sun in the green lion picture was John, crashed in the ocean just off the shore, and the seven red stars were the seven presidents following President Kennedy's murder, that led to the death of his son. The future had been predicted, but it was stolen just the same . . . maybe because, as a whole, we didn't recognize it, or were kept blind to it.

America, as always and as planned, would be kept in the dark. John was eliminated before he could expose the lies in his father's murder and the hardships of Robert Kennedy, Robert Bouck, Angela Novello, and Evelyn Lincoln in their courageous efforts to secure and preserve the truth. The interview would never come out now; there would be no story at all, except the story of another dead Kennedy.

***

A television set switched on, the tubes hummed loudly as they warmed up, the screen gave off a light glow, and a picture materialized. Fidel Castro addressed his people on a broadcast that was displayed on every television and heard over every radio in Cuba.

"I have sad news to tell you tonight; a fine young American, along with his wife and sister, has died in a plane crash into the ocean above New York. His name is John Kennedy Jr., the promising son of the former President of the United States." Castro held up his picture. "John was my friend, and Cuba's friend; I will miss him, and I will always wonder about what greatness we have lost but will never realize. I don't cry . . . but I cried today."

47

AMERI-CAN'T

PRISON TIME

The following day, as I re-mulched the small trees on the outside of the low security prison, I heard someone talking. I was kneeling down working the soil, trying to make everything clear in my mind. Something about the simplicity and purity of working with nature brought me back to a foundation; it reminded me of better times at my grandparent's farm when I was just a boy. The voice got louder; as I turned around there was a man standing over me, his head haloed by the sun. "We've got it down to a science, you know," he said. "No, it's more like an art." he was being boastful.

"Excuse me?" I said, shielding my eyes. I recognized the inmate, but I had never talked to him before.

"Car crashes, heart attacks, plane crashes," he pointed his finger at me and winked, "whatever needs to be done, we can do it without a trace." He grinned and walked away, shattering my attempt at forgetting current events.

I wanted to speak with Argus Gregorios. I remembered seeing a news clipping in his locker; I never read it, but it was something about the CIA. I needed to be open with someone, and Argus was the only guy around that I thought I could trust. After work, I sought him out to see if he could share any insight into my situation. I found him standing by his locker and asked about the guy who had talked to me outside.

"That motherfucker was in wet works. He's a real asshole."

"He said he could kill by heart attack; how do you fake a heart attack?" I asked.

"Nicotine," Argus said. "Concentrated nicotine, anyone can do it, really. The CIA prides itself on developing recipes from household items to kill without a trace, so operatives can travel anywhere in the world and kill a target without worrying about getting weapons across borders. For a heart attack, you get a big pot of boiling water and unwrap a couple packs of cigarettes, then just put the tobacco in. The nicotine separates and builds a film on top. Scrape off the film and put it on anything, a door handle, a coffee mug. Just be sure you wear protective gloves through the whole processes; as soon as the target touches it, it enters through the skin and causes a massive heart attack, untraceable."

It was a recipe I never wanted, and wished I hadn't asked for, but I was curious. "How do you know that?"

Argus just looked at me.

"Can I see that article?" I asked.

He removed the news story from his locker and handed it to me. It was an original clipping from the *Washington Post*, December 22, 1963, page A11, written by President Harry S. Truman:

> I think it has become necessary to take a look at the purpose and operations of our central intelligence agency—CIA. [...]
>
> For some time I have been disturbed by the way CIA has been diverted from its original assignment. It has become an operational and at times a policy-making arm of the government. This has led to trouble and may have compounded our difficulties in several explosive areas.
>
> I never had any thought that when I set up the CIA that it would be injected into peacetime cloak and dagger operations. Some of the complications and embarrassment I think we have experienced are in part attributable to the fact that this quiet intelligence arm of the president has been so removed from its intended role that it is being interpreted as a symbol of sinister and mysterious and foreign intrigue—and a subject for cold war enemy propaganda.
>
> [...] The last thing we needed was for the CIA to be seized upon as something akin to a subverting influence in the affairs of other people. [...]
>
> But now there are some searching questions that need to be answered. I, therefore, would like to see the CIA be restored to its original assignment as the intelligence arm of the president, [...] and that its operational duties be terminated or properly used elsewhere.
>
> We have grown up as a nation, respected for our free institutions and for our ability to maintain a free and open society. There

is something about the way the CIA has been functioning that is casting a shadow over our historic position and I feel that we need to correct it.

"Why do you have this in your locker?" I asked.

"To remind me it was those motherfuckers that put me in here and ruined my life. That article came out in the *Washington Post* thirty days after President Kennedy was murdered, and it never got a second glance. President Trumann felt such a responsibility for what had happened that he was compelled to draft that article himself and get it published. Allen Dulles, the Director of the CIA, that Kennedy had fired, did everything he could to dissuade Trumann from publishing, but he did it anyway.

"Truman had signed the National Security Act of 1947 and initiated and developed the CIA to get organized, non-biased intelligence to the president from one coordinated source rather than from every agency independently. At the beginning it worked, but when Eisenhower became president, the CIA convinced him they had to come up with plots and plans to keep America the global superpower, and that's where things started to change. It was funded by Wall Street, and they never let go. James Angleton developed the idea of feeding disinformation to the media, creating chaos. Too much opposing information was used as a way to hide true facts. From that point on, the Agency grew like a kid out of control, realized its own power, and came up with its own agendas.

"Both Eisenhower and Truman knew that men in the CIA had gone rogue. The real problem was plausible deniability; the national security directive in 1948."

"What do you mean?"

"Basically, it authorized the national security state to violate law—to lie to any official inquiry all the way up to the president—if that lie was important for national security. They can't be held accountable, and politicians can't do anything about it."

I remembered what Bouck had told me. Argus's wealth of knowledge on the matter confused me. "I thought you were a lawyer."

"I am; well, I was," he said with disgust. "I was contracted with the CIA for years; I had guts and balls and could get things done. They always contract that type of outside personnel, especially lawyers, to conduct investigations and file lawsuits; it keeps them off the hook."

"Did you always work for the Agency?" I asked.

"Yeah, since I was a young man, but not just them, others too. Once I was hired by Malcolm Forbes. He needed someone with my skill set to get his son, Steve, out of a cult."

"What did you do for the Agency?"

"Why do you want to know?" he asked.

"Because I believe you might be able help me. I need to talk to somebody about my case, and I think I can trust you. I can't imagine anybody faking the kind of anger you have."

"Faking?" he said. "If I had those motherfuckers in my sights right now they'd all have a bullet in the brain. But that isn't really me, I'm not a wet works guy like your new friend, I'm just a sucker lawyer that the Agency got to investigate Eric Holder."

"The deputy attorney general?"

"Yeah, they wanted to know everything about him, you know, whatever dirt I could find. But then the winds changed; they wanted to keep their money-driven presidential pardons, and keep the voting process rigged. But don't worry, Christopher, it's all legal . . . and America continues to go right down the toilet. Now the information I was directed to unearth is my prison sentence. How's that for an early retirement package!

"And things are only going to get worse. If you take one piece of my advice, let it be this: America has become a whore; take from her what you can, then get out. I highly recommend the Greek islands; that's where my family is from. It was the center of culture for thousands of years for a reason . . ." He paused and looked at me as if he had just remembered that I wanted to speak with him. "I'm just a very angry guy; Chris, what did you want to tell me about your case?"

"Everything."

I gave Argus my paperwork—my federal transcript and attorney correspondence—and told him every detail I could remember. I assumed he'd ask me questions, but Argus was cautious, a trained professional; he wanted to review it all in his own time first. We didn't speak about it for over a week, but one evening he approached me at chow just as I sat down to eat. "Let's walk," he said.

We went outside and began walking around the compound. "Just act like we're doing this for the exercise," he said, before he started in. "President Eisenhower had two heart attacks when he was in office; while he was recovering Allen Dulles held the reins. When Kennedy was elected president, he decided to take the CIA's power away; by 1962, it became a matter of survival or oblivion. Allen Dulles had brought the CIA a mission to make the world secure by means of profitability through U.S. corporate cooperation. The Agency overthrew democratically elected governments, replacing them with right-wing-dictators favorable to U.S. corporate interests. It was meant to keep everything in line: profit over people, profit over morality, profit over everything. Kennedy was wholly against such tactics and supported the world nations and their leaders with their own democracies. When the CIA's operation to get Kennedy in line with the Agency's position on Cuba resulted in his assassination, the CIA got a green light to continue their subversive manipulations.

"President Reagan barely escaped the assassination attempt on him, but the outcome was good for the Agency, anyway: Vice President Bush took over from that day on, and Congress allowed the FBI to become a private, taxpayer-funded cover-up committee for the White House. The CIA accomplished the goal that had been driving them since '63, getting their man in the White House: George H.W. Bush. Skull and Bones mandate number one is to put its members in the highest positions of power.

"Did you know Clinton signed away the free press in directive 68? It gives centralized control of the world press to the Agency, with full cooperation of defense, state, justice, commerce and treasury departments, and the FBI. All the bullshit you are hearing through the Pentagon about John Jr. right now is due to their ability to control the press worldwide. Now, with John Jr., the audacity is starting all over again. Only these are the updated versions of the old tricks: kill a concern before it even becomes a concern."

He was angry and kept ranting. "The men in the office of the president are not what you would consider presidential material anymore. I mean, a President of the United States of America should command authority and admiration, be able to give a speech or an interview without a teleprompter, and answer direct questions concisely and intelligently. They should instill confidence in their leadership. And we, the people, should feel good about the men in that position, making decisions for the future of our families and the future of our nation, and not be embarrassed, complacent and ambivalent. Instead we are made to feel scared and reliant."

I thought of Cutter's words about how you treat a woman, and discovered the relationship between a president and his people should be the same way: a strong partnership built on trust and respect.

Argus continued, "President Roosevelt used to do weekly broadcasts to the nation; he would speak to everyone as a loving father would. These presidents now are all weak," he said disdainfully, "weasels, back-door con men, they do the bidding of their masters, everything for the financial betterment of themselves and the super rich, not the country.

"The CIA learns from every source in the world. It studies models of the Mafia, Greek and Roman history, all the way up to the latest science fiction; it determines what works, and what doesn't. There have been so many secret deals made with the elite leaders of our government, they are more scared than ever of any outsider in Washington calling them out and doing things differently. Most of them have been black mailed into a corner and are owned. There is a real push to keep America feeling they need these individuals in power to keep us safe. There are big plans that include false flag acts of terrorism within our borders and the weakening of the commitment of the American people to their right to bear arms—which is one of the main things the elites are worried about. All of this will turn our country further away from what once made it great; John Jr. would have disrupted those plans.

"These federal camps, within driving distance from Washington D.C., house the individuals that are of most concern to the U.S. Government, but the bureau of prisons has a screening process for cases that cross-reference in any way. At first when I reviewed your case I thought you might have been sent here to do me harm. After some thought, I've come to the conclusion that you are not a plant, but the luckiest and unluckiest guy I've ever met. In the first place, I'm surprised you aren't dead already; I'm amazed at how well you've actually survived all of this so far. In the second, you managed to get yourself caught up in this mess to begin with.

"The system knows me, they know what I know; they turned on me because they changed direction and didn't want a loose cannon. Hell, they let me self-report to this shithole; my wife drove me here. But they were concerned about you. They put you through a gauntlet usually reserved for terrorists and enemies of the state. They wanted something from you, and obviously they got what they were looking for during your interrogations, or else you'd still be in it. That's why your sentence was reduced enough to get you into this camp. There were a lot of counts on you. It's rare they would take such trouble at documenting every single incident; they had you a hundred times over . . . I recognized all the lawyers' names in your case; you know Salvin's firm works for Ted Kennedy?"

"Yes."

"Do you know about Paul G. Kirk Jr.?"

"Who?"

"Paul Kirk. He was cc'd on everything in your case. He's Ted Kennedy's personal lawyer, and one of his most trusted confidants. He's chair of the National Democratic Committee, and chairman of the board of the JFK Library. He's close with Caroline Kennedy . . . And did you know Robert White's lawyer, Philip Adder, contracts out like I did? He's a highly valued asset."

"No," I said, starting to fume over the covert bullshit that had drug me through hell and landed me here.

"He's way up the food chain; his involvement in your case means you were a major concern. He fed you to the wolves . . . But most serious were the letters from Williams & Connolly, Nicole Seligman, who was representing John Jr. and Caroline . . . She demanded the return of the material evidence in Kennedy's assassination from you, and was upset that it was still scheduled for sale and not withdrawn. Do you know anything about Seligman?"

"No."

"She's in with the elite; she's the ultimate watchdog and problem-solver. She was Lt. Col. Oliver North's attorney during the Iran–Contra scandal. North said, 'Nobody messes with Nicole Seligman.' She's given the highest priority cases in the world: the White House, Mobile Oil, General Dynamics . . . Seligman is one of the selected few in the Clintons' inner circle; Hilary thinks the world of her. You know, the difference between White House counsel and these specialized private attorneys is client privilege. They evoke confidentiality where White House counsel can't."

"Jesus Christ!" I exclaimed.

"Oh, it gets better," Argus continued. "Seligman worked for the CIA, with directors William Webster, George Tenet, and Admiral William Crowe. And On July 23, she accompanied the president aboard *Air Force One* to the private funeral service for John Jr. . . . I bet she was in on your interrogations, too."

"There was a woman in the panel who asked me questions," I said. "She stated for the record that she thought I was much smarter than I was letting on."

"Likely Seligman," Argus stated bluntly.

I was choking on this inside. I had been devoured.

"Seligman and Emmet Flood are both partners at Williams & Connolly. They were President Clinton's personal lawyers; they defended him during the Monica Lewinsky scandal . . . That was at the exact same time Seligman sent you the demand letter.

"The Agency was involved in the combination and alignment of you, President Clinton, the release of JFK assassination records, and the Lewinsky scandal."

"You mean the CIA . . ."

"I wouldn't put it past the Agency to have arranged the diversion of the scandal to keep the president in a defensive mode, rather than concentrating on releasing the Kennedy assassination materials that came through you and White. They couldn't have all that information made public before the next election . . . and Clinton associated himself too closely with John Jr.'s agenda. My best guess is that the files on you and White, involving the agencies and the White House, have been classified or, more likely, removed altogether. The public will never be allowed to review them."

I felt sick, but it all made sense. It was incredible to have Argus share his insight openly with me. I continued to listen very intently.

"You see, Chris, Clinton was trying to get the ARRB to do their job for real, but the agencies weren't cooperating; they were withholding classified materials. The Secret Service went so far as to burn their records on the protection of the president in '63 rather than hand them over to the ARRB. The director of the board wrote a letter to the Secret Service calling their actions criminal. There have been so many crucial documents stolen from the National Archives; the American public has no idea.

"The board was supposed to be shut down in 1996, but with Clinton's support, they pushed for a one-year extension; when that time was up, they pushed for another year. It was granted and they tried to finish their job. When they finally had to call it quits, when was it, one month after your arrest? Yeah, it was the end of September '98. The board had members from the FBI, the CIA, the Department of State, the United States Army, the General Service Administration, and interestingly, one individual representing the Armed Forces was there for DNA and blood analysis . . . It wasn't just a panel of five people that the president trusted; it was a diplomatic mission between the office of the president and the intelligence community that was consistently failing. The ARRB wasn't just about fact-finding for the investigation into JFK's assassination; their main goal was to re-establish this country's confidence and trust in their government. It ended up being an exercise in futility.

"At the end of it, Judge Tunheim wasn't remotely satisfied. He knew there were huge gaps in the final report. He took it upon himself to fly to Russia, Minsk, offering $100,000 for the KGB files on Oswald. He was turned down. But in June 1999, as a good-will gesture, Yeltsin secretly gave Clinton part of the file directly. It showed the Russians had no hand in JFK's assassination, and that they wanted the truth to be exposed."

Argus's inside information was overwhelming. I was having trouble breathing. Argus and I slowed our pace; I was out of shape from being locked up, and it seemed Argus was out of shape from his wife's good cooking.

"We have something in common," he continued. "Let me share my side. Remember I told you my family is from Greece? I'm friendly with the Onassis family; even though we aren't close, we have a strong affiliation. In Greece, Aristotle Onassis is still a very important figure. Most people don't know it, but Ari was in the White House just after JFK's assassination. He flew in from West Germany with his security team to protect Jackie. Jackie was so scared; she thought that she and Bobby were the next targets.

"Onassis had big plans to take over oil production and refining in the United States, and was setting up business in the U.S. Gulf. He consoled and married Jackie Kennedy in hopes of being accepted into the U.S. to help his public image and gain control of the U.S. oil business.

"But his son was killed, then Ari had a stroke and died. Christina, Ari's daughter, was devastated and furious at the loss of her brother and father, and blamed Jackie for bringing the Kennedy curse to her family. However, she was very fond of her stepbrother, and asked me to keep an eye on him in New York.

"Anyway, Christopher, you told me part of what I was missing: John was covertly taking bold steps towards a public and legal disclosure of his father's murder and would use that as a platform to run for the U.S. Senate. People forget he was a lawyer like his uncle; he knew what to do, and how to do it. The forensic autopsy required by Texas law would have supplied certified evidence of the exact facts of JFK's murder, that everything was botched at Bethesda Naval Hospital, and the chain of evidence was broken. I heard Bobby Kennedy was saving evidence at that time. I know he was trying to avert World War III, but he was also the one who allowed the bullshit over how his brother was murdered to remain covered.

"CIA dispatch 1035-960 has been in full effect since '67 to discredit and mislead the American public regarding the assassination through the media, but American law is clear: the state of Texas owes the citizens of the United States a murder trial for the death of President John F. Kennedy. It would have been easy for John Jr. to file a case. With the evidence withheld by Bobby Kennedy that you sold him, and the Secret Service documents you gave him, a grand jury would have convened immediately. It would have been the beginning of the undoing of our current government.

"I should have known something was going on when John Jr. traveled to Cuba without his passport to interview Castro, and when I saw the photo ops he took at Mount Rushmore. He was gearing up. His magazine would have been the key. He would have released the information through *George* without fear of censorship, and coming from him, those facts would not have been questioned as to whether or not they were true.

"When I heard the news about his plane going down . . ." Argus looked at the ground and shook his head. "Christopher, now you can clearly see the necessity for taking away our good names and reputations, and putting us in this godforsaken place.

"This is how far we have fallen . . . We are both ruined, useless, and out of the way. But what still puzzles me is who made the decision to put us in the same place to serve out our sentence. Did someone make a mistake? What changed at your sentencing? Why was the recommendation of twenty-five years in a medium security facility altered? Why Loretto Camp? Why did the judge make the decision she did?"

I told Argus about the paper Callahan had put in my pocket and how the judge had ended the session, but that I didn't know what the paper had said.

"What did you tell them about John Jr.?"

"Nothing, I never said a word! Most of their questions had to do with the acquisition and development of the assassination evidence. I did notice a change in the room when I told them about the letter and affidavit from Evelyn Lincoln and Secret Service Agent Bouck. I had to tell them the new owner of the watch took possession of those documents when the evidence was transferred, but I never said John was the new owner."

"Don't worry, they would have already known about that. The forfeiture amount for substitute assets they were trying to get from you was almost the exact amount you received from John Jr. for the watch. They wanted to make sure any traces of that transaction disappeared. It's so obvious it's almost funny."

I saw the correlation, but I wasn't laughing.

"Now, Agent Callahan told you he investigated the hell out of you," Argus continued. "And he asked about the letter you wrote to the Clintons?"

"Yes."

"Reading the transcript, it was obvious to me that your federal prosecutor didn't want the judge's reasons to be published. The note from

Callahan made all the difference; that agent was your guardian angel. He must have been trying to help you *and* John Jr. I've been ruminating over this mess, and I think I've figured it out . . ." He looked at me, but as he did he saw the other inmates walking briskly back to the main building; it was time for a count.

If we weren't at our bunks for inspection it would be considered a blown count; they would have to do it over again. If we were missed on the second count they would assume we had escaped. If an inmate turned up after blowing two counts, disciplinary measures would be taken, but if they didn't, the marshals would be called to go hunting.

Argus and I walked quickly back to our bunks; we didn't have an opportunity to talk further that evening. I didn't know when we would get another chance to speak seriously in private, but I knew an opportunity would present itself before too long; until then it was just idle chatter in the mess hall or by the bunks.

48

THE MOST DANGEROUS MAN

PRISON TIME

As the seasons changed, the work outside became less enjoyable. We would get up when it was still dark, don our work boots, and head out into whatever inclement weather was brewing. Some days we were drenched in torrential downpours, others we were working with frozen earth, covered in a foot of snow. The cold was biting and icy wet; the slush seeped through our boots and assaulted our feet.

I was told to go clear debris at the edge of the federal property, close to the state highway. A heavy rain had just fallen and the grounds were slick with deep mud. At least I could be left in peace for a while. About half an hour into a fresh downpour, I watched a civilian car drive by. As it came around the bend, it hydroplaned and lost all control. I could see the driver madly spinning the wheel, but the car slid from the road and crumpled as it hit a phone pole.

My instincts were to rush to give aid, but I couldn't cross the road; it would mean another automatic five years for attempted escape, even if I was just trying to help someone in trouble. I stood there watching helpless, hoping to see someone get out of the vehicle, but there was no sound, no movement. I had no idea how many people were in the car. What if there were passengers? What if there were children?

I ran as fast as I could to the main building, but it was difficult trying to get uphill through the wet grass and mud. A CO stood just inside the front door; I knew he could get help sent to the victims. Between gulps of air I told him what had happened.

"That's off the Federal Reserve," he said, "it's out of our jurisdiction; it's none of our business."

"But there are people trapped or unconscious; you have to call someone," I urgently beseeched him.

He became instantly angry. "I don't have to do a goddamn thing, and if you try telling me what I should or shouldn't do ever again, I'll write you up and you can spend a month in the hole."

I felt like punching him in the face, breaking into the warden's office and phoning 911 myself, but I was immobilized by the threats of a petty CO. No help was called, and I was prevented from returning to the scene. I wondered how anyone could be so robotic, hold such little regard for life. This was an American? It takes a certain type to do this job, individuals with no humanity.

I wasn't allowed to work outside for the next few weeks, so they put me to work cleaning the main building. A CO sent me to get some supplies. I had to go up a flight of stairs to get to the storage room in the maintenance hut. When I opened the front door I found inmate Pelzer sitting on a chair at the top of the stairs jerking himself off. I immediately turned to leave, but he said, "You don't have to go."

"That's alright," I said, "you've got this," and promptly left him to his business.

Pelzer was one of the most unusual and unsavory characters at Loretto. He was a balding and tubby black guy in his early forties who owned a chain of funeral homes. He was convicted for having sexual relations with the recently deceased: man, woman, child, it didn't matter to Pelzer; he prided himself on trying it all. He paid the feds huge sums of money during his incarceration for the right to continue to maintain and operate his funeral homes; rumors abounded it was somewhere between $15,000 and $20,000 a month. His agreements with the feds kept him out of harm's way, but he was despised by all the inmates.

His bargain was typical, making it obvious that justice didn't mean a goddamned thing to the Federal Government. Forget "the right thing to do," it was all about their agenda, the deals they could make and what was in it for them. How could anyone respect that? Pelzer was in for necrophilia. In his business he was trusted to aid and comfort families in their time of ultimate loss and pain; instead he routinely had sex with their deceased loved ones. The man should have been put down, but because he was willing, and could afford to pay a tidy sum to the U.S. Government, Pelzer would be allowed to get right back to it before long.

***

One afternoon I was talking to Tone about the outside; I thought he might benefit from hearing how some things had changed before he was released. "Taps and toilets have motion sensors on them," I said. "You just wave your hand or stand up, and the water comes on and the toilets flush and you don't have to touch anything."

"Don't make shit up!" Tone yelled.

"No, Tone, I'm serious, it's like that in public bathrooms now."

"Stop fucking with me, Chris."

I would have thought it was funny that he didn't believe me, but it was legitimately upsetting him. He had been locked up for so long, and was about to go out into a world he didn't recognize anymore. It was sinking in just how much time had passed, how long he had been trapped in limbo while the world outside progressed without him. I sadly realized that I had hurt him instead of helped him. It was seriously concerning that this highly intelligent and capable man had permanent damage from his incarceration that would prevent him from retrofitting back into society. He had suffered and changed too much. I worried about how damaged I would be when it was my turn to be released.

The mantra throughout CCDC was, "Try not to die," but I guess I started to forget that in the soft surroundings of the camp. I was stuck working with a big-mouthed inmate named Curtis. If it wasn't bad enough having the COs tell us what to do, Curtis thought he could draw some kind of authority if he barked out his own orders, like some fucking incarcerated foreman. It was probably his coping mechanism, but I didn't care. I didn't know if it was my ineffectiveness during the car crash, my inability to have control over anything, or remembering what I had been taken away from, but something about this big stupid son of a bitch acting like he knew something infuriated me; I just fucking lost it.

"You goddamn son of a cocksucker," I exploded, "Who the fuck do you think you are? You haven't earned the right to boss me or anyone else here around. You haven't got a goddamn clue and I don't want to be the one to give it to you, but so help me God, if you keep opening your big stupid goddamned mouth I won't have a fucking choice."

He turned around with a surprised look on his face, but it quickly changed to a challenge and he came at me fast. I stood firm, ready to inflict serious injury. Tone was standing near me and quickly pushed between us to keep us from beating each other to death. Tone was strong and experienced with deadly conflict and diffusion; he was also very experienced with death. He forced Curtis aside and took a dominant position, pressing his face up to Curtis's to talk him down. I was still burning with insurmountable rage when Tone came to speak to me. "Let this motherfucker go, or it's going to end bad!"

I used to be afraid of death and didn't want to face it, but I had changed, and any price didn't seem too high just to regain a moment of control. "I can't," I said. My whole life had been turned around, inside out, torn apart and reconstructed into something I had no recognition of.

"Fine," Tone said sharply, "then go to the maintenance shed, find the claw hammer and put it in his skull. If you don't let this drop right fucking now, this moment of recompense will cost you five years for institutional murder." Tone looked at Curtis, who was ready to back off, but when he looked at me he still saw fire. He grabbed my shoulders. "Look, I had the same problem when I worked my way here from the penitentiary. It's a strange phenomenon; you get used to trying to survive in a place where every tiny detail means so much, everything is so intense, so you keep yourself under lock and key at all times, because one wrong move can mean death. Once you've experienced that, you don't realize the psychological impact of coming to a clown factory like this, where you have more freedom than you've had in years. Most of these guys haven't experienced things like you and I have, so they run their spoiled mouths and cry about every little thing; after a while it makes you snap. C'mon, Chris, you're too smart to get caught in this trap; c'mon, brother."

I stopped and actually weighed the value of proceeding or not. Taking the time to look at it logically cooled my blood. Tone was right, it was all or nothing, and I would lose either way.

Tone could see I had made up my mind, so he brought Curtis over to shake my hand and clear the air. I should have thanked him for saving me from myself, but it was hard to see it that way at the time.

Before I knew it, Tone's sentence was up and he was back on the outside. When he left, I lost an ally and true friend. He had a way of making things better, and when he was gone I could clearly see all the crazy surrounding me. I wondered how he was coping in the brave new world.

***

When I worked outside I was issued a tool chit with my number on it. I would exchange the chit for whatever tool I required to do a certain job; it was the same for every inmate. If the tool wasn't returned at the end of the work day, it was an automatic ticket to the hole. Guys would spend hours looking for a misplaced screwdriver or hammer after a hard day's work, because there were no exceptions: if you didn't return the tool, you went to the hole.

I stood outside CO Bauer's office waiting to trade my chit for a shovel. Bauer was a large, overweight man with short, buzz-cut grey hair. If he didn't act like such a backwards American hick, I could have imagined him standing alongside Adolf Eichmann in WWII. He had German ancestry and would have made the perfect Nazi: he was a racist bastard.

Bauer reserved the worst jobs for the Spanish guys and the black guys. The people he abused the least were the stupid redneck inmates that kissed his ass.

Bauer loved to search out information about an inmate, and use that miserable kernel of knowledge to make their life a living hell. If someone's wife had left them, Bauer would grind his mocking insults into them relentlessly, all day every day, until the next damning secret came to his attention. As if being incarcerated wasn't bad enough, we had assholes like him prying into our psyches with that bullshit.

While I stood waiting, a couple of Bauer's inmate cronies ran into his office. They were revved up and out of breath. "CO Cohen just had it out with CO Stiles over Cohen's wife," one said. Bauer's eyes got big at the prospect of public misery. There had been talk throughout the camp that Stiles had been sleeping with Cohen's wife.

The other inmate said, "They fought for a bit and it looked like Stiles had him, but when Cohen hit the ground, he pulled his gun and shot Stiles in the leg. Stiles went down screaming."

"Holy fuck, that's great!" Bauer said laughing. "I'm glad he got that little pissant Stiles; I wish I could have shot him myself. He's never going to hear the end of this." Apparently Bauer's bullshit wasn't limited to inmates; he tormented his fellow COs as well.

I naively anticipated CO Cohen's gun would be confiscated, the police would arrive, take statements, make a report, make an arrest, and an ambulance would pull up to take the wounded officer Stiles to the hospital. While working outside I heard everyone buzzing with the news, but I gathered from multiple conversations that none of those things had taken place; it was all kept quiet and handled within the Federal Reserve.

***

I eventually caught up with Argus Gregorios and expected him to furnish me with every unknown left in my case. Instead he handed me back my paperwork and said, "Listen, remember that asshole wet works guy that talked to you?"

"Yeah," I said, wondering what the problem was.

"He overheard us when we were walking outside, and passed that information along. Christopher, I don't want to be transferred from this camp. My relationship with my wife is already on a shoestring; if I'm transferred to some other facility in the middle of God-knows-where, I know it'll snap. We can't talk or be seen together for a while."

"Wait a minute, wait a minute," I pleaded, "you've got to tell me; I need to understand..."

Argus spoke in a hushed voice: "This is the last time I'll talk to you about it . . . Your prosecutor had a specific agenda, but you placed a note in front of the judge and your interrogation ended. Following that, you were sentenced to this camp contrary to the DOJ's recommendation. The prosecutor didn't want the reason for that decision recorded . . . I figure the note had something to do with your actions being sanctioned, that you were working for someone with enough power to alter the judge's decision.

"I thought about who the feds knew you had come in contact with or who you could have come in contact with. The Russians would have hurt you more than helped you, CSIS wouldn't have had enough juice, the Clintons had already written you and said they were staying out of it, and John Jr. wouldn't have had any pull in federal court. In my mind, that leaves one person: President Ronald Reagan. Robert White had met with him; it was likely the feds figured that you had, too. If the note said you had been sanctioned by him, the feds would believe it."

"It's incredible that you figured that out . . . What else can you tell me? What about John?"

"My best guess is that John Jr. was looking at making amendments to the Constitution that would take the power away from Washington and give it back to the individual states. I think he also would have pushed election reforms for the presidency. President Kennedy's death was determined to have been caused by a 'gunshot to the head,' which meets the 'suspicious death' threshold that is required, by law, for a proper forensic autopsy. You and John Jr. scared the shit out of everyone; in essence you were recreating the lost chain of evidence.

"In 1996 there was an official request made by U.S. Attorney John T. Orr Jr. He wanted bullet fragments, found by the Secret Service in Kennedy's limousine, to be re-examined to confirm different ammunitions were used during the assassination, proving there was more than one shooter. The request was given to Attorney General Janet Reno, who passed it on to FBI Director Louis Freeh. President Clinton and Congress established that the Department of Justice retained total jurisdiction over all matters relating to President Kennedy's assassination. The DOJ stated they would restrict their investigation based upon the expectation there would be no eventual prosecutions in the matter, so nothing has ever been done. But that wouldn't matter if a member of the Kennedy family wanted the DOJ to re-open an investigation. I know for a fact that the DOJ, by law, must also allow Texas investigative jurisdiction, so the FBI would be forced to cooperate with Texas officials if new evidence was tendered. That was the real threat you both posed.

"I would bet John Jr. would have requested his father's body be ex-humed for a proper modern forensic autopsy, or use that possibility as leverage to run for federal office. Even if they had exhumed the president and found that he had been cremated, from what you've told me, they still would have found the evidence that Bobby Kennedy had collected.

"John Jr. needed to be derailed before he caused irreversible damage to the status quo. The safe bet was to take you first—you were a high-value debrief. They needed to know what the plans were, what John Jr. had got his hands on. They were going to bury you for decades, couldn't have you walking around with documented evidence; you could have filed a case in Texas almost as easily as John Jr. could have.

"The ARRB's orders are to release all the Kennedy records to the public by October 2017. What people don't know is that there are three types of documents and evidence that will *never* be seen by the public: anything to do with the IRS and taxes (like Oswald's and Ruby's tax returns that would show government payment), grand jury information, and the records regarding Bobby Kennedy's withheld evidence that fell outside the deed of gift and outside the government's control: the real, genuine proof.

"The government built a very specific case against you. Your prosecution was established through the IRS, sealed grand jury indictments, and Bobby Kennedy's withheld evidence. Like I said before, your part in this will never be released. They had to ensure that if any of this leaked to the American public, that the transfer of the evidence to you was seen as illegal, fruit of the poisonous tree—useless in a court of law.

"Because Lyndon Johnson was complicit in President Kennedy's murder, it was simply an illicit and treasonous administration; you and John Jr. could have proven that. Since 1963, every president, federal regulation, order, policy, and law that was passed could be seen as illegitimate and illegal. That could be argued in court, but more importantly, it would have opened the door for radical change in this country, and that made you a very serious threat."

With JFK's assassination, the innocence of our country was lost, and our greatness degraded beyond recognition, and no one would ever be held accountable. There was no excuse so great as to counterbalance the lost loyalty and trust of the people of this nation to those who have been charged with protecting it.

I could see my position with more clarity: when this started, I had been pulled into decades of secret agendas I didn't understand. I naively believed it was my obligation to preserve the evidence and find the truth. I wished to God I had never been a part of any of it. I tried to figure out what Tech had told me . . . was this my fate, or just chance? I never felt more alone and unsettled in the truth of the history of my country.

Argus continued, "They had to put you away so that by the time you got out, if you said anything publicly, it wouldn't matter: you'd be a convicted felon with decades of dust on your story. But something happened in that courtroom that changed the situation. You were sentenced to less time, allowing you to make it into a camp, and then you were ordered to this specific camp by the judge.

"This place, specifically, has been famous for holding people with White House problems and CIA concerns. They mix us in with a bunch of high-profile drug cases so we don't stand out. Anyway, the piece of paper you put on the judge's bench made all the difference. It let you slip through.

"Here, take my contact information. Get hold of me when you get out, I think I can get you an audience with Ari's heir, Athena, and her guardian; they would have an interest in your involvement. Just be cautious: it's a violation to communicate or coordinate with fellow inmates for five years after being released from the federal system. You could be sent back to prison." He shook my hand and said, "Goodbye for now," then walked away.

I had gained a pivotal perspective on what had actually happened to me; I had finally been told the truth.

I figured Argus would calm down eventually and we would have plenty of time, years, to discuss everything at length, but it wasn't long after my conversation with him that I was summoned. "Fulton!" a CO yelled. "Report to the warden's office before work assignment." I left the main building and walked the ten steps to the administrative building. I tried to open the door but it was locked, so I knocked. A few moments later it was opened by the major, the head CO of the camp. He pointed to his right, "That way, Fulton, down the hall, on the left." He walked behind me and stood by the door as I went into the warden's office.

When I first arrived at Loretto, I had reported to the major, but this was the first time I had ever seen the warden. "Mr. Fulton," he said, "as you know, we are overcrowded here, so the bureau has decided to transfer you to Lewisburg Camp."

"Sir, I'm settled here; I'd prefer not to leave."

"There is no appeal process for this, Fulton; the bureau of prisons has decided to move some people around, and you are one of them. Get your stuff packed and ready to go. There's no need to report to your work station this morning; you're leaving this afternoon."

I left the warden's office alone; I was expected to exit out the security door at the end of the hall. As I put my hand on the door handle, I paused; I could have got into serious trouble for not leaving the hall right away, but really what could they do, send me to prison? I could hear the warden and the major talking back in the office. Their voices echoed through the doorway and bounced down the hall; I could hear every word. The warden said, "You know the government considers him and the Greek to be the most dangerous guys in here?"

I was one of the most dangerous?

I quickly and quietly opened the door and walked outside. I guess everything Argus had said was right, and now I was the one being transferred.

49

A GLINT OF TRUTH

PRISON TIME

It wasn't long before a bus came to collect me from Loretto prison. They put me in shackles; after having some freedom the steel encircling my wrists and ankles made my skin crawl. I wanted to question the marshal about the chains, but I knew it would be a waste of time. It must have been the policy for all levels of security during transport. My personal effects were transferred separately in a box, so when they took custody of me, it was just me and my chains. Although I lamented being taken away from Loretto, I was anxious to get to the freedoms of another camp as quickly as possible and establish another stabilizing routine.

The bus was full and I was assailed by the conversations of more serious offenders. I sat across from an old man who ranted and raved for the entire two-hour transport. I did my utmost to block him and the rest of the bus's clamor from my thoughts. That had become one of my survival skills, but today it was an impossible endeavor. "The battle of light and darkness has begun," the old man ranted. "Prophets were here to alert us to the consequences of our collective actions. They used their visions to give us time to change, and risked it all. They warned us, yet still we do nothing. We are all blind cowards . . . The hellish souls will now be reborn to earth as children, they are the dead rising."

As the bus slowed, his voice became louder. "The Kennedys were prophets, now the last one has been vanquished. It has begun, you are all witnesses . . . *You* are a witness, *you* saw it!" He said pointing at me, his shackles clanking at the black box around his waist. "You bore the evidence, you shook hands with God's angel of free will, then watched him cast down to the sea by the deeds of evil men. Did you cry with God? Did you?"

All I could do was stare back at him. My handcuffs were not the only things making my skin crawl. He seemed to be on the brink of insanity, but he clearly knew something. If I had met him in camp, maybe I could have delved deeper into the workings of his mind, but I had bigger problems now. As I turned my gaze away from the unsettling man, I saw it: a huge wall that towered over the bus. It was all stone with gun turrets that dominated the top. I could hear names being spoken by the inmates as we approached: John Gotti, Jimmy Hoffa, Al Capone, Nazi and Russian spies, American traitors . . . This was their home: Lewisburg Penitentiary. I prayed we would drop off the inmates quickly, and I could get to the satellite camp posthaste.

The bus pulled through the massive front gate; it closed behind us. Another gate in front opened, and we drove into the yard. We were all ushered off the bus, each man chained to the next. *God, I was being pulled out with the rest of the inmates!* We toed the line and a CO came out in a t-shirt that said: "The Big House," like he was a fan of the place.

"This is the big house," he bellowed. "I don't know where you've been or where you're coming from, but people die in here. Most of our inmates are lifers, so keep your shit wired at all times. Listen to any directions you are given, and follow them instantaneously. Lethal force is authorized for all personnel inside; they do not have to ask permission to take your life from you."

Why was I being taken to the penitentiary instead of the camp? This wasn't just any pen, it was the most notoriously dangerous and fearsome one in the entire country. It was an ominous prison; it looked like it belonged in an old horror movie like *Nosferatu*, and had the same sense of foreboding about it. We entered the castle-like prison; our ankle chains clanked noisily along the cold floor as we shuffled along, over the threshold and into a nightmare.

Once swallowed inside the doors, we were in the belly of the beast. I feared I would be forgotten, and digested by the iniquity confined here. Many strong-willed men had lost their lives in this place, not just the weak or unsure. I tried to keep my back to the wall and my mouth shut, listening and learning as quickly as I could. I couldn't believe I was in this position again, but I was determined to survive it.

Once unchained from each other and stripped and deloused, we were separated out into holding cells. Later a few of us were chained up again and taken down a stinking corridor where we were sized up by the resi-dent inmates. They were attempting to see if we were prepared to take a life to defend our own or not. Many of the inmates had magazines taped around their arms like armor to prevent shiv wounds. As we walked past the castration room, the CO threatened it was still in use. Threads of fishing line shimmered along the corridors, between cells, and between buildings. It was an intricate matrix of miniature highways strung to send things back and forth between inmates. This place was operating out of time, a place untouched by the modern and civilized world.

Was this my punishment for talking with Argus? Had I been reclassi-fied from a minimum security camp to maximum security penitentiary? I wondered what strings had been pulled to get me here, and by whom. When a cow is led to slaughter, nobody tells it what is about to happen. I was totally in the dark; it was torturous.

Once secure in my cell, I had a moment to close my eyes and imagine that I was somewhere else, anywhere else. I thanked God I didn't have a cellmate. Before I got the chance to escape my reality, there was a bang on my cell door. A CO was standing there. "You're in a federal penitentiary now. If there is a nuclear attack anywhere in the northern hemisphere, we're under direct orders to kill all prisoners. The government considers you all to be enemies of the state. It's nothing personal, but I will come and shoot you in the head." I thanked him kindly for the forewarning.

As I lay down on my bunk, the filthy striped pillow under my head, my eyes wandered to the cell window. The prison's copper roofing glinted in the sun, and I could see the flag in the middle of the yard: the Star Span-gled Banner, blowing in the breeze. *God Bless America, it's not personal, but I will shoot you in the head.* Until now, I never knew this America existed.

The flag was the last thing I saw before it happened . . . I had never before experienced what some would call a waking dream. I heard a voice speak to me directly, but I was completely alone. The tone was strong and reassuring, soothing and calm. A clearly audible voice said, "Do you un-derstand?" I felt like it was meant as a gift. Then the words were repeated: "Do you understand?" I sat on my bunk isolated in this experience which arrived not from a physical plain, but from a spiritual one. Had the stress broken my mind into fragmented, talking pieces, or had I had truly expe-rienced a divine visitation?

A CO brought me my first Lewisburg chow. There was steak with a baked potato, gravy, and a big roll of bread with tons of butter. I imagined this was what a prisoner's last meal would be like. When I asked the CO about it, he said everyone in the pen ate like this. "It's something to look forward to every day, keeps you guys happy so you won't kill each other as frequently." But I thought better: it was so the inmates wouldn't kill the COs as often. It was best meal I had eaten in a very long time.

I wanted to know what was going to happen to me, but I wasn't hopeful; you never get those kinds of answers in places like this. At night I dreamed I was back at Loretto: I was outside on a warm summer day, cutting the grass and mulching the trees, keeping myself to myself. I breathed in fresh air and felt the warm, brilliant sun on my face. Every time I woke to the cold grey stone and the stale sour air of Lewisburg, shock would ripple through my gut until I threw up.

I was left in continual unknowing, but luckily I was able to stay in my cell. A transfer to general population could come at any time, so I tried to prepare myself for a return to an endless state of survival mode. If I had to live out the rest of my sentence here, I had to get ready, mentally and physically.

Lewisburg was used for attitude adjustments; Warden Bledsoe was known for keeping guys shackled up for days, and the cells were so small that two men couldn't walk around at the same time. This hell hole paved the way for modern super max prisons where inmates are never allowed to see the light of day. Seventy-five years ago, prisons were meant to rehabilitate criminals; today they're designed to drive inmates crazy and keep the recidivism rate high. Imprisoning people has become a business.

On top of the ungodly sum of money allocated by the government for each federal inmate, which increases every year, there's the added benefit of what they call Unicore. Unicore is a government-run prison business where inmates strip millions of donated computers to recover resalable platinum and gold and are compensated with pennies a day. It's almost a pure profit business that runs all day, every day, under the guise of rehabilitation. The major shareholders of Unicore are the federal judges and district attorneys who put the men and women in prison to begin with, at an astronomical conviction rate.

The land of the free has become the most litigious country with the highest prison rate in the world. Back in CCDC, Cutter told me there were more black men incarcerated in America than all the men and women enslaved prior to the Emancipation Proclamation. Slavery was abolished in 1865, *except* for any man or women who committed a crime. In the federal world, the term crime has a very broad perspective, inflicted with vigor on those they choose, and ignored for those plugged into power within the system. The powerful men and women are not prosecuted and destroyed for their crimes against our society; instead they are protected and promoted because they can be controlled.

***

A month passed, and I still had no idea what my future held, until a guard came to my cell. "Fulton, come with me," he said with a blank expression on his face. My time had run out, I was going to be placed in general pop. I had been dreading this moment since I arrived, I had thought of nothing else. I decided to attack the first person I thought I could beat out in a fight, to keep the rest of the animals at bay and stay alive.

I followed the CO through the horrific corridors until I was back where I had first entered the pen. He escorted me out the main entrance, through the yard, and directed me to a side entrance by the front gate. He took off my cuffs and instructed me to walk through the door, turn left, and keep walking until I hit the camp. "Report to the major immediately," he ordered, and opened the door.

I couldn't believe what I was hearing. I was in one of the worst places in the world under the tightest security, and now I was being released to freely walk outside. I looked up at the gun towers. *Were they setting me up so they could take me out? Would they shoot me for escape?*

I walked through the door and turned my back to the immense walls. I concentrated on the ground under my feet, and expected to hear a crack and feel a sharp pain radiate before I died in a pool of my own blood, just outside the gates of Lewisburg Penitentiary.

If this was it, I didn't want to see it coming, but I wasn't going to run. I just kept walking, and waiting. I never heard the report of a rifle, and I never felt death touch me.

Welcome to Lewisburg Camp.

50

THE KEEPERS OF SECRETS

PRISON TIME

Lewisburg Camp was proportionately different from Loretto. As the satellite camp to Lewisburg Pen, it was massive, housing over 1100 men; it was also more strict and more oppressive. The COs did double duty in both the camp and penitentiary. They thought the inmates at camp had too many freedoms, so they restricted them whenever possible. The inmates had jobs maintaining the fence line and grounds around Lewisburg Pen. I hoped I could continue working outside by myself like I had at Loretto.

The camp was so big it was split into sections. I was housed in one of two main buildings which held the largest population of men. Very few here were in for political reasons, but I did meet a former leader in the Democratic Party. I had seen him on television and in magazines and was interested to hear his story. I introduced myself and asked how such a high-profile political figure ended up here.

"When I was working for the party we had the best time in the world," he explained. "For decades, everyone had money; we were swimming in donations and tax dollars. It was a perfect network of support and friendship, until it wasn't. I made the mistake of crossing a line and I fell on the wrong side of the party's interest. I may have lived high on the hog for years, but I sure felt their wrath when they turned on me. This was the result." That was all I ever got out of him, but it painted a clear-enough picture.

I also met an attorney general; a secretary of labor; an elderly U.S. diplomat from Russia who had worked for the CIA; a young man from the

NSA; Tony the Knife, who was in his seventies and had worked for the Mob and the government and was in on a gun charge; the brother of Pat Croche, the President of the Philadelphia 76ers; a New Jersey police officer; and Frank McCracken, "Mac," the first black councilman in Redding Pennsylvania, president of WTVE television station, and a minister. Mac was asked to roll over on the mayor of Philadelphia, and his refusal cost him dearly. He was indicted on tax evasion, and was serving a two-and-a-half-year sentence.

This place wasn't like Loretto, where people were sent to be hidden away with their secrets. These men had gone against the political grain and were sent to Lewisburg as punishment. They had made the government fight and forced them into court.

There were other quarters that were completely segregated from everything else. They were reserved for the Wall Street offenders, the men addicted to cocaine who were responsible for moving around America's money. They were behind monetary thefts too large to conceive. Their lawyers enrolled them in the drug rehabilitation program at Lewisburg Camp that catered to them specifically. They had their own building with their own track, and had the opinion they were better than everyone else. They weren't better, but they certainly weren't like the rest of us; they were high-living thieves and this was their slap on the wrist. We owe a big part of our country's mess to these fine men. The other inmates never fraternized with them except during chow.

At mealtimes everyone co-mingled in the mess hall. I got to know one of the Wall Street boys, Ellis. "How come you aren't in our wing?" he asked as we stood in line for chow. "You look like you belong with us."

"I don't," I said. "I'm in for something else."

"That's a shame. Everything's better for us over there. Know why I'm in? Too much money; too many good times. I got into the best school, graduated with a license to steal, and went to work for the biggest firm in New York." He puffed out his chest and had a stupid grin on his face I would have liked to punch off. I hated how he was so cavalier about crimes that were so costly to so many honest and hard-working Americans. This little punk didn't have any idea about life, real life. Privilege makes weak people.

"Aw, it was great," he continued, with a dreamy look in his eyes. "We were dropping 75k a night on hookers, and just as much on premium lines. If things went south at work with a big fish, we'd just say, 'DK, don't know.'" He laughed. "It might have been reflected in our pay check, but it usually wasn't. Man, I can't wait to get out of here and get back to it."

This place was maddeningly incongruent. I didn't have to worry about other guys trying to kill me; I was just worried about them driving me crazy.

My bunky, Kelly, who was 6'5 and over 300 pounds didn't talk much. I knew he was a biker and he was in on a drug charge, but that was it. He put himself on a strict oatmeal diet. I didn't think anyone could survive on oatmeal and water, but after a few months he was down to 170 pounds.

One day he asked me if I would stand with him while he lit a candle. I wondered where he got a candle from, but I said, "Alright, what's it for?"

"Every year I light a candle for my brother," he said. "I'd like you to be there with me." He pulled the candle from his locker, set it on top and lit it. We stood in silence for a moment before Kelly started talking; he had never opened up before. He was very matter of fact. "My brother Jeff and I were in a hotel. I'd had a problem with a drug transaction and was hiding out. I knew they were gunna try and kill me, but I was prepared to take as many of them as I could. We didn't have food with us, so Jeff had to go out to get supplies. When he didn't come back, I panicked; I was convinced they'd gotten him.

"Hours later the hotel room door swung open without warning; I was caught off guard. Out of reflex, I fired my 45 automatic; I hit the perpetrator one time square in the chest. It was Jeff; he fell to his knees. I threw the gun down and grabbed my brother before he hit the floor. I just held him in my arms, I didn't know what to do. I can still hear him saying, 'It hurts, it really hurts,' before he closed his eyes. That was it, he was gone. I had killed my baby brother.

"Someone reported the gunfire and the police showed up. When they came I was still holding him; I couldn't let go. The cops gave me my last free minutes with him before they put the cuffs on. I told them he was my brother . . . that I shot him by accident. I begged them to take me to my mother so I could tell her I was the one who took the life of her son.

"On this day I allow myself to think about those two moments: when I saw the life leave my brother by my own hand, and the look in my mother's eyes when I told her. I light a candle for him on the anniversary every year. Thanks for being here with me."

51

LIBERTY AND JUSTICE FOR ALL

PRISON TIME

I had been at Lewisburg Camp for a year and was settled into my surroundings and routine when I heard the Twin Towers had come down.
Tech had been right. I felt a supreme and overwhelming sadness, not
only for the people who lost their lives, but for their families, too. I thought
maybe if Tech hadn't been beaten to death in his cell he could have somehow warned someone, gotten word out, and maybe made a difference.

I heard on the radio that over 40,000 of Jacques Lowe's negatives had
been destroyed in the collapse. Jacques, himself, had passed away four
months earlier. I felt sorry I had never been able to send him the photo I
had once promised.

Following the horrors of 9/11, a fellow inmate, who was formerly a
New York police officer, sought me out. I came to realize he was in a pre-
dicament similar to the one I had found myself in at Loretto when John's
plane went down. He needed someone to talk to and I was that someone.

His name was Nick Lee and he possessed the mind of a shrewd de-
tective. He said he couldn't stand keeping quiet anymore; after 9/11 it
was just too painful. He shared his case paperwork with me and I quickly
understand who he was and why he was here.

He told me his story: "I used to get my hair cut at a small barbershop
in New Jersey; nobody knew I was a cop. I noticed Middle Eastern men
had started to gather there, talking to each other in Arabic. It seemed to
be their new hangout. Something bothered me about the situation, so I
took a tape recorder with me the next time I went in for a trim. I stayed in
the shop and recorded for as long as I could without looking suspicious.

"I gave the tape to someone who spoke Arabic and got them to translate it for me. I thought I was seeing things when I read the transcription. The men were discussing their progress with flying lessons, and their abilities to accurately hit targets in New York; they even said the words, 'the towers.' I took the recordings to the FBI right away and told them how I had gotten them. They told me they were aware of the situation and to stand down. I thought they must have undercover agents on it already. Later, an agent warned me that the CIA was trying to turn the suspects into double agents, and even the FBI was ordered to back off. I didn't want to get in the way or blow the investigation.

"Almost immediately after, I was arrested by the FBI for helping illegal immigrants get jobs in New York; I'd been doing that for years. My mom, you know, she came over illegally, but she worked hard and was able to make a life for herself and our family, and she made it right when she could. I just wanted to help other people get that same chance. I pled guilty and was sent here. Next thing I know the towers are down; why didn't they stop it?" Nick was distraught; it tortured him.

I remembered Tech's words and told Nick, "You and I aren't part of the world out there anymore. They put you in here for a reason, and I'm sure it wasn't because you were helping people find jobs; that's just what they could get you on. You knew too much about a situation they didn't want anyone to know about, so they locked you away, like me, cut you off from the outside world. I was told the towers were coming down, too, years ago while I was still in max security. The feds have known about it for a long time. Other than gaining the ability to control through fear, I don't know why they allowed it to happen, but they did. If something fits the government's agenda, they'll disregard the well-being of American citizens to achieve it."

There was no advice I could give him, or I would have given it to myself, so I suggested he start attending the camp's church services with me to try and assuage his soul.

Lewisburg's inmates divided themselves religiously: church services were held separately for Christians, Catholics, and Muslims. Mac led the worship for the Christian service; he was a talented pastor who played the piano and sang. Along with a fellow inmate who played the guitar, he brought music and life to us every Sunday. I enjoyed his sermons and his music. There was nothing like it at any other facility I had been to. I felt an overwhelming desire to be a part of it; it was positive in a well of negativity. The inmates benefited mentally as well as spiritually from the services. It was crucial for some men who had served long sentences under harsh conditions, and were looking for a way home. I respected the guidance Mac was bringing to the camp. He had a strong character, and I drew strength from him. Each Sunday became an important process for me as well.

After several months in attendance, Mac asked me to stay behind following one of his services. "I've seen how you react to things," he said, "and I think I know what kind of person you are. I've learned that paying close attention and making careful decisions about who to be friends with makes all the difference."

As time went on, Mac and I became close, more like brothers with a bond of blood rather than friendship. Sometimes I would come to him with what I thought was a severe dilemma, looking for direction. He would listen intently, then say, "And so?"

His answer always frustrated me.

"So, what comes next?" he tried to explain. "Every crossroads you come to, you can go left or right or straight through; the outcome will depend on your decision. You have to look ahead to decide which path will give you the best result. You can come to me with all your problems, and we can talk about the different roads you can take, but you have to decide for yourself what you want out of the situation and what each decision you make will mean to you. Truth, and choice, and right changes from man to man, so it's up to you to figure out what your roads will lead to. If you want any enjoyment out of life, it's your responsibility to try and find it and be a part of it. All we are here to do is live and die; it shouldn't torture you that much. You know better than most: knowledge can have a steep price, cost you everything. There is always a price to pay for learning and becoming better than you were, and sometimes you don't get to choose whether you want to pay or not.

"When I was in Vietnam, I was an intelligence officer working under the orders of President Johnson. My job was to direct the carpet bombing to demolish the morale of the Viet Cong by obliterating and killing everything: villages, women, children, animals. One day I was in the officers' tent when a pilot pushed his way through the flaps, walked up to me, and put a woman's severed arm on the table, on top of my paperwork. 'This is what you make us do,' he said. 'You know damn well the Viet Cong are dug in and protected; all we are doing is killing civilians.' A sergeant grabbed him and pushed him out of the tent, but I knew he was right. He shocked the distance out of what I was doing: directing orders for human destruction from a position of safety. The pilot brought it to me, made it real, physical; he made me take responsibility for my part in killing thousands of innocent people. The veil of my position in the cogs was removed. This wasn't simply a policy of demoralization to win a war, it went beyond that; I was part of a racial annihilation.

"I went to a front-line position. I outranked the commanding officer there and ordered him to place me in a fox hole on point that evening. He thought I was crazy, but it was something I had to do. I was stationed on the left, and there was a young corporal on the right. We were both armed with M16's, and could detonate claymore mines in front of us.

"At around three in the morning a large enemy force silently moved past us. I was supposed to set off the claymores to alert our guys, who were sleeping behind us, so they could engage. But the Viet Cong weren't advancing on our position; they were travelling past, from left to right. Their force far outnumbered our own; I knew setting off those claymores would cause every one of our boys to die. I sat motionless, thinking the corporal to my right would fire. If he did, we would be the first to die that night. I prayed to God. I said, 'If you want me to go this way, then I'm ready, but if you spare me, I'll devote my life to you.'

"The corporal didn't make a move. It was a miracle the Viet Cong passed through without altercation. The next morning I asked the young soldier why he didn't fire. He said, 'I don't know, sir; it just didn't feel like the right thing to do.' From that point on I studied to become a priest; I no longer worked for the destruction of humanity, but for its salvation. It was never easy for me to admit my responsibility for so much death; it takes a strong desire to change, to separate yourself from evil. Chris, I believe that you have been spared for a reason. God is using you for some purpose; it just hasn't been revealed to you yet. Remember, God has chosen all of us, but it's up to the individual to act."

What Mac told me was powerful. I appreciated him sharing with me the personal experience that had changed his life. If I could learn from the hardships of another to better my own life without having to experience that particular misery myself, I was very happy to do so. I felt I couldn't take much more of my own adversity; I just didn't have the capacity to survive it any more.

I felt alone in my own experiences, and Mac understood that. "This helps me," he said, "maybe it will help you too. When we start out on the tree of life, we begin on the bottom branch; we crawl out as far as we can to see what is beyond us. Then we grab the next branch and pull ourselves up so we can see more. This process can go on for as long as someone is physically and mentally able. Most people stop halfway up the tree and are satisfied with what they see. They aren't interested in the continued effort it would take to pull themselves higher or see further.

"Others are pushed into the climb by outside forces: tragedy, unexpected suffering, war, Vietnam for me; for you, going through the prison system as an enemy of the country. People on the branches below can't see what you see, and likely have no interest or belief in what you could tell them. The people on the branches above you don't want to look down; it scares them to be pulled backwards. But we each have our own unique experience in the tree, and it's our responsibility to share those experiences with others, regardless; that is an important part of being human.

"At the top of the tree the branches are few and far between so there are less people with whom you can truly communicate and call friends. Our lives are so short. Many spend their time worrying about things that ultimately have no consequence. If you are strong, you can start to eliminate those unnecessary excesses that so many others struggle with. But remember, with much wisdom comes much sorrow."

I thought of the name I was given by Cutter.

According to Mac's "tree of life," most people wouldn't believe what I had been through, and the ones who already knew, who really *knew*, didn't want to look back. The price of association in this long-buried and convoluted history had been far too costly. The dirty relationships had compromised everyone, and I was just one of the many casualties.

Mac could tell I was suffering deeply on the inside. "I know you told me you played music in your youth," he said. "Why don't we see if we can get access to the bass and get you playing with us for the services."

I played every Sunday from then on. We weren't afforded time to practice, we would just get up in front of the congregation and work through the hymns until we had them down. I was privileged; out of 1100 men there were only three positions open for playing music, and I had one of them.

Once we had played together a few times, we sounded pretty good. The Catholic priest approached me. "Christopher, do you know who I am?"

"Yes," I said, although all I really knew was that he had also been a priest when he was on the outside.

"I'd like to invite you to play for our services as well."

I said I would be very happy to do so. The Catholic congregation was predominantly Hispanic and appreciative of the music. Mac and I were

339

instantly made welcome, and they said they would be there for us if we were ever in trouble.

Between our jobs and playing music for the church, Mac told me that my situation was similar to soldiers at war, but the difficult difference was that a soldier had brethren to share the burden of experience with, whereas I had no one. Mac introduced me to men at Lewisburg he had come to respect and hold in high regard. These "old heads" had all had unusual experiences. Mac thought my talking to them would help me feel like I wasn't alone. These men normally never talked to anybody on a personal level; I only got to know them because Mac had arranged it.

My first introduction was to a refined gentleman in his seventies. Mac had shared enough of my case with him that we were able to start our conversation with a basic respect, openness, and trust of one another.

"Mac tells me you were a diplomat in Russia," I said.

"That's right. I spent the majority of my professional career overseas while I was on the Agency's payroll. You spent time in Russia, too?"

"Yes," I said, "I was a construction consultant updating flats in Moscow." "That's the only reason you were there?" he asked, raising an eyebrow. "Mostly, but it turned out to be a very different experience from what I expected."

"So, you probably understand better than most that America's ideas about Russia, and Russia's ideas about the U.S., are purposefully unfocused."

"Yes," I said, "I certainly got that feeling."

"Mac told me a little about your involvement with evidence from President Kennedy's assassination. That must be part of the reason you ended up here." He looked pityingly at me.

I nodded and said, "It's the main reason."

"A number of years ago I found myself engaged in part of that assassination story."

I didn't say a word. It was clear he had insider knowledge of the conspiracy; I wanted him to keep talking. Instead, he handed me a sheaf of letters. "These were given to me in secret, a favor for a favor; they're part of my case file . . . I can't tell you how I know, but I can tell you these letters have not been manipulated."

The letters were translated from Russian. The first was from 1963 and coded "Top Secret." It read:

> The American press has disseminated various slanderous fabrications regarding some Soviet and Cuban "connections" of Lee

Harvey Oswald, who was charged by the U.S. authorities with the assassination of U.S. President John F. Kennedy and who was then himself killed under mysterious circumstances. [. . .]

The Ministry of Foreign Affairs of the USSR and the KGB of the Council of Ministers of the USSR have prepared a statement for the Soviet press to debunk these allegations by the American media. The thrust of the draft statement is that the murder of Oswald himself reveals now even more clearly the identity of the groups who were behind President Kennedy's assassination and who are obviously trying to cover up their tracks. The question of whether it is advisable to publish such a statement requires special consideration, the final decision being contingent on how the investigation of the circumstances surrounding Kennedy's assassination turns out.

If the U.S. authorities request the Soviet embassy in Washington for information concerning Oswald's stay in the Soviet Union, they could be provided with a relevant report on this matter. [. . .]

It was signed by A. Gromyko on November 25, 1963, just three days after the assassination. Its powerful language and shocking threat caught me off guard. I had never read anything like it.

The next document was labeled: "Top Secret Cipher Telegram Highest Priority."

Please note Oswald's letter of November 9, the text of which was transmitted to Moscow over the line of nearby neighbors.

This letter was clearly a provocation: it gives the impression we had close ties with Oswald and were using him for some purposes of our own. It was totally unlike any other letters the embassy had previously received from Oswald. Nor had he ever visited our embassy himself. The suspicion that the letter is a forgery is heightened by the fact that it was typed, whereas the other letters the embassy had received from Oswald before were handwritten.

One gets the definite impression that the letter was concocted by those who, judging from everything, are involved in the president's assassination. It is possible that Oswald himself wrote the letter as it was dictated to him, in return for some promises, and then, as we know, he was simply bumped off after his usefulness had ended.

The competent U.S. authorities are undoubtedly aware of this letter, since the embassy's correspondence is under constant surveillance. However, they are not making use of it for the time being. Nor are they asking the embassy for any information about Oswald himself; perhaps they are waiting for another moment.

The question also arises as to whether there is any connection between the wait-and-see attitude of the U.S. authorities and the ideas conveyed by Thompson (though he himself may not be aware of this connection) on the desirability of some restraint on the part of the Soviet press and gradually hushing up the entire matter of Kennedy's assassination. Perhaps that is exactly what the federal authorities were inclined to do when they learned all the facts and realized the danger of serious international complications if the interested U.S. groups, including the local authorities in Dallas, continued to fan the hysteria over the "leftist" affiliations of Kennedy's assassin and the exposés we would have to issue in this case.

The main question now is: should we give the U.S. authorities Oswald's last letter if they ask for our consular correspondence with him (there is nothing else in it that can be used to compromise us). After weighing all the pros and cons, we are inclined to pass on this letter as well to the authorities if they request all the correspondence, because if we don't pass it on, the organizers of this entire provocation could use this fact to try casting suspicion on us. Please confirm (receipt).

Agreed upon with A. I. Mikoyan.

It was signed on November 26, 1963, by A. Dobrynin
I recalled my conversation with Lebed from so many years ago concerning the Russian Ambassador, Dobrynin, and Bobby Kennedy foreshadowing the fateful events in Dallas. I read the next document, written by A. I. Mikoyan, with rapt fascination:

[...] judging from everything, the U.S. Government does not want to involve us in this matter [...] it clearly prefers to consign the whole business to oblivion as soon as possible. Our reaction to these murders has already played its role. The [U.S.] President stated today publicly that a thorough investigation would be carried out.

Jesus! The Warren Commission was established because the Soviet Government needed to know they would not be publicly held accountable for President Kennedy's death. The commission wasn't just there to pacify Americans; it also had to satisfy the Russians, providing a benign accounting of the events in Dallas. We have all been blinded...

One more letter particularly struck me, it was also a top-secret cipher telegram, highest priority, written by Mikoyan:

Immediately after the requiem at Arlington Cemetery, I and other foreign representatives who attended Kennedy's funeral went to the White House, where the late president's widow, Jacqueline Kennedy, had arranged a reception. The guests were greeted by members of the Kennedy family, but Jacqueline herself did not show up until the end of the reception. Those in attendance filed by the late president's spouse and shook her hand. It struck us that Jacqueline Kennedy, who exchanged only two or three words with the persons introduced to her, looked very calm and even appeared to be smiling. However, when we were presented to her and when we conveyed our heartfelt condolences to her on behalf of Nina Petrovna, N.S. Khrushchev, and Rada, and Alyosha Adzhubey, as well as on behalf of the Soviet government, the Soviet people, and myself, Jacqueline Kennedy said, with great emotion and nearly sobbing: "I am sure that Chairman Khrushchev and my husband could have been successful in the search for peace, and they were really striving for that. Now you must continue this endeavor and bring it to completion."

We replied that we fully shared her opinion and agreed that both sides should continue striving to develop friendly relations between our countries for the benefit of peace throughout the world. We emphasized our sorrow over the misfortune that had befallen her.

In conclusion, Jacqueline Kennedy expressed her sincere gratitude to N.S. Khrushchev and us for our sympathy and for the special trip we had made to the United States to attend her husband's funeral. She said all this with inspiration and deep emotion. During the entire conversation she clasped my hand with her two hands, trying to convey as convincingly as possible her feelings and thoughts regarding the cause of peace, to which her husband had devoted his efforts, and her own desire that our countries complete this endeavor.

Her fortitude is most impressive.

It was signed November 25, 1963.

It was touching and devastating. It made me sick and angry; a feeling of helplessness and finality swept over me. This was all so long ago, but it had managed to change my life, and the ramifications continued to change the fate of the world, without most people even realizing it. And they never would; all the information seemed to be in the ground or locked behind bars.

The diplomat gave me a moment to process. I'm sure he clearly saw the tide of changing emotions ebb and flow over my face. When he started to speak again, it was quietly. "I've been in the intelligence field for thirty-five years and I can tell you, the United States is worse now than Russia ever was. In Russia, people knew how corrupt the government was; it was frightening, but they knew what to expect. In America, the general populace has no clue; they've been blinded by media and government propaganda . . . They still think the government is there to help them, which is even more frightening.

"When George W. took office, he contacted all agency heads and informed them not to cooperate with sensitive Freedom of Information requests. His personally appointed attorney general, Ashcroft, will back him up. They're re-classifying and removing JFK-related documents from the national archives that were released by President Clinton's administration and the ARRB. They are doing it silently, no fanfare, no disclosure of their actions, just tucking it all back out of sight. All of America is conveniently too distracted with the war on terror to notice." He handed me several classified U.S. Government documents prepared through the CIA.

"How did you get all of these in here?" I asked.

"They were part of my legal defense."

As I read the documents, I couldn't believe what I was seeing: the U.S. Government had stipulated numbers of how many civilians could be killed in different scenarios, in different cities across the U.S., that would still be considered acceptable losses. They were recipes for death. It shocked me; it gave me a perspective I never would have even imagined, growing up American. It was hard for me to come to terms with how naïve I really was about the brutal policies of our government. Who could know how far they would go? Even children weren't safe from the grand plan. Considering what I had been put through, this piece of the puzzle should not have surprised me: it fit, and what it meant for me and my fellow Americans was deeply concerning.

He continued, "From all I have seen and experienced, it is my opinion that there are no good governments anywhere." He looked sullen. "When every true patriot and great American has been imprisoned, killed, or has left of their own accord, what will our country be then?"

He had given the majority of his life in service to the States, and this is where it landed him: an old man with no wife, children, or grandchildren, locked away with 1100 other men in a miserable prison camp, maybe for the rest of his life. I thought back to a story Argus Gregorios told me at Loretto about his work when he was a younger man, from before he was imprisoned for doing his job.

While on a plane, heading towards a clandestine meeting to deliver important and confidential material, Argus was approached by a flight attendant who claimed to be with MI 6. She said the British Government would pay him ten million dollars to hand over the case attached to his wrist and abandon his directive. He declined, and completed his assignment.

Looking back, I'm sure he regretted not taking the money and just buggering off. For all his service, for all his time and energy and the work he put his life into, he was now being rewarded with a membership to federal prison camp Loretto.

52

It's Nothing Personal

Prison Time

The next man Mac introduced me to was Tony the Knife. Tony had been playing government and Mafia games, bouncing between the two his whole life. He was a loner, rarely talked to anyone, but everyone in the camp knew he was a top dog back in the fifties and sixties.

"Why do they call you 'Tony the Knife'?" I asked. My question sounded stupid when I heard myself say it out loud, but I did want to know.

"Kid, I'm only talking to you because Mac said you're a good guy with a special case. Look, I've been around a while; you may have even read about me in a few books. I worked for the FBI when they needed me, and I worked for the Mob when they needed me; I was what you'd call an equal opportunity employee. Back then, that's just the way things worked; sometimes it worked out good, sometimes not so good.

"One time I had this FBI agent pull up to my house. He came in fast-like; I thought he was gunna be trouble so I got ready for him, but he sez, 'Do yourself a favor, wear your vest today.' Son of a bitch saved my life. Only reason he warned me was 'cause I was still valuable to them. Back then loyalties was built on being close, and being responsible for each other's lives. There was respect; it's not like that anymore. Technology has made everything impersonal. All the old guys have been replaced by these kids who don't know shit, and don't give a shit about anybody; they're just mindless, soulless fucks who do what they're ordered to do.

"Like your case, all that Kennedy mess; the government covered up all of it, they only told people what they wanted them to know. Christopher, you weren't valuable, in fact, you were dangerous; you had something that could expose the past bullshit, and they didn't know what you were gunna do with it. So, they had to destroy you; it wasn't personal."

Why was everyone telling me it wasn't personal, it was the epitome of personal; this was my goddamn life, how much more personal can you get?

"Take me," he said, "when I was a useful man, to whoever, I stayed alive and free and had a good life. It didn't matter what I did, and believe me, kid, I did it all. The most important thing I can tell you from experience is that you can do anything you want to and get away with it, as long as you don't tell nobody about it, ever; remember that. Anyway, this new crop of feds, these young kids, they come to my house, see all my guns and automatic weapons, and they charge me for having arms I shouldn't have. I had that shit all my life; they've always known about 'em, but now these young jackasses make a case out of it? Shit, I used those same guns when their fathers hired me, and now they put me in jail over it. Bullshit.

"It's alright, it ain't nothin'; when they want you they get you,' is all it is. When you become a liability, that's when your time becomes short. If you ain't useful no more, or they think you're a threat, they'll find something to bring you in on."

"Can you tell me anything about my case?"

"What about it? The Kennedys, the Mob, the Agency?"

"Yes, everything," I said. If Tony had been around for so long playing both sides, I hoped he could enlighten me about the pieces of the puzzle that still remained in shadow; maybe he could tell me what Argus couldn't.

"Well, kid, it starts back a ways, before JFK got in the White House, back when the Mob and the government was thick thieves. Boss Mossello controlled photographs of J. Edgar Hoover having oral sex with his fag buddy Clyde Tolson, so Hoover and the FBI wouldn't take no action against them. When JFK ran for president, Hoover used the same tactic and blackmailed him, forced him to take Johnson as V.P. Johnson was there to protect the Mob and Hoover's secrets. Anyway, Johnson asked the Mob to do him a favor and buy the election votes in Chicago, West Virginia, and Texas, putting both JFK and Johnson in the White House." He laughed, "Sam Giancana told me JFK fuckin' hated Hoover."

"Kennedy knew Giancana?" I asked.

"Yeah, he knew Sam, and he knew Johnny Roselli, too. When JFK was running for president, he asked to meet Sam to get him the votes he needed to win. But after JFK had been in the White House for a while, they had a falling-out. Anyway, Johnson tried to protect the Mob, but JFK and Bobby cut Johnson down to size. I remember Johnson was pissed because he wasn't allowed on *Air Force One*, ever, and the Kennedy brothers made it clear that anything Johnson said didn't represent the views of the American Government, which totally humiliated him.

"Anyway, until the brothers came to the White House the FBI had no formal training or divisions that addressed organized crime at all; it was totally hands off. But Bobby wasn't havin' none of it; he declared war against the Mob and was hitting 'em real hard; that little son of a bitch put over seven hundred Mafioso in prison. The president was making big changes, giving his brother carte blanche against the Mafia and making moves to weaken the CIA. The brothers was making serious enemies, and not just with the Mob boys. It was the Kennedys versus the kings, and the Kennedys was outnumbered.

"Then there was Lee Oswald, a young motherfucker born in New Orleans. That kid wanted to be somebody, so he became a Marine. The CIA trained him in Japan under the Office of Naval Intelligence and sent him off to Russia as a fake defector. Lee took radar reports the CIA wanted the Ruskies to have. When Lee came back from Russia, the CIA thought he was a hot number, so they were gunna use him to kill Castro."

Bouck had told me the same thing.

"The CIA had been working with the Mob boys, hell, since WWII. In '63, all those guys wanted Fidel dead, dead, dead, fuckin' in the ground. Meyer Lanksy had an agreement with Castro, that if he took over Cuba, he would allow the Mob to continue to own and operate their hotel casinos, but two months after he came into power, Castro shut everything down. Lansky put a million-dollar bounty on Castro's head, but he cancelled it, because the CIA was so eager to kill Castro, they were going to pay the Mob to do it. Everyone was pissed because they were losing millions after Castro fucked them all.

"Nobody knew it was Bobby Kennedy who got Lee back to the States in '62. It would have been the news event of the year: 'American defector moves back home from Russia,' but Bobby made sure that didn't show up nowhere. He was real careful to make sure there was no paper trail between 'em. He trusted Lee because the kid's information was good. Bobby thought Lee was the perfect person to spy on everyone for him, so Bobby had him inform through the FBI."

"Wait, you're saying Lee Harvey Oswald worked for the Kennedys?" I asked, taken aback.

"Yeah, kid. If I remember right, Lee's code was *T or S, 179*. He was an informant for Division Five of the FBI. Uh, I think he was agent 110669;

goddamn, I still remember! You won't find that in your history books, kid; Allen Dulles had all Lee's informant and payment records destroyed." He laughed. "One day you're in, next day you're out . . . Anyway, Bobby could read his reports, and no one would know who it was coming from. That's what I heard from my contacts at the Bureau. Lee actually sent a warning note to his Dallas fed contact five days before JFK's assassination. The note was destroyed after.

"If that wasn't all fuckin' dangerous enough, the CIA was trying to get Lee into Cuba, and next to Castro to kill him. But Castro was a smart bastard, and wouldn't even let him in the country, so they needed something big to convince Castro that Lee was a Russia-loving, Castro-loving son of a bitch.

"The Kennedys had been lied to by the Agency, which was operating around their orders. When JFK left the CIA hangin' out to dry at the Bay of Pigs, well, they all turned on him. That's when Bobby Kennedy hired Lee, to keep him informed, keep on top of what was really going on, to protect his brother.

"It was pretty fucked up: Lee was reporting back to Bobby about doctors who were trying to figure out how to inject Castro with cancer cells. They were using prisoners with life sentences as guinea pigs, real Nazi shit. Well, I guess it was fair play—Castro hired all the old Nazi SS to help protect his island. Anyway, the CIA never could get Castro.

"Lee was playin' the most dangerous game in history, and he was ready to lay down his life for the cause. Let me tell you somethin', kid, you heard about spies? James Bond shit? Lee was the biggest of them all, super-classified counterintelligence. The kid infiltrated everything and reported back to Bobby. He had balls the size of coconuts. At that time he literally had the fate of the world in his hands. After JFK's assassination, the press was jawing about his bad character, his weak chin . . . they even got his mother to corroborate their story, bullshit! It was all crap.

"Anyway, a handful of intelligence operatives was told there was going to be a demonstration against JFK by Castro sympathizers that pointed to communists, to force the president's hand politically on Cuba. It was a false flag operation. If any information ever leaked, there was plausible deniability for all.

"The president was going to be shot at in Chicago on November 2, '63. There was supposed to be a lot of witnesses to blame the whole thing on Castro. Lee was on the inside testing the weapons that would be fired, shit like that . . . Lee warned Bobby about the Chicago trip, and JFK cancelled; the rogues knew someone leaked.

"The next setup in Tampa went bust because Lee tipped Bobby again and JFK left early by helicopter. The weapons for Tampa had to be transferred to Dallas because Dallas was the last shot, set up by Johnson. They found out Lee was Bobby's mole and fed him false bullshit, then fed him to the sharks.

"Dallas wasn't just a Mob or CIA town, it was a Lyndon Johnson town, and Johnson put his two cents in to make sure the hit would go down all the way and get covered. Johnson needed it to happen in Texas so the investigation could be controlled. If he wasn't in control, he was finished; he was out for '64, going to fuckin' prison, like us! You think Johnson was happy about that shit? It was Johnson's attorney, Edward Clark, who put the fellas together for Dallas, got two million cash from Texas oil. He even got the Secret Service IDs for the shooters; Johnson helped him with that. Once Johnson got Kennedy to Dallas he was never gonna let the president leave that city alive.

"Lee was told Texas was aborted, and at the time it was, so he told Bobby, who told his brother, and JFK went to Texas. JFK wasn't worried about the reports coming in, he thought he had the best insider information, but Lee was made a pawn. The green light was given the night before the twenty-second; no chance of a leak that time. I heard that sure perked up Johnson's spirits.

"On the twenty-second the driver of the limo knew not to pass the 'kill zone' until he was ordered to. Kennedy was supposed to be hit from behind so they could blame one guy: Lee. Lee was the perfect fall guy—Johnson knew Bobby Kennedy couldn't pursue anything against Lee and would shut down . . . But the shooter couldn't get the fuckin' head shot until it was too late, and the last-resort shooter fired. I heard Jackie was too close to the president in the car after he got hit in the back; made 'em nervous. It was Johnson's attorney's decision to have a last-resort shot; it was a military round that blew the president's head apart. Damn thing had mercury in it, for God's sake, made a fuckin' mess. I know they were under orders *not* to hit Jackie, so that last shot made sense. But that's why Jackie got Non-Hodgkin's lymphoma years later; she got the fuckin' mercury vapors all over her. So now the new U.S. Government, as Ruby described it, had to sell the biggest fuckin' lie in history to the world."

"My God!" I said, surprised and saddened by the sickening information. "I never realized Jackie died of cancer because of her exposure to the mercury."

"Yeah, it was all fucked up, kid. They planned that exact scenario for Lee to take out Castro, but they used it to kill JFK instead. Hell, Lee was on the second floor of the book depository drinking a cola when JFK's head exploded. When he found out what happened, he panicked; he hadn't been told the right facts, and that let him know he was on the outs—just a little late, eh kid?

"After that, Lee needed to get to his controller. He went to the movie theater because it was their rendezvous point. That info was leaked and made it easy for the intelligence community to tip off the Dallas cops on his exact whereabouts. Officer Tippet was killed and an 'all points, shoot-on-sight' order was given on Lee. The Dallas cops were supposed to flush him out the back exit of the theater where more cops were waiting to fill him full of holes, but the smart bastard kept screamin' and makin' a scene yelling, 'I am not resisting arrest!' The cops had to arrest him in the theater, around witnesses. Whoops!

"It's funny you know, when Lee was asking for legal help on TV, for someone to come forward and help him, he was talkin' to Bobby. The kid wasn't nervous, he was working for the CIA *and* Bobby fuckin' Kennedy. He was an informant for the FBI, for Christ's sake; he figured someone would come get him."

"Why didn't Bobby help him?" I asked.

"How could he get involved? Lee was his informant—*his* man was being blamed for the murder of the president; if the story got out, Bobby would be caught up in his own brother's murder. Lee was a patriotic and dedicated son-of-a-bitch Marine, but just a dumb young kid too willing to sacrifice his life. He got his wish didn't he?

"When the Pentagon was hit on 9/11, it was the Offices of Naval Intelligence that were destroyed. Lee's file was kept next to Kennedy's in a safe, so where are they now? Poof . . . The records, the real dirty shit, all gone. A lot of problems were solved and a lot of dirt and messy secrets were destroyed with 9/11.

"Anyway, Lee knew about the plots against foreign governments and the president, so Johnson had to move quick. He was nervous as a long-tailed cat in a room fulla rockin' chairs when Lee was taken in by the Dallas police. Like I said, the kid was supposed to get shot, not arrested.

"Because of his training, Lee wouldn't say a word until his controller, George de Mohrenschildt, told him what to do. De Mohrenschildt was a close family friend of Jackie Kennedy; she used to bounce on his knee as a kid and call him 'Uncle George.' Anyway, Johnson made sure Lee's call never went through. Wouldn't have mattered if he had. anyway: it was most likely de Mohrenschildt who spilled the beans that Lee was working for Bobby.

"Having it end at Lee put Bobby Kennedy in the clear, and put Bobby in Johnson's pocket. Hell of a chess move, eh kid? The plan was for Lee to die anyway; too bad for Ruby it had to be done so publicly. Ruby had helped the Mob in Cuba; he was also an informant for the FBI in the '50's and ran guns for the CIA, hell, he even worked for Nixon when Nixon was in Congress. Ruby was an equal-opportunity employee, like me. Before he shot Lee, he was told he would be released as a national hero: a gift from Johnson. But he wasn't used to all the spotlight attention; he kept running his mouth: 'A whole new form of government is going to take over our country,' so they left him in prison to rot to keep control of him. Kind of like what they're doing to us.

"The government doesn't care what you know, kid, but it does care what you could do. Like Robert Oppenheimer—they fuckin' destroyed him after he gave them the atom bomb . . . poor bastard.

"When the Warren Commission came out, those fucks knew Lee was on the FBI payroll but never said a goddamned thing. The attorney general of Texas called those SOBs at the Commission personally, told 'em Lee was FBI, but they covered it. They all became made men in the new government.

"The DA in New Orleans, Garrison, was the only guy that tried to do something for real, started knockin' on doors in his neighborhood. But the CIA's domestic contract files from New Orleans had already been loaded into a U-Haul and transported back to Langley, never to be seen again.

"Bobby Kennedy did everything he could to stop Garrison's investigation secretly so the shit wouldn't hit the fan; Bobby needed his shot at the White House. But the men who put JFK into the ground would never let Bobby get the presidency. Shit, he knew everything, so when he pushed for the White House, he had to go. That's how Nixon became president. It was fuckin' important to Johnson who came to the White House after him. He never left anything to chance, made sure he had the dirt on Nixon receiving a half a million in campaign funds from Greece's military dictators, so Nixon could never turn the tables back on him.

"You know, people still talk about this bullshit because it's a riddle. They can't believe the amount of deceit that came from the government. You ever see a marionette show? People wonder how the puppets move like that. It's the men pulling the strings who make everything happen, but nobody sees them, so nobody talks about them. Anyway, this is all ancient history—well, maybe not for you," he chuckled. "Mac asked me to talk to you as a favor, said all this shit touched you . . . What evidence did you have anyway?"

"I had the wristwatch the president was wearing when he was assassinated, the one that wasn't supposed to be there. Bobby Kennedy wouldn't turn it over to the government, so he hid it, and thirty-one years later, I got it."

"Oh yeah, I remember something about that: for years the Agency, the Mob, even the fuckin' royal family of England, was looking for the shit Bobby held back. Everybody wanted to be the keeper of the trump cards. But I heard he put it all in JFK's grave; I guess not, eh kid?" He laughed again and said, "I'm an old man, Chris, I'm tired now, but if you wanna talk later, maybe I'll tell you how to survive a shootout . . . Oh yeah, and you wanted to know about my name?

"Well, I was talkin' to this kid, right, but the lover boy was daydreaming or somethin', so I took out my knife, reached across the table, and cut his ear off. He sat there with this stupid look on his face while blood was gushing out the side of his head. I held his ear up to my mouth real close and whispered, 'You hear me now?'" Tony smiled at the memory. "That's why they called me 'the Knife.'"

I had grown used to the brutality of the men I had to share my life with now; Tony's "earcapade" didn't have anything on Spielberg.

Tony was Bouck's opposite; he was a guy who had been there and done that, but from the other side. I hadn't expected to learn more about the history tied to my case since I left Loretto, but I was in a unique position in which Tony shared his inside knowledge with me. Without Mac's introduction, there wouldn't have been a chance in hell he would have ever talked to me. I would never have been able to put everything together without being sentenced to these prison camps.

53

JUST BEING ALIVE IS A GIFT

PRISON TIME

I hadn't received any letters since I had arrived at Lewisburg Camp, until I got one from Henry McRobie.

> Dear Christopher,
>
> I hope this letter finds you alright. I have only just found out that you're in prison; why didn't you tell me? I assume you were trying to keep me out of it; I appreciate that, but you should have let me know.
>
> I received a letter from Robert White's attorney, Philip Adder, requesting me to disclose any and all information relating to your dealings with Robert White. I found it extremely improper; that information is client privileged, so of course I told him to go jump off a bridge. However, I was notified in his letter that Robert White died from a heart attack on October 11 of this year.
>
> I called his wife to give her my condolences; we're practically neighbors here in Catonsville. I also wanted to see if I could find out any information about Adder's letter. She told me a few things I thought I better share with you: first, she was not aware that the attorney had sent me the request; second, she said that Caroline Kennedy hounded her husband mercilessly; and third, even though he was under immense stress following his inheritance, White was healthy, so his heart attack was very sudden and unexpected.
>
> After his death, both the JFK Library and the National Archives intervened in his estate and came to a settlement with his wife. She said she had little choice, and was too tired and scared to fight any longer.
>
> Before he died, White did open his museum for a while in St. Petersburg, Florida, but in 1999 the FBI were sent down to review

his remaining items that weren't in the auction in New York and they took another 100 documents for national security. Then Caroline Kennedy got the museum shut down.

All of this comes off as highly suspicious and is extremely concerning to me, considering JFK Jr. is now dead, and your life is being wasted in jail. It makes my stomach turn and keeps eating at me; I wish there were something I could do. We can always discuss it through client privilege; tell me if there is anything I can do to help you.

Regards,
Henry McRobie

I was shocked to hear about Robert's death, particularly concerning how it had occurred.

People linked to the inheritance were dying. McRobie was connecting dots on the outside. I wrote him back immediately and thanked him for his letter, but told him there was nothing he could do for me now. I said we'd talk about everything when I got out in four years.

Once I finished writing my response to Henry, a CO came through the barracks and informed us that officials from the U.S. Senate would be coming through in the afternoon. "Most of you will be at your jobs," he said, "but if you see them, don't pay any attention. You are prohibited from engaging them. If they ask you a direct question, answer in a positive way, or you will be sent to the hole."

I saw the officials when they came through. There were four: a senator and three other government representatives, along with six children. I couldn't fathom why they would bring children to a place like this. I felt like an exhibit at the zoo. Nobody talked to me or asked me any questions; they just walked though, looking around to see how we lived, and then they were gone. I understood the Senate would determine how much money to allocate each institution. God forbid the prison's and camp's funding be cut and the tax money dry up. We all kept our mouths shut, made complicit in their abuse of the system.

***

It was Christmas. I had been playing the church services for two years. The Catholic congregation wanted to negotiate more time in the church, so they marched 300 strong in peaceful protest outside the major's office. One of the COs rotating in from the pen was an asshole bigot. He was pissed off that the Hispanic inmates had mobilized like that.

He punished them by locking the instruments up and banning any music for their services over the holidays.

Mac asked me to come in after his service; he was sitting at the piano, but the bass and guitar were locked in the cabinet, and the CO had the only key. Mac told me the situation: we were still allowed to play for the Christian worshippers because they weren't part of the protest. We both didn't feel good about it. "This is shit," I said, "those guys have treated us like brothers, and we're just going to roll over and do what some prick CO says?" I wasn't going to let that happen. I grabbed the cabinet door and pulled as hard as I could; the lock stayed intact, but the hinge broke away from the wood. The other guitar player had left the camp some time before, so I reached in, grabbed the guitar, and turned back to Mac.

"You realize we're both going to the hole for this?" he said.

"Yeah, and so?"

The Catholic congregation was surprised and very happy to see us playing music for mass. When the CO found out, he was fuming, and I prepared myself for a month in the hole at Lewisburg Pen. I felt bad that Mac would have to pay the same price for my actions, but I wasn't able to bend over for this; there comes a time when you have to cover the ground you stand on.

The following morning Mac came up to me, put his hand on my shoulder, and said, "Are you ready to go?"

I didn't know what he was smiling about, but I knew he had never set foot in the pen before. He sat on my bunk and rubbed his hand over his head. "God is good," he said.

"What are you talking about? We're going to the hole for a month."

"Yeah, Officer yokel had the papers drawn up; we were gone this afternoon, but . . ."

"But?"

"Somehow the Spanish guys got word to the warden at the pen. He knew about our services and is a huge music lover; he tore up the orders for us to go to the hole. Merry Christmas!" he said, and smiled again.

It was the most meaningful Christmas present I had ever received. "You've got another job too," he said.

"What is it?"

"You'll be working with me at Allenwood."

Allenwood was another facility twenty minutes north of Lewisburg that consisted of low, medium, and high security facilities. A few trusted inmates from Lewisburg Camp were chosen to work for the COs there, maintaining the huge federal property.

The next morning I got on a bus with Mac and a few other inmates, and we headed to Allenwood. When the bus stopped, the COs were already waiting to pick up their individual workers. A CO named Oakley came up and spoke to me. "Mac told me you guys almost got thrown in the hole."

I didn't say anything; I didn't know him.

"That's ok," he said, "you'll get used to things here; there's a lot more latitude and freedom. Mac said your case was pretty interesting . . . if you wind up getting a book or movie deal, I want to be in it," he laughed.

Oakley wasn't an asshole, and he wasn't trying to be demeaning, he just seemed lighthearted. So far I didn't have anything against him.

"If any of the other COs here give you a hard time, remind them you're my inmate," he said. "They should come to me if they have a problem."

Before Mac and I got into his truck, another CO drove up and asked Oakley to recommend dependable inmates for a sensitive project. He volunteered us along with a handful of others.

Each morning we were transported to a mess hall, well fed, then taken to our discreet job: the condemned man's "daycation." We were told the feds had shut down and abandoned a camp. A multitude of lawsuits had been filed against the feds because numerous inmates from that camp had contracted, or died, from cancer while manufacturing paint for the B-2 stealth bombers. The surviving inmates had been dispersed to other camps all over the country. Our job was to destroy the remaining records and the medical buildings, everything, including blood work results, dental records, and biological samples. If there wasn't any evidence to support the cases, they would all be thrown out of court.

We were given axes, sledgehammers, and heavy machinery, and told: "Use whatever you need to get the job done, except fire. Get to work." Not only was it physically freeing, but there was also an incredible release of frustration and stress. I felt the anger in me build as I took the first few swings with a sledgehammer, shattering glass and splintering wood cabinetry. Most days I had to keep it way down, forget the irritation, fury, and brimming insanity, ignore it, numb myself to my circumstance, so I could get through without any problems. But the activity let it all out, intensified my rage and brought it forward; it overflowed from its previous confines. The twisted propulsion moved me to shatter everything within my reach. I began to enjoy myself. I bludgeoned my way through the offices, smashing and tearing, leaving absolute ruin in my wake, until it hit me: I was helping the very institution that had placed me in this position to begin with. I was now being employed to do their dirty work, and I wanted to, because it was my only chance to feel a bit of control again, and I hated that. I hated that I was doing their bidding, and enjoying it.

I felt sorry for the poor sots who had gone through this camp. They were dying now, used up as the government's disposable slave labor. The government learned from big corporations that it's easier to take a small loss and harm people rather than own up, pay, and revamp the system; that way everything remains easy and they never have to admit error. Just cover the tracks, pretend nothing happened, and eradicate the evidence before it can be used against them. And here I was helping them.

Despite all of that, I enjoyed the power I gained back through this job. Creation or destruction is gratifying. If you don't have the capability to create something, destroy it, because there is still power in that, power and control. I was just sad I was on the wrong side of it.

It took us about two weeks to raze everything. The day the job was completed, my attention was drawn to a grassy hill on the other side of the road. Atop sat a long-abandoned church with a cemetery fenced in by wrought iron. Sunlight glinted through its stained-glass windows; I knew God was still there. I asked the only accompanying CO if I could go over and look around. "You're Oakley's inmate?" he asked.

"Yes."

"Go ahead."

The gate had no lock; it creaked open and I walked into the graveyard. The stone markers were from the Civil War; many of the boys who fought for the North were buried here. In this place, the past was set in stone. This was federal land: no civilians allowed. Nobody had visited these men for a very, very long time. They lay forgotten, isolated by the very government they had fought for.

Out of respect, I spoke each of their names aloud. It was likely the first time their names had been uttered in over a hundred years. Ancient Egyptians believed that saying a name aloud and remembering a person would keep them living on after death. I felt, in reading the names, that perhaps some part of them would come back to life, or at the very least not remain forgotten, and I would be connected to them. Jesus said the very stones would cry out in his honor if he received no honor elsewhere. As I read the epitaphs, I became caught up by the late souls. I understood the silent stones, how they could speak to those who listened. More stoic and patriotic, I continued to read aloud until I was called back.

I remembered an acquaintance of mine from many years ago. He pointed out a picture on a wall: "Come over here and look at this," he said.

The photo was of men in Civil War uniform. It was crisp and clear, like it had been taken just days before. "Do you know what the most interesting thing about this picture is?" he asked.

"No," I replied.

"They're all dead, but you and I are alive, right now, in this moment . . . What are we going to do with it?"

Just being alive is a gift.

54

One Hell of a Story

January 5, 2006

McRobie sat in his office watching another TV show about JFK Jr.'s death. He got up, turned off the box, and said, "That's it, I can't stand this anymore." His law partner, Shaw, asked what he was talking about. "Don't worry about it," he said.

Henry packed up the paperwork on his desk, got in his car, and drove east a short distance to the offices of the *Baltimore Sun* newspaper. He didn't know who to talk to. He figured it was a big story, so he went to the front desk and said, "Take me to the editor's office, please."

"Do you have an appointment?"

"No, but I'm sure as hell he'll want to speak to me."

The receptionist told Henry to wait at the desk, then disappeared to find the editor. She knocked on his office door, opened it, and said, "I'm sorry, there's a man at the front desk who says he wants to speak with you right away. He says it's urgent."

"That's fine, Judy."

Judy went back, told Henry to follow her, and led him to the private office. "Mr.?" the editor queried, as Henry walked through the door.

"McRobie, Henry L. McRobie. I'm an attorney."

"What can I do for you, Mr. McRobie?"

Henry began to tell the editor everything he knew. The editor got up and closed the door to his office as Henry continued. After twenty minutes the editor said, "That's a hell of a story. Can you back up what you're saying?"

"Yes."

"Are you prepared to do an interview and stand behind it?"

"Yes."

"How far do you want me to go with this?"

"I want you to run it on the front page! You're lucky your office is closer or I would have gone to the *Washington Post*."

"Ok, I'll talk to legal about it right away, then I'll assign a reporter to interview you for the complete story. I'll call you when we're ready."

"Fine, just please make it soon."

They shook hands and McRobie left feeling satisfied. Something was finally going to happen.

January 7, 2006

Henry often worked long hours into the weekend. At the end of the day, he stepped out of his office and fumbled to get his keys in the car door. It had been a long day and he was tired; he was looking forward to getting home to ease the stress of the day with a tot of scotch.

Driving a steady seventy miles an hour along Highway 32, Henry felt an oppressive tightening in his chest. Trying to keep one hand on the wheel, he ripped at his shirt with urgency; it felt like his heart was going to explode.

At the same moment, a tractor-trailer was headed in the opposite direction. The truck driver was making good time.

The pain in Henry's chest consumed him. His car crossed the double yellow line right into the path of the oncoming big rig. The head-on collision was devastating, but incredibly the impact did not kill Henry. Although he was rushed to the hospital, he died, age sixty-four, from the massive heart attack that struck him while driving.

Judy sat at her computer at the *Baltimore Sun* and typed up an obituary for Henry L. McRobie: a former Marine and Maryland state attorney in good standing.

Prison Time

When our secret demolition job was finished, I went back to work for CO Oakley every day. He initially put me on tasks that enabled me to earn his trust. I could take charge of small projects and make my own decisions. He didn't usually watch over me; instead, he gave me general directives, and let me get to it. He allowed me a little bit of freedom, a little bit of life. I learned how to weld, and operate a Bobcat loader; I fixed and repaired things. It was the most freedom I'd had since being arrested in '98.

One morning Oakley said, "Fulton, you're with me today." While we drove to our destination, another truck approached on our left and stopped next to us. Oakley and the other driver rolled down their windows and spoke openly as if I wasn't there.

"Did you ever think we'd have it this good?" said the other CO.

"No, I didn't," Oakley responded.

"There's plenty of surplus this month; I'll make a tidy profit, just like last month," he laughed. "When I applied for the job, I didn't know about the debit cards, to purchase whatever we need . . . for the prison." He laughed again, but Oakley didn't laugh. "Our garage is like a storage unit for all the new stuff," he continued, "but I really want an Escalade."

"Off the confiscation lists?" Oakley asked.

"Yeah, but I'm waiting for a black one with low miles."

This CO was a cheat, a thief, and obnoxious to boot, but I was the one who was incarcerated.

As we pulled away, Oakley said, "I don't like that guy. There's a lot of guys here like that."

We drove up to an office building. "You're ok with numbers," he said as we walked inside. Oakley showed me to a desk in a private office. "I want you to log these receipts on the computer. Let me know when you're done," and he walked out of the room. I began sorting the receipts and recognized they were from the credit cards the other CO had been talking about: issued to Allenwood to buy whatever was needed for the maintenance of the facilities. Items were bought in multiples: not just one air conditioner, but ten; not just one pane of glass, but a hundred. Whatever was left over went to the COs, who then sold the surplus, off the books, at their leisure, for personal profit. From what I could see, the overstock revenue was in the tens of thousands of dollars . . . all taxpayer money . . . and this was just one Federal Reserve out of countless across the United States.

After I finished importing the figures, Oakley came back in and said, "I know you'll be out of here soon; take the truck and take the day, pretend to get some supplies at the warehouse, just be back before the bus leaves." I drove to the large storage building and parked the truck facing downhill towards the main road.

On the opposite side of the road was a federal facility that, for all intents and purposes, did not exist; it wasn't on any map, it wasn't listed as part of Allenwood, and it had no address. The perimeter was walled, but there were no guards. The windows on the outside of the main building were all blacked out. It was one of the most secured federal facilities in the country. The inmates called it the Cheesecake Factory. I heard the food was top notch: New York steaks, lobster, the best food the government could provide. These inmates were special: they all had something the government wanted or needed. They were all high-profile rats doing the governments bidding.

I watched as a van approached, its windows blacked out. The electronic gate opened, and closed again behind the van. Although I couldn't see them, I knew there was a pair of binoculars trained on me to ascertain whether or not I was a concern, but whoever was looking could see I was just a nothing convict sent to get something for my CO.

I had gone from being on the most wanted list, in chains, held in max security facilities, to sitting in a pickup truck, on my own, watching a new inmate being transferred to a Cheesecake Factory that didn't exist . . . strange life. I thought about my release; I was still a prisoner, but freedom was close.

***

I was required to see the doctor before being allowed to depart Lewisburg on my discharge date. He did the normal tests: took my blood pressure, checked my reflexes, took three vials of blood, and x-rays of my chest. "While you've been in federal custody, you've been exposed to many diseases," he said. "I'll be testing you for TB, and AIDS. If your test results come back positive for AIDS you cannot be released. The FBI already has samples of your DNA at Quantico, Virginia. Before your release they will match it with the blood I just took from you. Remember, your BOP number is yours for life; if you get three strikes, another two convictions, it doesn't matter what they are for, you will get an automatic life sentence."

The thought made me feel ill. I remembered a man I'd met in transit; he had been arrested for driving under the influence and blowing over the legal limit of alcohol on a federal highway in Washington D.C. First conviction, first offense, family man with kids: he got six months in prison. If I ever made a stupid mistake like that, twice, I would end up incarcerated for the rest of my life.

When the test results came back they were all clear and I was released after eight and a half years of misery. Although my life had been a living hell, it was my privilege and honor to serve my time with a handful of the best and brightest Americans I would ever meet.

OCTOBER 2006

I couldn't call my mother; I couldn't see her, or hear her voice, or tell her I'd made it. So many things had changed irreversibly while I was locked up. I could never feel, or see, or think the same way again.

I had to report to a halfway house in Baltimore for four months before I would be able to truly be my own man. Perhaps it was for the best; I might need the time to come to terms with what it meant to live free again. But I burned to get back to Canada and see if there were any remnants of my old life. I'd thought of Shauna every day since I'd been taken, even after I found out she'd left me. I needed to get back, to ensure she and the dogs were having a good and happy life.

I tried to buy work clothes with the little money they gave me upon my discharge. I went to a shopping mall but quickly became disoriented, angry, and completely panic-stricken. It was all too much. I heard a couple arguing about what color curtains they were going to buy. Their argument wasn't worth the breath they wasted on it. Having to wait in line, the noise, the people, not being able to see every entrance, not being able to protect my own back . . . how was I ever going to survive in "normal" society again? How was I ever going to find work?

The halfway house was an old converted hotel in a very bad part of the inner city; there was a lot of poverty, drug dealing, prostitution, and violence. I had to get a job. I didn't have a car, so I searched for something within walking distance until I found a Kentucky Fried Chicken. I told the manager straight as I could that I'd just served eight and a half years for bank fraud and structuring to avoid reporting requirements, and I needed a job. I told him I would take anything he would give me, and I would work very hard. "Well," he said, "you can start by picking up garbage from the parking lot, and we'll see how that goes."

There was a tremendous amount of garbage in the lot. It wasn't the volume that concerned me, but rather the kind of garbage: dirty needles and used condoms from the previous night's activities. Even though I wore gloves, I had to take care not to accidently infect myself. I would feel pretty stupid having made it this far only to die from something I picked up in a KFC parking lot.

After a few days, the manager told me he had never seen the parking lot so clean. He showed me trust and respect; he even went so far as to ask me to go with him every day to drop off the bank deposits. The new position helped me feel my own worth again.

One day when I was near the back door of the restaurant, I noticed two men sitting in a running car smoking cigarettes. They were casing the place, waiting to make a move in broad daylight. I took a firm stance in their point of entry. The driver looked at me and showed me his gun, a way of telling me to step aside. I shook my head and let him know I wasn't going to. The driver must have thought I was out of my mind. He looked at his partner, then at me, and drove away.

I told the manager, and got him to call 911. When the police showed up I gave them a description of the men, the car, and the license plate number. The cop said, "You're either pretty brave or pretty stupid. Those guys have been robbing fast-food restaurants all over the city; they've already shot and killed one man."

I asked the cop if he could keep me out of his report; I had just done time and couldn't afford any problems. I had learned from prison that you don't interfere, but I was on the outside again; someone could have been hurt or killed, and I couldn't have that on my conscience. Better I take the hit than someone in the restaurant who had a life.

Back at the halfway house, I was called to the case worker's office. "Get in here, Fulton," she said angrily. "Where the hell have you been?"

"At work."

"Well I don't know who you know, but you should've been here this morning. You're responsible for this!"

"For what?"

"Some fancy-dressed woman came in here from the Bureau of Prisons in D.C. sayin' she was responding to a request from the Maryland State Senator's Office, and they want you to go home as soon as possible. I don't want to lose my job over this, Fulton. Don't report here anymore. I don't want to see you again."

"Ma'am, I don't know anything about that, but I'm going to keep reporting here. No one will say I didn't do what I was supposed to."

I wouldn't breach my agreement with the government and give them any more power over me. I continued to report every day until I could get my final release papers.

Before they were issued to me, I was called into the main meeting room. A man had come in from Washington and I was told I wouldn't be discharged until he spoke to me. I had no idea who he was or what he wanted.

"I need to ask you a few questions before you go home, Mr. Fulton."

"Alright," I said, getting uncomfortable flashbacks of my proffer sessions.

"Where do you plan on residing?"

Considering I had done my time at the halfway house, and there was no required supervision of me at this point, he had no business asking me any questions or preventing me from leaving. But I didn't want to push the issue, so I told him I had to go back to Canada.

"What will you do for work?"

"I don't know yet."

"We recommend you get a job that doesn't involve computers or the press. Do you have any children?"

"No."

"Are you sure?"

"Yes, I'm sure." *What was this?*

He looked down at some papers, spoke to the caseworker, and said, "I'll be notifying them of his release."

I didn't know who *them* was.

"Thank you, Mr. Fulton; that will be all," he said. I got my release papers and left.

I was free...

55

TIME WAITS FOR NO ONE

FEBRUARY 2007

With the precious little money I had, I bought myself a backpack, a few clean clothes, some food, a compass, and a map.

I figured the cheapest way to get back to Canada was to buy a bus ticket, get as close as I could to the border, walk across, then buy another bus ticket in Quebec to get back to Vancouver.

The Greyhound got me to about twenty miles from the Canadian border. I wanted to walk through the countryside, not along the highway. A few farmhouses dotted the landscape, but there was not much around as I started walking away from the road. By the time I made it through the fields to the edge of the forest, I was beginning to feel a stinging pain in my feet from the long hike in second-hand shoes.

It was early afternoon, and the sun shone through the canopy, leaving dappled shadows on the forest floor. Despite having to navigate the occasional boulder, berm, or fallen tree, it was a pleasant trek. I actually felt a sense of peace for the first time in a very long time. There was silence, and solitude, and tranquility. I imagined I'd had this life all along, and was just out for an afternoon hike, that the absolute hell I'd been living for the last eight and a half years had never happened.

I came to a gully with a stream at the bottom. It wasn't deep or wide, but the soil was loose. I almost made it to the bottom without a problem, but my last step was a mistake; the soil gave way and I tumbled into the stream. I landed on my back, with steep banks on either side. As soon as I hit, the water began flowing over me. My backpack must have snagged on a root or rock because I couldn't get up. I was angled backwards, my weight pushing my head farther under the surface. With the pressure of the water running over my face and limbs, sitting up felt impossible; I was a turtle on its back, stuck, helpless, and drowning. I stretched up my arms hoping to find something I could use to pull myself out. There was nothing but loose soil on either side; my hands flailed, grabbing at nothing but sandy earth. I kept my eyes open and could see the hazy glimmer of trees and light though the flowing water. If I had been able to breathe I would have lingered in the beauty of it, but now it seemed my life would end at the hands of a two-foot-deep playful stream in the middle of a peaceful forest. Life is funny; apparently death is too.

During my desperate struggle, I managed to unhook myself from whatever had snagged my backpack. I rolled onto my side and grabbed a breath of air, then stood up soaking wet and freezing. I gulped in all the air I could, and thanked God. I crawled on all fours to get up the other side of the bank, my stomach snaking along the damp earth.

Once out of the gully, I was not only cold and wet, but muddy and exhausted. I needed to rest for the night. I still felt uneasy; it wasn't as if they were looking for me, or even cared, but I had lived though situations that lacked all reason or sensibility. I knew how quickly circumstances could deteriorate. I built a fire and laid my clothes out to dry. As soon as I could, I put something on that wasn't dripping wet, and I tried to sleep.

The next day started when the sun came up. I had lost the compass when I fell in the river, but I still had my map, and a pretty good feel for what direction I needed to go. I had also worn holes clear through the soles of my shoes. I tried to pad them, but every step I took made me painfully aware of their presence.

The trees thinned, and I could see a paved road. As I emerged from the forest, I saw a huge twelve-point buck standing on the far side. He froze where he stood, and looked at me. He tried to jump for cover, but his way was blocked by a sheer, fifteen-foot-high rock face. As the buck looked back at me I could have sworn he said, "Watch this." Revealing the incredible power in nature, he ascended the cliff, straight up and over, and showed me that the impossible was indeed possible. I thanked him for the demonstration.

The border crossing was all but deserted. There was one man in a booth waiting for anyone to come by. He didn't expect to see me come out of the forest. I approached and handed him the little documentation I had and hoped he would accept it as proof of my Canadian citizenship. We exchanged few words, and he let me pass onto Canadian soil.

I walked for another three hours before I stopped at a gas station to ask where the nearest motel was. The attendant looked me up and down and pointed north. He had a thick French accent. "Four blocks up the main road, and take a left on Rue Bouchard. Walk another four blocks and you'll see it on the right, the Lascelles Motel." I thanked him politely and decided to try and freshen up a little in the restroom.

I got a key from the attendant, and made my way around the side of the station where the bathroom was. It was like a four-star hotel compared to where I had spent the last eight and a half years of my life. I splashed some water on my face and arms and wiped myself down as best I could with the rough brown paper towels. Where most people would leave that gas station feeling grimy, I felt cleaner. That's just how everything was now, back to front and inside out. My life no longer had a parallel with anyone I knew; hell, most people wouldn't be able to understand how I saw things now at all.

The streets I walked through were clean. The sidewalks were even and bright, with little trees planted at perfect intervals. Picket fences lined the rows of mowed lawns and tidy houses; the place looked like Mayberry. I walked up the concrete steps of the Lascelles Motel and opened the door to find a young woman standing behind the counter. She didn't seem bothered by my dirty clothes, or that I looked a little worse for wear. A welcoming smile lit up her face. "Can I help you?" she asked. She had a vulnerable, naïve ease about her; until that moment, I had forgotten what innocence looked like.

I got a key to my room and made my way to number 8. As soon as I locked the door behind me, I headed to the bathroom and started filling the tub. My feet throbbed as I took off my shoes and socks. I took off my pants, stepped into the bath, and sat on the outside edge. I closed my eyes and took in a deep breath. As I exhaled I looked into the water; it had turned a crimson red. Walking in worn-through shoes had done more damage than I had anticipated. I lifted up my foot; the sole was torn and gouged. The warm water must have softened the dried blood and got it flowing again. The watery blood ran down my foot and dripped back into the bath water, adding to the swirling red at my other ankle.

All I wanted to do was immerse my whole body, but the idea of soaking in my own blood somehow lessened the appeal. I drained the water and turned on the shower, took off the rest of my clothes, and stepped in. The dirt snaked in rivers down my body and circled the drain, a swirl of brown and red as it mingled with the blood from my feet.

It was a strange feeling: to be in a private bathroom, in a room I had all to myself, with no other inmates. I didn't have to be on guard for survival, I could just bathe, and breathe, and be. I don't know how long I stood in the shower; I had almost nine years of filth to wash away. Once I felt clean, I stepped out and lay on top of the bed. I instantly fell asleep, and was totally dead to the world.

***

I woke up back in maximum security at Lewisburg Pen. As he locked me in my cell, I asked the guard, "How long am I going to be here?"

"As long as it takes," he responded with a sneer, and walked away.

The cell walls slowly started to grind towards me. I beat my fists and yelled through the door, "Get me out of here! Somebody, anybody, I'm not supposed to be here anymore!"

The walls moved closer: my eight-by-eight cell was now six by six. Another guard walked up and told me I'd better keep it down, or he'd throw me in the hole. "YES, fine," I said, "just get me out of here!" The walls inched closer as he walked away. I looked around wildly, and yelled to anyone who might hear, "How much longer do I have to stay here? The walls keep getting closer, the cell is too small!" Another guard walked up and looked at me, then looked past me at the moving walls. "I'll see what I can find out." He was gone for five, ten, fifteen minutes. I waited, and began to sweat as my cell became three by three. I searched for a way out: a loose stone or a broken hinge on the door... there was nothing. I started to lose hope and hung my head in despair. The walls were grinding closer and closer, if he didn't come back soon I'd be compressed to death. Finally he walked into view.

"Did you find out?" I shouted, "I need to get out of here!"

"You're never going home," he said coldly.

The walls were so close now I had to hold my body diagonally so I wouldn't be crushed. "Take me out now," I pleaded, "I'm not going make it!"

"Sorry," he shrugged, indifferent, "that's just the way it is." With that, he turned and walked away from my shrinking cell. I could feel the stone firmly press against my shoulders. I held them tight up to my neck, and tried to fight the walls that threatened to take me over. I called out again as I felt the devastating force that was bearing down on my bones. My arms were pinned by my sides, pushing into my ribs. I couldn't breathe. The last remaining air in my lungs expelled as pain exploded in my shoulders, hips, and ribs. Tears rolled down my face as I heard my own bones crack throughout my body. My life was being crushed from me, my existence snuffed out. I would die here. This cell would be my tomb; they would board up the door, and I would remain eternally sealed in stone.

I woke up dripping with sweat.

Was this how it was going to be every time I went to sleep?

After I left the hotel, I bought a pair of shoes and a bus ticket. The bus trip took five days. I didn't sleep at all; the thought of being sucked back into the illusion of prison was enough to keep me awake.

56

You Can't Go Home

March 2007

I arrived in Vancouver and called my father to pick me up at the bus station. He didn't want to; he made excuses, excuses not to pick up his own son. Eventually he gave in. My own family had become afraid of me; I was a pariah. My father kept me waiting at the station for hours before pulling up. "Where do you want to go?" he asked.

"I need to see Shauna."

"Are you sure? I don't think you're ready . . ."

Anger welled inside me. "GODDAMNIT, I think I fucking know what I can and can't take!" Considering the outburst, maybe he was right; perhaps seeing Shauna, who had left me in my darkest hour, wasn't the best idea. But I calmed myself; I had resigned myself to the fact that she had left me years ago. I just needed to see for myself that she was happy, and see that my dogs had a good life. Once that was done I could move forward.

We got on the Sea to Sky Highway. It was a long drive; we didn't talk. I had enough voices in my head to keep me preoccupied. I guessed Shauna was still living in the house that we had bought together, but as we approached our street, my father missed the turn; I asked him where he was taking me.

"To see Shauna; I'm so sorry, Christopher."

I was sorry too, but I felt there was still hope; nothing was final, nothing was set in stone. We pulled into a drive and the sign out front said: "Squamish Funeral Chapel."

"What is this?" I said. "Why are you taking me here?" Panic gripped me. "What are we doing here?" I yelled.

"I told you I didn't think you were ready; we can go back," he said in a very quiet voice.

"No!" I shouted.

He got out of the car and walked me to a columbarium. An engraved brass plaque was set in the cold marble vault: "Shauna Tyler 1972–1999." I shivered in shock and disbelief; I turned to my father. "What is this?"

"Oh my God," my father said, reading it in my face, "you didn't know." I raced back to the car and my father followed.

"They said Shauna left me . . . Where are my dogs?" I shouted at him, starting to break.

"I don't know about the dogs, but Shauna never left you, Son, not in that sense. After you were taken she changed; she got into drugs. Her parents wrote to you to try and spare you while you were locked up; that's what we all did."

This was all wrong, it didn't make any sense. This wasn't my Shauna he was talking about.

"She was speeding along the highway when her car flipped; she was hopped up on something. Nobody came along that stretch of road until it was too late . . ."

I felt sick. As I sat down in the passenger seat I completely lost it; my fist shot forward, smashing into the windshield. The cracks spidered outwards in all directions and fractured along the top clear to the left side. I didn't say a word, and neither did my father. We sat in silence. My breathing was heavy and ragged with anger and hate. "It couldn't have happened like that," I said finally. My heart shriveled in my chest.

"Your house is up for sale; here's the number if you want to call." Useless. I told my father to take me to a hotel. I knew I wasn't in denial,

I just knew it had to be a mistake. She was out there somewhere. I would figure it out. My father put the car in gear and we rolled out of the parking lot. The sound of the tires echoed the scratching of a record that would never play. He drove me to a hotel, and paid for a week in advance. It was enough time for me to come up with a plan.

He told me to get some rest. It had been five days since I slept. I started laughing, what else was I going to do? There was nothing left to do. This all had to be some sort of cosmic joke, so I laughed. Maybe, if I hadn't just got out of prison and discovered some conspiracy surrounding my wife, I could close my eyes in peaceful slumber . . . but now, as far as I was concerned, I would never sleep again. I was so wired I decided I would live out the rest of my life awake; I could make up for lost time, always be on guard, and never have to worry about the nightmares again.

I left my father behind somewhere down the hall, got into my room, and sat on the foot of the bed to try and figure out my next move. I fell back on the bed, blinked, and was out cold.

The nightmares came again: a swirl of prison stints, court dates, help-less dogs, and a wife who kept vanishing and reappearing through the haze. They played over and over again while I slept, joined by the intense, unforgiving emotions that accompanied the rotating themes. A rhythmic beating bludgeoned its way into my pain-filled subconscious. It was unre-lenting. I saw Tech's head open and bloodied, then JFK's head surrounded by a halo of gory mist, then it was footsteps disappearing in darkness . . .

"Room service."

I sat bold upright, but I was exhausted, mentally drained, and confused. I called to the maid to please leave me be. So this was my life of freedom: plagued by nightmares. I had to find out for myself about Shauna; I had to know what had happened for sure.

I picked up the phone and dialed the number my father had given me.

A real estate agent named Susan answered.

"I wanted to inquire about the house for sale in Lions Bay," I said.

"Oh, you will just love that house," she gushed, and went on to tell me all the virtues of my former home.

"What's the asking price?" I pressed.

The figure she told me was five times the amount Shauna and I had paid nine years earlier. "Are the owners willing to negotiate?" I asked.

"Well, I'm the owner."

"How long have you had it?"

"I bought it from the bank after it fell into arrears in 1999."

"As an investment?"

"Yes. It really is a lovely home."

"Why was the bank selling it in the first place?"

***

Susan did her best to put a positive spin on the story, but the need for disclosure could really inhibit her sales ability on this house. She thought of the previous owner: what absolute scum, filthy low-life . . . and the four dog carcasses decaying on the kitchen floor—the smell had made her puke in the sink. But it was all polished and clean now, and she hoped she had found her buyer.

***

"Well," Susan said. I could hear her sunny disposition falter for a moment. "The last owner was a drug addict; she got high and flipped her car and died. Nobody knew she had dogs in the house; they all died locked inside. But that was so long ago," she said, and I heard the smile return to her voice. "It's really quite lovely now."

I was mentally shutting down. "I have to go," I said, and hung up the phone.

***

I found myself walking . . . I was on our old street. I had been drawn there and I couldn't turn back. It was nighttime and the air was cool but still. Every house I passed had their lights on, and a gentle yellow glow spilled out the windows onto the damp grass below. I held my breath. It felt like my heart had stopped beating. I didn't know what I expected to find.

Then I saw it, our home on the corner; it also had a calm brightness that illuminated every window. My heart jumped and my pace quickened. I *knew* there had been a mistake, Shauna was still alive; she was there with our dogs in our home. I couldn't hold back, I ran up the walkway and looked through the window. God, there she was in the kitchen, a smile on her face as she bent down to feed Kelley leftovers from her dinner plate. The sight jump-started me.

I ran up the steps to the front door and flung it open, calling her name as I turned into the kitchen. The look of surprise and joy on her face was everything I had waited for. I ran to her and wrapped my arms around her. She held my face in her hands and kissed me, and Kelley and Tao, and Bear and Leo all came to welcome me home. I closed my eyes as I breathed in the smell of Shauna's skin and hair, felt the gentle touch of her hand. For the first time in almost nine years I felt true peace, and love, and hope. I held her tightly and closed my eyes to try and take in every detail of that moment.

When I opened my eyes again the house had grown dark and cold. Shauna was gone, the dogs were gone, there was no light . . . It wasn't real; none of it had been real.

There was a fine layer of dust on the floor, disturbed by the dried dead leaves that tumbled in through the open door. I had seen her, had touched her, but now everything lay silent and still, lifeless, except for my body convulsing in absolute agony on the kitchen floor. I cried so hard no sound came out. I pushed myself not to breathe in: the longer I went without breathing, the closer I felt to death, and that was all I wanted, the pain was too great . . . but with every inhalation, oxygen surged back into my bloodstream, and I kept living.

I stumbled out of the God-forsaken house, tripped and skidded, and landed face first on the turf. As I lay there it started to rain; the wet and the dirt mixed as I tried to feel the world breathing. Maybe if I could get in sync, if I could feel the rhythm in the soil beneath me, I'd find a reason for living. The rain began to beat down and I rolled on my back to let the cold, swollen drops break apart on my face. I focused on the trails forged as the water pooled and overflowed down my cheeks; the rain was crying for me. Finally I breathed out, and let the tension drain from my body and exit through every surface that touched the earth.

***

"Doctor, he's waking up."

I heard a woman's voice that I didn't recognize. I opened my eyes to a stark white room with a physician standing over me and checking a monitor on my left. He looked back at me. "Mr. Fulton, can you hear me? How do you feel?"

"Yes, I can hear you."

"Do you know where you are?"

"No."

"You're in Lions Gate Hospital. What's the last thing you remember?"

"I don't know . . . I was on the phone . . . I was walking down the street . . . I don't remember."

"Mr. Fulton, you were found in an excavation pit on a construction site in Lions Bay. An ambulance was called, and you were brought here. You haven't suffered any permanent damage; your vitals have been strong and consistent, but you were unconscious for some time.

"Your father came to visit. I'll notify him you're awake so he can come back and see you. I want to keep you under observation for the next two days; if everything looks good, I'll discharge you. Are you hungry?"

"Yes." My head was aching and I was trying to process everything the Doctor told me.

The first thing I wanted to ask was if Shauna knew, but then I remembered. I was disoriented and dizzy; I thought I might lose consciousness again.

"Good. Nurse, please arrange for some food to be brought to Mr. Fulton."

When the nurse came back with a lunch tray she said I had a visitor and asked if I was up to seeing them.

"Who is it?" I asked.

"Her name is Loretta. She said she was your wife's best friend."

Loretta? I hadn't seen her in almost nine years; how did she know I was here? "Yes, that's fine," I said, "I'll see her."

When she walked in I was taken aback; she looked different, older. I could only imagine how I had changed.

She grabbed a chair and put it next to the bed. "How are you feeling?"

"Alright, I guess, considering. I don't remember anything that happened; I only know what the doctor told me. How are you? How have you been?"

"I'm alright," Loretta said. "I've wanted to talk to you. I didn't even know you were out."

"How did you find out I was here?"

"Your dad called me."

"What did you want to tell me?" I asked.

"I don't know . . . Maybe now isn't the best time . . . maybe when you are out of the hospital and feeling better . . ."

"No, no, I'm fine; if you've got something to say, tell me now." I had learned not to let moments pass.

"This has been bothering me since Shauna was killed," Loretta said sadly. "The police said she was using drugs and she died from an overdose and ran off the road. But I can tell you that's not what happened. I saw her that day, we had dinner together. All she could think about was you . . . She was sad and stressed out, but she definitely wasn't using drugs. You knew her, she barely even touched alcohol. The whole time you were gone, I was the one she was leaning on; she never turned to anything else."

Listening to her was like cutting open stitches before a deep wound had healed. But I sat quietly, trying to hold back my emotions.

"We were supposed to go to a movie after dinner but I had a headache; I still think if we had just gone to the theater, things wouldn't have happened the way they did. It was the last time we could get together before I left on my trip to Australia. By the time I heard what'd happened it was too late. They ruled it a drug related-death, and your dogs . . . I'm so sorry, Christopher." She grabbed a tissue. Exhuming the guilt brought on waves of emotion and she had to pause for a moment to regain her composure.

"It wasn't your fault," I said as I grabbed her hand, "I'm glad you came to talk to me."

"I don't know what happened, or why someone would have killed her, but it had to be some sort of set-up. She was her usual self when I last saw her. She had a hard time coping with losing you, but she was strong. I tried to tell the police, but no one would listen. They all dismissed me, saying the stress cracked her, but it didn't, Christopher, I know it didn't. That's why I needed to come; I needed to let you know . . . What are you going to do now?"

"I don't know. I don't have a place to live, I hardly have any money; I need to be able to take care of myself before I can take care of the past."

"How would you feel about moving back to the States; you were born there, right?"

"Why?" I asked.

"Just a thought . . . My grandfather passed away a few weeks ago, but my grandmother is still living out in the California desert by herself. She has a ranch out in the Mojave with a couple of houses on her property. She's looking for someone to stay in her guest house and run errands for her so she can feel safe and continue living in her own home."

The people who destroyed my life and murdered the ones I loved were still in the States. "That sounds perfect," I said.

57

A New Future

Late March 2007

The thought of going back to the States frightened me. I wasn't concerned about death, but the thought of being locked up again, of losing my life while still living, made my blood run cold. But I couldn't see any other way around it: I had something important to do, and I needed somewhere to do it.

I arrived at Loretta's grandmother's ranch in the Mojave Desert. It was perfect: open land as far as you could see, and a backdrop of rugged mountains on the western horizon. The brick houses were built in the forties, and it seemed like nothing in the area had changed since then.

Freedom was tangible here. I could think of no better place in the world for me to be. The house I was staying in was small but comfortable: it had a kitchen, a bedroom, and a bathroom. The last time anyone had lived in it was during the seventies.

Loretta's grandmother, Martha, was an elderly, strong-willed religious woman who prided herself on her independence. After losing her husband and finding herself alone in the desert, she felt insecure for the first time in her life. She was happy to have someone working the ranch for her. There was more to be done than time in a day; I worked hard. Martha had me use her husband's 1960 Ford pickup to drive into town and get groceries and do chores around the ranch. Sunday was always a day of rest; that was my time.

On my fourth Sunday, I drove into the small town, but not for food. I bought rubber gloves and ten cartons of cigarettes without filters at the drug store. The little house still had cupboards full of dishes, cutlery, and pans, so I didn't need anything else. When I returned, I put a pot of water on the stove to boil, then lay down on the sofa and waited.

There was a knock at the door and I heard Martha's voice: "Christopher?" I jumped off the sofa and opened the door. Martha was on the front porch smiling. "I know it's Sunday, and God knows you need a rest, but I'd like to donate some things to the church and they have to be taken in by the end of the day. Could you help me load the truck?"

"Of course," I said, smiling back.

I turned off the stove and we drove to the main house; I loaded everything she had put aside. Then she pointed to something with a black cover on it; it was very heavy. "What is this?" I asked.

"That's Harold's IBM. He was a war correspondent and that was his favorite electric typewriter. He bought it during the Vietnam War."

"Did he write many pieces?" I asked.

"Yes, he did. He was a good man; he wrote about things that mattered. Some of his exposés were so important he couldn't even get them published. If it interests you, why don't you take it for yourself? Harold would like that, and it would make me feel good if you took it and gave it a good home."

"I wouldn't know what to do with it," I said.

"Well, you keep it anyway, and take that ream of bond paper with you, too; maybe you'll want to write a letter to someone."

"Alright, thank you, Martha."

When we finished dropping the belongings off at the church, Martha asked if we could go to the Bakersfield National Cemetery. She said she didn't want to take up my whole Sunday with her errands, but leaving her husband's things at the church made his absence ever poignant. She wanted to see him, speak to him, feel close to him again.

We drove an hour out of the desert and down the 58 to the cemetery hidden in the hills above Bakersfield. We parked and got out of the truck. I could smell the grass and I felt a cool breeze against my face as we made our way to her husband's headstone. I left so Martha could be alone with him.

The cemetery was set amongst rolling hills studded with ancient oak trees. The leaves were just starting to turn. I looked out across the markers; they were cool and bright, a uniform white that reflected the sun. Each monument was adorned with an American flag; the motion of the red, white, and blue rippling in the breeze added a chorus of patriotic color to the lonely stones.

I had seen this place before, only with endless additions to the dead, as far as the eye could see. A shiver ran through me. I stood still and did not make a sound.

When Martha was done speaking with her husband, she beckoned me to her side, and I escorted her back to the truck. "Harold always said, 'Live forward, but think in reverse.' Do you understand?"

"No," I said, feeling another chill up my spine. I helped Martha into the truck. "What did he mean?"

"Don't take something to your grave as a regret. Do what you need to do, and say what you need to say, while there is still breath in your lungs. You always have to move forward, but keep the end in your mind; make sure in your life you accomplish the things that mean the most. Harold wrote the truth, and whether it got published or not, he had peace at the end because he always stayed true to himself. If others chose to see it or not, it didn't matter ..."

As we drove back to the desert, Martha fell asleep in the passenger seat. I was happy to have been able to help her, but doing so had deviated me from my original plans. I was anxious to get back.

When we returned to the ranch I helped Martha into her home, and I carried Harold's typewriter into my little brick house. I was curious about the machine. I sat it on the table and took off the cover. It had a long cord out the back that was looped together with a rubber band. I went to take the band off but it crumbled at my touch. I wondered if it would still work. I plugged it in and flicked the switch on. It instantly hummed to life; it worked flawlessly, as if it was new. Martha said it was the top of the line when her husband had bought it. I grabbed a fresh piece of paper and reached to remove the old single sheet still in the machine; it had been used. I pulled it from the paper bail, and read it before inserting the fresh sheet.

May 8, 1962, Convention Hall, Atlantic City

[...] Now I know there are some people who say this isn't any business of the President of the United States, and who believe that the President of the United States should be the honorary chairman of a great fraternal organization and confine himself to ceremonial functions. But that is not what the Constitution says, and I did not run for President of the United States to fulfill that office in that way. [...]

[...] I believe it is the business of the President of the United States to concern himself with the general welfare and the public interest, and if the people feel that it is not, then they should secure the services of a new President of the United States. [...]

April 27, 1961, Waldorf Astoria Hotel, New York City

[...] the dangers of excessive and unwarranted concealment of pertinent facts far outweighed the dangers which are cited to justify it. [...] And there is very grave danger that an announced need for increased security will be seized upon by those anxious to expand its meaning to the very limits of official censorship and concealment. That I do not intend to permit to the extent that it is in my control. And no official of my Administration, whether his rank is high or low, civilian or military, should interpret my words here tonight as an excuse to censor the news, to stifle dissent, to cover up our mistakes or to withhold from the press and the public the facts they deserve to know. [...]

Today no war has been declared--and however fierce the struggle may be, it may never be declared in the traditional fashion. Our way of life is under attack. [...]

[...] this is a time of peace and peril which knows no precedent in history. [...]

[...] I am asking your help in the tremendous task of informing and alerting the American people. For I have complete confidence in the response and dedication of our citizens whenever they are fully informed. [...]

Without debate, without criticism, no Administration and no country can succeed--and no republic can survive. That is why the Athenian lawmaker Solon decreed it a crime for any citizen to shrink from controversy. And that is why our press was protected by the First Amendment--the only business in America specifically protected by the Constitution--not primarily to amuse and entertain, not to emphasize the trivial and the sentimental, not to simply "give the public what it wants"--but to inform, to arouse, to reflect, to state our dangers and our opportunities, to indicate our crises and our choices, to lead, mold, educate and sometimes even anger public opinion.

[...] [The] government in all levels must meet its obligation to provide you with the fullest possible information [...]

[...] [I am] confident with your help man will be what he was born to be: free and independent.

– President John F. Kennedy

The words on the page startled me, ripped through me. Was it part of an editorial Harold was working on? I realized the statements were as relevant today as they were when they were penned. Everything Kennedy said had come to pass. I switched off the machine, replaced the cover, and walked into the kitchen. I tried to put Kennedy's words out of my mind and return to my day's intention: I had to test the recipe. I turned on the stove, lay back on the sofa, and waited for the water to boil again. I stared at the ceiling to clear my mind; I had done it so often while I was up against it in lockup, like a meditative trance.

Everything had been taken from me, not only the life I had lived, but the future I had dreamed of. It was all gone.

I wanted retribution, I wanted justice.

I saw my future, not the one that stretched to my old age with my wife and my children and grandchildren, but something for right now. It didn't matter what came after, because death was still attractive . . . but I couldn't keep Kennedy's words out of my mind.

I looked at the stove. The boiling water was angry, violently spilling over the sides. Then the silent typewriter pulled my gaze.

I felt something, like a pinprick between my lungs in the bottom of my heart, and I could have sworn I felt Shauna's hand on my cheek. Did she know what I planned to do?

I had been dragged through years and years of hell, channeled, against my will, from the very beginning into the narrowest of existences. Nothing remained of me but a burned-out cinder of what was once a happy and fruitful existence. But somehow I had survived it. I was forged by fire, changed, broken, and poorly fit back together, but I *had* survived. The question was, *Why? What did it mean?* But the real question was, *What would I do with the gift of my continued existence?* It reverberated in my skull.

If this happened to me, and my love, and my life, how many more Americans would have their futures destroyed? I had met enough men in prison to know I was not a special case; people are destroyed all the time without a second thought, unvalued pawns in someone else's chess game. Ever frequently, we are all becoming nothing more than pawns.

I thought of Robert Kennedy. He came to the reasoning that it was far more important to gain the White House to help the world rather than seek vengeance solely to avenge his brother's murder. Then I thought of Evelyn Lincoln: the sacrifices she had made and the burden she had carried for so long. Did she ever worry that her efforts would be in vain? Did she hope the country would find out the truth because of her diligence? And John Jr.—his death still wrenched at my guts. There was so much hope, so much promise, and then nothing.

This information, these secrets, these truths were not just Bobby Kennedy's mantle, or Evelyn Lincoln's or Robert Bouck's, John Jr.'s, or even Robert White's or mine; they belonged to the country. They belonged to all of us.

I was likely the last player in this part of JFK's narrative who was still alive. So what could I do?

I could say what needed to be said.

Again I felt Shauna, and I knew . . .

I took the pot of boiling water off the stove and poured it down the drain; with it went my plans for revenge. I sat at the table with my inherited typewriter in front of me. This machine had been an instrument of truth and knowledge during a time of war, and now it was my turn to use it for the same purpose. I would stay in the country where I was born, strike the keys, and use the narcotics of words to stave off the desire to end life, use them to print the experience and texture of my own personal war, and illuminate what hides in the shadows.

I flicked on the switch; the typewriter sat humming, waiting for me to make my move. I fed it a new sheet, took a deep breath, and started to type:

"Today started out differently . . ."

DOCUMENTS
&
PHOTOGRAPHS

Evelyn Lincoln at the eternal flame.

Christopher Fulton and his father at the eternal flame.

Christopher Fulton and his mother at the White House in 1967.

Christopher Fulton's mother.

Christopher Fulton's family

Christopher Fulton

Christopher Fulton

Kelly

Leo

Tao

Christopher Fulton in Vancouver, B.C., 1997

One of Christopher Fulton's job sites in Vancouver, B.C.

TO WHOM IT MAY CONCERN

Certificate of Good Standing

This is to Certify that

THE TWELVE GLOBAL LIMITED

Incorporated under the Companies Ordinance 1981 on the 24th day of February, 19 97 is in good standing with this Office at the date hereof.

Given under my hand and seal this 30th day of March, 1998.

DEBORAH C. ASHTON
Registrar of Companies
Turks & Caicos Islands

Registered No. E.20260

SPRING FASHION PREVIEW/GAY TALESE'S "UNTO THE SONS"

GQ

FOR THE MODERN MAN
JANUARY $3.00

The Furor Over
"JFK"

Oliver Stone
Defends His Movie
by Jennet Conant

The Real Jim Garrison
by Nicholas Lemann

GQ cover featuring Jacques Lowe's photo of Senator
John F. Kennedy wearing the Cartier watch.

J.F.K.
8·12·57

JFK's Cartier watch

000075

October 29, 1966

Honorable Lawson B. Knott, Jr.
Administrator of General Services
Washington, D. C.

Dear Mr. Knott:

The family of the late President John F. Kennedy shares the concern of the Government of the United States that the personal effects of the late President which were gathered as evidence by the President's Commission on the Assassination of President Kennedy, as well as certain other materials relating to the assassination, should be deposited, safeguarded and preserved in the Archives of the United States as materials of historical importance. The family desires to prevent the undignified or sensational use of these materials (such as public display) or any other use which would tend in any way to dishonor the memory of the late President or cause unnecessary grief or suffering to the members of his family and those closely associated with him. We know the Government respects these desires.

Accordingly, pursuant to the provisions of 44 U.S.C. 397(e)(1), the executors of the estate of the late President John F. Kennedy hereby transfer to the Administrator of General Services, acting for and on behalf of the United States of America, for deposit in the National Archives of the United States, all of their right, title, and interest in all of the personal clothing of the late President now in the possession of the United States Government and identified in Appendix A, and in certain x-rays and photographs connected with the autopsy of the

001131

MD 112

Page one of the seven page Kennedy family donor agreement for personal effects. Complete document available at https://www.history-matters.com/archive/jfk/arrb/master_med_set/md112/html/md112_0001a.htm

THE WHITE HOUSE
WASHINGTON

September 15, 1989

Dear Robert:

The dark tinted, brown rimmed sun glasses,
encased in a black, soft, hook on, leather case,
which you now have in your possession, were used
by John F. Kennedy during his Presidency. The
words "Fidelity U.S.A." are on the black case.
These glasses were discarded after someone sat
on them breaking the frame.

Sincerely,

Evelyn Lincoln
Personal Secretary to
the late President
John F. Kennedy

Robert L. White
304 Bloomsbury Avenue
Catonsville, Md. 21228

U.S. DEPARTMENT OF JUSTICE FULTON CASE FILE: Letter from Evelyn Lincoln to Robert White and one of Christopher Fulton's Guernsey's consignments.

THE WHITE HOUSE
WASHINGTON

June 5, 1992

Dear Robert:

This gold Cartier Lord Elgin watch with brown wrist band and "JFK 9-12-57 " engraved on the back, which you now have in your possession, was worn by President John F. Kennedy for a short while, but he then discarded it because he didn't like the wrist band.

Sincerely,

Evelyn Lincoln

Evelyn Lincoln
Personal Secretary to
our late President
John F. Kennedy

Robert L. White
304 Bloomsbury Ave.
Catonsville, Md. 21228

The original White House letter for President Kennedy's Cartier from Evelyn Lincoln to Robert White.

Evelyn describes the watch adding the word "Lord Elgin", which was the embossed name found on the inside of the brown wriststrap used to replace the original black wriststrap.

On the date of Evelyn's letter, June 5, 1992, the Secret Service documents pertaining to President Kennedy's Cartier watch and the assassination remained classified and had not yet been released to the public.

U.S. DEPARTMENT OF JUSTICE FULTON CASE FILE: Letter to Robert White from Evelyn Lincoln..

THE ROBERT L. WHITE
COLLECTION ON
PRESIDENT JOHN F. KENNEDY

John Fitzgerald Kennedy

February 6, 1993

Dear Mrs. Lincoln:

Thank you for the most insightful and informative letter I think I've ever received.

I felt compelled to write and again stress to you I was in no way inferring that you were in error with regard to the documentation on that little money clip. Deep down inside me something said it could'nt be and your lengthy words really cleared up the mystery that Manchester's book creates.

Thank you again for setting the record straight and I'm proud to have your original .letter with that little money clip of the President's.

My best to Mr. Lincoln as always and my family all wish you both the best.

Sincerely yours,
Love,

Robert

WANTED: ANY DOCUMENTED PERSONAL ITEMS, AUTOGRAPHS, LETTERS, PHOTOS OR ANYTHING ON
JOHN F. KENNEDY AND THE KENNEDY FAMILY. ANY PERIOD—EARLY YEARS,
CONGRESS, SENATE, PRESIDENTIAL AND ASASSINATION RELATED.

CALL OR WRITE ▬▬▬▬▬ BALTIMORE, MARYLAND 21228

CHRISTOPHER FULTON'S PERSONAL DOCUMENT: Letter from Robert White to Evelyn Lincoln regarding President Kennedy's St. Christopher money clip and the truth about its involvement during the assassination.

TOP SECRET

Memo. #246

oximately 1:00 P. M., I was asked to clear the way for Vice President Lyndon
. and Mrs. Johnson, who came out of Minor Surgery Division completely surrounded
·t service men, in order that they may exit through the back door of the
·cy area.

oximately 1:00 P. M., I was notified that a casket would arrive soon at the
·cy. We were asked to lend all assistance possible in letting them in. When
·ket arrived it was accompanied by Pegg Oneal, owner of Oneal Funeral Home.
·assisted in moving the casket into the area where the late President's body
·pproximately thirty minutes later, the casket was brought out through the door.
·old that it contained the body of the late President. It was accompanied by
· service men, Mr. Oneal, and Mrs. Jacqueline Kennedy, who walked beside it with
·d on the casket. We cleared the hallway and assisted this party out of the
·cy area.

·thereafter, Miss Bowron, R. N. in the emergency room, handed me a wrist watch
·as informed the watch belonged to the late President, Mr. John F. Kennedy. I
·the watch in my pocket and as soon as I could find time to get to a telephone,
·ied Mr. Forrest Sorrells, Agent-in-charge of the Secret Service in Dallas, Texas,
·was in possession of a watch that was reported to be that of the late President.

·ells told me to keep the watch and he would send an agent, either here or to
·, to pick up the watch. I carried the watch in my pocket for several days and
·ch had not been picked up. I again called Forrest Sorrells and reminded him
·was still in possession of the watch. He told me that he had not forgotten it
·not had the manpower to send for it, but that he would send for it soon.

·ch was picked up on November 26, 1963, at 4:05 P. M. by Mr. Roger Warren, an
·f the United States Secret Service.

·oximately 1:00 P. M., Chief Curry of the Dallas Police Department came to me
·d if I could possibly get a telephone out of the building so he could call the
·Department. We could not get an outside line on the hospital trunk lines, so
·to my office and used my private line to relay a message for him. The message
·Clear the area around the reloading place where the President and his party
·depart". The message was not to be broadcast but that they were to send officers
·d see that this area was kept clear of all unauthorized people. I then went back
·emergency room where I assisted in every way to keep this area secure until approxi-
·2:00 P. M.

·en informed that we had considerable traffic in the main lobby in front of the
·l. I sent two security officers to this area and cleared the hallway of all un-
·ted people, so that authorized persons could move about in this area. Chief
·d I again conferred and he told me that until there was no further need he
·ntinue to furnish me with the needed number of city police officers to secure
·ital. Two men were kept on the emergency entrance, two men on the main entrance
·t of the hospital, and two men on the personnel entrance that leads out by
·service to the staff residence. This security was maintained until 11:00 P. M.
·ht when it was deemed no longer necessary. The security officers were removed
·was turned over to the State Highway Patrol, State Rangers, who had moved into
·l by this time. In fact they started moving in immediately after 4:00 P. M.,
·up press rooms, Governor's offices on the main floor in front of Nursing Service,
·ing part of Administrative offices, and tightly securing the second floor where
·rnor was being treated.

TOP SECRET

PRICE EXHIBIT No. 29—Continued

NATIONAL ARCHIVES AND RECORDS ADMINISTRATION: Parkland Hospital's recorded statement by O.P. Wright.

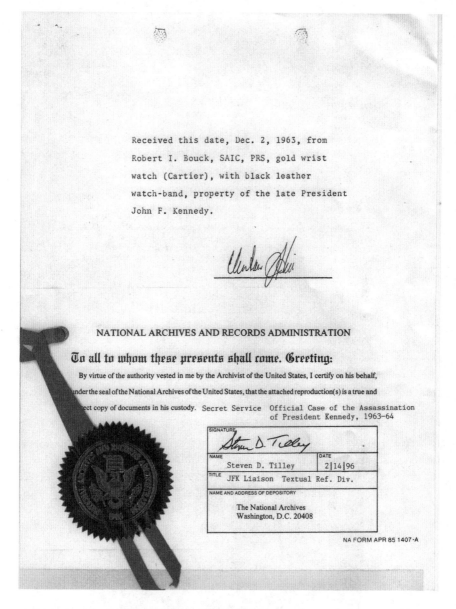

Received this date, Dec. 2, 1963, from Robert I. Bouck, SAIC, PRS, gold wrist watch (Cartier), with black leather watch-band, property of the late President John F. Kennedy.

NATIONAL ARCHIVES AND RECORDS ADMINISTRATION

To all to whom these presents shall come. Greeting:

By virtue of the authority vested in me by the Archivist of the United States, I certify on his behalf, under the seal of the National Archives of the United States, that the attached reproduction(s) is a true and correct copy of documents in his custody. Secret Service Official Case of the Assassination of President Kennedy, 1963–64

SIGNATURE	
NAME Steven D. Tilley	DATE 2|14|96
TITLE JFK Liaison Textual Ref. Div.	

NAME AND ADDRESS OF DEPOSITORY

The National Archives
Washington, D.C. 20408

NA FORM APR 85 1407-A

NATIONAL ARCHIVES AND RECORDS ADMINISTRATION: Secret Service receipt for Cartier watch.

ROGER C. WARNER
Special Agent, Secret Service
Dallas, TX 1963.

Statement given February 29,1996.

I was sent to pick up the President's wristwatch from O.P. Wright, the 26th of November, 1963. I did not look at the watch, I was not interested in seeing it. We were very busy at the time. I do not recall exactly how we sent it back to Washington. Because the watch was the personal possession of President Kennedy, we were not required to testify about it, so a specific receipt was not issued to me. But everything in the assassination went back and through PRS section of the Secret Service in Washington, D.C. where careful documentation took place. That was our clearance house for the items from Dallas.

Roger C. Warner: _Roger C Warner_

Date: _11 March 1996_

Notary: _Catherine M. Frank_
my commission expires 2-28-2000
State of Virginia
County of Fairfax

U.S. DEPARTMENT OF JUSTICE FULTON CASE FILE: Sworn statement that Christopher Fulton received from Secret Service Agent Roger Warner.

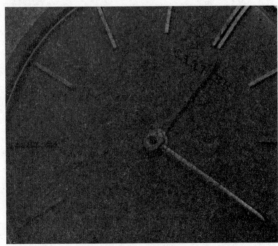

U.S. DEPARTMENT OF JUSTICE FULTON CASE FILE: Photo of Christopher Fulton's Guernsey's consignment: Cartier Watch. Picture shows striations and small cracks in the watch's crystal

ROBERT J. GRODEN
212 EMILY LANE
BOOTHWYN, PA 19061

6/12/96

Dear Chris:

Thank you for all your help.

Here are the 8x10 photographs from the DCA film. I hope they are
what you needed.

As a bonus for your generosity and help, I am including original
35mm slides of the 5 frames. This may be of further help to you.

In addition, I am including a copy of each of my two video tape
productions, JFK:The Case for Conspiracy and The Assassination
Films as a gift to you.

Thanks again for your help.

Robert Groden

CHRISTOPHER FULTON'S PERSONAL RECORD: Letter from Robert Groden

CHRISTOPHER FULTON'S PERSONAL RECORD: Frame from the DCA film from Robert
Groden showing President Kennedy in the limousine on November 22, 1963, wearing
the Cartier watch and no cufflinks.

399

AFFIDAVIT

This is to confirm that Chris Fulton owns 2 JFK watches from my collection.

First being a Nastrix 57 jewel waterproof wristwatch taken from JFK's desk drawer in the Oval Office by Evelyn Lincoln just after the assassination, then gifted to Evelyn by Jackie, then given to me by Evelyn on August 5th, 1991.

Second is a Cartier 18K round, serial number, #345090, that JFK wore for many years and was wearing the day of the assassination in Dallas. It was returned to Jackie by the Secret Service after it was logged as evidence and gifted to Evelyn Lincoln by Jackie, then given to me on June 5th, 1992.

Robert L. White.

Date: _July 11, 1996_

CHRISTOPHER FULTON'S PERSONAL RECORD: Notarized letter from Robert White regarding President Kennedy's Cartier watch.

This is a true and correct image of John F. Kennedy's watch as I received it on June 5th, 1992 from Evelyn Lincoln, JFK's personal secretary of 12 years. Evelyn spoke little of this watch, other than it was a gift to her from Jackie as a memento of President Kennedy. It has recently been discovered through photos and Secret Service documentation that this is indeed the watch he wore for many years and was wearing the day of the assassination in Dallas. The original black Cartier alligator strap with gold deployant buckle was removed by the Secret Service and replaced with the Lord Elgin leather strap before the watch was returned to Mrs. Kennedy on December 2nd, 1963. His most personal possessions gifted between he and Jackie were initialed J.F.K. as this watch is. The date engraved, September 12, 1957, was their fourth wedding anniversary.

Description as follows: Cartier, 18K gold, 18 jewel, manual wind, serial number: 345090, movement number: 486411, number 156 appears on reverse of case lug, inscribed on back: "J.F.K. 9.12.57", crystal shows fine scratches, original strap replaced.

Robert L. White

Notary

Jacquelyn E. White
7/1/94

CHRISTOPHER FULTON'S PERSONAL RECORD: Notarized letter from Robert White regarding President Kennedy's Cartier watch.

SOTHEBY'S
FOUNDED 1744

1334 York Avenue
New York, New York 10021
Telephone: (212) 606-7000

CONFIDENTIALITY AGREEMENT

September 12, 1996

BY FACSIMILE - (604) 922-2813

Mr. Chris Fulton
Vancouver, Canada

Dear Mr. Fulton:

In consideration of your (the "Client") interest in a possible transaction between Sotheby's, Inc. ("Sotheby's) and the Client, Sotheby's understands that the Client intends to provide Sotheby's with certain information that is confidential information that has not heretofore been made available to the public. Sotheby's agrees that it shall treat all confidential, non-public information furnished to Sotheby's by the Client, on and after the date of this Agreement (herein collectively referred to as the "Evaluation Material") as follows:

1.   Sotheby's recognizes that certain Evaluation Material may be proprietary in nature. Sotheby's agrees that the Evaluation Material will be used to evaluate the material may be disclosed to any Sotheby's agents, attorneys or accountants who need to know such information for the purpose of evaluating a possible transaction with the Client.

2.   Without the prior written consent of the other party hereto, neither Client nor Sotheby's will disclose to any person either the fact that discussions or negotiations are taking place concerning a possible transaction with the Client or any of the terms, conditions or other facts with respect to any such possible transaction including the status thereof; nor will any of them disclose that the Evaluation Material has been made available to Sotheby's.

U.S. DEPARTMENT OF JUSTICE FULTON CASE FILE: Letter from Sotheby's to Christopher Fulton.

SOTHEBY'S
FOUNDED 1744

3.   Sotheby's shall have no obligation hereunder with respect to any information in the Evaluation Material to the extent that such information is already known to Sotheby's or if such information has been, or will be, made public other than by acts by Sotheby's in violation of this Agreement. In either event, Sotheby's shall have no further obligation in respect to such Evaluation Material.

4.   In the event that any Sotheby's Representatives are legally requested or compelled to disclose any of the Evaluation Material, Sotheby's will provide prompt written notice to the Client (provided that Sotheby's is not otherwise precluded by law from doing so) so that the Client may seek a protective order or other appropriate remedy at Client's expense and/or waive compliance with the provisions of this Agreement.

This Agreement shall be governed by and construed and enforced in accordance with the laws of the State of New York. In the event of a dispute hereunder, the Client agrees to submit to the jurisdiction of the state courts of and the federal courts sitting in the State of New York.

If the Client is in agreement with the foregoing, please countersign this letter in the space provided below and return to us an original, executed copy of this letter.

Very truly yours,

SOTHEBY'S, INC.

By: _____

Warren P. Weitman, Jr.
Executive Vice President

Received and agreed to this 12th
day of September, 1996.

_____

G:\WINWORD\AGTS.CONFIDEN-FULTON.DOC

TOTAL PAGE.002

U.S. DEPARTMENT OF JUSTICE FULTON CASE FILE: Letter from Sotheby's to Christopher Fulton.

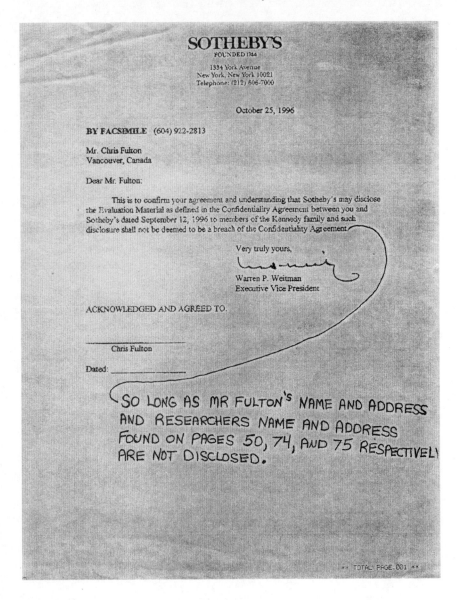

SOTHEBY'S
FOUNDED 1744

1334 York Avenue
New York, New York 10021
Telephone: (212) 606-7000

October 25, 1996

BY FACSIMILE (604) 922-2813

Mr. Chris Fulton
Vancouver, Canada

Dear Mr. Fulton:

This is to confirm your agreement and understanding that Sotheby's may disclose the Evaluation Material as defined in the Confidentiality Agreement between you and Sotheby's dated September 12, 1996 to members of the Kennedy family and such disclosure shall not be deemed to be a breach of the Confidentiality Agreement.

Very truly yours,

Warren P. Weitman
Executive Vice President

ACKNOWLEDGED AND AGREED TO.

_____
Chris Fulton

Dated: _____

SO LONG AS MR FULTON'S NAME AND ADDRESS
AND RESEARCHERS NAME AND ADDRESS
FOUND ON PAGES 50, 74, AND 75 RESPECTIVELY
ARE NOT DISCLOSED.

** TOTAL PAGE.001 **

U.S. DEPARTMENT OF JUSTICE FULTON CASE FILE: Fax from Sotheby's to Christopher Fulton.

SOTHEBY'S
FOUNDED 1744

1334 York Avenue
New York, New York 10021
Telephone: (212) 606-7000

October 30, 1996

BY FACSIMILE (604) 922-2813

Mr. Chris Fulton
Vancouver, Canada

Dear Mr. Fulton:

This is to confirm your agreement and understanding that Sotheby's may disclose the Evaluation Material as defined in the Confidentiality Agreement between you and Sotheby's dated September 12, 1996 to members of the Kennedy family and such disclosure shall not be deemed to be a breach of the Confidentiality Agreement, so long as Mr. Fulton's name and address and researcher's name and address found on pages 50, 74, and 75, respectively, of the Evaluation Material are not disclosed.

Very truly yours,

Warren P. Weitman
Executive Vice President

ACKNOWLEDGED AND AGREED TO:

Chris Fulton

Dated: Nov 6 1996

U.S. DEPARTMENT OF JUSTICE FULTON CASE FILE: Fax from Sotheby's to Christopher Fulton.

EXAMPLE LETTER

Dear _____:

First, let us congratulate you on your marriage and wish you nothing but happiness.

Second, we wish to inform you that we are in contact with a corporation which had acquired 2 personal items belonging to your father through his late secretary Evelyn Lincoln. This corporation has stated that our auction on behalf of your mother was so well done that they have expressed an interest in selling one of their acquired pieces. They wish no publicity on their behalf however, so, we have signed non-disclosure agreements.

The item of discussion is the documented Cartier wristwatch your Father had worn in Dallas November, 22. Because of the highly personal nature of this piece it is the opinion of said corporation and ourselves that you should be contacted before any public sale.

The corporation suggests that if sold by Sotheby's, 15% of the proceeds shall be given to the JFK library and another 10% to a cause of your choice, and if handled in a fitting manner of praise and highest regard, a worthy buyer should come forth. Your concerns, suggestions, and or participation would be encouraged and appreciated. If you are adamantly opposed to a public sale, they ask for a letter stating your feelings as such: "I wish this piece not to be auctioned publicly" and they would honour your wishes. The other piece in their possession, if sold, should pose no consequence for your family.

Thank you and best wishes to you and your wife.

U.S. DEPARTMENT OF JUSTICE FULTON CASE FILE: Sample letter to JFK Jr. through Sotheby's.

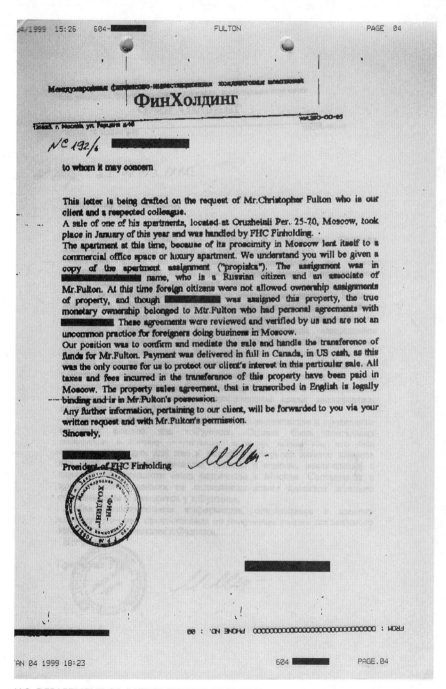

ФинХолдинг

NC 192/6

to whom it may concern

This letter is being drafted on the request of Mr. Christopher Fulton who is our client and a respected colleague.

A sale of one of his apartments, located at Oruzheinii Per. 25-70, Moscow, took place in January of this year and was handled by FHC Finholding.

The apartment at this time, because of its proximity in Moscow lent itself to a commercial office space or luxury apartment. We understand you will be given a copy of the apartment assignment ("propiska"). The assignment was in ■■■■■■ name, who is a Russian citizen and an associate of Mr. Fulton. At this time foreign citizens were not allowed ownership assignments of property, and though ■■■■■■ was assigned this property, the true monetary ownership belonged to Mr. Fulton who had personal agreements with ■■■■■ These agreements were reviewed and verified by us and are not an uncommon practice for foreigners doing business in Moscow.

Our position was to confirm and mediate the sale and handle the transference of funds for Mr. Fulton. Payment was delivered in full in Canada, in US cash, as this was the only course for us to protect our client's interest in this particular sale. All taxes and fees incurred in the transference of this property have been paid in Moscow. The property sales agreement, that is transcribed in English is legally binding and is in Mr. Fulton's possession.

Any further information, pertaining to our client, will be forwarded to you via your written request and with Mr. Fulton's permission.

Sincerely,

■■■■■
President of FHC Finholding

U.S. DEPARTMENT OF JUSTICE FULTON CASE FILE: Letter concerning Christopher Fulton's time in Moscow, Russia.

To: jeremy
cc: brian
From: Dave Montague/ARRB
Date: 01/27/97 04:35:54 PM
Subject: Initial conversation w/ Robert White's attorney

CALL REPORT Issue # 78

Document's Author: Dave Montague/ARRB   **Date Created:** 01.27.1997

Who initiated the call?   ○ We initiated call
                ● Individual initiated call

Evelyn Lincoln Project

Subject: **Initial conversation w/ Robert White's attorney**
Description of the Call

    I was called today by a "David Glassman" who said he is an attorney &
represents White. Glassman said White asked him to call the Review Board & find
out the "specifics" of what we're looking for. He doesn't want the Review Board to
waste time visiting White if he doesn't have records re: the Lincoln Estate. Glassman
also asked what the "Review Board" stands for. I gave him a brief explanation of our
purpose & told him I'd give him a call in the morning w/ the specifics he requested. He
said that would be fine.

    I verified his phone number & thanked him for his call.

    *Brian Rosen & I had a brief discussion w/ White last Friday, during which <u>White
said he has no problem dealing w/ the Review Board & would like to talk in person
as opposed to over the phone.</u>

    David Glassman, Esq.
    215.563.7100

    Philidelphia Bar Association
    215.560.6296
    *I tried to verify his identity, but I need to call back due to volume of callers

she wrote something

ASSASSINATIONS RECORDS REVIEW BOARD: Evelyn Lincoln Project. Internal memo regarding access to Robert White.

To:	jeremy, brian
cc:	douglas
From:	Dave Montague/ARRB
Date:	01/29/97 04:23:53 PM
Subject:	CORRECTED: In-depth conversation w/ David Glassman re: access to Robert White

CALL REPORT Issue # 78

Document's Author: Dave Montague & Brian Rosen of ARRB   Date Created: 01.29.1997

Who initiated the call?   ○ We initiated call
                            ● Individual initiated call

Evelyn Lincoln Project

Subject: In-depth conversation w/ David Glassman re: access to Robert White
Description of the Call

Glassman returned our call today. We explained the nature of the Review Board & our desire to discuss the Lincoln Estate & possible assassination related records which White may have or know of.

Glassman was not cooperative w/ our suggestion to clarify the distribution process re: assassination related records. We offered to send Glassman some explanatory material & copy of our legislation so he could become familiar w/ our purpose & authority; Glassman said sending such material to him is irrelevant because his client is not in possession of **any** assassination related material.

We specifically asked if Glassman was representing to us that his client did/does not have any specific types of records such as:

-Evelyn Lincoln's diaries
-appointment books
-personal papers re: the assassination
-photographs of the assassination &/or autopsy
-correspondence re: the assassination

We explained that we interpret assassination related records to include these types of items. Glassman said: "...I'm representing to you that my client does not have any assassination related records...as you describe them". He later said he does not feel comfortable in anyway about our approaching his client & that he didn't like the idea of his client being "...singled out ahead of the other beneficiaries..." We explained that the Review Board makes determinations as to what items are assassination related & Glassman insisted we accept his representation that White is not in possession of any such records. We discussed possible avenues for gaining White's cooperation & Glassman mentioned the word "subpoena" (for which we made clear was

ASSASSINATIONS RECORDS REVIEW BOARD: Evelyn Lincoln Project. Internal memo regarding access to Robert White.

not the purpose of our discussion). We explained that we were merely speaking w/ various beneficiaries & thought White might be able to explain the distribution of certain JFK related items & that he appeared to be one of the principle beneficiaries of the will. We also explained we know White completed an appraisal of items & that we specifically would like to know more about "file 5" as listed on White's inventory. Glassman reiterated that his client never had & does not now have anything related to what we're looking for & that if we started asking White questions, it may "open the door" to other parties seeking access to his collection.

We mentioned to Glassman that as recently as last Friday, White encouraged our visiting his home to discuss our request once he realized our purpose. Glassman agreed to speak w/ White re: our request, but said he doesn't think it will make a difference. We told Glassman we'd send him some explanatory material anyway, look forward to hearing the response from White & thanked him for his time.

David J. Glassman, Esq.
Executive Office Building, Suite 700
1125 Atlantic Avenue
Atlantic City, NJ 08401
609.822.6464
215.563.7100 (to his Philadelphia office)

To: jeremy
cc: brian
From: Dave Montague/ARRB
Date: 01/29/97 01:49:31 PM
Subject: 2nd attempt to reach Robert White's attorney

CALL REPORT Issue # 78
Document's Author: Dave Montague/ARRB   **Date Created:** 01.29.1997

Who initiated the call?   ● We initiated call
                           ○ Individual initiated call

Evelyn Lincoln Project
Subject: 2nd attempt to reach Robert White's attorney
Description of the Call
Brian Rosen & I called his office again & left word for him to call. Glassman previously asked for detail re: the Review Board's interest in White and the Lincoln Estate. Prior to that, we had a conversation w/ White who said he has no problem dealing w/ the Review Board & would like to talk in person as opposed to over the phone.

David Glassman, Esq.
215.563.7100

ASSASSINATIONS RECORDS REVIEW BOARD: Evelyn Lincoln Project. Internal memo regarding access to Robert White.

AKKB   (617) 223-9289   P.02
@001

FILE COPY

Assassination Records Review Board
600 E Street NW · 2nd Floor · Washington, DC 20530
(202) 724-0088 · Fax: (202) 724-0457

February 3, 1997

David J. Glassman, Esq.
Executive Office Building
Suite 700
1125 Atlantic Avenue
Atlantic City, N.J. 08401

Dear Mr. Glassman:

Enclosed is a copy of a letter sent by the Assassination Records Review Board to Robert White and the other beneficiaries of the estate of Harold and Evelyn Lincoln. As Brian Rosen and David Montague of our staff discussed with you in a January 29, 1997 telephone conversation, the Review Board is attempting to contact Lincoln estate beneficiaries because we have reason to believe that the estate may have contained some records that would be useful for understanding issues related to the assassination of President Kennedy that were disbursed by the terms of the Lincolns' wills. We are particularly interested in meeting with Mr. White because he performed an inventory of the estate and, even if not in possession of assassination-related material himself, is in the best position to provide an overview of the contents of the estate and direct us to potential assassination records in the possession of other parties.

A member of our staff will telephone you again in the near future in order to attempt to arrange a meeting with Mr. White to discuss these issues. Please feel free to call me if you have any questions. We look forward to your cooperation.

Sincerely,

T. Jeremy Gunn
General Counsel

Enclosures

ASSASSINATIONS RECORDS REVIEW BOARD: Evelyn Lincoln Project. Letter to Robert White's attorney.

FYI

Assassination Records Review Board
600 E Street NW • 2nd Floor • Washington, DC 20530
(202) 724–0088 • Fax: (202) 724–0457

February 5, 1997

Mr. Robert L. White
302 Bloomsbury Ave.
Baltimore, Maryland 21228

Dear Mr. White:

I am writing to you on behalf of the Assassination Records Review Board, an independent Federal agency established pursuant to the John F. Kennedy Assassination Records Collection Act, 44 U.S.C. § 2107 (Supp. V 1994). The Review Board, whose members are appointed by the President and confirmed by the Senate, is responsible for collecting records and information related to the assassination of President Kennedy. The Review Board is not seeking to reach conclusions regarding the assassination but primarily is concerned with locating, identifying, clarifying and making available to the public assassination records. I am enclosing some explanatory materials about the Review Board and its mandate.

As part of our efforts to locate assassination records, we are contacting all of the benficiaries of the estate of Harold and Evelyn Lincoln. A version of this letter is being sent to each person listed on the attachment. Our review of the Lincolns' wills and the inventory of the Lincolns' estate indicates that some of the items left by the Lincolns may be assassination records. In order to make this determination, we are seeking to locate and review any diaries, notes, papers, correspondence, appointment books or other materials bequeathed by the Lincolns that may directly relate to or provide historical context to the assassination of President Kennedy. We have already contacted the John F. Kennedy Library and obtained their cooperation with our efforts.

A member of our staff will be telephoning you in the near future to discuss potential assassination records among the items left to you by the Lincolns. If you have any questions, please feel free to contact Brian Rosen, an attorney on our staff, at the number listed above. We look forward to talking with you soon.

Sincerely,

David G. Marwell
Executive Director

Enclosures

cc: David J. Glassman, Esq.

ASSASSINATIONS RECORDS REVIEW BOARD: Evelyn Lincoln Project. Letter to Robert White.

k
ARRO
(617) 223-9289
P.03
003

DAVID JAY GLASSMAN
ATTORNEY AT LAW

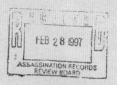

FILE COPY

LAW LEISE OFFICES
1528 ATLANTIC AVENUE
SUITE 700
ATLANTIC CITY, NEW JERSEY 08401
(000) 822-6464
FAX (000) 345-8080

MEMBER OF N.J. & PA. BAR

FEB 28 1997

ASSASSINATION RECORDS
REVIEW BOARD

February 24, 1997

T. Jeremy Gunn, Esquire
Assassination Records Review Board
600 E. Street NW
2nd Floor
Washington, DC 20530

        Re: Robert White

Dear Mr. Gunn:

        Please be advised I am in receipt of your correspondence
dated February 3, 1997 and have reviewed its contents with Robert
White.

        Presently, I can confirm that Mr. White did not receive
nor is he in possession of any assassination related artifacts
and/or memorabilia originating from the Lincoln Will or from
any other source.

        In regard to the fact that Robert White performed an
"inventory" of the Lincoln Estate, as you are no doubt aware,
the inventory which Mr. White performed was the subject of recent
litigation, in which it was alleged that the "inventory" of
which you refer was inadequate, incomplete, unprofessional and
cursory at best.

        I have discussed your inquiry with Robert White and can
confirm that to the best of his knowledge, information and belief
he is not aware of the existence of any assassination related
item or items that were inventoried by him or part of a
distribution to any beneficiary of which he is aware of.

ASSASSINATIONS RECORDS REVIEW BOARD: Evelyn Lincoln Project. Letter from Robert White's attorney.

413

David Jay Glassman, Esquire
January 24, 1997
Page 2

I regret that we cannot be of any further assistance to the Committee in this regard, however as I previously advised you, the focus of Mr. White's Collection is not in anyway, shape, or form geared to the assassination of President Kennedy; rather it is a celebration of his life and times.

I trust that this correspondence sufficiently addresses any outstanding questions you may have.

Thank you for your attention.

Very truly yours,

David Jay Glassman, Esquire
Counsel for Robert White

DJG/gh
Certified Mail R.R.R.

ASSASSINATIONS RECORDS REVIEW BOARD: Evelyn Lincoln Project. Letter from Robert White's attorney.

ₗk
ARKB   (617) 223-9289   P.05
                                       ₆₀₀₅

Assassination Records Review Board
600 E Street NW · 2nd Floor · Washington, DC 20530
(202) 724-0088 · Fax: (202) 724-0457

February 28, 1997   **FILE COPY**

BY TELECOPIER

David Jay Glassman, Esq.
1125 Atlantic Avenue
Suite 700
Atlantic City, New Jersey 08401

Re: Evelyn Lincoln Papers and Mr. Robert White

Dear Mr. Glassman:

Thank you very much for your February 24, 1997 response to my letter of February 3.

Although we had not thought that your client, Mr. Robert White, had possession of "any assassination related artifacts and/or memorabilia originating from the Lincoln Will or from any other source," we appreciate your confirmation of that fact for us. We also appreciate your having discussed with Mr. White the nature of Mrs. Lincoln's records and your informing us that he was unaware of any assassination-related material in the Lincoln Papers. Although we have no reason to doubt his or your sincerity in this matter, it is of course entirely possible that information that may look unremarkable to him might be of significant importance to us in our work.

Let me offer one example. It is our understanding that the U.S. Federal government provided Mrs. Lincoln with an office in the National Archives after the assassination. During that time, she had custody of materials that had been prepared at the autopsy of President Kennedy. These materials were subsequently donated to the U.S. government by the Kennedy family. At the time the autopsy materials were inventoried, however, it was determined that some of the materials were missing. I am sure that you can understand that the U.S. Government has an interest in pursuing all leads relative to materials that had been in the custody of Mrs. Lincoln and that subsequently were found to be missing. For this reason, cryptic notes that might appear innocuous to one reader might be highly relevant to us. As a lawyer, I am sure that you understand that there may be a substantial difference between what a lawyer might (honestly) say about what he believes his client knows, and what his client might be able to describe to others.

ASSASSINATIONS RECORDS REVIEW BOARD: Evelyn Lincoln Project. Letter to Robert White's attorney.

(617) 223-9289   P.06

David Jay Glassman, Esq.
February 28, 1997
Page 2

Although we certainly would assume that the vast majority of Mr. White's collection of Kennedy memorabilia constitutes a "celebration of his life and times," we continue to be interested in receiving a conscientious understanding of the records that Mrs. Lincoln left. Thus, we still wish to have an informal discussion with Mr. White at a time and place that would be convenient for him. Most people whom we have contacted in the course of our work have been agreeable to such discussions. Others, because of the nature of their testimony, have requested that we issue subpoenas. (We also have employed our statutory authority to provide witness immunity.) Although we prefer not to issue subpoenas unless necessary, we would be perfectly willing to do so if you believe that to be the most effective and advisable manner for us to proceed.

Again, we would simply prefer to have an informal discussion with Mr. White, but we are willing to proceed differently if you so advise.

I appreciate your timely response to my first letter and I trust that you will again respond promptly. Please do not hesitate to contact me if I can answer any of your questions.

Sincerely,

T. Jeremy Gunn
General Counsel

U.S. DEPARTMENT OF JUSTICE FULTON CASE FILE: Photos of Robert White, with Evelyn Lincoln and Dave Powers respectively, from Guernsey's JFK auction catalog.

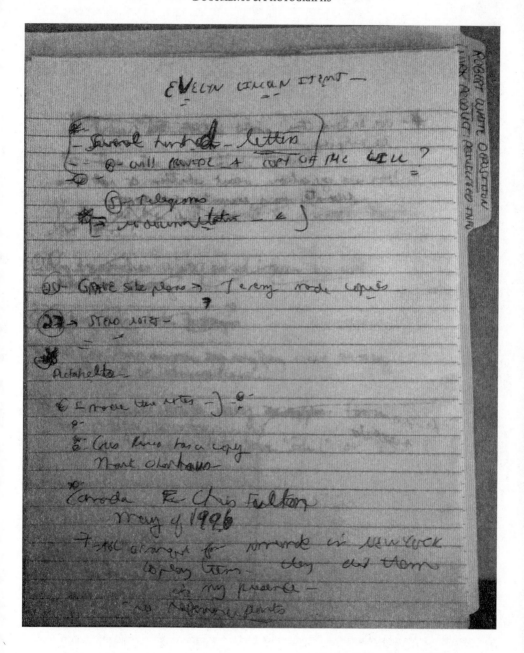

ASSASSINATIONS RECORDS REVIEW BOARD: Evelyn Lincoln Project. Notes on Robert White's deposition made by a federal official, who was reporting to President Clinton.

"*Dictabelts—

[...]

*Canada Chris Fulton May of 1996."

The date and location were misstated. The recordings were transferred to Christopher Fulton in May of 1997, in Baltimore, Maryland.

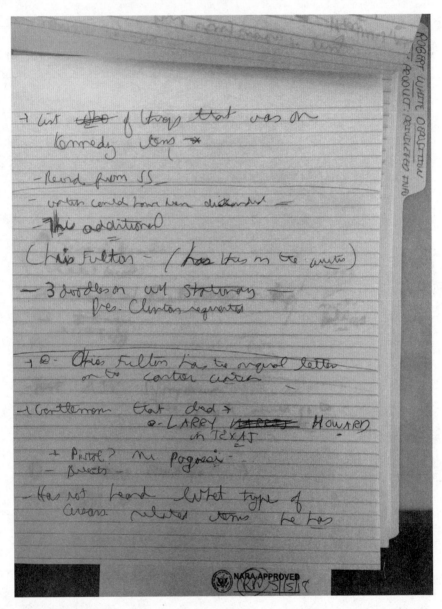

ASSASSINATIONS RECORDS REVIEW BOARD: Evelyn Lincoln Project. Notes on Robert White's deposition made by a federal official, who was reporting to President Clinton.
"Record from SS [Secret Service]—
—watch could have been discarded—
[. . .]
—Chris Fulton—(has item [. . .])
[. . .]
Pres. Clinton requested
Chris Fulton has the original letter on the cartier watch"

2   1k   (617) 223-9289   P.07

MEETING REPORT

Document's Author: Brian Rosen/ARRB   **Date Created:** 04/10/97

Meeting Logistics

Date:	04/10/97
Agecny Name:	General Public
Attendees:	Brian Rosen, Dave Montague, Robert White and David Glassman
Topic:	Evelyn Lincoln Estate

Summary of the Meeting

We met with Robert White and his attorney, David Glassman, in order to discuss his involvement with the estate of Evelyn Lincoln. Mr. White informed us that he first contacted Mrs. Lincoln in the early sixties by letter and received a polite reply and an autograph. He next wrote to her in the early seventies and again received a polite response, along with a PT 109 tie clip. Their relationship evolved from there to occasional correspondence and lunches. Throughout this time, Mrs. Lincoln occasionally began to give Mr. White items of Kennedy memorabilia for his collection and to authenticate items he wished to add to his collection from other sources. He assisted her by acting as a buffer between her and other collectors and researchers that approached her regarding Kennedy. By the eighties, the two had become family friends and remained so until her death. Despite their close friendship, Mr. White stated that Mrs. Lincoln rarely spoke about the assassination. According to White, she was psychologically and emotionally damaged by the assassination and it remained a very traumatic and troubling topic for her. White acknowledged that she had some "strange" ideas about Lyndon Johnson, but stated that she never spoke of or showed him any documents or evidence to support her ideas.

Prior to Mrs. Lincoln's death, White stated that he never knew of or viewed the trunks and file cabinets dispensed by the Lincolns' wills. After Mrs. Lincoln's death, Mr. Lincoln showed White where the file cabinets were located in the Lincolns' apartment, but they were unable to open any of the combination locks that sealed the cabinets. Mr. Lincoln died about forty days later. Approximately two weeks after the funeral, Mr. White viewed the contents of all the trunks and file cabinets with Stephen Blakeslee, executor of the will, and Frank McGuire, a beneficiary of the will, for the purpose of creating an inventory and appraisal of the estate at Blakeslee's request. Mr. White described his review of the contents of the trunks and cabinets as a "cursory inspection." He stated that he opened all the trunks and cabinets but only "eyeballed" individual items, most of which were in piles or files that he did not sort through (White stated that he thought Blakeslee felt this general inspection was sufficient because the trunks and cabinets were pre-labled and he wanted to save money for the estate).

This inventory process went from only 10:00 - 11:30 and then 1:00 - 2:30 on a single day. White stated that Blakeslee and McGuire were with him the entire time, and that this occasion was the only time in which he viewed the contents of all the trunks and cabinets cited in the will. White then stated that soon after the inspection he forwarded his notes and blank business stationary to Blakeslee, who created the final letter, inventory and appraisal that is included in the estate's formal papers (White merely signed the papers at Blakeslee's request). He stated that he does not know what happened to his original notes from the inventory after he passed them on to Blakeslee, and that he did not keep any copies. White could only speculate as to how the file cabinet and trunk numbers in the inventory correspond to the numbers in the will because he claimed that Blakeslee, for reasons unknown to White, rewrote the numbers and descriptions from White's notes when he created the formal papers.

White provided us with a list and descriptions of the items he received from the Lincoln estate, all of which are "memorabilia" unrelated to the assassination. He reiterated that he did not receive any items from the Lincolns that are related to the assassination. He also stated that his inventory did not reveal

ASSASSINATIONS RECORDS REVIEW BOARD: Evelyn Lincoln Project. Report on the meeting with Robert White.

ık   (617) 223-9289   P.08

any items related to the assassination, other than the diaries or appointment books that went to the JFK Library. He described the diaries as day journals with red covers packed together in a single average sized box. He claimed that he did not read the diaries and could only guess at their contents. Despite stories by Mr. Lincoln of diaries being burned, he always believed they existed because Mrs. Lincoln usually referred back to some source material in order to answer his questions and was often able to answer with great recall. Other than Mr. Lincoln's stories, White had no evidence that any diaries had been destroyed. He also speculated that Evelyn Lincoln was the type of person who would have made sure anything of historical significance would have gone to the JFK Library.

White did express concern that some items from the estate that he should have received because they related to Kennedy may have been removed by Maria Ray, the residuary beneficiary of the will. Apparently, Ray and her husband stayed for a short time in the Lincolns' apartment after the cabinets and trunks were opened for the inventory. White was unsure what the Rays had access to but claimed they filled several boxes with items from the estate before returning to Florida. However, he stated that it is unlikely that they took any "assassination records" because they probably only were interested in things they could identify as having monetary value and were not educated enough to identify a vauable document or record.

ASSASSINATIONS RECORDS REVIEW BOARD: Evelyn Lincoln Project. Report on the meeting with Robert White.

My Copy

CONTRACT

This contract made May 1,1997 is between Robert White, Chris Fulton ▮▮▮ ▮▮▮▮▮ It is made with the terms and conditions set out below.

A) All parties agree to work towards publication of a picture book on JFK

B) Robert White will provide access to his collection and all necessary information on the Kennedy's

C) Chris Fulton will provide access to his Kennedy items. He will also provide funding until the completion of a contract with a publisher and arrange for complete funding for a published book.

D) ▮▮▮▮▮▮▮▮▮▮▮▮▮▮▮▮▮▮▮▮▮ provide all necessary photographic and computer expertise.

E) All net profits from this project will be shared ▮▮▮▮ to each party named above.

F) Chris Fulton and Robert White reserve the right to determine which photos will be used in the book.

G) Chris Fulton is authorized to negotiate and sign a publishing contract for all parties.

H) Credit for this book will be given to all ▮▮▮ parties.

I) No other book project based on JFK will be started by any of the parties involved until this project is completed. All parties agree to a sequel book together if this book is published.

Agreed to by: *[signature]*

Robert White
Baltimore MD

[signature]
Chris Fulton
West Vancouver B.C.

▮▮▮▮▮▮▮▮▮▮▮▮▮▮▮▮▮▮▮

U.S. DEPARTMENT OF JUSTICE FULTON CASE FILE: Contract between Robert White and Christopher Fulton.

August 21, 1997

Mr. Chris Fulton (CEO International Investments)
The Twelve Global Ltd
1395 Marine Drive
Suite 27006
West Vancouver, BC
V7T 1B6 CANADA

Dear Chris:

This letter will serve as an agreement between us concerning your engagement of Richard Curtis Associates, Inc. as your exclusive literary agents in the negotiation of publishing contracts for PICTURE BOOK OF KENNEDY MEMORABILIA, hereinafter referred to as "The Work," in the trade book market. In the event we are unable to license The Work to a United States book publisher within six months of this date, this contract shal terminate and we shall have no further obligations to each other.

You shall have sole and final approval of all contracts we negotiate on your behalf.

You also engage us as your exclusive agents for four months from this date in the exploitation of any rights to The Work which we may reserve for you in the name The Twelve Global Ltd. for which Chris Fulton is the signing authority, included but not limited to first serial rights, British and foreign language publication rights, motion picture and television dramatizations and audiocassette, videocassette, multimedia and other electronic adaptations.

We shall collect all moneys due under the terms of agreements we negotiate for you, and shall remit all net moneys to you within ten days of our receipt of same.

Our commissions are as follows:

On all revenue derived from the licensing of book or magazine publication in the United States and Canada, fifteen percent (15%).

On all revenue derived from the licensing of British or foreign translation publication rights, twenty percent (20%).

On all revenue derived from the licensing of motion picture, television, audiocassette, videocassette, multimedia and other electronic adaptations, fifteen percent (15%).

The commisions of sub-agents we may use to license any of the above rights shall be paid out of our commisions.

We shall also be entitled to deduct from moneys we disburse to you certain out-of-pocket expenses beyond the normal cost of doing business, such a s photocopy of manuscripts, express mail, messenger deliveries and pickups, and purchases of copies of The Work for submission to other markets. We must request your

CHRISTOPHER FULTON'S PERSONAL RECORD: Introduction letter from literary agent, Richard Curtis.

express permission before incurring any such expense of more than $50.00, and shall furnish you with detailed statements of deducted expenses whenever we remit moneys to you.

If we successfully place The Work with a publisher, with a contract between the parties, this agreement shall be extended to your next related book length work written for trade publication.

If the above is acceptable to you, please sign below and return one copy of this agreement to me.

Sincerely,

RICHARD CURTIS

AGREED: _____

DATE: AUG 21 1997

AGREED: _____

DATE: September 2, 1997

SOCIAL SECURITY NUMBER: ███████████

AGREED: _____ DATE 9/2/97

RICHARD CURTIS ASSOCIATES INC.

CHRISTOPHER FULTON'S PERSONAL RECORD: Introduction letter from literary agent, Richard Curtis.

Richard Curtis Associates, Inc.

AUTHORS' REPRESENTATIVES

RICHARD CURTIS
PRESIDENT

September 5, 1997

Dear Chris:

As per our conversations, I'm enclosing the signed agency agreement.

I now look forward to receiving that introduction along with more detailed essays or captions about the provenance of the sample items in the photographs. These will, I'm sure, make for an irresistible and commercial book. Remember, the more anecdotal the better.

Also, when you have a chance, I'll need addresses and, for an American citizen among you, Social Security numbers.

All best wishes.

Sincerely,

RICHARD CURTIS

Members, Association of Authors' Representatives
171 EAST 74TH STREET / NEW YORK, NEW YORK 10021
TELEPHONE 212/772-7363 FAX 212/772-7393
http://www.curtisagency.com

CHRISTOPHER FULTON'S PERSONAL RECORD: Letter from Richard Curtis.

1 of 4

October 12, 1997

Richard Curtis Associates, Inc.

Dear Richard :

This letter will serve as an agreement between us concerning the engagement of Richard Curtis Associates, Inc. Hereinafter referred to as "the Agent" as our exclusive literary agents in the negotiation of publishing contracts for PICTURE BOOK OF KENNEDY MEMORABILIA, hereinafter referred to as "The Work," in the trade book market. In the event the agent is unable to license The Work to a United States book publisher within six months of this date, this contract shall terminate and we shall have no further obligations to each other.

It is understood that the Agent is an independent contractor, this is not an employment contract nor is it a partnership agreement with the agent.

The agent agrees to reveal if he has any conflicts of interest with any similar work before the contract is signed.

The contract shall be between Richard Curtis Associates, Inc. and
Mr. Robert White (Represented by Mr. Fulton)
304 Bloomsbury Ave.
Baltimore Md.
21228

Mr. Chris Fulton (CEO International Investments)
The Twelve Global Ltd.
1395 Marine Drive
Suite 27006
West Vancouver, BC
V7T 1B6 CANADA

Hereinafter referred to as "The Partners"

CHRISTOPHER FULTON'S PERSONAL RECORD: Contract with Richard Curtis.

████████████████████████████ Chris Fulton will receive credit for writing. All partners shall receive appropriate credits for their work involved. The partners will share copyright for the finished work equally, ████████████████
████

This contract shall take precedent over any previous contracts with the agent. Specifically the contract dated August 21, 1997 between Richard Curtis Associates, Inc. and Mr. Chris Fulton (CEO International Investments) The Twelve Global Ltd. This contract dated August 21,1997 shall be considered null and void and of no effect upon the signing of this new contract dated September 22, 1997 this is agreed to here by

_____   _____
        Richard Curtis   Chris Fulton

The Partners also engage you as our exclusive agents for six months from this date, in the exploitation of any rights to The Work which you may reserve for us in the name of the Partners, included but not limited to first serial rights, British and foreign language publication rights, motion picture and television dramatizations and audiocassette, videocassette, multimedia and other electronic adaptations.

Chris Fulton ████████████████, shall have sole and final approval of all contracts that are negotiated on our behalf. Chris Fulton will negotiate with the publishers on behalf of all of the partners equally, on any contract supplied by the agent.

The agent shall collect all moneys due the Partners minus his commissions which shall be.

On all revenue derived from the licensing of book or magazine publication in the United States and Canada, fifteen percent (15%).

On all revenue derived from the licensing of British or foreign translation publication rights, twenty percent (20%).

On all revenue derived from the licensing of motion picture, television, audiocassette, videocassette, multimedia and other electronic adaptations, fifteen percent (15%).

CHRISTOPHER FULTON'S PERSONAL RECORD: Contract with Richard Curtis.

(10) TEN BUSINESS DAYS

The agent shall remit all moneys due the partners within ~~seven days~~ of his receipt of same. The agent shall disperse monies in a confidential manner. These funds shall be kept in a separate Escrow account and not included with the agents general funds and shall be treated as trust funds on behalf of each individual partners. ~~The agent shall pay a 1/2 percent interest (.5%), per day, on any funds that are not paid out on time.~~ The Agent shall pay the funds out in equal ▮▮▮▮▮▮ each of the above mentioned partners: ▮▮ to Robert White, ▮▮ to Chris Fulton and or twelve global ltd., ▮▮▮▮▮▮▮▮▮▮ The agent shall pay these funds directly to each party by the agent. The partners will individually have the right to privately direct where the agent should pay their ▮▮▮▮▮▮▮▮ The agents commissions shall be paid only on monies collected by the agent from the publisher and not on monies owing..

The commissions of sub-agents that the agent may use to license any of the above rights shall be paid out of the agent's commissions.

The agent shall not receive any commission on any subsequent sale of any item that appears in the book whether or not the publisher has referred the buyer, nor will he receive any commission on revenue derived from any item that appears in this book unless the agent has arranged for it.

The agent shall also be entitled to deduct from moneys to be disburse to us certain out-of-pocket expenses beyond the normal cost of doing business, such as photocopy of manuscripts, express mail, messenger deliveries and pickups, and purchases of copies of The Work for submission to other markets. The agent must request Chris Fultons express permission before incurring any such expense of more than $50.00, and shall furnish the partners with detailed statements of deducted expenses whenever he remits moneys to the partners. The agent will provide a full accounting every three months if requested by any partner.

If the agent successfully places The Work with a publisher, with a contract between the parties, this agreement shall be extended to our next related book length work written for trade publication.

The agent can not assign this contract to any other parties.

This contract shall terminate if the agent goes into bankruptcy or becomes insolvent.

CHRISTOPHER FULTON'S PERSONAL RECORD: Contract with Richard Curtis.

10/12/97 SUN 17:36 FAX 804 303 0115   KINKO'S RICHMOND B.C.   @001

4 of 4

If this contract is terminated and monies are still due the partners, then the partners shall individually and privately have the right to direct payment of their share of the outstanding moneys due. The agent shall disperse monies in a confidential manner.

All parties agree to indemnify the publisher if requested. ████████████ when requested.
Chris Fulton will give a release for any of his writing to the publisher when requested.

Sincerely,

Chris Fulton on behalf of the partners

AGREED: _____ DATE: 10/12/97
RICHARD CURTIS

AGREED: _____ DATE: 10/12/97
CHRIS FULTON (representing ROBERT WHITE)

AGREED: _____ DATE: 10/12/97
CHRIS FULTON

████████████████████

CHRISTOPHER FULTON'S PERSONAL RECORD: Contract with Richard Curtis.

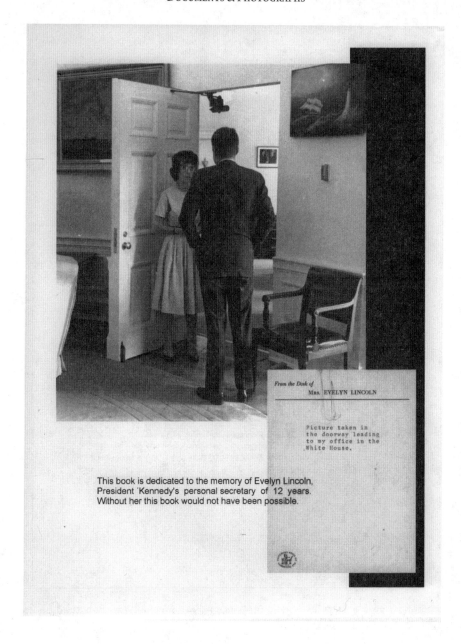

From the Desk of
MRS. EVELYN LINCOLN

Picture taken in
the doorway leading
to my office in the
White House.

This book is dedicated to the memory of Evelyn Lincoln,
President Kennedy's personal secretary of 12 years.
Without her this book would not have been possible.

CHRISTOPHER FULTON'S PERSONAL RECORD: Pages from the never-published photo book, *The Evelyn Lincoln Collection.*

Although all of the items in this book are special, it was the anniversary gifts from Jackie that were most treasured by Jack. Jackie chose this elegant gold Cartier watch for their fourth wedding anniversary and inscribed it "JFK 9, 12, 57".

CHRISTOPHER FULTON'S PERSONAL RECORD: Page from the never-published photo book, *The Evelyn Lincoln Collection*.

Waiting for the final returns election night!

CHRISTOPHER FULTON'S PERSONAL RECORD: Page from the never-published photo book, *The Evelyn Lincoln Collection.*

For their first anniversary, Jackie presented JFK this gold St. Christopher money clip, inscribed "For Jack Sept. 12, 1954". Although the clip was not used for bills, it was always with Jack in his wallet, to the extent that the reverse image of the St. Christopher design was imprinted in the leather.

CHRISTOPHER FULTON'S PERSONAL RECORD: Page from the never-published photo book, *The Evelyn Lincoln Collection*.

Shown is the gold St. Christopher money clip that President Kennedy always kept in his wallet, over his heart. It was held back on November 22, 1963, by Lyndon Johnson's Secret Service agent. It was not worn by President Kennedy when he was killed. Although Jackie Kennedy desperately wanted it placed in her husband's coffin, at Robert Kennedy's request it was kept by Evelyn Lincoln. After Robert Kennedy's assassination in 1968, it remained in her possession. Before her death, she gifted it to Robert White. Prior to the Guernsey's JFK auction, Robert White signed an agreement with the Justice Department and was forced to relinquish the money clip, along with the president's wallets, to the government.

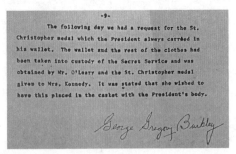

-9-

The following day we had a request for the St. Christopher medal which the President always carried in his wallet. The wallet and the rest of the clothes had been taken into custody of the Secret Service and was obtained by Mr. O'Leary and the St. Christopher medal given to Mrs. Kennedy. It was stated that she wished to have this placed in the casket with the President's body.

George Gregory Burkley

NATIONAL ARCHIVES: Admiral George Burkley's statement regarding President Kennedy's St. Christopher money clip.

432

JFK's personal physician, Janet Travell, recommended that the president sit at this antique signing table, which he used adjacent to the oval office desk, to help ease his constant back pain. He also wore a medical corset and a lift in his left shoe as further remedies. Other than the few times in his life where he required crutches, the only public display of pain was the grimace he made taking that awkward straight-down step from the presidential helicopter.

CHRISTOPHER FULTON'S PERSONAL RECORD: Page from the never-published photo book, The Evelyn Lincoln Collection.

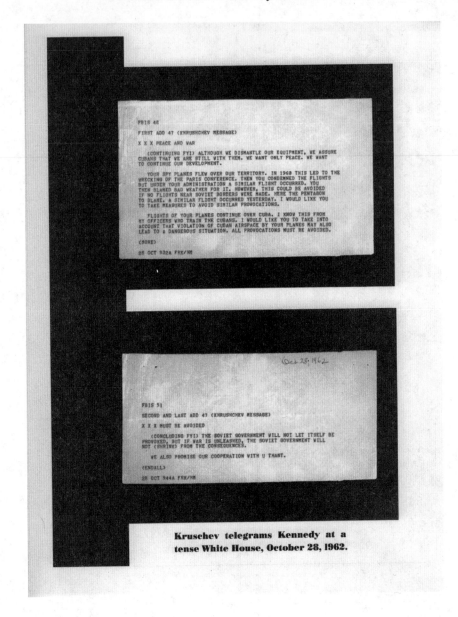

FBIS 46

FIRST ADD 47 (KHRUSHCHEV MESSAGE)

X X X PEACE AND WAR

(CONTINUING FYI) ALTHOUGH WE DISMANTLE OUR EQUIPMENT, WE ASSURE CUBANS THAT WE ARE STILL WITH THEM. WE WANT ONLY PEACE. WE WANT TO CONTINUE OUR DEVELOPMENT.

YOUR SPY PLANES FLEW OVER OUR TERRITORY. IN 1960 THIS LED TO THE WRECKING OF THE PARIS CONFERENCE. THEN YOU CONDEMNED THE FLIGHTS BUT UNDER YOUR ADMINISTRATION A SIMILAR FLIGHT OCCURRED. YOU THEN BLAMED BAD WEATHER FOR IT. HOWEVER, THIS COULD BE AVOIDED IF NO FLIGHTS NEAR SOVIET BORDERS WERE MADE. HERE THE PENTAGON TO BLAME. A SIMILAR FLIGHT OCCURRED YESTERDAY. I WOULD LIKE YOU TO TAKE MEASURES TO AVOID SIMILAR PROVOCATIONS.

FLIGHTS OF YOUR PLANES CONTINUE OVER CUBA. I KNOW THIS FROM MY OFFICERS WHO TRAIN THE CUBANS. I WOULD LIKE YOU TO TAKE INTO ACCOUNT THAT VIOLATION OF CUBAN AIRSPACE BY YOUR PLANES MAY ALSO LEAD TO A DANGEROUS SITUATION. ALL PROVOCATIONS MUST BE AVOIDED.

(MORE)

28 OCT 932A FRK/HH

Oct 28, 1962

FBIS 51

SECOND AND LAST ADD 47 (KHRUSHCHEV MESSAGE)

X X X MUST BE AVOIDED

(CONCLUDING FYI) THE SOVIET GOVERNMENT WILL NOT LET ITSELF BE PROVOKED, BUT IF WAR IS UNLEASHED, THE SOVIET GOVERNMENT WILL NOT (SHRINK) FROM THE CONSEQUENCES.

WE ALSO PROMISE OUR COOPERATION WITH U THANT.

(ENDALL)

28 OCT 944A FRK/HH

Krushev telegrams Kennedy at a tense White House, October 28, 1962.

CHRISTOPHER FULTON'S PERSONAL RECORD: Page from the never-published photo book, *The Evelyn Lincoln Collection.*

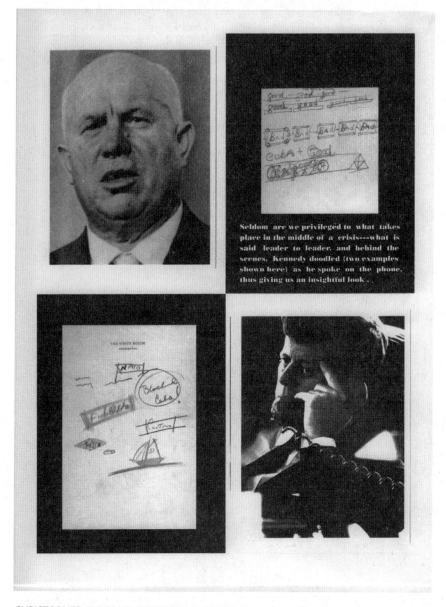

CHRISTOPHER FULTON'S PERSONAL RECORD: Page from the never-published photo book, *The Evelyn Lincoln Collection*.

CHRISTOPHER FULTON'S PERSONAL RECORD: Page from the never-published photo book, *The Evelyn Lincoln Collection*. A coded message that President Kennedy was going to add to his speech when he delivered it at the Trade Mart in Dallas, Texas.

From page 77: Robert handed me a piece of paper with the header Air Force One. In Kennedy's untidy hand it read: "Government reform, we are going forward." Evelyn's letter said it was the last thing the president had written: an addition to the speech he was going to give at the trade mart."

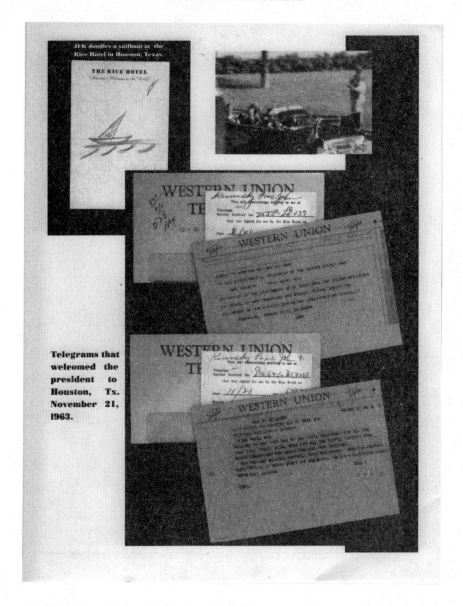

CHRISTOPHER FULTON'S PERSONAL RECORD: Page from the never-published photo book, *The Evelyn Lincoln Collection*.

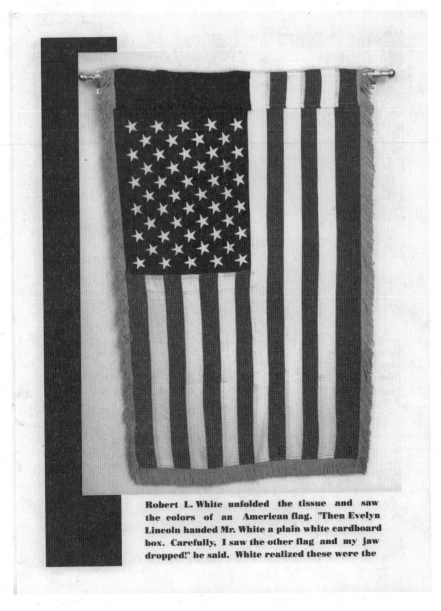

Robert L. White unfolded the tissue and saw the colors of an American flag. "Then Evelyn Lincoln handed Mr. White a plain white cardboard box. Carefully, I saw the other flag and my jaw dropped!" he said. White realized these were the

CHRISTOPHER FULTON'S PERSONAL RECORD: Page from the never-published photo book, *The Evelyn Lincoln Collection*.

hand-embroidered silk presidential flags... the ones that streamed from the fenders of John F. Kennedy's convertible in Dallas, November 22, 1963. Wax wiped from the fenders is as apparent on the gold fringe as if thirty-five years ago were yesterday.

CHRISTOPHER FULTON'S PERSONAL RECORD: Page from the never-published photo book, *The Evelyn Lincoln Collection*.

U.S. DEPARTMENT OF JUSTICE FULTON CASE FILE: Photo of Robert White meeting with President Ronald Reagan about the Evelyn Lincoln inheritance.

CHRISTOPHER FULTON'S PERSONAL RECORD: The two JFK wallets owned by Robert White.

On behalf of President Clinton, thank you for your letter.

The former President understands your concerns. While he is unable to assist, he encourages you to contact your local representative or the current White House for appropriate guidance.

President Clinton is glad you took the time to write and sends his best wishes.

Sincerely,

U.S. DEPARTMENT OF JUSTICE FULTON CASE FILE: President Clinton's response to Christopher Fulton's federal case.

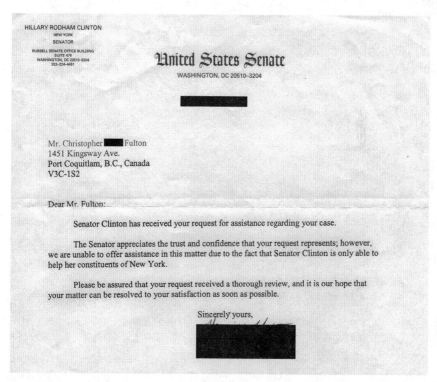

HILLARY RODHAM CLINTON
NEW YORK
SENATOR

RUSSELL SENATE OFFICE BUILDING
SUITE 476
WASHINGTON, DC 20510–3204
202-224-4451

United States Senate

WASHINGTON, DC 20510–3204

Mr. Christopher ▮▮▮ Fulton
1451 Kingsway Ave.
Port Coquitlam, B.C., Canada
V3C-1S2

Dear Mr. Fulton:

Senator Clinton has received your request for assistance regarding your case.

The Senator appreciates the trust and confidence that your request represents; however, we are unable to offer assistance in this matter due to the fact that Senator Clinton is only able to help her constituents of New York.

Please be assured that your request received a thorough review, and it is our hope that your matter can be resolved to your satisfaction as soon as possible.

Sincerely yours,

U.S. DEPARTMENT OF JUSTICE FULTON CASE FILE: Hillary Clinton's response to Christopher Fulton's federal case.

THE KENNEDY COLLECTION
ROBERT L. WHITE

oct 97

Chris —

Thanks for talking to Allan Burns & think it was good & productive.

We looked at the few pages of the book project on his computer screen. Conceptually they are good, I found the photographs very nice but the write-ups had huge mistakes ie.... "JANET GRAVEL" (the President's doctor its JANET TRAVELL. I know you said its a first draft but details especially simple one's are just that! I like the look and I guess that's important to show a prospective client. Herewith is

CONSULTANT ∝ CURATOR
Specializing in Tactile History Relative to
JOHN F. KENNEDY AND THE KENNEDY FAMILY
Call or Write: 304 Bloomsbury Ave. • Baltimore, Md. 21228 • (410) 788-7471

CHRISTOPHER FULTON'S PERSONAL RECORD: Letter to Christopher Fulton from Robert White regarding photo book

THE KENNEDY COLLECTION
ROBERT L. WHITE

a tape which has Dateline NBC, a local big
morning T.V, show "Rise & Shine" and a no
audio Franklin Mint tape which gives you an
idea of what was there.

OK, I need very badly those tapes
of JFK's mic sock, they are my
only copy and I need them ASAP!
Thanks!

Well take care, glad some of this
staged stuff is behind us and lets
move forward

Best,
Robert

CONSULTANT & CURATOR
Specializing in Tactile History Relative to
JOHN F. KENNEDY AND THE KENNEDY FAMILY
Call or Write: 304 Bloomsbury Ave. • Baltimore, Md. 21228 • (410) 788-7471

CHRISTOPHER FULTON'S PERSONAL RECORD: Letter to Christopher Fulton from Robert White regarding photo book

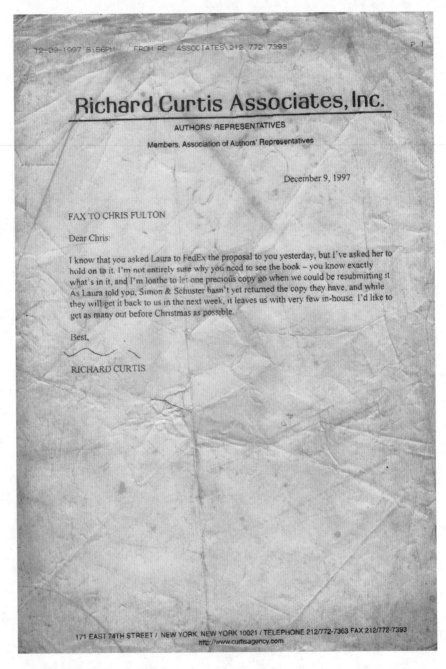

Richard Curtis Associates, Inc.

AUTHORS' REPRESENTATIVES

Members, Association of Authors' Representatives

December 9, 1997

FAX TO CHRIS FULTON

Dear Chris:

I know that you asked Laura to FedEx the proposal to you yesterday, but I've asked her to hold on to it. I'm not entirely sure why you need to see the book — you know exactly what's in it, and I'm loathe to let one precious copy go when we could be resubmitting it As Laura told you, Simon & Schuster hasn't yet returned the copy they have, and while they will get it back to us in the next week, it leaves us with very few in-house. I'd like to get as many out before Christmas as possible.

Best,

RICHARD CURTIS

171 EAST 74TH STREET / NEW YORK, NEW YORK 10021 / TELEPHONE 212/772-7363 FAX 212/772-7393
http://www.curtisagency.com

CHRISTOPHER FULTON'S PERSONAL RECORD: Letter to Christopher Fulton from Richard Curtis.

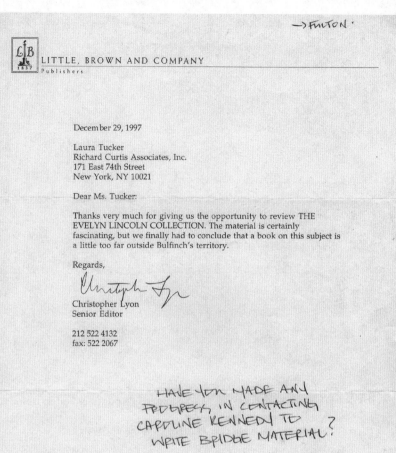

CHRISTOPHER FULTON'S PERSONAL RECORD: Turndown letter from Little Brown.
"Have you made any progress in contacting Caroline Kennedy to write bridge material?"

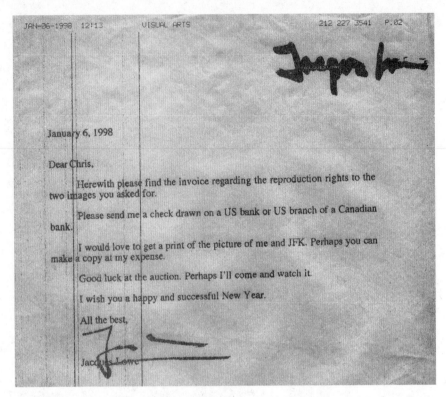

January 6, 1998

Dear Chris,

Herewith please find the invoice regarding the reproduction rights to the two images you asked for.

Please send me a check drawn on a US bank or US branch of a Canadian bank.

I would love to get a print of the picture of me and JFK. Perhaps you can make a copy at my expense.

Good luck at the auction. Perhaps I'll come and watch it.

I wish you a happy and successful New Year.

All the best,

Jacques Lowe

CHRISTOPHER FULTON'S PERSONAL RECORD: Letter to Christopher Fulton from President Kennedy's photographer, Jacques Lowe.
"Good luck at the auction. Perhaps I'll come and watch it."

CHRISTOPHER FULTON'S PERSONAL RECORD: Unpublished photo of Jacques Lowe with President Kennedy. Christopher Fulton promised to give this photo to Jacques Lowe, but he never got the opportunity to do so.

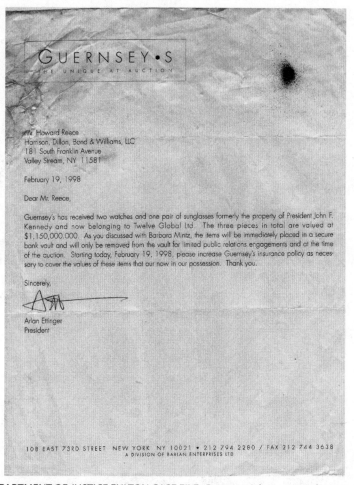

U.S. DEPARTMENT OF JUSTICE FULTON CASE FILE: Guernsey's letter regarding insurance for Christopher Fulton's consignments.

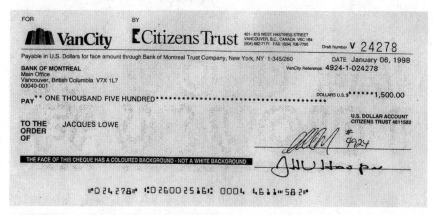

U.S. DEPARTMENT OF JUSTICE FULTON CASE FILE: Christopher Fulton's check to Jacques Lowe for the use of Lowe's photos in Guernsey's JFK auction.

U.S. DEPARTMENT OF JUSTICE FULTON CASE FILE: Photo of Christopher Fulton at Guernsey's JFK auction before the auction began. The Cartier watch's display frame is visible in the background, in the middle, on the left-hand side.

DEMOCRAT AND CHRONICLE ▪ WEDNESDAY, DECEMBER 24, 1997   5B

JFK MEMORABILIA ON BLOCK

The Associated Press

Hotelier Donald Trump tries out one of John F. Kennedy's rocking chairs yesterday at a Trump Tower display of Kennedy-linked goods that will be auctioned March 18 and 19 by Guernsey's. Most of the goods once belonged to the president's personal secretary, Evelyn Lincoln.

U.S. DEPARTMENT OF JUSTICE FULTON CASE FILE: Associated Press news story on Donald Trump's involvement with the JFK auction.

Richard Curtis Associates, Inc.

AUTHORS' REPRESENTATIVES

Members, Association of Authors' Representatives

February 24, 1998

Chris Fulton
1395 Marine Drive
Suite 27006
West Vancouver, BC V7T 1B6
CANADA

By Fax and Mail

Dear Mr. Fulton:

It seems that we have been unsuccessful in marketing THE EVELYN WHITE
COLLECTION, the collection of photographs of John F. Kennedy memorabilia.

We hereby release you from all obligations to us. You are free to contact other agents and
publishers about this project.

Sincerely,

RICHARD CURTIS

171 EAST 71 STREET / NEW YORK, NEW YORK 10021 / TELEPHONE 212/772-7363 FAX 212/772-7393
http://www.curtisagency.com

CHRISTOPHER FULTON'S PERSONAL RECORD: Letter to Christopher Fulton from Richard
Curtis officially terminating the already suppressed photo book publication.

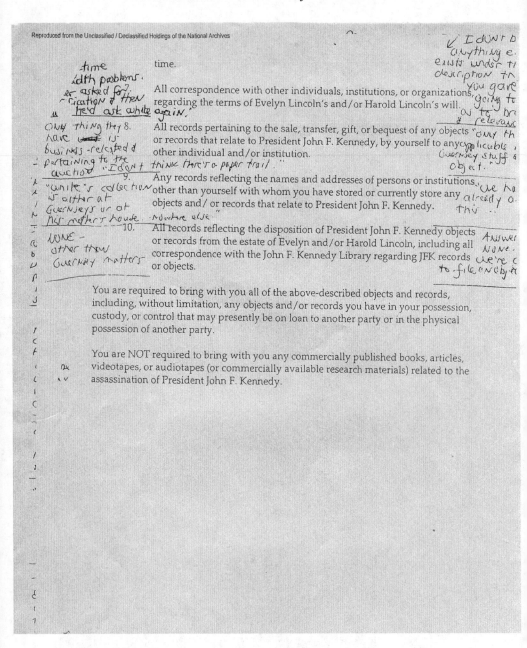

time.

7. All correspondence with other individuals, institutions, or organizations regarding the terms of Evelyn Lincoln's and/or Harold Lincoln's will.

8. All records pertaining to the sale, transfer, gift, or bequest of any objects or records that relate to President John F. Kennedy, by yourself to any other individual and/or institution.

9. Any records reflecting the names and addresses of persons or institutions other than yourself with whom you have stored or currently store any objects and/or records that relate to President John F. Kennedy.

10. All records reflecting the disposition of President John F. Kennedy objects or records from the estate of Evelyn and/or Harold Lincoln, including all correspondence with the John F. Kennedy Library regarding JFK records or objects.

You are required to bring with you all of the above-described objects and records, including, without limitation, any objects and/or records you have in your possession, custody, or control that may presently be on loan to another party or in the physical possession of another party.

You are NOT required to bring with you any commercially published books, articles, videotapes, or audiotapes (or commercially available research materials) related to the assassination of President John F. Kennedy.

U.S. DEPARTMENT OF JUSTICE: A drafted page for Robert White's federal subpoena. This subpoena was crafted to force Robert White's submission regarding his Evelyn Lincoln inheritance. Robert White and his attorney used it to paint Christopher Fulton as non-cooperative with Justice Department. Fulton never knew about the subpoena or the position it had placed him in until after his arrest.

ATTACHMENT A

DEFINITIONS AND INSTRUCTIONS

1. "You" means Robert White, any of ~~your~~ *Mr. White's* agents, representatives, partners, or any other person who may have possession, custody or control of ~~your~~ *Mr. White's* records and objects that are identified in this subpoena.

2. "And" and "or" and the use of the singular or plural of any noun should be understood in the broadest reasonable sense and should be construed inclusively in favor of producing the largest number of records and objects.

3. "Object" means all physical entities *except* "records" as herein defined. "Objects" include memorabilia such as rocking chairs, tie clips, ash trays, clothing, toiletries, picture frames, model ships, etc.

4. "Records" should be understood broadly to include, without limitation, *tape recordings* memoranda, documents, handwritten notes, typewritten notes, journals, diaries, entries, drawings, photographs, electronic recordings, dictabelts, motion pictures, correspondence, contracts, computer files or databases, agreements and legal instruments.

5. "JFK Act" means the *President John F. Kennedy Assassination Records Collection Act of 1992*, 44 U.S.C. Sec. 2107 (Supp. V 1994).

6. To the extent that it is impossible to comply with any of these requests, you should comply fully with all remaining requests and be prepared to explain the reasons why you cannot comply with any request.

7. To the extent that you are unable to make available one or more records and/or objects that would otherwise be responsive to this subpoena, provide a list that identifies (for each record and/or object that is not produced): (a) a description of the record and/or object; (b) the source from whom you obtained the record and/or object; © the date that you originally obtained the record and/or object: and (d) the reason why you are unable to make the record or object available.

U.S. DEPARTMENT OF JUSTICE: A drafted page for Robert White's federal subpoena. This subpoena was crafted to force Robert White's submission regarding his Evelyn Lincoln inheritance. Robert White and his attorney used it to paint Christopher Fulton as non-cooperative with Justice Department. Fulton never knew about the subpoena or the position it had placed him in until after his arrest.

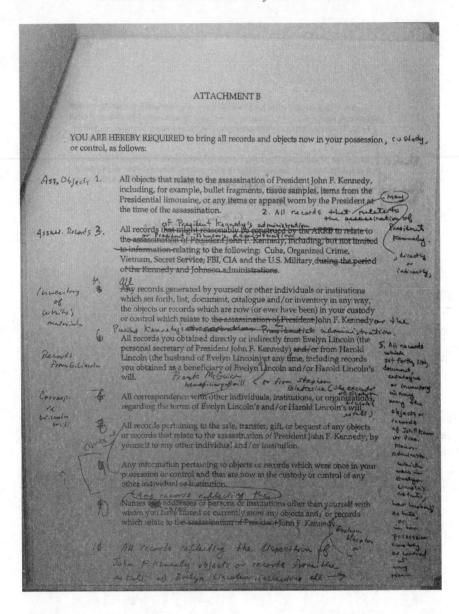

ATTACHMENT B

YOU ARE HEREBY REQUIRED to bring all records and objects now in your possession, *custody,* or control, as follows:

Ass. Objects 1. All objects that relate to the assassination of President John F. Kennedy, including, for example, bullet fragments, tissue samples, items from the Presidential limousine, or any items or apparel worn by the President at *(may)* the time of the assassination. 2. All records *that relate to the assassination of the president*

Assass. Records 3. All records *of President Kennedy's administration* that might reasonably be construed by the ARRB to relate to the assassination of President John F. Kennedy, including, but not limited to information relating to the following: Cuba, Organized Crime, Vietnam, Secret Service, FBI, CIA and the U.S. Military during the period of the Kennedy and Johnson administrations. *directly indirectly*

4. *all*

Inventory of white's materials 5. Any records generated by yourself or other individuals or institutions which set forth, list, document, catalogue and/or inventory in any way, the objects or records which are now (or ever have been) in your custody or control which relate to the assassination of President John F. Kennedy *or the President Kennedy's* Presidential administration.

Records from E. Lincoln 6. All records you obtained directly or indirectly from Evelyn Lincoln (the personal secretary of President John F. Kennedy) and/or from Harold Lincoln (the husband of Evelyn Lincoln) at any time, including records you obtained as a beneficiary of Evelyn Lincoln and/or Harold Lincoln's will. *Frank McGuire or from Stephen Blakeslee Gibbs executed beneficiary will* **5. All records which set forth, list, document, catalogue or inventory in any way, any the objects or records of JohF Kennedy or Pres. Kennedy admin. which were once in Evelyn Lincoln's estate, her husband's estate or in his possession or control of any such person**

Corresp. re Lincoln will 7. All correspondence with other individuals, institutions, or organizations regarding the terms of Evelyn Lincoln's and/or Harold Lincoln's will.

8. All records pertaining to the sale, transfer, gift, or bequest of any objects or records that relate to the assassination of President John F. Kennedy, by yourself to any other individual and/or institution.

9. Any information pertaining to objects or records which were once in your possession or control and that are now in the custody or control of any other individual or institution.

10. *Any records reflecting the* Names and addresses of persons or institutions other than yourself with whom you have stored or currently store any objects and/or records which relate to the assassination of President John F. Kennedy. *Evelyn thicpn or*

11. All records reflecting the disposition *of* John F Kennedy objects or records from the estate of Evelyn Lincoln *including all* →

U.S. DEPARTMENT OF JUSTICE: A drafted page for Robert White's federal subpoena. This subpoena was crafted to force Robert White's submission regarding his Evelyn Lincoln inheritance. Robert White and his attorney used it to paint Christopher Fulton as non-cooperative with Justice Department. Fulton never knew about the subpoena or the position it had placed him in until after his arrest.

/ ﹏﹏﹏﹏ ﹏﹏ENT PRIVILEGE

ATTACHMENT B

YOU ARE HEREBY REQUIRED to bring all records and objects now in your possession, custody, or control, as follows:

PRIOR CONVERSATION

[handwritten: WEDNESDAY 1-28-97 CONV.]

[handwritten left margin: "WHERE has no bullet fragments, no tissue samples, no items, no apparel, no sunglasses. Has limo switches.]

1. All objects that relate to the assassination of President John F. Kennedy, or *[handwritten: will produce]* to his trip to Texas in November, 1963, including for example, bullet *[handwritten: limo switches]* fragments, tissue samples, items from the Presidential limousine, or any *[handwritten: letter to Salinger, welcome]* items or apparel worn by President Kennedy at the time of the *[handwritten: to Texas program]* assassination. *[handwritten: Letter to Salinger "Welcome to Texas program."]*

[handwritten left margin: - Nothing except Connally hospital bill, Easter card w/ LHO's signature, pamphlet in Ruby's pocket, Ruby's notes. Still coming from Ruby]

2. All records that may relate, directly or indirectly, to the assassination of *[handwritten: Will produce]* President John F. Kennedy including, but not limited to, records *[handwritten: previously]* pertaining to Jacqueline Kennedy, Governor and Mrs. Connally, Lee *[handwritten: discussed item]* Harvey Oswald, Jack Ruby, J.D. Tippit, President Kennedy's trip to Texas in November, 1963, etc.

[handwritten left margin: EL's Cuban missile crisis calender. Krushiv's telegram, certain de helts "may or may not hurt info on Cuba and/or Vietnam]

3. All records of President Kennedy's administration or President Lyndon *[handwritten: will produce]* Johnson's administration that relate to the following: Cuba (including, for *[handwritten: previously]* example, any records that refer to the Bay of Pigs or the Cuban Missile *[handwritten: discussed, etc.]* Crisis), Organized Crime, Vietnam (including, for example, any records that refer to President Kennedy's conversations with Maxwell Taylor relating to the Vietnam War), the Secret Service, the FBI, the CIA, and the U.S. Military.

[handwritten left margin: military consignment list. Is it Davidy's memo. White wrote to Adler in response to our subpoena.]

4. All records that set forth, list, document, index, catalogue, inventory or *[handwritten: Eve already]* identify in any way, the objects or records that are now (or ever have *[handwritten: read to you]* been) in your custody or control that relate to President John F. Kennedy *[handwritten: what write]* or the Kennedy Administration. *[handwritten: her listed in his memo to me. I won't A/C Privilege]*

[handwritten left margin: "Big-time breadth problem"]

5. All records you obtained directly or indirectly from Evelyn Lincoln (the personal secretary of President John F. Kennedy), Harold Lincoln (the husband of Evelyn Lincoln), Frank McGuire (beneficiary of Lincoln's will), or from Stephen Blakeslee (the executor of Evelyn Lincoln's estate), at any *[handwritten: will agree]* time, including records you obtained as a beneficiary of Evelyn Lincoln's *[handwritten: in its]* and/or Harold Lincoln's will. *[handwritten: entirety.]*

[handwritten left margin: - No inventories. Executor did not inventory anything that was in the file cabinets.]

6. All records that set forth, list, document, index, catalogue, inventory or *[handwritten: There's no]* identify the objects or records of President John F. Kennedy or the *[handwritten: such document]* Kennedy administration that were in Evelyn Lincoln's estate, Harold *[handwritten: it doesn't]* Lincoln's estate, or in either of their possession, custody, or control at any *[handwritten: exist.]* *[handwritten: We're not going to produce anything else."]*

U.S. DEPARTMENT OF JUSTICE: A drafted page for Robert White's federal subpoena. This subpoena was crafted to force Robert White's submission regarding his Evelyn Lincoln inheritance. Robert White and his attorney used it to paint Christopher Fulton as non-cooperative with Justice Department. Fulton never knew about the subpoena or the position it had placed him in until after his arrest.

453

U. S. Department of Justice

Civil Division

IAN 2

Washington, D.C. 20530

SUBPOENA DUCES TECUM
FOR THE PRODUCTION OF DOCUMENTS
AND APPEARANCE FOR TESTIMONY
BEFORE THE ASSASSINATION RECORDS REVIEW BOARD

TO: Mr. Robert White
      302 Bloomsbury Avenue
      Baltimore, Maryland 21228

YOU ARE HEREBY REQUIRED AND DIRECTED, PURSUANT TO 44 U.S.C. § 2107, TO
APPEAR BEFORE:

T. Jeremy Gunn, Executive Director and General Counsel of the Assassination Records
Review Board at 600 E Street, N.W., Washington, D.C. 20530, on the 12th day of February
1998, at 9:30 a.m., or at such other mutually agreeable time and place, and at the same time
each day thereafter until the taking of testimony is complete, to testify under oath regarding
any records or objects relating to President John F. Kennedy.

YOU ARE HEREBY REQUIRED to bring with you, to produce and to make available for
inspection and copying or reproduction at said time and place all objects and records as
defined in Attachment A hereto, that are in your possession, custody or control, and that
are described in Attachment B hereto.

The production of documentary material in response to this subpoena must be made
under a sworn certificate in the form set forth, by the person to whom this subpoena is
directed or, if not a natural person, by a person or persons having knowledge of the factsu
and circumstances relating to such production. Accordingly, please review and execute the
attached Certificate of Compliance to verify that you have complied with the subpoena.

Inquiries concerning compliance with this subpoena should be directed to: Kim Herd,
Senior Attorney, Assassination Records Review Board, 600 E Street, N.W., Washington,
D.C., 20530, (202) 724-0088; (FAX) (202) 724-0457.

ISSUED AT *Washington, D.C.*

THIS *9* DAY OF *January*, 1998

By: *[signature]*
      FRANK W. HUNGER
      Assistant Attorney General

U.S. DEPARTMENT OF JUSTICE: The signed federal subpoena for Robert White.

ATTACHMENT A

DEFINITIONS AND INSTRUCTIONS

1. "You" means Mr. Robert White, any of Mr. White's agents, representatives, partners, or any other person who may have possession, custody or control of Mr. White's records and objects that are identified in this subpoena.

2. "And" and "or" and the use of the singular or plural of any noun should be understood in the broadest reasonable sense and should be construed inclusively in favor of producing the largest number of records and objects.

3. "Object" means all physical entities *except* "records" as herein defined. "Objects" include memorabilia such as rocking chairs, tie clips, ash trays, clothing, toiletries, picture frames, model ships, etc.

4. "Records" should be understood broadly to include, without limitation, memoranda, documents, handwritten notes, typewritten notes, journals, diaries, entries, drawings, photographs, electronic recordings, dicta belts, tape recordings, motion pictures, correspondence, contracts, computer files or databases, agreements and legal instruments.

5. To the extent that it is impossible to comply with any of these requests, you should comply fully with all remaining requests and be prepared to explain the reasons why you cannot comply with any request.

6. To the extent that you are unable to make available one or more records and/or objects that would otherwise be responsive to this subpoena, provide a list that identifies (for each record and/or object that is not produced): (a) a description of the record and/or object; (b) the source from whom you obtained the record and/or object; (c) the date that you originally obtained the record and/or object; and (d) the reason why you are unable to make the record or object available.

U.S. DEPARTMENT OF JUSTICE: The signed federal subpoena for Robert White.

time.

7. All correspondence with other individuals, institutions, or organizations, regarding the terms of Evelyn Lincoln's and/or Harold Lincoln's will.

8. All records pertaining to the sale, transfer, gift, or bequest of any objects or records that relate to President John F. Kennedy, by yourself to any other individual and/or institution.

9. Any records reflecting the names and addresses of persons or institutions other than yourself with whom you have stored or currently store any objects and/or records that relate to President John F. Kennedy.

10. All records reflecting the disposition of President John F. Kennedy objects or records from the estate of Evelyn and/or Harold Lincoln, including all correspondence with the John F. Kennedy Library regarding JFK records or objects.

You are required to bring with you all of the above-described objects and records, including, without limitation, any objects and/or records you have in your possession, custody, or control that may presently be on loan to another party or in the physical possession of another party.

You are NOT required to bring with you any commercially published books, articles, videotapes, or audiotapes (or commercially available research materials) related to the assassination of President John F. Kennedy.

U.S. DEPARTMENT OF JUSTICE: The signed federal subpoena for Robert White.

ITEMS WE RECEIVED FROM ROBERT WHITE ON 3-3-98

- We viewed several letters (many from Jacqueline)

- We reviewed one love letter from Jacqueline to JFK - seven pages

- We reviewed two Christmas Cards with JFK/JBK and Caroline (we returned)

- We went through all the stray items that he had not yet produced.

- Five Telegrams

- Grave site plans

- Steno notes

- Dictabelts

    - I made these notes (on the outside of the envelope)

    - Gus Russo has a copy

    - Mark Oberhaus has a copy

    - I gave my copies to "Chris Fulton" in Canada, in May, 1996

    - ABC arranged for someone in New York to play them - they did them in my presence.

1. Texas Trip advance sheets

2. Ruby notes

3. Letters

4. Letter from Dr. Robert Shaw to "David" Lee

5. Letter to Ronald Wade from H.D. Holmes

6. "Last moments with Pres. Kennedy" - Oscar Huber

U.S. DEPARTMENT OF JUSTICE FULTON CASE FILE: The government prepared lists of items to be removed from Robert White's collection for review and classification. The many items that were classified for national security were federally deposited and not returned. The most sensitive items were mixed in with innocuous items.

"Dictabelts

—I gave my copies to 'Chris Fulton' in Canada, in May, 1996"

As stated before, the date and location are incorrect. The recordings were transferred to Christopher Fulton in May of 1997, in Baltimore, Maryland.

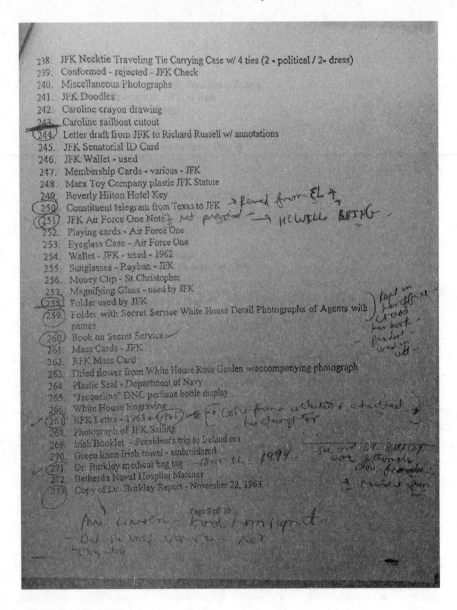

238. JFK Necktie Traveling Tie Carrying Case w/ 4 ties (2 - political / 2- dress)
239. Conformed - rejected - JFK Check
240. Miscellaneous Photographs
241. JFK Doodles
242. Caroline crayon drawing
243. Caroline sailboat cutout
244. Letter draft from JFK to Richard Russell w/ annotations
245. JFK Senatorial ID Card
246. JFK Wallet - used
247. Membership Cards - various - JFK
248. Marx Toy Company plastic JFK Statute
249. Beverly Hilton Hotel Key
250. Constituent telegram from Texas to JFK
251. JFK Air Force One Note
252. Playing cards - Air Force One
253. Eyeglass Case - Air Force One
254. Wallet - JFK - used - 1962
255. Sunglasses - Rayban - JFK
256. Money Clip - St Christopher
257. Magnifying Glass - used by JFK
258. Folder used by JFK
259. Folder with Secret Service White House Detail Photographs of Agents with names
260. Book on Secret Service
261. Mass Cards - JFK
262. RFK Mass Card
263. Dried flower from White House Rose Garden w/accompanying photograph
264. Plastic Seal - Department of Navy
265. "Jacqueline" DNC perfume bottle display
266. White House Engraving
267. RFK Letter - 1963
268. Photograph of JFK Sailing
269. Irish Booklet - President's trip to Ireland era
270. Green linen Irish towel - embroidered
271. Dr. Burkley medical bag tag
272. Bethesda Naval Hospital Matches
273. Copy of Dr. Burkley Report - November 22, 1963

Page 9 of 10

U.S. DEPARTMENT OF JUSTICE: The government prepared lists of items to be removed from Robert White's collection for review and classification.

Files of Kim Herd

Folder Title List
Volume: 4.4 feet
For questions about these records or copying information, please write to the Special Access and FOIA Staff at the National Archives at College Park, Room 6350, 8601 Adelphi Road, College Park, MD 20740-6001, call at (301) 837-3190, or e-mail: specialaccess_foia@nara.gov.
Box 1:

- CIA documents-179 Series-10038-10459

Box 2:

- CIA documents- 179 Series-10271-10336
- Untitled
- Robert White Depositions
- Robert White
  o Robert White Deposition
  o Robert White Items Received During Deposition
  o Robert White Appraisal
  o Robert White Inventories
  o Robert White Subpoena
  o Robert White Guernsey's Lists
  o AARB Correspondence with National Archives

Box 3:

- Dineen Appeal: Drafts
- Dineen Appeal: Herd's Background Notes
- Dineen Appeal: Warren Commission Index Cards at NARA
- The Record
- Dineen Appeal D.C. Mental Health Court Info.
- Dineen Appeal: Warren Commission Testimony of R. Bouck
- Dineen Appeal: Background from Internet
- Dineen Appeal: Pertinent Correspondence
- Dineen Threat Sheets Master List of Names
- Medical Journal Articles
- Dineen Documents: Background Research at NARA

NATIONAL ARCHIVES: Assassination Records Review Board's files. "Robert White" and "Evelyn Lincoln Project" appear multiple times.

- Financial Crimes Enforcement Network (FINCEN)
- Choice Point
- Appeal: Doctor's Letters

Box 4:

- Untitled
- Sheridan Miscellaneous
- Walter Sheridan Discovery Information
- Untitled
- Expert's Conference
- Correspondence w/Marty Underwood
- Dillon Committee Documents
- Final Report
- Secret Service Materials already at NARA
- ONI direction
- January, 1998-Round Meeting
- July, 1998 Board Meeting
- Secret Service: LBJ Library Referrals
- Secret Service: LBJ Library Referrals
- Kodak (Empty)

Box 5:

- Legal JFK Act
- Larry Haapanen
- Legal Subpoenas generally
- Harrison Livingston
- HSCA referrals
- Public Contacts

Box 6:

- DOS Compliance
- Untitled
- Materials Received from Robert White at his deposition
- Warren Commission
- Robert White Materials Received at Deposition
- Untitled

NATIONAL ARCHIVES: Assassination Records Review Board files.

"January, 1998 – Round Meeting" and "July, 1998 Board Meeting" under "Box 4" most likely contain decisions that were made on the executive level and the intelligence level regarding the Evelyn Lincoln Project and Guernsey's JFK auction.

Following a weeklong search, and a thirty-day formal investigation, the National Archives recognized that box 4 existed but was (and still is) officially missing from the archives with no removal slip left by any agency.

Box 7:

- 7.178 Evelyn Lincoln Project
- Untitled
- Lincoln Will Dispute: Conversation w/Presiding Judge
- Evelyn Lincoln's Will

Box 8:

- Correspondence
- Herd: Work Product
- Robert White: Herd's Notes
- Robert White: Background from ARRB
- Robert White-ist Mts.
- Robert White Correspondence with Robert Adler
- Secret Service Appeal of Eileen Dineen Document

Box 9:

- Legal-Walter Sheridan Settlement
- ARRB v. Connick
- Correspondence w/OPM Re: Redlich Documents
- Legal: Background Cases
- OPM- Correspondence Re: DeMohrenshildt Documents in HSCA files
- Board Meetings
- Ford Library
- April, 1998 Board Meeting

Box 10:

- Secret Service: December 31, 1997
- Secret Service: Correspondence Misc.
- Secret Service: March 12, 1998 Correspondence
- Secret Service-Background Investigation
- Secret Service-Correspondence
- Secret Service-June, 1998 Fine Request Letter
- Secret Service-Compliance
- Secret Service: Potential Additional Requests
- Secret Service: Interviews w/Former USSS Employees
- Secret Service: Inventories
- Secret Service: Materials Reviewed on 2-13-98

NATIONAL ARCHIVES: Assassination Records Review Board files.

Agenda
Assassination Records Review Board
January 22, 1998
TENTATIVE

Estimated Time	Subject
6:30-9:30	Individual review of classified memoranda
9:30-9:45	Closed Meeting on CIA issue and on green issues
9:45-10:00	Break and telephone calls
10:00-10:45	Executive Director Briefing/Board-Staff Meeting
10:45-11:15	Individual review of classified memoranda on NBR issues CIA "Monster" Memo CIA OPR

11:15-12:00	Closed meeting
	NBR Issues
	     CIA "Monster" Memo
	     CIA OPR
	
	Designation of Secret Service Records
	
	State records
	
	Joint Chiefs of Staff histories (tentative)
	
	Begin review of non-green issues (if time permits)
	     CIA
	     NSA

12:00-1:30	Lunch at 701
1:30-3:00	Continue closed meeting
3:00-3:15	Break
3:15-4:45	Continue closed meeting (if necessary) Discuss *Experts Conference*

Exec Director briefing

     Experts' Conference
     Personnel issues
     Public Affairs issues
     Ford visit
     NBC litigation
     Medical experts
     NARA and fragment testing
     Other issues of concern to the Board
     Robert White

NATIONAL ARCHIVES: Assassination Records Review Board files.

Assassination Records Review Board
600 E Street NW • 2nd Floor • Washington, DC 20530
(202) 724–0088 • Fax: (202) 724–0457

To: Kim Herd/ARRB
cc:
From: Tom Samoluk/ARRB
Date: 02/04/98 04:13:18 PM
Subject: Question for Robert White

Kim:

I have learned that given the admission by White that he does, in fact, have dictabelts, a relevant question is does he possess any analog tapes? Based on what the JFK Library told me, there is analog tapes of meetings that they believe exist, but do possess. Thus, the possibility that Evelyn Lincoln took some analog tapes, as well as dictabelts. An additional question is does White possess any logs or other records relevant to the dictabelts or analog tapes. You may recall that I asked him about logs related to the dictabelts when we interviewed him. He said that he did not. I want to make sure we get him on record about this whole area.

Thanks.

Tom

ASSASSINATION RECORDS REVIEW BOARD: Internal memo regarding analog tapes secured by Evelyn Lincoln. Robert White gave those analog tapes to Christopher Fulton.

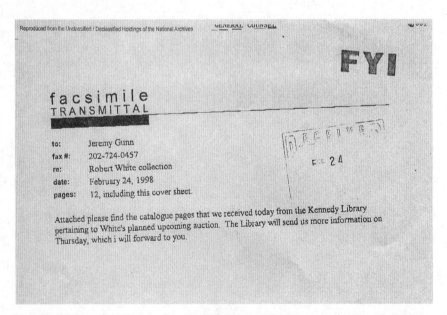

To: Kim
cc: Jeremy
From: Tom Samoluk/ARRB
Date: 02/06/98 03:35:23 PM
Subject: Additional Information Regarding Potential White Holdings

An anonymous person called the JFK Library last week, and advised Frank Rigg, of the JFK Library staff that White had dictabelt recordings of President Kennedy's telephone conversations (the description is a virtual match of what we have on the cassette tapes, so the source has good information), in addition to other materials.

Perhaps most important of what the caller claimed was the following: Among the textual materials is a file on the Dallas trip containing seating plans for the various events and motorcade arrangements for the various locations. One of these documents bears a handwritten reference to a "bubble top."   This description appears to match what we have heard from other sources and is obviously very important to us.

The caller made other claims that we can talk about at some point, but I was very interested in the additional information provided above.

ASSASSINATION RECORDS REVIEW BOARD: Internal memo.
"Perhaps most important of what the caller claimed was the following: Among the [Robert White's] textual materials is a file on the Dallas trip containing seating plans [...] and motorcade arrangements for the various locations. One of these documents bears a handwritten reference to a 'bubble top.' This description appears to match what we have heard from other sources and is obviously very important to us."

GENERAL COUNSEL

FYI

facsimile
TRANSMITTAL

to: Jeremy Gunn
fax #:   202-724-0457
re: Robert White collection
date: February 24, 1998
pages: 12, including this cover sheet.

Attached please find the catalogue pages that we received today from the Kennedy Library pertaining to White's planned upcoming auction. The Library will send us more information on Thursday, which i will forward to you.

ASSASSINATION RECORDS REVIEW BOARD: First page of internal memo regarding the ongoing coordination between the John F. Kennedy Library and the ARRB about Guernsey's JFK auction.

Assassination Records Review Board
600 E Street NW • 2nd Floor • Washington, DC 20530
(202) 724–0088 • Fax: (202) 724–0457

—SECRET—

HAND DELIVERY BY NATIONAL SECURITY CLEARED COURIER

March 3, 1998

Mr. Steven Garfinkel
Director
Information Security Oversight Office
700 Pennsylvania Avenue, N.W., Room 100
Washington, D.C. 20408

RE: Possible National Security Classified Records in the Possession of
Robert L. White

Dear Mr. Garfinkel:

As the Security Officer of the Assassination Records Review Board, I am transmitting herewith four sets of records that may contain national security classified information. We obtained these records during in the course of our deposition of Robert L. White, 304 Bloomsbury Avenue, Baltimore, Maryland 21228, who appeared with the records at our offices pursuant to a subpoena *duces tecum* that was issued by the United States Department of Justice.

It is our understanding that Mr. White obtained these records from the late Evelyn Lincoln, the personal secretary to President John F. Kennedy. According to his deposition testimony, Mr. White intends to sell these records at a public auction in New York City at the firm of Guernsey's later this month. The enclosed records are copies made from the records brought to the deposition by Mr. White. On the first page of the records are handwritten numbers (164, 165, 167, and 169), which correspond to the Robert L. White Consignment Inventory, which I also am enclosing.

—SECRET—
Declassified when Separated from Enclosures

ASSASSINATION RECORDS REVIEW BOARD: Classified, hand-delivered letter to the Information Security Oversight Office (the ISOO is responsible for classifying materials and information necessary for the security of the United States) stating that Robert White was in possession of National Security materials.

Mr. Steven Garfinkel
March 3, 1998
Page 2

—SECRET—

Given the circumstances of his acquisition of these records, and other testimony he provided today, we perceive it as highly likely that Mr. White may have additional national security classified records at his home in Baltimore.

Please do not hesitate to contact me if you have any questions.

Sincerely,

T. Jeremy Gunn
Executive Director

cc: Mr. Robert M. Adler (w/o enclosures)
      Attorney for Mr. White

Enclosures

—SECRET—
Declassified when Separated from Enclosures

ASSASSINATION RECORDS REVIEW BOARD: Classified, hand-delivered letter to the Information Security Oversight Office (the ISOO is responsible for classifying materials and information necessary for the security of the United States) stating that Robert White was in possession of National Security materials.

GENERAL COUNSEL ☑002

National *Archives* at College Park

8601 Adelphi Road   College Park, Maryland 20740-6001

BY FACSIMILE TRANSMISSION AND
FEDERAL EXPRESS

March 10, 1998

Arlan Ettinger
President
Guernsey's Auction House
108 East 73rd Street
New York, New York 10021

       Re: Request for the Return of Artifacts and Documents Relating to the Life,
            Career, and Presidency of John F. Kennedy

Dear Mr. Ettinger:

It has come to our attention that Guernsey's Auction House (Guernsey's) intends to
present for auction on March 18 and 19, 1998, certain documents, artifacts and audio-
visual materials relating to the life, career, and presidency of John F. Kennedy. We have
reason to believe that many of these documents, artifacts and audio-visual materials
belong to the United States. Items belonging to the U.S. will have to be returned to the
custody of the National Archives and Records Administration (NARA) for deposit in the
John F. Kennedy Library.

We also have reason to believe that some of the items listed for auction may contain
information that is classified for national security reasons. Materials containing national
security information must be stored in an approved Government repository under
appropriate security until the information can be reviewed for declassification. Therefore,
you will need to make arrangements with us immediately to safeguard the items
containing potential national security information.

The Kennedy Library was established as a part of NARA in accordance with federal law
and the wishes of the late President and his family. Through several deeds of gift
executed pursuant to 44 U.S.C. §§ 2111 and 2112, President Kennedy's estate and heirs
donated to the Library and NARA the official papers and artifacts of President Kennedy's
Administration, as well as numerous other items related to his life and career. Many of
the documents, artifacts and audio-visual materials donated to the Library and NARA
under these deeds of gift have been improperly alienated from the collection, and many of
the alienated materials appear in the Guernsey's auction catalogue. The alienation of

NATIONAL ARCHIVES: Threatening letter to Guernsey's Auction House to place them on
notice that some of the items being offered for sale in their JFK auction were of concern
for national security.

GENERAL COUNSEL   ☑ 003

2

these items has resulted in a loss of the documentation of the administration of John F. Kennedy and our national heritage. We ask that you immediately assist the Government in correcting this situation. Among the documents and artifacts listed in the catalogue to which we believe the Kennedy Library and NARA hold title are the following (as listed in the catalogue).

- Lot 7   John F. Kennedy's Inauguration Speech
- Lot 8   John F. Kennedy's Drop Leaf Signing Table
- Lots 41 - 42   John F. Kennedy's Notes and Correspondence on the Cuban Missile Crisis
- Lot 47   John F. Kennedy's Memorandum for the Secretaries of State and Defense
- Lot 48   John F. Kennedy's Memorandum for Secretary of State
- Lot 49   John F. Kennedy's Memoranda to Secretaries of State and Defense
- Lot 53   Report to the Nation About the Berlin Crisis
- Lot 78   JFK's Last Scribbles and Doodles (relating to the Dallas trip, and possibly an assassination related record.)
- Lot 79   Notes from Meeting with Khrushchev
- Lot 99   John F. Kennedy's Assorted Memoranda (includes memos to the Secretary of State, to the Director of the Office of Emergency Planning, and to the Secretary of Defense.)
- Lot 109   Budget Submission to Congress
- Lot 125   Trip to Mexico
- Lot 415   John F. Kennedy's White House Stereo

This is not a complete listing of the materials listed in the auction catalogue to which we think we hold title. However, this list does illustrate both the official nature of many of the items listed in the catalogue and their historical significance to the presidency of John F. Kennedy. We need to examine the items scheduled to be auctioned, as well as your information on their provenance, so that we can then provide you with a complete listing of the documents, artifacts and audio-visual materials that we believe belong to the Kennedy Library and NARA. This examination will also enable us to determine whether specific items do not belong to us. It is our desire to recover only those historical materials that belong in the Kennedy Library.

With respect to items listed in the auction catalogue that may contain national security information, we are required to safeguard such information pursuant to Executive Order 12958 and the Information Security Oversight Office Directive on National Security Information, 32 C.F.R. chapter 20, parts 2000-2003. These authorities, which govern the handling of national security information, require that information bearing a classification stamp or dealing with national security should be reviewed by the national security agency that generated the information for current classification or declassification, before

NATIONAL ARCHIVES: Threatening letter to Guernsey's Auction House to place them on notice that some of the items being offered for sale in their JFK auction were of concern for national security.

"With respect to items listed in the auction catalog that may contain national security information, we are required to safeguard such information pursuant to Executive Order 12958 and the Information Security Oversight Office Directive on National Security Information [. . .]."

GENERAL COUNSEL

☑004

3

release to the public. Some of the items in your catalogue are from the Presidential papers of John F. Kennedy and deal with foreign relations topics such as Berlin, NATO, the Soviet Union, and Cuba, as well as conversations between Heads of State. It is possible that some of this information has not been declassified.

The best way to address these national security concerns and to ensure that classified items are not prematurely released, is to transfer the aforementioned items to an approved federal repository. We could then arrange for a declassification review by the appropriate agencies. We will arrange to pick up and store these national security items, as well as other items properly belonging to NARA.

Theodore Carter of the Department of Justice's Commercial Litigation Branch and Kevin Jessar of my office are handling this matter for NARA. Mr. Carter will be contacting you on March 11 to discuss our request to examine the items in the Guernsey's catalog that we believe belong to us.

Finally, I must inform you that if Guernsey's sells or attempts to sell items properly belonging to the United States, appropriate action will be taken to protect the interests of the United States. In addition, the failure to return these items to NARA's custody, or the damage, destruction, or loss of the items that are such an integral and important part of our nation's history, may cause immediate action to be taken against Guernsey's by the United States.

Thank you for your attention to this serious matter. We will be informing Robert White of this letter and its contents.

Sincerely,

CHRISTOPHER M. RUNKEL
Acting General Counsel

cc: Robert White

        Bradley S. Gerratt
        Director, John F. Kennedy Library

NATIONAL ARCHIVES: Threatening letter to Guernsey's Auction House to place them on notice that some of the items being offered for sale in their JFK auction were of concern for national security.

"Theodore Carter of the Department of Justice's Commercial Litigation Branch and Kevin Jessar of my office are handling this matter for NARA."

U.S. DEPARTMENT OF JUSTICE FULTON CASE FILE: Photo of Christopher Fulton's Guernsey's consignment and display note from the Guernsey's Auction offering.

THE JOHN F. KENNEDY CARTIER DISPLAY

The display is the collaborated effort of many artisans commissioned to do justice to President Kennedy's legacy and is in itself a piece of art. It contains five (5) original photographs, and four prints, each showing the President wearing the Cartier.

The blue background was chosen to match the carpet in the Oval Office. The removable watch housing is a revolving cylinder of glass and sterling silver allowing a 360 degree view of the Cartier which reveals the President's monogram 'JFK' on the reverse. The magnificent plaque of sterling silver bears the emblem seal of the President of the United States.

The inscription reads:

The John F. Kennedy Cartier.
One of the most personal possessions of
John F. Kennedy
was the gold Cartier wristwatch
given to him by Jackie on their fourth wedding anniversary
inscribed: "J.F.K. Sept. 12, 1957"
President Kennedy wore it for the last time
with Jackie by his side in Dallas, Texas
November 22, 1963

"History, after all, is a memory of the nation"
John F. Kennedy.

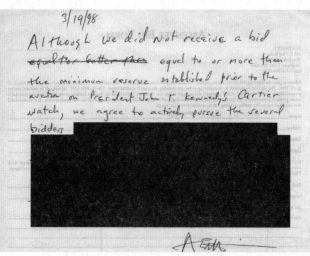

GUERNSEY•S

LOT STATEMENT

Consignor: ~~Christopher Fulton~~ The Twelve Global Ltd.
2558 WESTHILL CLOSE
WEST VANCOUVER B.C.,
CANADA V7S3E6

Date: 3/16/98
Reference: _____
Telephone: 604 925 0565
Evening: _____
Fax: _____

This schedule of property, including the following item or items consigned to Guernsey's, is incorporated into the consignment contract and made a part thereof.

CODE	LOT	DESCRIPTION OF PROPERTY	ESTIMATE
	153	JFK CARTIER WATCH	RESERVE 950,000
	154	JFK NATRIX WATCH	RESERVE 65,000
	431	JFK SUNGLASSES	RESERVE 15,000

The above is an accurate description of the property consigned.

Consignor Signature _____ Date 3.17.98

GUERNSEY•S, 108 EAST 73RD STREET, NEW YORK, NY 10021•212.794.2280 /FAX 212.744.3638

U.S. DEPARTMENT OF JUSTICE FULTON CASE FILE: Guernsey's lot statement for Christopher Fulton's consignments.

3/19/98

Although we did not receive a bid ~~equal to or better than~~ equal to or more than the minimum reserve established prior to the auction on President John F. Kennedy's Cartier watch, we agree to actively pursue the several bidders

CHRISTOPHER FULTON'S PERSONAL DOCUMENT: Note signed by Guernsey's President, Arlan Ettinger, that was slipped to Christopher Fulton during Guernsey's JFK auction.

MAR-16-98 MON 18:37 WILLIAMS & CONNOLLY   2024345061   P.02

LAW OFFICES
WILLIAMS & CONNOLLY

725 TWELFTH STREET, N.W.

WASHINGTON, D. C. 20005

(202) 434-5000

EDWARD BENNETT WILLIAMS (1920-1988)
PAUL R. CONNOLLY (1922-1978)

NICOLE K. SELIGMAN
(202) 434-5064
FAX (202) 434-5081

March 16, 1998

Via Facsimile and U.S. Mail
617-951-2125

Molly H. Sherden, Esquire
Peabody & Arnold
50 Rowes Wharf
Boston, MA 02110-3342

Dear Ms. Sherden:

As I believe you are aware, on February 6, 1998, I wrote to ▮▮▮▮▮▮
Esquire, attorney for Robert White, with regard to the ownership of items in Mr. White's
possession that he had received from Evelyn and/or Harold Lincoln. The items whose
ownership my clients contest, and whose return they have demanded, include items in
your client's scheduled auction, as we understand you and your client have been advised.

I write now with regard to an additional item in your client's auction, which
I now understand was not consigned by Mr. White: Item No. 153, the Cartier
Wristwatch. Mrs. Kennedy sought to gather the possessions her husband had with him
on November 22, 1963. From your client's catalogue, I understand you believe the watch
was among those possessions. If your description is accurate, the watch never was given
to Mrs. Lincoln for her personal ownership.

Please advise me as soon as possible as to the consignor of this watch, so
that we may directly demand its return. If you cannot disclose the consignor's identity,

U.S. DEPARTMENT OF JUSTICE FULTON CASE FILE: Letter from Williams & Connolly attorney, Nicole Seligman, to Guernsey's regarding Christopher Fulton. He was not shown the letter until after the auction.

"Please advise me as soon as possible as to the consignor of this watch, so that we may directly demand its return. If you cannot disclose the consignor's identity, please inform him or her immediately of this claim by Caroline and John Kennedy, and their demand that the watch be returned immediately to them."

It was demanded that the watch be returned directly to Caroline and John Kennedy, not to the National Archives or the JFK Library. In the press, John Kennedy and Caroline Kennedy used the words "intensely personal" to describe the watch and were careful not to use the words "national security."

At that time, Attorney Nicole Seligman was President Clinton's personal attorney; she defended him during the Monica Lewinsky scandal.

WILLIAMS & CONNOLLY
Molly H. Sherden, Esquire
March 16, 1998
Page 2

please inform him or her immediately of this claim by Caroline and John Kennedy, and their demand that the watch be returned immediately to them.

Thank you for your assistance.

Very truly yours,

Nicole Seligman

Nicole K. Seligman

NKS/mtp

cc: Paul G. Kirk, Jr., Esquire

PEABODY & ARNOLD LLP

COUNSELLORS AT LAW

50 ROWES WHARF

BOSTON, MASSACHUSETTS 02110-3342

TELEPHONE (617) 951-2100

FAX (617) 951-2125

ONE CITIZENS PLAZA. 8TH FL.
PROVIDENCE, RHODE ISLAND 02903
TELEPHONE (401) 831-8330
FAX (401) 831-8359

DIRECT DIAL NUMBER
(617) 951-2023
Internet: mhs@p-a.com

March 17, 1998

VIA FACSIMILE AND FIRST CLASS MAIL

Nicole K. Seligman, Esquire
Williams & Connolly
725 Twelfth Street, N.W.
Washington, D. C. 20005

Dear Ms. Seligman:

I am responding to your letter of yesterday concerning your clients' demand for the Cartier wristwatch, which is designated as Lot No. 153 in the Guernsey's auction catalog. As you have requested, I have put the consignor on notice of this demand and have provided the consignor with a copy of your letter.

I have reviewed the provenance of this item that was provided to Guernsey's. According to this information, the watch was removed from President Kennedy's wrist at Parkland Hospital in Dallas on November 22, 1963. The watch was then in possession of Nurse Diana Bowron who turned it over to Parkland Hospital Head of Security, Mr. O. P. Wright. Mr. Wright delivered the watch to Dallas Secret Service agent Roger C. Warner, who was sent to pick it up at 4:00 p.m. on November 26, 1963. Agent Roger Warner sent the watch from the Dallas Secret Service offices, via their liaison, who delivered it to the PRS Section of the Secret Service in Washington D. C. Robert I. Bouck, Special Agent in charge of the PRS Section, released it to Jacqueline Kennedy's Secret Service agent Clinton J. Hill for its return to Mrs. Kennedy on December 2, 1963. I enclose a copy of a receipt for the watch bearing this date, signed by Mr. Hill and authenticated by the National Archives and Records Administration. Mr. Hill returned the watch to Mrs. Kennedy the same day.

According to sources who prepared the provenance on the watch, this item was too vivid a reminder to Mrs. Kennedy of her late husband and, therefore, she gave it as a special gift to Evelyn Lincoln when she moved from the White House to Georgetown in 1964.

U.S. DEPARTMENT OF JUSTICE FULTON CASE FILE: Guernsey's counsel's response to the letter demanding the Cartier watch's return.

PEABODY & ARNOLD LLP

Nicole K. Seligman, Esquire
March 17, 1998
Page 2

Other consignors to the auction have confirmed that Mrs. Kennedy expressed her desire to have many of the late President's personal effects removed from the White House and discarded or given away because she did not want to have them or to have to see them after the assassination. I have spoken personally with an individual who was in the service of the Kennedys at the time in question and who has substantiated this account.

I am just now leaving for New York so that if you should need to reach me after you receive this letter, I can be contacted through Guersney's office at 212-794-2280.

Very truly yours,

Molly H. Sherden

MHS:itt
Enclosure

U.S. DEPARTMENT OF JUSTICE FULTON CASE FILE: Guernsey's counsel's response to the letter demanding the Cartier watch's return.

PEABODY & ARNOLD LLP

COUNSELLORS AT LAW

50 ROWES WHARF

BOSTON, MASSACHUSETTS 02110-3342

TELEPHONE (617) 951-2100

FAX (617) 951-2125

ONE CITIZENS PLAZA, 8TH FL.
PROVIDENCE, RHODE ISLAND 02903
TELEPHONE (401) 831-8330
FAX (401) 831-8359

DIRECT DIAL NUMBER
(617) 951-2023
Internet: mhs@p-a.com

March 17, 1998

VIA FACSIMILE AND FIRST CLASS MAIL

Christopher Fulton, CEO
The Twelve Global, Ltd.
2558 Westhill Close
West Vancouver, B.C.
Canada V7S3E6

Dear Mr. Fulton:

I represent Guernsey's auction house in connection with the auction of JFK documents and artifacts that will take place tomorrow in New York. I received this morning a copy of the enclosed letter from Nicole Seligman, who is the attorney for John and Caroline Kennedy.

I have already written a response to this letter on behalf of Guernsey's, which I also enclose. I have not disclosed your identity or provided any other information to Ms. Seligman besides what is contained in the letter. I do not believe there is any merit the Kennedy children's claim to ownership of the Cartier wristwatch. They have taken no legal action to stop the auction or to prohibit the sale of any item in the auction. All government agencies have reached a final resolution with Mr. White and no government agency is any longer challenging the ownership, authenticity or provenance of any remaining items.

Should you feel that any additional response to Ms. Seligman is required, I would be happy to assist you or your counsel in any way. I am leaving just now for New York and can be reached through Guernsey's office there.

Very truly yours,

Molly H. Sherden

MHS:itt/enclosures

U.S. DEPARTMENT OF JUSTICE FULTON CASE FILE: Guernsey's counsel's letter to Christopher Fulton. He did not see the letters until after the auction. According to Guernsey's, the situation had been handled.

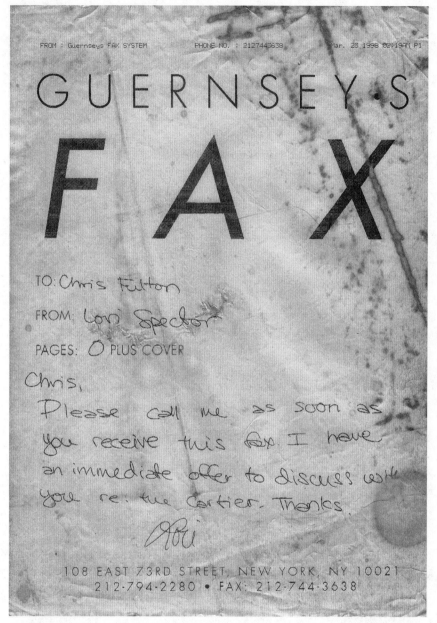

U.S. DEPARTMENT OF JUSTICE FULTON CASE FILE: Guernsey's fax about the after-sale offer on the Cartier watch.

GUERNSEY·S

108 ½ EAST 73ʳᴰ STREET, NEW YORK, NEW YORK 10021
212-794-2280 • FAX 212-744-3638
AUCTION LIC. # 795-147

NO.

DATE   March 24, 1998

NAME   The Twelve Global Ltd.
ADDRESS _____
                                        ZIP _____
PHONE (DAY) _____ (EVE) _____
RESALE _____ ON FILE _____

NOTES:

LOT	ITEM	PRICE
153	John F. Kennedy's Cartier Watch	$ 650,000
	less Guernsey's commission	40,000
	less insurance charges	6,000
	Total	604,000

CHECK # 1412

For $604,000⁰⁰

Received 3-24-98

U.S. DEPARTMENT OF JUSTICE FULTON CASE FILE: Guernsey's receipt of sale.

U.S. DEPARTMENT OF JUSTICE FULTON CASE FILE: Guernsey's sub-company's check to Christopher Fulton's corporation for President Kennedy's Cartier watch. It was sent to Switzerland to open a bank account.

GUERNSEY·S

108 ½ EAST 73RD STREET, NEW YORK, NEW YORK 10021
212-794-2280 • FAX 212-744-3638
AUCTION LIC. # 795-147

NO.

DATE April 23, 1998

NAME Chris Fulton — Turtle Global Ltd.
ADDRESS 2558 Westhill Close
West Vancouver,BC, CANADA   ZIP V753E6
PHONE (DAY) _____ (EVE) _____
RESALE _____   ON FILE _____

NOTES:

JOHN F KENNEDY
CONSIGNOR

LOT	ITEM		PRICE
153	JFK's CartierWristwatch	NET	$604,000.00
154	President JFK's Gold Nastrix Watch	PAID	
431	President JFK's Sunglasses		40,000.00
			40,000
	lot 153 Paid 604,000 check#		4,000
	1412		1,802
			$34,220
			No invoice
			charge
	Paid # 1454		
	*34,200.00		
	4/14/99		

U.S. DEPARTMENT OF JUSTICE FULTON CASE FILE: Guernsey's receipt of sale.

In 1998, Guernsey's conducted the first of its two auctions focused on the life and career of President John F. Kennedy. The inch thick catalogue produced for the event documented the extraordinary artifacts and documents included in the unprecedented event. With previews at The New-York Historical Society (NYC's oldest museum) and the auction at the Park Avenue Armory, the world's media flocked to cover the sale while buyers participated from around the globe. As one might have assumed, prices were extraordinary and included $1 million each being spent on the late President's wristwatch and briefcase. The surprise of the auction was a Kennedy-owned yacht that was bid to an astounding $6 million!

Guernsey's followed its own 1998 Kennedy Auction by selling the famed Robert White Collection in 2005. A life-long Kennedy collector, Mr. White's family chose Guernsey's to present his museum-quality Collection at auction. Buyers not only came to the Park Avenue auction site but participated on-line from everywhere as prices matched the levels of the first Kennedy Auction years earlier. Noteworthy among the thousands of items sold were important hand written notes from the late President and First Lady and the flags that flew from the Dallas motorcade.

Guernsey's involvement with American Presidents didn't stop with John F. Kennedy. Indeed, the firm's auction entitled "The Presidency" featured items relating to many Presidents and included the rarest Presidential White House flags, previously unseen White House photography and the magnificent collection of White House engraved and handwritten invitations from the late Sanford Fox, assistant to eight consecutive Presidents.

Guernsey's yet again became immersed in important Presidential documents and memorabilia when the firm began preparations for the Franklin Delano Roosevelt Auction. The extraordinary, inherited collection that was consigned to Guernsey's (imagine a magnificent oversized handwritten four-page letter from Benito Mussolini to FDR calling for world peace just before the outbreak of WWII) was in the process of being catalogued when Guernsey's was able to interest several parties in buying the collection intact. The negotiations that ensued resulted in a private treaty sale netting our consignors amounts so high that it was hard for them to imagine.

://www.guernseys.com/v2/about.html   Page 3 of 9

U.S. DEPARTMENT OF JUSTICE FULTON CASE FILE: Guernsey's website states that President Kennedy's Cartier watch sold for one million dollars. At the time of this book's publication, that information is still published by Guernsey's.

Item	Received From	Given To	Date	Agency	Record Number
The autopsy descriptive sheet	James J. Rowley	Robert H. Bahmer	10/2/67	HSCA	180-10109-10370
Two certificates dated 11/24 by Dr. Humes	James J. Rowley	Robert H. Bahmer	10/2/67	HSCA	180-10109-10370
Official autopsy report	James J. Rowley	Robert H. Bahmer	10/2/67	HSCA	180-10109-10370
Original Autopsy protocol dated 11/22/63 signed by Cmdr. J. J. Humes - std Form 503, six pages. Countersigned by Cmdr. J. Thornton Boswell & Lt. Col. Pierre A. Finck	United States Secret Service	John F. Simmons	10/3/67	HSCA	180-10109-10369
Skipped 180--10109-10368					
Naval Bethesda Hospital's autopsy report		Orrin Bartlett, FBI	12/23/63	HSCA	180-10109-10379
Clothing worn by President Kennedy when assassinated	Robert I. Bouck, USSS William R. Greer, USSS	PRS, Section, USSS Orrin Bartlett, FBI	11/23/63	HSCA	180-10109-10378
Gold wrist watch (Cartier) of the late President Kennedy			12/2/63	HSCA	180-10109-10378
Skipped 180-10109-10366					
Skipped 180-10109-002631					

Item	Received From	Given To	Date	Agency	Record Number
burning certain preliminary draft notes relating to NMS Autopsy Report # A 63 #272					
Small Neman Markus box about 2 ½" x 3 ½"	Roy Jevous, FBI	George G. Burkley Dr. James Young	11/27/63	HSCA	10910385
Specimen of bone that appears to be from a skull (marked Fragment No. 2)	David Burros	United States Secret Service		HSCA	10910385
Specimen of bone that appears to be from a skull (marked Fragment No. 2)	Robert I. Bouck, USSS	George G. Burkley		HSCA	10910385
Original and seven copies of Autopsy Rpt A63-272, each of six pages, & each having attached original or certified copies of three receipts for certain materials, & each having two certificates signed by J.J. Humes attached.	J.H. Stover, Jr.	George G. Burkley	11/24/63	HSCA	180-10109-10371
Autopsy notes & holograph original of Autopsy Rpt A63-272	J. H. Stover, Jr.	C.B. Galloway George G. Burkley	11/24/63	HSCA	180-10109-10371
Handwritten notes by Dr. J. J. Humes, including the holographic draft	James J. Rowley	Robert H. Bahmer	10/2/67	HSCA	180-10109-10370

U.S. DEPARTMENT OF JUSTICE FULTON CASE FILE: HOUSE SELECT COMMITTEE ON ASSASSINATIONS document. Blank "received from" and "given to" sections pertaining to President Kennedy's Cartier watch. This information was classified and not available to the HSCA during their investigation of President Kennedy's assassination.

AGENCY INFORMATION

```
           AGENCY : HSCA
    RECORD NUMBER : 180-10087-10095
   RECORDS SERIES : NUMBERED FILES
AGENCY FILE NUMBER : 000640
```

DOCUMENT INFORMATION

```
       ORIGINATOR : USSS
             DATE : 12/02/63
            PAGES : 1
    DOCUMENT TYPE : OTHER TEXTUAL
         SUBJECTS : KENNEDY, JOHN, ASSASSINATION; EVIDENCE; CLOTHING,
                    KENNEDY, JOHN F.
   CLASSIFICATION : UNCLASSIFIED
     RESTRICTIONS : OPEN IN FULL
   CURRENT STATUS : OPEN
DATE OF LAST REVIEW : 07/27/93
         COMMENTS : RECEIPT OF WRIST WATCH (CARTIER).  BOX  16. FOLDER
                    TITLE:
```

Hit 31 of 50

AGENCY INFORMATION

```
           AGENCY : HSCA
    RECORD NUMBER : 180-10087-10096
   RECORDS SERIES : NUMBERED FILES
AGENCY FILE NUMBER : 000640
```

DOCUMENT INFORMATION

```
       ORIGINATOR : W.C.
             FROM : BOUCK, ROBERT L.
             DATE : 11/23/63
            PAGES : 1
    DOCUMENT TYPE : LIST

         SUBJECTS : KENNEDY, JOHN, ASSASSINATION; EVIDENCE; CLOTHING,
                    KENNEDY, JOHN F.
   CLASSIFICATION : UNCLASSIFIED
     RESTRICTIONS : OPEN IN FULL
   CURRENT STATUS : OPEN
DATE OF LAST REVIEW : 07/27/93
         COMMENTS : BOX  16. FOLDER TITLE:
```

Hit 32 of 50

AGENCY INFORMATION

```
           AGENCY : HSCA
    RECORD NUMBER : 180-10087-10162
   RECORDS SERIES : NUMBERED FILES
AGENCY FILE NUMBER : 008452
```

NATIONAL ARCHIVES: Receipt for President Kennedy's Cartier watch in Box 16. In part, Box 16 is comprised of Robert Kennedy's private papers from the John F. Kennedy Library.

COVINGTON & BURLING
UNION TRUST BUILDING
WASHINGTON 5, D. C.

REPUBLIC 7-5900

ROBERT F. KENNEDY PAPERS
SENATE CORRESPONDENCE
PERSONAL FILE 1964 - 1968
BOX 16

FOLDER:
JOHN F. KENNEDY LIBRARY
CORRESPONDENCE, 5/27/65

27 May, 1965

Honorable Robert F. Kennedy
United States Senator
4700 Chain Bridge Road
McLean, Virginia

Dear Senator:

There is enclosed a notebook containing the original and one copy of the transcriptions of the notes that I took on the contents of President Kennedy's files still in the possession of Mrs. Lincoln.

Because of the nature of much of the material, as well as my own time problem, these notes are elliptical and as abbreviated as possible. I did, however, try to make a note of anything which you might wish to withdraw from the Deed of Gift. I have assumed in general that you would not want to withdraw documents dealing with national security or military matters (even though some may require indefinitely delayed release dates) except possibly by substituting copies for the originals of particular pieces of correspondence.

It should be clear from the enclosed notes that the files are for the most part not well organized. If the files were to be made available at all to anyone at this time, their condition would raise a serious immediate problem. As long as they are kept isolated, however, there is no urgency about the very large job which would be involved in reorganizing them, and in taking steps to ensure the indefinite physical preservation of original documents, such as speech drafts and some of the correspondence, which are beyond price and irreplaceable.

It should be noted that the documents and categories noted in the enclosed lists do not include everything in Mrs. Lincoln's possession which is covered by the Deed of Gift. In addition to what is listed, there are in the vault the following:

NATIONAL ARCHIVES: First page of a etter to Robert Kennedy about items in Evelyn Lincoln's possession and the deed of gift to the government. It is from Robert Kennedy's personal file 1964-1968, box 16 file folder.

205 Mt. Auburn Street
Cambridge, Massachusetts 02138
Telephone: (617) 868-6251

June 22, 1998

Dear Chris,

Since I haven't received acknowledgement from you on my letter and package of April 22, I assume you don't wish to pursue the idea.

I left a message for you on your business telephone, and the home phone number you gave me had a Fax signal.

Please feel free to tell me if you think the material is not worthwhile. I will not be offended!

If you have no interest in further conversation about this, I would be most appreciative of your sending all the papers back to me.

Thank you

Sincerely,
Deidre

Mr. Chris Fulton
1395 Marine Drive
West Vancouver, B.C.
V 9 T 1 B 6, Canada

CHRISTOPHER FULTON'S PERSONAL RECORD: Letter to Christopher Fulton from President Kennedy's aide, Deidre Henderson. Ms. Henderson consigned President Kennedy's European diary at Guernsey's JFK auction, in 1998.

U.S. DEPARTMENT OF JUSTICE FULTON CASE FILE: Photo of Deidre Henderson that appeared in Guernsey's JFK auction catalog.

483

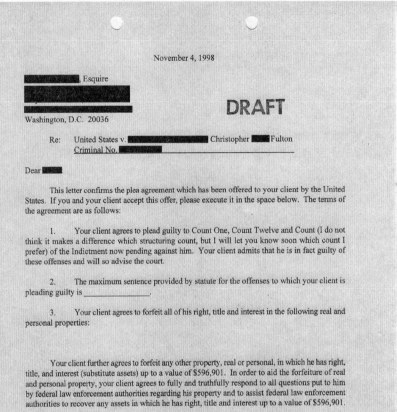

November 4, 1998

███████, Esquire

████████████████

████████████████
Washington, D.C. 20036

DRAFT

Re: United States v. ██████████████ Christopher ████ Fulton
    Criminal No. ████████

Dear ████:

This letter confirms the plea agreement which has been offered to your client by the United States. If you and your client accept this offer, please execute it in the space below. The terms of the agreement are as follows:

1. Your client agrees to plead guilty to Count One, Count Twelve and Count (I do not think it makes a difference which structuring count, but I will let you know soon which count I prefer) of the Indictment now pending against him. Your client admits that he is in fact guilty of these offenses and will so advise the court.

2. The maximum sentence provided by statute for the offenses to which your client is pleading guilty is _____.

3. Your client agrees to forfeit all of his right, title and interest in the following real and personal properties:

Your client further agrees to forfeit any other property, real or personal, in which he has right, title, and interest (substitute assets) up to a value of $596,901. In order to aid the forfeiture of real and personal property, your client agrees to fully and truthfully respond to all questions put to him by federal law enforcement authorities regarding his property and to assist federal law enforcement authorities to recover any assets in which he has right, title and interest up to a value of $596,901.

The United States agrees that it will not voluntarily disclose any information provided by ███████████ in response to the questions posed by federal law enforcement authorities to any other law enforcement authorities.

4. Your client understands that a sentencing guideline range for this case will be determined by the Court .. (standard language)

5. The United States and your client understand, agree and stipulate to the statement of facts attached as Exhibit A (not attached) and the following applicable sentencing factors:

U.S. DEPARTMENT OF JUSTICE FULTON CASE FILE: Early draft of Fulton's plea bargain.

7.   Paragraph on relinquishment of constitutional rights.

8.   In return for fulfillment by your client of all of his obligations under this agreement, the United States agrees as follows:

a.   After ███████ appears before the Court and enters a guilty plea, and after he is initially debriefed by federal law enforcement agents pursuant to the terms of paragraph 3, and after the United States is satisfied that ███████ is providing full and truthful information, the government will agree to his release from his current custody pending sentence, under maximum Pretrial Services supervision, and as long as there is an appropriate third party custodian, and as long as his whereabouts are monitored electronically, and as long as ███████ remains in full compliance with the terms of this agreement.

9.   In order to permit your client to make disclosures to the government pursuant to this agreement, any information or documents that he discloses to the government during the course of his debriefing pursuant to paragraph 3 will not be used against him, directly or indirectly, by the United States in any criminal or civil case, except, as provided by this agreement, in the case of a breach of the agreement by your client.

10.   Other than the offenses to which your client has agreed to plead guilty, he will not be charged with any other violations of federal criminal law in this United States District Court for any conduct occurring prior to the date of this agreement of which this Office or any of its agents is aware or of which this Office or its agents may become aware as a result of disclosures made by your client during his cooperation. This office represents that it is not aware of any other conduct by ███████ occurring prior to the date of this agreement which may subject him to prosecution elsewhere and this Office does not intend to take any actions to cause ███████ to be prosecuted by other law enforcement authorities for conduct occurring outside of this United States District Court.

Similarly, this Office agrees not to prosecute any member of ███████ family with any violations of federal criminal law occurring prior to the date of this agreement of which this office is aware nor to take any actions to cause any member of ███████ family to be prosecuted by other federal, state, or local law enforcement agencies.

11.   Standard paragraph on waiver of Speedy Trial rights and understanding that sentencing may be delayed until his cooperation is completed. However, the parties agree and stipulate to use good faith efforts to complete the cooperation expeditiously, so that ███████ may begin service of any sentence of imprisonment imposed by the Court as soon as possible.

Sincerely,

DRAFT

███████, Esquire
United States Attorney's Office

U.S. DEPARTMENT OF JUSTICE FULTON CASE FILE: Early draft of Fulton's plea bargain.

MEMORANDUM

TO: ▓▓▓▓ File

FROM: ▓▓▓▓▓▓▓▓

DATE: November 10, 1998

RE: Kennedy Memorabilia

Evelyn Lincoln dies - June July, 1995

Lincoln leaves ▓▓▓▓ White items in her will, including filing cabinet in which White finds dictabelts from Kennedy.

White goes to dicta belt company in Melbourne Florida with Russeau and dictabelt makes cassette copies of the dictabelt recordings

▓▓▓▓▓▓▓▓▓▓▓▓▓▓▓▓ contact White. Idea of book is ▓.

▓▓▓▓▓▓▓▓▓▓▓▓ meet with White to discuss book idea. Actually sign a contract , 1996, 1997. White lawyer, ▓▓▓▓▓, later sends ▓▓▓▓▓▓▓▓▓ a letter cancelling contract to split proceeds on the book.

White gives ▓▓▓▓ the cassettes to be turned into CD to become pocket part of book. (▓▓▓▓▓▓▓▓▓▓▓▓▓▓ take alot of photos of White memorabilia for book).

After contract cancelled, White wants tapes back. ▓▓▓▓ supposed to give tapes back at auction.

White eventually donates original dictabelts to Kennedy Library in 2/98. White currently wants cassettes back to establish value of donation he makes for charitable deduction. According to ▓▓▓▓, dictabelts are either capable of being heard or are capable of being copied onto cassettes as before.

▓▓▓▓ has tapes.

The watch

▓▓

Fulton got watch from ▓▓▓▓, maybe purchase.

U.S. DEPARTMENT OF JUSTICE FULTON CASE FILE: DOJ memorandum regarding Christopher Fulton.

Fulton brought watch to NY auction of White's stuff. Bids taken by phone. Apparent bid for watch of $700,000. Auctioneer never clsoed sale. Cut off phone.

Fulton later told Alan Burt, White's business manager, that someone paid cash for the watch. Lear Jet at Airport. Burt made memo of Fulton conversation, which IRS SA has.

Fulton may also have sold pair of glasses.

U.S. DEPARTMENT OF JUSTICE FULTON CASE FILE: DOJ memorandum regarding Christopher Fulton.

███████████████

ATTORNEY AT LAW

EXECUTIVE SUITES ████████   MEMBER OF NJ & PA BAR

ATLANTIC CITY, NEW JERSEY 08401
(609) ████████
FAX (609) ████████

████████████

Mr. Chris Fulton
1395 Marine Drive
Suite 27006
West Vancouver, B.C.
Canada V7T 1B6

Dear Mr. Fulton:

Please be advised I represent Robert L. White.

Upon careful review of the "Contract" executed on May 2, 1997, Mr. White has elected to terminate in full the referenced agreement and any further participation with you on a book project. You are directed to cease any and all activities on his behalf.

It is my understanding that you are in possession of certain photographs which are the property of Robert L. White. Accordingly, I am requesting that they be returned immediately. Kindly forward them to me at the above-stated address.

Further, in accordance with the terms of this termination, Mr. White does not consent for you or anyone acting on your behalf to use, display, exhibit and or utilize for any purpose whatsoever the photographs taken of his collection during the week of April 26 through May 2, 1997.

Pursuant to Mr. White's request, please direct all further inquiries regarding this matter directly to my attention.

Thank you for your anticipated cooperation in this regard.

Very truly yours,

████████████, Esquire
Attorney for Robert L. White

DJG/gh
Transmitted via telecopier
& Express Mail R.R.R.

cc: ████████████
    Mr. Robert L. White

U.S. DEPARTMENT OF JUSTICE: Robert White's attorney, in coordination with the DOJ.

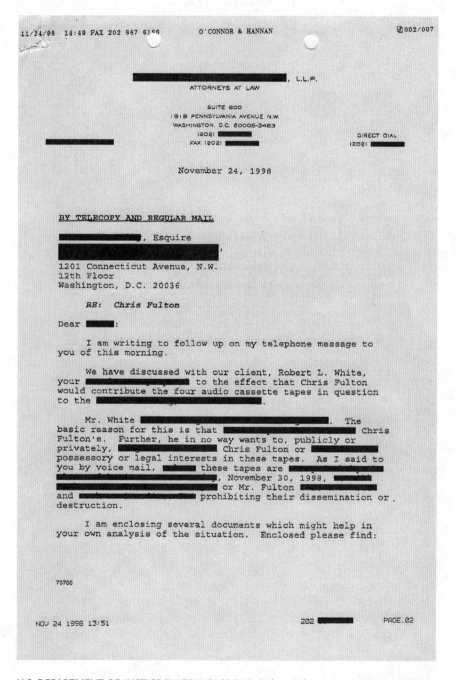

████████████████████████, L.L.P.
ATTORNEYS AT LAW

SUITE 800
1919 PENNSYLVANIA AVENUE N.W.
WASHINGTON, D.C. 20006-3483
(202) ▮▮▮▮
FAX (202) ▮▮▮▮

DIRECT DIAL
(202) ▮▮▮▮

November 24, 1998

BY TELECOPY AND REGULAR MAIL

████████████, Esquire
██████████████████████,
1201 Connecticut Avenue, N.W.
12th Floor
Washington, D.C. 20036

RE: Chris Fulton

Dear ████:

I am writing to follow up on my telephone message to you of this morning.

We have discussed with our client, Robert L. White, your ████████████████ to the effect that Chris Fulton would contribute the four audio cassette tapes in question to the ████████████████.

Mr. White ████████████████████████████. The basic reason for this is that ████████████████ Chris Fulton's. Further, he in no way wants to, publicly or privately, ████████ Chris Fulton or ████████ possessory or legal interests in these tapes. As I said to you by voice mail, ████ these tapes are ████████████████████, November 30, 1998, ████████ ████████████████ or Mr. Fulton and ████████████ prohibiting their dissemination or destruction.

I am enclosing several documents which might help in your own analysis of the situation. Enclosed please find:

70700

NOV 24 1998 13:51   202 ████████   PAGE.02

U.S. DEPARTMENT OF JUSTICE FULTON CASE FILE: Robert White's attorney, in coordination with the DOJ, attempted to secretly place President Kennedy's recordings in federal court without them being destroyed or released to the public. There were discussions about Christopher Fulton donating the recordings to the John F. Kennedy Library.

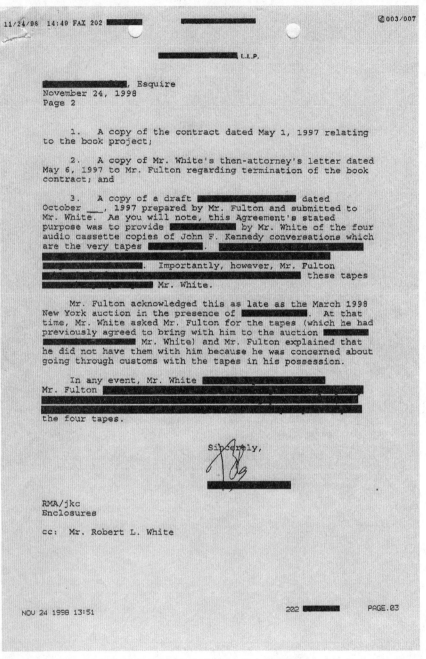

███████████, L.L.P.

██████████████, Esquire
November 24, 1998
Page 2

    1.   A copy of the contract dated May 1, 1997 relating to the book project;

    2.   A copy of Mr. White's then-attorney's letter dated May 6, 1997 to Mr. Fulton regarding termination of the book contract; and

    3.   A copy of a draft ██████████████████ dated October ___, 1997 prepared by Mr. Fulton and submitted to Mr. White. As you will note, this Agreement's stated purpose was to provide ███████████ by Mr. White of the four audio cassette copies of John F. Kennedy conversations which are the very tapes ██████████. ████████████████████████ ██████████████████. Importantly, however, Mr. Fulton ████████████████████████████████ these tapes ████████████████ Mr. White.

    Mr. Fulton acknowledged this as late as the March 1998 New York auction in the presence of ████████████. At that time, Mr. White asked Mr. Fulton for the tapes (which he had previously agreed to bring with him to the auction ████████ ██████████████ Mr. White) and Mr. Fulton explained that he did not have them with him because he was concerned about going through customs with the tapes in his possession.

    In any event, Mr. White ██████████████████████ Mr. Fulton ████████████████████████████ ██ the four tapes.

                       Sincerely,

RMA/jkc
Enclosures

cc: Mr. Robert L. White

U.S. DEPARTMENT OF JUSTICE FULTON CASE FILE: Robert White's attorney, in coordination with the DOJ, attempted to secretly place President Kennedy's recordings in federal court without them being destroyed or released to the public. There were discussions about Christopher Fulton donating the recordings to the John F. Kennedy Library.

WASHINGTON, D.C. 20036
TELEPHONE: (202) ▇▇▇▇▇▇
FAX: (202) ▇▇▇▇▇▇

FACSIMILE TRANSMISSION
COVER SHEET

TO: Jack Fulton

FAX NO. 604-▇▇▇▇▇

FROM: ▇▇▇▇▇▇

CLIENT NO. ▇▇▇▇▇

DATE: November 25, 1998

NO. OF PAGES (including cover sheet) -

If you experience any problems in receiving this transmission, please call Barbara Thomas at (202) ▇▇▇▇▇▇

****

Jack:

You may wish to discuss this with ▇▇▇. If the tapes are to be donated to the Kennedy Library, there is not much time.

****

U.S. DEPARTMENT OF JUSTICE FULTON CASE FILE: Lawyers were concerned about President Kennedy's tapes being donated before Christopher Fulton's federal sentencing.

JAN   1999

Judge ███████████████
Federal District Judge, U.S. Courthouse
6500 Cherrywood Ln
Greenbelt MD. 20720

Dear Judge ████████,

████████████████████████████

I'm writing on behalf of Chris Fulton. My name is Fr. ████
████. I am a Roman Catholic Priest from the Diocese of Des
Moines Iowa. For the last four months I've been an inmate at the
Charles County Detention Center in La Platta Md. I'm here for my
participation in a non-violent nuclear weapons protest at Andrews
Air Force Base last May 17. It's during my time here at the
Charles County Detention Center that I've had the pleasure to met
Chris Fulton.

Chris and I are part of a dayly Bible Study and Prayer Support
Group in Cell Block B/C. Through this support group I've gotten to
know Chris well. As you might imagine, this has not been an easy
time for him. His whole life has radically changed. Much of who he
was before his arrest and imprisonment will never be recovered.

At the same time, its not been an entirely bad experience
either. For the first time in his life Chris is seriously exploring the
central issues of his Faith and what it means to trust in God.
He is asking himself some basic questions about life and what is
Really important. He knows his done wrong and knows he'll
need to serve some prison time for the laws he has broken.
More importantly he knows he needs to change the way he's
been living if he is ever to be truely happy and Full.Filled. As
he grows in his new found Faith, he is eager to start that
new life.

I'm writing to ask you to consider the lowest possible
jail sentence that is permitted in Chris's case. Serving any

U.S. DEPARTMENT OF JUSTICE FULTON CASE FILE: Letter, regarding Christopher Fulton, written by an incarcerated Roman Catholic priest to the judge in the Fourth Circuit Federal Court. The priest spent six months at Charles County Detention Center (CCDC) for his demonstration against the storage and use of nuclear weapons.

More jail time than is absolutely necessary will be of no benefit for the Government, society or Fr Chris.

Thank you for your consideration

Fr. [redacted] B/C 15
Charles Co. Detention Center
P.O. Box 1430
La Plata Md. 20646

Upon Release March 22, 1999
%o Diocese of Des Moines
P.O. Box 1816
Des Moines Iowa 50306

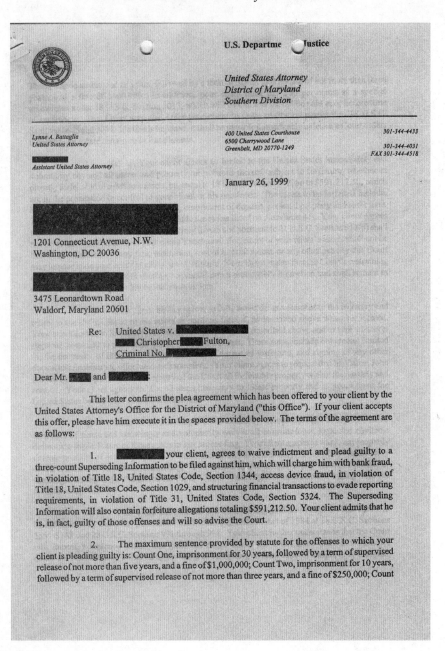

U.S. DEPARTMENT OF JUSTICE FULTON CASE FILE: Fulton's signed plea agreement from DOJ.

this Office will also recommend (i) that your client be required to pay restitution to the victim financial institutions and access device companies consistent with the loss amounts described above and your client's ability to pay and (ii) that as a condition of supervised release, your client be required to continue his cooperation with this Office, law enforcement agencies, and the United States Marshals Service with respect to the execution of this Court's forfeiture orders. Your client reserves the right to recommend any sentence within the guideline range determined by the Court after the resolution of disputed guidelines issues and requests for downward departure. The parties will jointly recommend that the Court enter forfeiture orders consistent with paragraph 3.

(b)   This Office reserves the right to bring to the Court's attention at the time of sentencing, and the Court will be entitled to consider, all relevant information concerning your client's background, character and conduct.

(c)   After the Court imposes sentence on the superseding information and enters final forfeiture orders, this Office will move to dismiss the original indictment in this case.

(d)   This Office agrees not to bring or cause any other prosecutor's office to bring any further charges or to seek any further forfeiture against your client relating to conduct which occurred prior to the date of this agreement of which this Office is aware. This Office further agrees not to bring any further charges against members of your client's family relating to the conduct charged in the indictment and superseding information. This Office reserves the right to bring civil actions charges against your client's father relating to the transfer, sale, concealment or other disposition of potentially forfeitable assets and violations of the Court's October 15, 1998 Order.

7.   Your client and the United States knowingly and expressly waive all rights conferred by 18 U.S.C. Section 3742 to appeal whatever sentence is imposed, including any issues that relate to the establishment of the guideline range, reserving only the right to appeal from an upward or downward departure from the guideline range that is established at sentencing. Nothing in this agreement shall be construed to prevent either your client or the United States from invoking the provisions of Federal Rule of Criminal Procedure 35, and appealing from any decision thereunder, should a sentence be imposed that exceeds the statutory maximum allowed under the law.

8.   Your client expressly understands that the Court is not a party to this agreement. In the federal system, sentence is imposed by the Court, the Court is under no obligation to accept this Office's recommendations and the Court has the power to impose a sentence up to and including the statutory maximum stated above. If the Court should impose any sentence up to the maximum established by statute, your client cannot, for that reason alone, withdraw his guilty plea, and will remain bound to fulfill all of his obligations under this agreement. Your client understands that neither the prosecutor, you, nor the Court can make a binding prediction of, or promise him, the guideline range or sentence that ultimately will apply to his case. Your client agrees that no one has made such a binding prediction or promise.

5

U.S. DEPARTMENT OF JUSTICE FULTON CASE FILE: Fulton's signed plea agreement from DOJ.

9.   Your client must understand that by pleading guilty he will be giving up the following constitutional rights. Your client has the right to plead not guilty. He has the right to be tried by a jury, or if he wishes and with the consent of the government, to be tried by a judge. At that trial, he would have the right to an attorney and if he could not afford an attorney, the Court would appoint one to represent him. During that trial, your client would be presumed innocent and a jury would be instructed that the burden of proof is on the government to prove his guilty beyond a reasonable doubt. Your client would have the right to confront and cross-examine witnesses against him. If your client wished, he could testify on his own behalf and present witnesses in his own defense. On the other hand, if your client did not wish to testify, that fact could not be used against him and a jury would be so instructed. He would also have the right to call witnesses on his own behalf. If your client were found guilty after a trial, he would have the right to appeal that verdict to see if any errors had been committed during the trial that would require either a new trial or a dismissal of the charges. By pleading guilty, your client will be giving up all of these rights except the limited right to appeal his sentence set forth in paragraph 7. By pleading guilty, your client understands that he may have to answer questions posed to him by the Court both about the rights he will be giving up and about the facts of this case. Statements made by your client during such a hearing would not be admissible during a trial except in a criminal proceeding for perjury.

10.   Your client reserves the right to seek reconsideration of the order of pretrial detention in this case. This Office reserves the right to oppose such a request.

11.   This letter states the complete plea agreement in this case. There are no other agreements, promises, undertakings or understandings between your client and this Office.

If your client fully accepts each and every term and condition of this letter, please sign and have your client sign the original and return it to me promptly. The enclosed copy is for your file.

Very truly yours,

Lynne A. Battaglia
United States Attorney

By: _____

Assistant United States Attorney

6

U.S. DEPARTMENT OF JUSTICE FULTON CASE FILE: Fulton's signed plea agreement from DOJ.

February 9, 1999

Ms. Berger
Credit Suisse
P.O. Box
Private Banking
Zurich, Switzerland 8070

    Re: The Twelve Global, Ltd.

Dear Ms. Berger:

    I am one of the signatories to an account with the Private Banking Group at Credit Suisse. The account is in the name of The Twelve Global Ltd. I hereby request that you provide my counsel in the United States, ███████████, a copy of all records related to this account. Mr.███████████████████████████████ 12th floor, Washington, D.C. 20036.

    If you have any questions regarding this matter, please call Mr.████ at 202/████████

Christopher/████Fulton

U.S. DEPARTMENT OF JUSTICE FULTON CASE FILE: Christopher Fulton's under-duress signature for the release of his Swiss bank account records.

AO 110(Rev. 12/89) Subpoena to Testify Before a Grand Jury - US DISTRICT COURT (Rev. 3/98)

United States District Court
District of Maryland

TO:

███████ Christopher ███ Fulton

SUBPOENA TO TESTIFY BEFORE GRAND JURY

SUBPOENA FOR:

☐ PERSON ☐X DOCUMENT(S) OR OBJECT(S)

YOU ARE HEREBY COMMANDED to appear and testify before the Grand Jury of the United States District Court at the place, date and time specified below.

USAO #███████████

PLACE	SUITE
United States Courthouse 6500 Cherrywood Lane Greenbelt, MD 20770	400
	DATE AND TIME March 3, 1999 @ 9:00 a.m.

YOU ARE ALSO COMMANDED to bring with you the following document(s) or object(s):*

☐ Please see additional information on reverse.

This subpoena shall remain in effect until you are granted leave to depart by the court or by an officer acting on behalf of the court.

U.S. MAGISTRATE JUDGE OR CLERK OF COURT	DATE
(signature) (BY) DEPUTY CLERK	2/10/99

This subpoena is issued upon application of the United States of America. Lynne A. Battaglia United States Attorney	NAME, ADDRESS AND PHONE NUMBER OF ASSISTANT U.S. ATTORNEY AUSA ███████████ United States Courthouse 6500 Cherrywood Lane, Suite 400 Greenbelt, MD 20770-1249 (301) 344-4433

*If not applicable, enter "none."

U.S. DEPARTMENT OF JUSTICE FULTON CASE FILE: Fulton's subpoena to testify for documents or object.

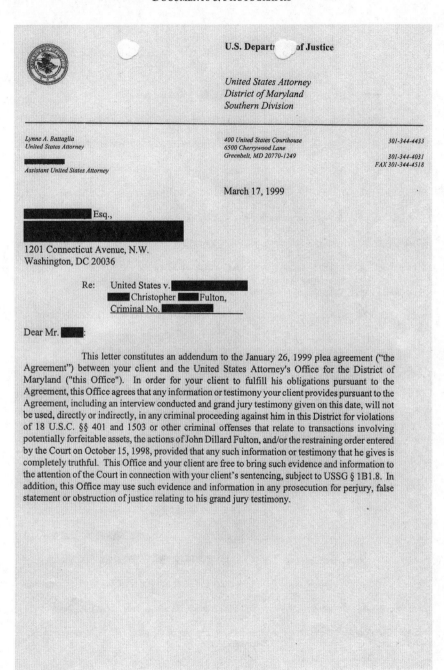

U.S. DEPARTMENT OF JUSTICE FULTON CASE FILE: Plea agreement addendum based on testimony.

As background, the Court should understand the following facts:

In 1995, after committing the offenses in Maryland to which he has pled guilty, ███ ██████ moved to Vancouver, Canada. There he became associated with two legitimate business ventures, I Rock Concrete and I Rock Pumping. Both companies were involved in the construction industry. Jack Fulton, the defendant's father, who had more substantial prior experience in concrete and construction, joined his son and worked for the companies. In 1995, ████████████ lawfully acquired various items of Kennedy memorabilia, which he and his father lawfully sold in 1998 in connection with an auction at Guernsey's auction house.

████████ was indicted in February, 1998 and arrested in August, 1998. The indictment sought not only the forfeiture of the proceeds of his unlawful conduct in Maryland many years earlier, but the forfeiture of "substitute assets". As could be expected, ████████ no longer had the proceeds of his fraud. He had spent the proceeds in numerous subsequent business and personal transactions. Despite the fact that he could have contested the Government's right to seek the forfeiture of "substitute assets", given that his then existing assets had either been legitimately earned or were not traceable to his fraud, he agreed to forfeit to the United States all of his existing assets, up to the value sought by the United States. His current assets are designated in an attachment to the Plea Agreement and will be turned over to the Court.

During the numerous plea discussions between ████████ and the United States, which discussions lasted several months, ████████ told the Government ████████████ owned the Kennedy watch which had been sold at auction ███████████████ controlled the funds in the Credit Suisse account. Prior to entry of the plea, he was debriefed at length on more than one occasion about his assets, including the Kennedy watch. Indeed, these pre-plea proffers were a condition precedent to the Government's acceptance of the plea. While the Government

U.S. DEPARTMENT OF JUSTICE FULTON CASE FILE: In this confidential memorandum, The DOJ was forced to disclose information to the presiding judge before Christopher Fulton's sentencing.

cooperation with respect to the most significant items of property. In particular, he has failed to provide the United States with records relating to the Swiss bank account into which the bulk of his assets were transferred during 1998.

By way of background, while defendant Fulton was living in Vancouver, British Columbia (███████████████ Christopher ███ Fulton), he established a corporation called The Twelve Global Ltd. ("Twelve Global"), which was based in the Turks and Caicos Islands, a known tax haven. ████████████ maintained two bank accounts with Credit Suisse bank in Zurich, Switzerland, one in his name and one in the name of Twelve Global. ███

██

In late 1995, ████████████ purchased two watches from ████████████ ██████████████████████████. These watches ████████ belonged to President John F. Kennedy. One of them, which cost approximately ████████ was ██████████ the watch worn by President Kennedy at the time of his assassination ("the JFK assassination watch").

████████████ handled this transaction himself and there are no contemporaneous documents available to us indicating that his father, John Fulton, played any part in the transaction.

████████████, again by himself, then took steps to authenticate the JFK assassination watch's pedigree ██████████████.

On January 7, 1998, ████████████████ "Chris Fulton, CEO" of Twelve Global, executed a consignment agreement relating to the JFK assassination watch with Guerney's auction house in New York, which was coordinating a sale of Kennedy items to be held in March 1998. On March 17, 1998, ████████████ Chris Fulton, executed a "lot statement" or

2

U.S. DEPARTMENT OF JUSTICE FULTON CASE FILE: In this confidential memorandum, The DOJ was forced to disclose information to the presiding judge before Christopher Fulton's sentencing.

schedule of property which was incorporated into the consignment contract. ▐▉▉▉▉▉▉▉

▉Fulton, also conducted other correspondence with Guerney's. While the JFK assassination watch did not sell as part of the main auction, it was sold in a separate sale in March 1998 for $650,000. After commissions, expenses and insurance, Twelve Global was to receive $604,000.

▉▉▉▉▉▉▉▉▉ sent his father, John Fulton, to New York to exchange the JFK assassination watch for a check. The check, payable to Twelve Global and drawn on the account of Guerney's corporate parent, was dated March 24, 1998 in the amount of $604,000. It was then deposited into Twelve Global's account at Credit Suisse. The following month, ▉▉▉▉▉▉

▉▉▉▉received, via mail or courier, a check for $34,200 from Guerney's to Twelve Global relating to the sale of a pair of President Kennedy's sunglasses, ▉▉▉▉▉▉▉▉▉

▉▉▉▉▉▉▉▉ This check was deposited to the same Credit Suisse account. On April 23, 1998, Guerney's sent a receipt to "Chris Fulton – Twelve Global Ltd." in West Vancouver, Canada confirming the two sales. The two checks issued to Twelve Global were endorsed in a manner that does not disclose the number of the Credit Suisse account into which they were deposited.

In August 1998, ▉▉▉▉▉▉▉▉ was arrested. Since then, he has taken the position that the JFK property ▉▉▉▉▉▉▉▉▉▉▉ the funds from the Guerney's sale. ▉▉▉▉▉▉▉▉▉▉▉

▉▉▉▉▉▉▉▉▉▉▉▉▉▉

▉▉▉▉▉▉▉▉▉. In addition, ▉▉▉▉▉▉▉▉ has admitted that after he was arrested and advised of the charges and forfeiture allegations against him, he met with his father at a jail in Washington State and, at a minimum, tacitly suggested that his father take steps to

3

U.S. DEPARTMENT OF JUSTICE FULTON CASE FILE: In this confidential memorandum, The DOJ was forced to disclose information to the presiding judge before Christopher Fulton's sentencing.

hide the funds that had been deposited into the Credit Suisse account. This Office and the law enforcement agents associated with this case do not know where the funds are at this time.

As part of the plea agreement, the United States requested that ▓▓▓▓▓▓ execute a waiver and request copies of his account records from Credit Suisse. These records would enable law enforcement agents to begin tracing the funds. To date, ▓▓▓▓▓▓ has not provided the United States with any records from the Credit Suisse account. Nor has he provided any information about the current whereabouts of the money from the Guerney's sale. Meanwhile, John Fulton has been served with a copy of the Court's pretrial restraining order relating to forfeiture matters. Despite repeated requests from law enforcement agents that he repatriate the assets to the Registry of the Court ▓▓▓▓▓▓▓▓▓▓▓▓▓▓▓▓ ▓▓▓▓▓▓▓▓▓▓▓▓, Fulton has refused to turn over the money. ▓▓▓▓▓ ▓▓▓ claims that he has been unable to persuade his father otherwise. Even if this is so, what ▓▓▓▓▓▓ can do, and has not done, is to assist the agents in tracing more than $600,000 in missing, forfeitable funds. Until ▓▓▓▓▓▓ completes his part of the plea agreement, he should not receive the benefits provided by the remainder of the agreement.

Accordingly, the United States requests that the Court postpone the sentencing in this case until, at a minimum, ▓▓▓▓▓▓ provides law enforcement agents with all relevant records relating to his Credit Suisse accounts.

Respectfully submitted,

Lynne A. Battaglia
United States Attorney

By: ▓▓▓▓▓▓▓▓▓▓▓▓

Assistant United States Attorney

4

U.S. DEPARTMENT OF JUSTICE FULTON CASE FILE: In this confidential memorandum, The DOJ was forced to disclose information to the presiding judge before Christopher Fulton's sentencing.

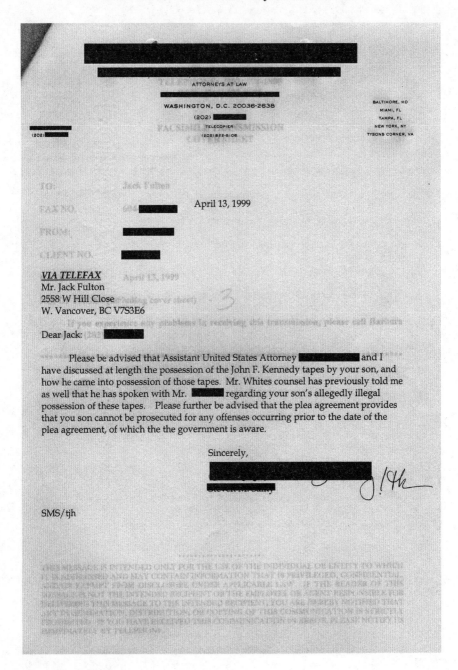

U.S. DEPARTMENT OF JUSTICE FULTON CASE FILE: Lawyer's letter to Mr. John Fulton:
"Please be advised that Assistant United States Attorney — — and I have discussed at length the possession of the John F. Kennedy tapes by your son, and how he came into possession of those tapes. [. . .] Please further be advised that the plea agreement provides that your son cannot be prosecuted for any offences occurring prior to the date of the plea agreement, of which the government is aware."

United States District Court

District of Maryland

UNITED STATES OF AMERICA	**JUDGMENT IN A CRIMINAL CASE** (For Offenses Committed on or After November 1, 1987)
v.	Case Number: ████████
████████████ Christopher ████ Fulton	Defendant's Attorney: ██████████████
	Assistant U.S. Attorney: ██████████

THE DEFENDANT:

☒ pleaded guilty to count(s) <u>one, two, and three of the superseding information</u>

☐ pleaded nolo contendere to count(s) _____, which was accepted by the court.

☐ was found guilty on count(s) _____ after a plea of not guilty.

Title & Section	Nature of Offense	Date Offense Concluded	Count Number(s)
18 U.S.C. § 1344	Bank Fraud	9/9/94	1
18 U.S.C. § 1029	Access Device Fraud	1/13/95	2
31 U.S.C. § 5324	Structuring Financial Transactions to Evade Reporting Requirements	11/2/94	3

The defendant is sentenced as provided in pages 2 through ___8___ of this judgment. The sentence is imposed pursuant to the Sentencing Reform Act of 1984.

☐ The defendant has been found not guilty on count(s) _____

☒ Count(s) <u>1 - 17 of the original indictment</u> are dismissed on the motion of the United States.

    IT IS FURTHER ORDERED that the defendant shall notify the United States Attorney for this district within 30 days of any change of name, residence, or mailing address until all fines, restitution, costs, and special assessments imposed by this judgment are fully paid.

Defendant's SSN: ████████

Defendant's Date of Birth: ██████

Defendant's U.S.M. No.: ████████

         <u>April 19, 1999</u>

         Date of Imposition of Judgment

Defendant's Residence Address:

         ███████████████████ *Apr 21, 1999*

                                            Date

         United States District Judge

Defendant's Mailing Address:

████████████████

Columbia, Maryland 21044

Name of Court Reporter:

C/m 4-21-99

U.S. DEPARTMENT OF JUSTICE FULTON CASE FILE: Judgment in criminal case.

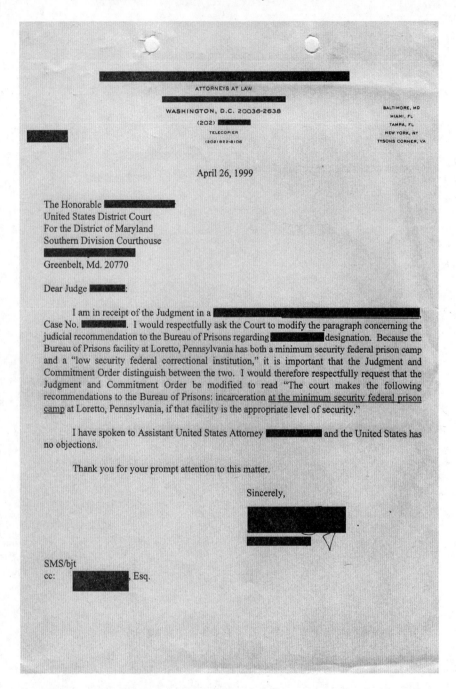

ATTORNEYS AT LAW

WASHINGTON, D.C. 20036-2638
(202) ▓▓▓▓▓
TELECOPIER
(202) 822-8106

BALTIMORE, MD
MIAMI, FL
TAMPA, FL
NEW YORK, NY
TYSONS CORNER, VA

April 26, 1999

The Honorable ▓▓▓▓▓▓▓▓▓
United States District Court
For the District of Maryland
Southern Division Courthouse
▓▓▓▓▓▓▓▓▓▓
Greenbelt, Md. 20770

Dear Judge ▓▓▓▓▓:

I am in receipt of the Judgment in a ▓▓▓▓▓▓▓▓▓▓▓▓▓▓▓▓▓▓▓▓▓▓▓▓.
Case No. ▓▓▓▓▓▓. I would respectfully ask the Court to modify the paragraph concerning the judicial recommendation to the Bureau of Prisons regarding ▓▓▓▓▓▓ designation. Because the Bureau of Prisons facility at Loretto, Pennsylvania has both a minimum security federal prison camp and a "low security federal correctional institution," it is important that the Judgment and Commitment Order distinguish between the two. I would therefore respectfully request that the Judgment and Commitment Order be modified to read "The court makes the following recommendations to the Bureau of Prisons: incarceration at the minimum security federal prison camp at Loretto, Pennsylvania, if that facility is the appropriate level of security."

I have spoken to Assistant United States Attorney ▓▓▓▓▓▓▓ and the United States has no objections.

Thank you for your prompt attention to this matter.

Sincerely,

SMS/bjt
cc: ▓▓▓▓▓▓, Esq.

U.S. DEPARTMENT OF JUSTICE FULTON CASE FILE: Letter to presiding judge, from Christopher Fulton's attorney, regarding Loretto Federal Facility.

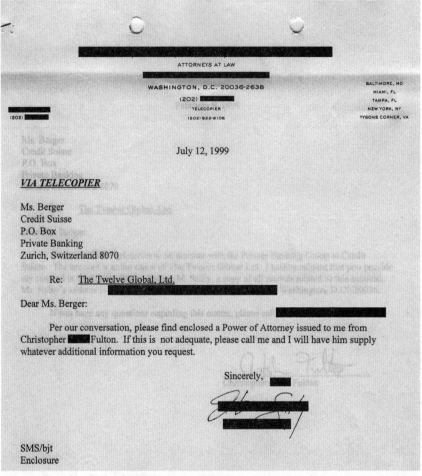

ATTORNEYS AT LAW

WASHINGTON, D.C. 20036-2638

(202) ▮▮▮▮
TELECOPIER
(202) 822-6106

BALTIMORE, MD
MIAMI, FL
TAMPA, FL
NEW YORK, NY
TYSONS CORNER, VA

(202) ▮▮▮▮

July 12, 1999

VIA TELECOPIER

Ms. Berger
Credit Suisse
P.O. Box
Private Banking
Zurich, Switzerland 8070

Re: The Twelve Global, Ltd.

Dear Ms. Berger:

Per our conversation, please find enclosed a Power of Attorney issued to me from Christopher ▮▮▮▮ Fulton. If this is not adequate, please call me and I will have him supply whatever additional information you request.

Sincerely,

▮▮▮▮ Fulton

SMS/bjt
Enclosure

U.S. DEPARTMENT OF JUSTICE FULTON CASE FILE: Letter to Swiss bankers requesting additional information.

CHRISTOPHER FULTON'S PERSONAL PHOTO: Frank (Mac) McCracken (right), who became Christopher Fulton's closest friend at Lewisburg Camp, working with President Obama (left).

REFERENCE SERVICE SLIP
SHADED BOXES FOR NARA USE ONLY

DATE (MM/DD/YYYY): 5/1/2018

TRACKING NUMBER: 44 1389

LAST NAME (PRINT): Fulton

FIRST NAME (PRINT): John

RESEARCHER CARD NUMBER: 181039

SERIES OR COLLECTION NAME: Files of Kim Herd

RECORD GROUP NUMBER/ COLLECTION DESIGNATION: 541

ENTRY NUMBER: 22

NATIONAL ARCHIVES IDENTIFIER (OPTIONAL):

BOX/ITEM NOS. REQUESTED: Box 4

STACK: 650L1

ROW: 67

COMPARTMENT: 23

SHELF: 4

NUMBER OF BOXES/ITEMS PULLED:

OTHER RECORD IDENTIFICATION INFORMATION [SPECIFY FOLDER TITLE(S)/FILE NUMBER(S)]

JUN 1 AM 11:21

REQUEST REVIEWED BY

REQUEST PULLED BY

RECEIVED BY

DATE (MM/DD/YYYY)

REFILED BY

DATE (MM/DD/YYYY)

NATIONAL ARCHIVES AND RECORDS ADMINISTRATION

DO NOT REMOVE FROM RECORDS

NA 14001 (08-16)
Required by NARA 1572

PROBLEMS WITH YOUR REQUEST FOR RECORDS

_____ The records are charged out to:

_____ you

_____ another researcher

_____ reproduction order

_____ a government agency

_____ Maximum 16 archival boxes or 6 FRC boxes. Submit a new request for the remainder.

_____ Records are on microfilm available in Room 4050.

_____ Records are classified.

_____ Records require screening.

X Unable to find at the given location.

_____ Unable to find with the information given.

_____ Records must be requested under the FOIA or Special Access.

_____ Other: _____ Staff: _____

No box 4 on shelf, there isn't room on shelf for another box. It was not in surrounding locations.

NATIONAL ARCHIVES: Weeklong investigation at the National Archives facility in Maryland. Box 4 is missing.

---------- Forwarded message ----------
From: **Gene Morris** <eugene.morris@nara.gov>
Date: Wed, Jun 20, 2018 at 1:37 AM
Subject: Re: [18-42822] 'Files of Kim Herd' (JFK) Box 4

Mr. Fulton:

This is in response to your request for information about the records of the JFK Assassination Records Collection. Specifically, you are interested in the whereabouts of box number 4 of the Files of Kim Herd, part of the Assassination Records Review Board (ARRB) records.

The box is currently considered as missing. We checked the other boxes to see if the records had been re-boxed and the number 4 simply skipped when the boxes were labeled. This was not the case. There is a box and folder list for the Files of Kim Herd on our website and none of the files listed as being in box 4 are in any of the boxes. There is no pull slip on the shelf to indicate who last removed the box, but there is a space where box 4 should fit. At the moment, it believed that the box was improperly re-shelved. We did a quick survey of the space and could not locate the box. We have put out notice that the box is not in it's proper location. Finding the box may not be a quick process. We will advise you when we have found the box.

We regret any inconvenience that this may cause you. If you have any further questions, please feel free to respond by return email or by calling (301) 837-1993.

Gene Morris
Archives II Textual Reference Branch (RDT2)
Room 2400

NATIONAL ARCHIVES: Response from the National Archives regarding a thirty-day investigation over missing Box 4, which most likely contains records of meetings with all agencies and President Clinton regarding the Evelyn Lincoln Project.

Index

A

Adder, Philip 134-138, 147-149, 157-160, 171, 258, 313, 354
Affair to Remember, An 142
Almeida, Juan 62, 101, 102
Angleton, James 22, 309
Assassination Records Review Board (ARRB) 11, 22, 44-46, 55, 74, 132, 134, 144-146, 149-152, 176, 203, 293, 314, 324, 344

B

Baltimore Sun 360, 361
Baranovsky, Pyotr 59
Barman, Stewart 5, 6, 13, 14, 40, 47, 48, 85, 86, 257, 265, 269-273, 275-277, 284-287, 289-291
Bartlett, Orrin 148
Bessette, Carolyn 304
Bolshakov, Georgi 63
Boston Globe 170
Bouck, Robert 26-29, 81-84, 93-97, 99, 100, 102, 103, 105, 112, 113, 116-121, 127-130, 148, 177, 257, 276, 278, 285, 305, 309, 316, 348, 353, 384
Bowron, Diana 29-31, 83, 111, 112
Brezhnev, Leonid 50
Burkley, George 77, 82, 158
Bush, George H.W. 11
Bush, George W. 4, 22, 23, 294, 311, 344

C

Cabell, Earle 102
Callahan, Joe 3, 4, 11, 69, 151-155, 157, 183, 217-219, 257, 264, 265, 269, 270, 272, 281-284, 287, 289, 291, 292, 316, 317
Capone, Al 192, 328
Carter, Jimmy 11, 23, 115

Cartier 16, 17, 24, 26, 28, 33, 34, 41, 42, 72, 81-83, 92-94, 106, 109, 110, 113, 118, 120, 122, 140, 141, 148, 149, 158, 161, 162, 168-173, 176, 182-184, 276
Castro, Fidel 62, 98, 99, 101, 102, 106, 117, 178, 186, 305, 306, 316, 348-350
Central Intelligence Agency (CIA) 10, 11, 13, 17, 22-24, 63, 72, 86, 87, 98-103, 114-117, 146, 147, 149, 152, 178, 307-315, 325, 332, 336, 344, 348-352
Chadawick, Judge 290, 291, 294
Churchill, Winston 37, 244
Clark, Edward 350
Clinton, Bill 11, 12, 40, 46, 61, 74, 149, 151, 152, 176, 185, 186, 206, 218, 277, 290, 294, 313, 314, 324, 344
Clinton, Hillary Rodham 203, 211, 313
CNN 140, 161, 169
Connally, John 104, 107, 108, 114
Couric, Katie 161, 162
Croche, Pat 333
Crowe, William 313
Curtis, Richard 90, 131

D

Dateline 161
Day of the Jackal, The 119
Death of a President, The 26
Decker, Bill 102
de Mohrenschildt, George 351
Dobrynin, A 62, 342
Dulles, Allen 68, 98, 117, 309, 310, 349
Dyer, James 155, 156

E

Eichmann, Adolf 322
Eisenhower, Dwight 87, 98, 99, 114, 309, 310
Entertainment Tonight 140, 161
Ettinger, Arlan 132, 133, 137, 140, 156, 157, 161-163, 165-168, 170, 171, 175, 182-184
Evelyn Lincoln Project 11, 151, 152, 185, 277, 293

F

Federal Bureau of Investigation (FBI) 3, 10, 11, 25, 26, 30, 32, 63, 82, 83, 113, 115-118, 121, 135, 147, 148, 151, 155, 157, 158, 176, 183, 198, 208, 219, 235, 239, 244, 245, 257, 264, 265, 294, 296, 311, 314, 324, 336, 346-348, 351, 352, 354, 363

Flash II 141, 164

Flood, Emmet 313

Forbes, Malcolm 310

Forbes, Steve 310

Ford, Gerald 11, 121, 379

Forsyth, Frederick 119

Freeh, Louis J. 11, 294, 324

Fulton, Christopher 5, 6, 16, 18, 20, 27, 28, 31, 38, 42, 49, 60, 67, 72, 73, 79, 84, 90, 93, 95, 96, 103, 105, 106, 113, 121, 130, 131, 136-143, 148, 149, 152-154, 158, 162, 170, 175, 178, 183, 184, 189, 190, 192, 197, 198, 200, 202, 203, 206, 207, 231, 234, 235, 240, 243, 245, 247, 250, 253, 254, 260, 261, 264, 265, 267, 269, 278, 290, 293, 296, 298-300, 303, 310, 315, 316, 323, 339, 346, 354, 372, 377, 378, 380

Fulton, John 265

Fulton, Shauna 13-16, 26, 30, 33, 36-39, 48, 52, 66, 67, 69, 70, 76, 77, 79, 132, 140-142, 161, 163, 164, 166-169, 173, 175, 179, 184, 187, 188, 199, 203, 205-207, 212, 214, 232, 238-240, 257, 261, 272, 278-280, 297, 299, 303, 304, 364, 372-377, 383, 384

Fulton, Wendy 265

G

Garfinkel, Steven 149

Garrison, Jim 75, 352

George (magazine) 178, 198, 294, 316,

Giancana, Sam 347

Glazier, Jarrod 44-46, 55-58, 140

Glenn, John 98

Good Morning America 161

Gotti, John 328

Greer, William 31, 107-109, 148, 180, 285, 292

Gregorios, Argus 298, 307-311, 313-317, 322, 323, 325, 326, 329, 344, 345, 347

Groden, Robert 33, 34, 285

Gromyko, Andrei 341

Guernsey's Auction 132, 136, 137, 141, 148, 150-153, 156, 157, 161, 163, 170-173, 175, 177, 181, 182, 184, 277, 284, 286

Gunn, T. Jeremy 144, 149

H

Hagan, Joe 32

Hagen, Joe 285

Harris, Judge 278, 287, 290

Henderson, Deirdre 90-92, 140, 141, 163

Herd, Kim 55, 146, 151

Hill, Clint 26, 27, 107, 110, 111, 119

Hoffa, Jimmy 328

Honey Fitz 166, 167

Hoover, J. Edgar 104, 114-116, 121, 347

Hughes, Howard 5

Hunger, Frank W. 144

J

JFK (movie) 33

John F. Kennedy Library 8, 10, 24, 285

Johnson, Dwayne 281

Johnson, Lyndon 5, 56, 63, 64, 75, 81, 82, 103-105, 107, 108, 110, 113-115, 118-127, 324, 337, 347, 348, 350-352

Jonathan "Tech" 235, 237, 241, 245-247, 252, 255, 261, 267, 291, 300, 305, 325, 335

Jones, Ronald 31, 111, 285

K

Katzenbach, Nicholas 121

Kellerman, Roy 109, 292

Kennedy, Caroline 42, 43, 72, 78-80, 131, 132, 134, 136, 140, 147, 152, 165, 167, 172, 175-177, 180, 313, 354, 355

Kennedy, Edward (Teddy) 43, 75, 152, 177, 186, 231, 305, 312, 313

Kennedy, Jacqueline 20, 26, 34, 63, 72, 76, 77, 84, 96, 97, 100, 103, 104, 106, 107, 108, 109, 110, 111, 113, 119, 120, 121, 122, 128, 143, 158, 315, 343, 350, 351

Kennedy, John F. v, 1, 7-11, 16, 17, 19-22, 24-28, 30-34, 38, 41, 45, 47, 56, 62, 63, 69, 71, 72, 75, 76, 78, 79, 81-83, 86-89, 91-93, 96-102, 105-110, 113-118, 120-130, 134, 141, 143, 145-150, 153, 156, 158, 162, 164, 166, 169, 170, 172, 175, 184, 185, 190, 198, 203, 247, 276, 284, 285, 292, 293, 304-306, 309, 315, 323, 324, 340, -342, 382

Kennedy, John Jr. 129, 130, 172, 190, 198, 246, 306, 311-317, 323, 324, 335, 383, 384

Kennedy, Joseph P. 92, 99

Kennedy, Robert F. 5, 8-11, 21, 22, 34, 62, 63, 64, 65, 73-77, 81-84, 86, 89, 93, 96, 97, 99, 104, 113-124, 127-130, 143, 152, 153, 158, 171, 177, 180, 198, 276, 285, 293, 305, 315, 324, 342, 347-353, 383, 384

Khrushchev, Nikita 62, 63, 78, 99, 100, 101, 102, 343

Kirk, Paul G Jr. 312, 313

L

Landregan, Steve 31, 285

Lawford, Peter 100

Lebed, Alexander 60-69, 72-74, 85, 178, 277, 342

Lee, Nick 335

Lemay, Curtis 98

Lennon, John 287

Lewinsky, Monica 40, 153, 185, 313, 314

Lincoln, Abraham 20, 21, 37, 71, 77, 100, 130

Lincoln, Evelyn 7-11, 13, 21-24, 41, 45, 46, 55-57, 65, 72-81, 83, 85-88, 90, 93, 94, 95, 97, 105, 113, 116, 122, 128-134, 136, 140, 141, 143, 145-152, 154-156, 158, 164-166, 171, 172, 176, 177, 185, 198, 257, 276-278, 284-286, 293, 294, 305, 316, 383, 384

Lincoln, Harold 8, 10, 55, 56, 81, 145, 171

Little, Brown and Company 131

Lowe, Jacques 16, 34, 142, 143, 162, 175, 285, 335

Luken, Sasha 17, 18, 143

M

Mack, Gary 27, 33

Mafia 17, 24, 63, 101, 115, 312, 346, 348

Manchester, William 26, 113

Mancini, Clara 3, 4, 69, 151, 152, 153, 154, 155, 156, 157, 183, 217, 218, 219, 257, 264, 265, 271, 281, 282, 283, 289

Mansfield, Jayne 303

Marciano, Rocky 258

Margolin, James 155, 156

Marwell, David G. 45

McCone, John 86, 87, 116, 117

McCracken, Frank 333

McKinnon, Father 266, 267, 268, 270, 292

McRobie, Henry 73, 80, 81, 83, 84, 93, 130, 184, 354, 355, 360, 361

Mehran 15, 38, 48, 49, 50, 52, 53, 59, 60, 61, 62, 64, 66, 68, 85

Mikhailov, Mehran 15, 38, 48, 68, 85

Mikoyan, A. I. 342

Mitnz, Barbara 171

Monroe, Marilyn 100

Moyers, Bill 114, 115

N

NARA 146, 153, 158

NASA 6, 100

National Archives 10, 12, 21, 22, 25, 26, 45, 65, 82, 128, 156, 158, 165, 175, 176, 186, 314, 354

Newton, Isaac 242, 246, 253

Nixon, Richard 23, 96, 98, 178, 179, 247, 265, 352

North, Oliver 313

Novello, Angela 8-10, 74, 82, 83, 129, 305

NSA 10, 101, 146, 155, 243, 333

O

Oakley, CO 357, 358, 361, 362

Offices of Naval Intelligence 351

Onassis, Aristotle 34, 315

Onassis, Christina 315

Onassis, Jacqueline Kennedy 34

Ono, Yoko 287

Operation Bobwhite 134

Oppenheimer, Robert 352

Orr, John T. Jr. 323

Oswald, Lee Harvey 29, 117, 118, 314, 324, 341, 342, 348

P

Pentagon 10, 62, 63, 97, 98-101, 115, 155, 277, 311, 351

Pontius, Ron 105

Powers, Dave 110, 111, 185

Prelude to Leadership 91

Price, C.J. 31, 285

R

Ready, John 108

Reagan, Nancy 20, 21

Reagan, Ronald 11, 19-23, 38, 44, 73, 74, 76, 84, 152, 203, 277, 287, 290, 311, 323

Reno, Janet 13, 151, 152, 183, 185, 186, 207, 210, 238, 278, 293, 294, 324

Richards,Captain 188

Rigg, Frank 146

Riggs Bank 196

Rigoletti, Toni "Meatball" 236, 237, 249, 258, 259, 282

Roberts, Emory 109

Rockefeller, Lawrence 294

Roosevelt, Franklin 93, 96, 311

Roselli, Johnny 178, 347

Roth, Ryan 55, 56, 57, 58

Rowley 82, 117, 118

Ruby, Jack 324, 350, 352

Runkel, Christopher M. 156

S

Salvin, Stephen N. 4, 231, 232, 238, 272-274, 281, 289, 290, 312

Samoluk, Tom 55, 57, 146

Sanders, Joe 112

Schumer, Larry 195, 196, 197

Security Oversight Office 147, 149, 153, 158, 176, 277

Seligman, Nicole 147, 171-173, 175, 313

Sharron, Mitchell J. 103-105, 107, 108

Sherden, Molly 171, 172, 173

Shipman, Thomas 292

Shriver, Maria 170

Sinatra, Frank 302

60 Minutes 166

Sklar, Zachary 33

Sleepless in Seattle 142

Somaluk, Tom 57

Sorensen, Ted 91, 163, 171

Sorrels, Forrest V. 27-29, 83, 113, 117, 285

Sotheby's 34, 40-43, 140, 177

Stein, Roger 27, 28, 30, 32, 83, 93, 197-199, 206, 207, 238, 285

Stockdale, Grant 77

Stone, Oliver 22, 33, 34

T

Taylor, Maxwell 31, 87

Tenet, George 313

Thomas, George 103

Today 3, 161, 163, 205, 382, 384

Tolson, Clyde 347

Tripp, Linda 40, 153

Trotter, William 207-210, 212, 214

Truman, Harry S. 96, 118, 308, 309

Trump, Donald 61, 132, 137, 141, 142, 152, 166
Tunheim, Judge 147-149, 314
Twelve Global Ltd 47, 154, 172

U

U.S. Secret Service 20, 21, 25-28, 30, 32, 81-83, 93, 96, 97, 102-109, 111-116, 118-120, 123, 146, 148, 154, 158, 177, 180, 276, 278, 285, 292, 314-316, 323, 350

V

Vaughn, John C. 6
Vaughn, William Jr 6

W

Wade, Cable 16-18, 24, 64, 143
Wallach, Justice 207-209
Walton, Bill 63
Warne, Kate 100, 130
Warner, Roger 27-30, 32, 35, 83, 93, 285
Warren, Earl 22, 30, 40-43, 118, 121-124, 127, 342, 352
Washington, George 96, 100
Washington Post 308, 309, 361
Webster, William 313
Weitman, Warren P., Jr. 40, 41, 42, 43
White, Jacquelyn 10, 19
White, Robert L. 5,-11, 13, 19, 20, 24-26, 32, 37, 38, 44-47, 50, 55-58, 63-65, 69, 70, 75, 76, 81, 85-87, 91-93, 96, 99, 100, 105, 113-115, 120, 121, 124, 127, 128, 131-138, 140, 142, 144-154, 157-160, 164-166, 170-173, 175-177, 180, 186, 198, 209, 211, 212, 218, 234, 243-245, 247, 258, 275, 276, 278, 284, 286, 293, 294, 311, 313-315, 323, 325, 343, 347, 348, 352, 354, 383, 384
Williams & Connolly 171, 313
Wilson, Lamar "Cutter" 234, 235, 239, 245, 258-263, 300, 304, 311, 330, 339
Wright, Elizabeth L. 31, 285
Wright, O.P. 1, 29-32, 112, 113, 285
Wynn, Steve 228

Y

Yeltsin, Boris 52, 61, 314
Youngblood, Rufus 105, 107, 112
Yusuf "Spielberg" 235, 237, 239, 241, 247, 353

Z

Zapruder, Abraham 71